Raising Churchill's Army

Raising Churchill's Army

The British Army
and the War against Germany
1919–1945

DAVID FRENCH

OXFORD
UNIVERSITY PRESS

OXFORD
UNIVERSITY PRESS

Great Clarendon Street, Oxford, OX2 6DP
Oxford University Press is a department of the University of Oxford.
It furthers the University's objective of excellence in research, scholarship,
and education by publishing worldwide in

Oxford New York

Athens Auckland Bangkok Bogotá Buenos Aires Calcutta
Cape Town Chennai Dar es Salaam Delhi Florence Hong Kong Istanbul
Karachi Kuala Lumpur Madrid Melbourne Mexico City Mumbai
Nairobi Paris São Paulo Singapore Taipei Tokyo Toronto Warsaw

and associated companies in Berlin Ibadan

Oxford is a registered trade mark of Oxford University Press
in the UK and certain other countries

Published in the United States
by Oxford University Press Inc., New York

British Library Cataloguing in Publication Data

Data available

Library of Congress Cataloging in Publication Data

French, David, 1954–
Raising Churchill's army : the British army and the war against Germany, 1919–1945 /
David French.
p. cm.
Includes bibliographical references and index.
1. Great Britain. Army—History—World War, 1939–1945. 2. World War,
1939–1945—Great Britain. I. Title.

D759.F76 2000   940.54'1241—dc21   99-057301

ISBN 0-19-820641-0

1 3 5 7 9 10 8 6 4 2

Typeset in Imprint by Regent Typesetting, London
Printed in Great Britain
on acid-free paper by
T. J. International Ltd,
Padstow, Cornwall

To my FATHER
And the memory of
my MOTHER

Acknowledgements

I have amassed a large number of intellectual debts in the course of writing this book. I would particularly like to thank Mr Jeremy Barnett, Mrs Christine Bielecki, Dr John Bourne, Professor David Edgerton, Professor John Ferris, Dr Tim Harrison-Place, Dr Paul Harris, Dr Stephen Hart, Dr Brian Holden Reid, Lieutenant-Colonel Philip Pratley, Dr Gary Sheffield, and Mr Keith Simpson for sharing their insights with me, for suggesting possible sources and lines of investigation, and for securing access to material for me. The staff of the Imperial War Museum, the Public Record Office and the Liddell Hart Centre for Military Archives at King's College London gave me every possible assistance and made working in their institutions a pleasure. Once again Professor Keith Neilson placed me in his debt by taking immense time and trouble to read a draft of my manuscript and to give me the benefit of his copious suggestions. None of the above are responsible for what appears here, but I am grateful to them all. I alone am responsible for any errors of fact or interpretation. I am also most grateful to my editors at OUP, Tony Morris and Ruth Parr, and to their colleagues, for their patience and assistance.

The following individuals and institutions have kindly given me permission to quote from material to which they own the copyright: Mrs G. H. C. Abram; the Reverend Hugh Temple Bone; Mr Victor Bonham-Carter; the Master and Fellows of Churchill College, Cambridge; Mr E. A. Codling; the Rt. Hon. Sir R. Dunn MC; Mrs N. R. Edwards; Mr Tom Flanagan; Mr Ronald Gladman; Lieutenant-Colonel E. L. Jones MC; Miss Rosemary Lewin; Mrs Patricia Lothian; the Trustees of the Liddell Hart Centre for Military Archives, King's College London; the Department of Documents and the Department of Sound Records of the Imperial War Museum and the Montgomery Collections Committee of the Trustees of the Imperial War Museum and Viscount Montgomery of Alamein CBE; Mr Len Waller. Crown copyright material appears with the kind permission of the Controller of Her Majesty's Stationary Office. Despite my best endeavours, I was unable to contact the copyright holders of the papers of Sergeant E. P. Danger. I would like to apologize to them, and to anyone else whose copyright I may have inadvertently infringed.

The process of researching this book was made much easier than it might have been because I was the recipient of a Small Personal

Research Grant from the British Academy. I would like to thank the Academy for their support. This book is dedicated to my father and the memory of my mother.

David French
University College London
14 September 1999

Contents

Abbreviations

AA	Anti-Aircraft
AASF	Advanced Air Striking Force
ABCA	Army Bureau of Current Affairs
ACIGS	Assistant Chief of the Imperial General Staff
AFHQ	Allied Forces Headquarters
AFV	Armoured Fighting Vehicle
AGRA	Army Group Royal Artillery
AMD	Army Medical Department
AOC	Air Officer Commanding
AOP	Air Observation Post
AP	Armoured Piercing
APM	Assistant Provost Marshal
ASC	Air Support Control
ASSU	Air Support Signals Unit
ATM	*Army Training Memorandum*
AWM	Australian War Memorial
Bde.	Brigade
BEF	British Expeditionary Force
BGGS	Brigadier General General Staff
BGS	Brigadier General Staff
BLA	British Liberation Army
C3	Command, Control, and Communication
C3I	Command, control, communications and intelligence
Capt.	Captain
CAS	close air support
CCC	Churchill College, Cambridge
C-in-C	Commander-in-Chief
CGS	Chief of the General Staff
CIGS	Chief of the Imperial General Staff
CCRA	Corps Commander Royal Artillery
CO	Commanding Officer
COS	Chief of Staff
Col.	Colonel
CRA	Commander Royal Artillery
DAFV	Director of Armoured Fighting Vehicles
DAK	Deutsches Afrika Korps
DCGS	Deputy Chief of the General Staff
DCIGS	Deputy Chief of the Imperial General Staff
DDMO	Deputy Director of Military Operations
DDMS	Deputy Director, Medical Services
DDSD	Deputy Director of Staff Duties
DGTA	Director General Territorial Army

DMO	Director of Military Operations
DMO&I	Director of Military Operations and Intelligence
DMO&P	Director of Military Operations and Plans
DMT	Director of Military Training
DPM	Deputy Provost Marshal
DQMG	Deputy Quarter-Master General
DRAC	Director Royal Armoured Corps
DSD	Director of Staff Duties
DTI	Director of Tactical Investigations
EMF	Experimental Mechanised Force
FM	Field Marshal
FMC	Field Maintenance Centre
FOO	Forward Observation Officer
FSR	*Field Service Regulations (Operations)*
	Followed by date of publication.
GC&CS	Government Code and Cipher School
Gen.	General
GOC	General Officer Commanding
GOC-in-C	General Officer Commanding in Chief
GSO	General Staff Officer
HE	High Explosive
IG	Inspector General
ITC	Infantry Training Centre
IWM	Imperial War Museum
LHCMA	Liddell Hart Centre for Military Archives
Lt.	Lieutenant
Lt.-Col.	Lieutenant-Colonel
Lt.-Gen.	Lieutenant-General
Maj.	Major
Maj.-Gen.	Major-General
MGGS	Major General General Staff
MGO	Master General of the Ordnance
MTP	*Military Training Pamphlet*
nco	non-commissioned officer
OCTU	Officer Cadet Training Unit
ORS	Operational Research Section
PIAT	Projector, Infantry, Anti-tank
PRO	Public Record Office
psc	passed staff college
PUS	Permanent Under Secretary
QMG	Quarter-Master General
RA	Royal Artillery
RAC	Royal Armoured Corps
RAF	Royal Air Force
RAOC	Royal Army Ordnance Corps
RASC	Royal Army Service Corps
RE	Royal Engineers

REME	Royal Electrical and Mechanical Engineers
RHA	Royal Horse Artillery
RSM	Regimental Sergeant Major
r/t	radio telephony
RTC	Royal Tank Corps
RTR	Royal Tank Regiment
SHAEF	Supreme Headquarters Allied Expeditionary Force
'sigint'	signals intelligence
tac/r	tactical reconnaissance
TEWT	Tactical Exercise Without Troops
VCIGS	Vice Chief of the Imperial General Staff
WO	War Office
WOSB	War Office Selection Board
w/t	wireless telegraphy
2i/c	second in command

Introduction

During the first two years of the Second World War British politicians and generals could explain away the string of defeats that their army suffered in Norway, France, Greece, and North Africa as being the result of Britain's unpreparedness for the war that began in September 1939. But, by late 1941, that explanation was beginning to wear thin, and many of them started to wonder if something much more fundamental was wrong with the army. They harboured intense private doubts about the professional competence of the senior officers in command of the army in the field and the morale of their soldiers. In September 1941 Churchill, contemplating the possibility of a landing in Western Europe, decided that it 'could only have one outcome. The War Office would not do the job properly; indeed it was unfair to ask them to pit themselves against German organisation experience and resources. They had neither the means nor the intelligence.'[1] On 2 February 1942, the CIGS, Sir Alan Brooke, recorded in his diary, 'As usual, most unpleasant remarks by various ministers in connection with defeats of our forces. As we had retired into Singapore island and lost aerodromes, besides being pushed back in Libya, I had a good deal to account for.'[2] Four months later, Churchill accounted the surrender of Tobruk as a disgrace that reflected poorly on the morale of the British army.[3] As late as July 1944, Churchill was still capable of turning on his generals with venomous criticisms.[4] Although Brooke stoutly defended his senior subordinates in the face of Churchill's charges, he privately shared some of the Prime Minister's concerns. Brooke blamed the army's poor performance on the holocaust of the Western Front in the First World War that had deprived it of its best leaders and the spread of decadence at home. He spent hours pouring over the *Army List* in search of suitable divisional commanders. In July 1942, at the nadir of the army's fortunes, he wrote to Sir Archibald Wavell, the C-in-C in India, that

I agree with you that we are not anything like as tough as we were in the last war. There has been far too much luxury, safety first, red triangle, etc., in this

---

[1] J. Colville, *The Fringes of Power. Downing Street Diaries 1939–1955* (London, 1985), 443.

[2] LHCMA Alanbrooke MSS 5/1/5, Diary entry, 2 Feb. 1942.

[3] W. S. Churchill, *The Second World War*, iv. *The Hinge of Fate* (London, 1951), 343–4.

[4] M. Gilbert, *Road to Victory. Winston S. Churchill 1941–45* (London, 1986), 844.

country. Our one idea is to look after our comforts and avoid being hurt in any way.[5]

Wavell agreed, laying much of the blame on a growing moral decadence in society.[6]

After the war most senior field commanders took care to mute or entirely omit criticisms of the morale of their troops in their published memoirs, although some of them were less reticent about criticizing their fellow generals. The first major account of the North West European campaign, for example, was prepared under Montgomery's guidance in 1946 by his operations officer, Major-General David Belchem. It contained no hint that anything had been wrong with the morale, training, or equipment of 21st Army Group.[7] Montgomery and his Chief of Staff, Major-General Sir Freddie de Guingand, maintained a similar reticence in their own memoirs. Indeed, the former claimed that the morale of his troops had been 'second to none'.[8] The official historian of the Normandy campaign, Major L. F. Ellis, intimated that some units and formations had fought better than others. But he concluded his monumental study with the laudatory assessment of Montgomery's army, that its performance 'gives little occasion for adverse criticism'.[9]

Ellis's book was published in 1962. It was not greeted with universal approbation. One critic privately concluded that it had passed over awkward episodes which did not reflect well on individuals or units and that 'the truth has been polished out of existence in deference to Monty's subordinate commanders'.[10] A more critical school had already emerged and was gathering momentum. It has now come to dominate the historiography of the British army during the Second World War. In 1952 Chester Wilmot, a war correspondent who had worked for the BBC in the North West Europe campaign, published a best-selling examination of the European war, *The Struggle for Europe*, in which he highlighted a number of the army's apparent shortcomings. They included the inability of the British to exploit successful attacks, their often poor morale, their preference for fighting at a distance, using their overwhelming air and artillery support, and their reluctance to engage in face to face combat with the enemy.[11] Wilmot's arguments have become

[5] LHCMA Alanbrooke MSS 6/2/6, Brooke to Wavell, 5 July 1942.

[6] LHCMA Alanbrooke MSS 6/2/6, Wavell to Brooke, 31 May 1942.

[7] FMVisc. Montgomery of Alamein, *Normandy to the Baltic* (London, 1946), *passim*.

[8] FM Montgomery, *The Memoirs of Field-Marshal Montgomery of Alamein* (London, 1958), p. xi; Maj.-Gen. Sir F. de Guingand, *Operation Victory* (2nd edn., London, 1960). Montgomery was, of course, not at all backward in criticizing the operational conduct of some of his predecessors in command of 8th Army.

[9] Maj. L. F. Ellis, *Victory in the West*, i. *The Battle for Normandy* (2nd edn., London, 1974), 491.

[10] LHCMA Liddell Hart MSS 1/269/20, Essame to Liddell Hart, 26 Feb. 1963.

[11] C. Wilmot, *The Struggle for Europe* (London, 1954), 477.

the staple of most critical accounts of the British army's combat capability in the war against Germany and Italy. Numerous commentators, beginning with Sir Basil Liddell Hart in his book, *The Other Side of the Hill*, have contrasted the supposed tactical excellence of the German army, not just in Normandy, but throughout the war, with the ineptitude of the British. In particular, they have drawn attention to the chronic difficulty that the British experienced in practising combined arms tactics and have concluded that the British only won when they enjoyed overwhelming material superiority.[12]

Their explanations for these apparent shortcomings range from the strategic to the social. The army was the product of its parent society. It was the victim of politicians who, anxious to avoid another bloodbath on the scale of the First World War, kept it short of funds and decreed that its main function was to act as a colonial police force. It could not successfully practise combined arms tactics because it lacked a combined arms doctrine, because it did not take training seriously, and because it was a product of Britain's class-based social structure. The rank and file were too poorly educated to be able to think for themselves on the battlefield. The army could not train its junior leaders to exhibit initiative because to do so was 'basically contrary to the whole hierarchic and class system within the British army'.[13] The result, it was argued, was that at the tactical level many British units were slow to manoeuvre and they lacked the flexibility and drive of their German counterparts. Middle-ranking officers at brigade and battalion level were incapable of mounting anything other than set-piece assaults. The inter-war regular officer corps, the men who dominated the army's higher ranks between 1939–45, contained a few men who took their profession seriously but

---

[12] This analysis is informed by the following: C. d'Este, *Decision in Normandy* (New York, 1983); idem, 'The Army and the Challenge of War, 1939–45', in D. Chandler and I. Beckett (eds.), *The Oxford Illustrated History of the British Army* (Oxford, 1994), 298–9; M. Hastings, *Overlord. D-Day and the Battle for Normandy* (New York, 1984); A. Horne with D. Montgomery, *The Lonely Leader. Monty 1944–45* (London, 1994); J. Man, *The Penguin Atlas of D-Day and the Normandy Campaign* (London, 1994); W. Murray, 'British Military Effectiveness in the Second World War', in A. R. Millett and W. Murray (eds.), *Military Effectiveness*, iii. *The Second World War* (London, 1988), 90–135; R. Callaghan, 'Two Armies in Normandy: Weighing British and Canadian Military Performance', in T. A. Wilson (ed.), *D-Day 1944* (Lawrence, Kan., 1994), 261–81; C. Barnett, *The Desert Generals* (2nd edn., London, 1983); S. Bidwell, 'The Gentleman versus the Players', *Journal of the Royal United Services Institute*, 121 (1976), 82–3; M. Howard, 'The Liddell Hart Memoirs', *Journal of the Royal United Services Institute*, 111 (1966), 58–61; D. Fraser, *And We Shall Shock Them. The British Army and the Second World War* (London, 1983); J. Ellis, *Brute Force. Allied Strategy and Tactics in the Second World War* (London, 1990); B. H. Liddell Hart, *The Other Side of the Hill* (2nd edn., London, 1951). Only very recently has a younger generation of historians begun to reassess this consensus. See S. A. Hart, 'Field Marshal Montgomery, 21st Army Group, and North West Europe, 1944–45', Ph. D. thesis (London, 1995); idem, 'Montgomery, Morale Casualty Conservation and "Colossal Cracks": 21st Army Group's Operational Technique in North West Europe, 1944–45', *Journal of Strategic Studies*, 19 (1996), 132–53.

[13] Horne and Montgomery, *The Lonely Leader*, 191.

too many of them looked on soldiering as an agreeable pastime and saw the army as a refuge from the industrial world. They ignored the ways in which industrial and technical changes were altering the conduct of war. Placing cavalry officers in tanks was a mistake because they had no love for, or understanding of, machinery or how it ought to be used.[14] Men got to the top of the army because of their social standing, rather than their professional competence. Cleverness and ambition were less highly prized than good manners, courage, and chivalry. The regimental system, to which they were emotionally committed, helped to sustain morale, but it also encouraged a dangerous parochialism, which was one reason why the different arms found it so difficult to co-operate on the battlefield. The final outcome for many historians, was that whenever the British or Americans 'met the Germans in anything like equal strength, the Germans prevailed'.[15] An American historian, Colonel Trevor N. Dupuy, claimed to have discovered that the German army enjoyed 'a ground combat effectiveness superiority of about 20 per cent over the Western Allies'.[16] His findings, apparently based upon extensive statistical analysis, have formed the basis of several widely read studies.[17] Historians left with the task of explaining why the Anglo-American forces did finally win the war in the West have been forced back on the explanation that they enjoyed an overwhelming material superiority. From late 1942 until the end of the war the British army was eventually successful because it employed a combination of 'brute force' and a reversion to the methods of 1918. This book will suggest that although these explanations of the limitations of the British army's combat capability are not wrong, they are in some respects superficial, incomplete, and based upon a limited analysis of the available evidence. The purpose of this book is to provide a fuller and better documented account of why the British army fought the war against Germany in the way that it did.

Wilmot had the advantage that he was an eyewitness of many of the events that he wrote about. However, he based many of his more critical comments about the combat capability of the British army on translations of captured German assessments of their opponents and the post-war interrogation reports of senior German officers. He quoted with approbation, for example, a report written by General Bayerlein, the commander of the Panzer Lehr division, who contended that British infantry rarely exploited a successful break-in, their morale was

---

[14]   PRO CAB 106/1060, Reports from Normandy, 1944, 6 June–10 July 1944, by Brig. J. Hargest, New Zealand Army observer with XXX Corps.

[15]   Hastings, *Overlord*, 24.

[16]   Colonel T. N. Dupuy, *Numbers, Predictions and War. Using History to Evaluate Combat Factors and Predict the Outcome of Battles* (2nd edn., Fairfax, Va., 1985), p. ix.

[17]   See e.g. Hastings, *Overlord*; Horne and Montgomery, *The Lonely Leader*.

generally poor, and, rather than engage their opponents in close combat, they preferred to rely upon artillery and air support.[18] His successors have followed suit, for it is easy to ransack these reports for critical comments about British morale and combat capability.[19] At the operational level, by October 1941, the Germans had concluded that 'English leadership in large scale engagements is slow and cumbersome.'[20] After the CRUSADER offensive in North Africa in November and December 1941, Panzer Gruppe Afrika concluded that

there was scarcely any deviation [by the British] from cumbersome and methodical tactics. Orders were inflexible and went into very great detail. This gave intermediate and lower HQs very little freedom of action, and the high command was usually slow in adapting itself to new situations which arose as the battle developed.[21]

The 8th Army's commanders had violated one of the fundamental principles of war in failing to concentrate their forces at the decisive point. Following the fall of Tobruk in June 1942, the DAK reported that 'The slowness and clumsiness [of the 8th Army], the lack of initiative and tactical versatility observed up to date has not changed. There was no alteration in tactical planning as the battle developed in a way which had not been expected beforehand.'[22] Two years later, according to General Leo Geyr von Schweppenburg, who commanded Panzer Gruppe West in Normandy until early July 1944, it was still the case that 'The British leadership in Normandy proceeded slowly and methodically'.[23] Attacks were carried out only after thorough reconnaissance and were preceded by intense artillery fire.[24] The British 'attempt to smash the enemy by means of their heavy weapons and to occupy ground without having to fight for it, thereby avoiding heavy casualties'.[25] They also criticized the British for failing to exploit early successes. General Diestel, whose 346th Infantry division began to

[18] Wilmot, *The Struggle for Europe*, 477.

[19] Ellis, for example, quotes Wilmot quoting Bayerlen. Ellis, *Brute Force*, 535–6.

[20] AWM 3 DRL/6643/1/2Bii, GHQ MEF, Daily Intelligence summary, Part 2, Appendix B no. 602, 12 Jan. 1942: Captured German document, School for armoured troops, Experiences from the African theatre of war, 16 Oct. 1941. (I am most grateful to Prof. John Ferris for bringing this document to my attention.)

[21] PRO CAB 146/10, Enemy Documents Section, Axis Operations in North Africa, Part 2. Nov. 1941–Feb. 1942, Appendix 9: Appreciation of the fighting, 11 Nov. 1941–6 Feb. 1942, trans. from Panzergruppe Afrika's battle report.

[22] PRO CAB 146/15, Enemy Documents Section, Appreciation no. 9, Part IV, Appendix 9: Nehring, DAK 1a, DAKs report on fighting, May–July 1942, 10 Aug. 1942.

[23] LHCMA Liddell Hart MSS 15/4/95, von Schweppenburg, 'Reflections on the Invasion', July 1963.

[24] LHCMA Dempsey MSS, 2 Army Intelligence summary no. 46, 20 July 1944, Appendix C, Trans. of enemy doc., Panzer Lehr, Subject: Report on experiences.

[25] PRO WO 232/25, Directorate of tactical investigation, German MIRS papers, Special tactical studies no. 29: German views of allied combat efficiency, 17 Nov. 1944.

arrive in Normandy on 8 June, was only one of many German generals who commented that the British

attacks were too well-organised and lacking in originality to take full advantage of a completely defeated enemy. The allies failed to follow through and quickly press home their gains. Particularly was this so at night-time, when after a masterful advance during daylight, the troops would stop to prepare the next day's operation.[26]

Combined-arms co-operation seemed, to the Germans, to be poor or even non-existent. In 1942 DAK believed that apart from a few instances, 'there was no close co-operation between infantry and armoured formations; the tanks followed up very slowly and were not nearly quick enough in exploiting successes gained by the Lorried Infantry'.[27] At the tactical level, many German reports concluded that British junior leaders were lethargic, lacked initiative, and were tactically inept, all faults which the Germans attributed to a lack of proper training.[28] At Anzio in 1944, they criticized British infantry for attacking at a walking pace, and for failing to take advantage of features of the terrain which might have protected them. In July 1944 the commander of the 304th Panzer Grenadier Regiment in Normandy concluded that 'Regarding British inf[antry] it is known that their patrols do not use much skill in approach and that they can be allowed to approach and be shot up'.[29]

The Germans attributed British failures to press forward to their low morale. German intelligence reports noted that British tank crews in Normandy turned back when faced with even slight German opposition.[30] Similarly, the commander of the German 276th Infantry division insisted that 'The English infantryman is certainly no hero. When fired on, he stays under cover or withdraws. He even does this when his tanks have pushed ahead of the infantry.'[31] His opinion was shared by other German officers. The Ib [intelligence officer] of LXXXIX Corps, writing of the infantry of 7th Armoured division, concluded that 'The inf[antry]. soldier is regarded by our own t[roo]ps as medium. He fights if he has got the support of t[an]ks and art[iller]y; otherwise he takes evasive

[26] PRO WO 205/1021, Interrogation reports German Generals, vol. 1: Interrogation of General Diestel; see also H. Ritgen, *The Western Front 1944. Memoirs of a Panzer Lehr Officer* (Winnipeg, Man., 1995), 76.
[27] PRO CAB 146/15, Enemy Documents Section, Appreciation no. 9, Part IV, Appendix 9.
[28] Ibid.
[29] LHCMA Dempsey MSS, 2 Army Intelligence summary no. 69, 12 Aug. 1944. Extract from log of 326 Infantry divn. captured Area 8847, 21 July 1944.
[30] PRO WO 219/1908, SHAEF, G-2 Records, SHAEF Operational Intelligence Section, Intelligence Notes no. 21, 3 Aug. 1944.
[31] LHCMA Dempsey MSS, 2 Army Intelligence summary: Trans. of extracts from Divn. Daily Orders of 276 Infantry divn., 5 Aug. 1944.

action.'[32] Once deprived of artillery support, British infantry under attack were apt to surrender or run away. After two weeks in combat, Panzer Lehr was particularly critical of the British propensity to remain on their objective rather than press forward to take advantage of a defeated enemy and believed that 'It is best to attack the English, who are very sensitive to close combat and flank attacks at his weakest moment—that is, when he has to fight without his art[iller]y'.[33]

The Germans insisted that the only reason that the British regularly defeated them after October 1942 was because they enjoyed overwhelming material superiority. Grenadier Hubert Wallner of the 987th Panzer Grenadier Regiment wrote in his diary on 23 July 1944 that 'We are only afraid of his [the British] artillery and his tanks, which he has in sufficient quantities. His infantry is not so hot.'[34] Allied air superiority meant, in the opinion of General von Eberbach, who succeeded von Schweppenburg as Commander of Panzer Gruppe West, that, while the British could move at will in daylight, the Germans had to confine their movements to the few hours of the summer night, were starved of supplies, and suffered terrible losses from air attacks.[35] In Von Schweppenburg's opinion, 'The British leadership gave the impression of aiming at a gradual "wearing down" of the enemy through British superiority in material. In this way Montgomery adhered to the British school.'[36]

However, before we take this evaluation at its face value, four provisos must be noted. This picture of British ineptitude has been contested by observers with actual experience of fighting the Germans on the ground. Sydney Jary, who commanded an infantry platoon from August 1944 to May 1945 in North West Europe, noted in 1987 that

Over the past twenty years it has become the custom of some of our younger military writers to extol the professional ability of the Wehrmacht whilst decrying that of our own fighting arms, particularly our armour and infantry. This

[32] LHCMA Verney MSS II/4, Trans. of a captured document: Appreciation of 7 Armoured divn. on the front, 4 Oct. 1944.

[33] LHCMA Dempsey MSS, 2 Army Intelligence summary no. 46, 20 July 1944, Trans. of enemy doc. Panzer Lehr. Critics of the morale of the British army, particularly in Normandy have also relied heavily upon two other pieces of evidence, a report written by the New Zealand observer in the beachhead, Brig. James Hargest, and the collapse of morale of the 6 Duke of Wellintgon's Regt. in June 1944. I have shown elsewhere that such isolated items of evidence cannot be accepted as a surrogate for an analysis of the morale of 2 British Army in 1944. See D. French, '"Tommy is no Soldier": The Morale of the Second British Army in Normandy, June–August 1944', *Journal of Strategic Studies*, 19 (1996), 154–78.

[34] LHCMA Dempsey MSS, 2 Army Intelligence summary: Trans. of extracts from diary of Hubert Wallner of 3 Coy, 987 PGR (now PW), n.d.

[35] PRO WO 205/1022, Special Interrogation Report, General Han Eberbach, Commander, Panzer Gruppe West (5 Panzer Army c.25 July 1944), 9 Dec. 1946.

[36] LHCMA Liddell Hart MSS 15/4/95, von Schweppenburg, 'Reflections on the Invasion', July 1963.

has perplexed me because it runs contrary to my experience. My 18 Platoon were better soldiers than any we fought. So was 'D' Company and the whole of 4th Battalion, The Somerset Light Infantry. Admittedly it was a good battalion but I find it hard to believe that it was unique.[37]

Secondly, Dupuy's work provoked a lively and critical response, aimed in particular at his methodology. One critic accused him of employing a biased sample and skewing his findings in favour of the German army by choosing engagements in which some of the best formations of the Wehrmacht were pitted against an average sample of US divisions.[38] A similar criticism can be made of his treatment of the British army. The core of his findings are based upon an analysis of a total of eighty engagements in the European theatre fought by US or British divisions between September 1943 and December 1944. However, the sample as a whole is heavily biased towards the Italian campaign. Sixty out of the total of eighty engagements took place in Italy. Only twenty-six of them involved British divisions, and all of the 'British' engagements were fought in Italy between September 1943 and June 1944. None of them, whether fought by British or American divisions, took place in the Normandy campaign.

Dupuy's sample of British divisions is extremely small and, in at least two important respects, misleading. He included only a single armoured division, the 7th, and five infantry divisions, the 1st, 5th, 46th, 50th, and 56th. This is not a representative cross-section of the British army. In July 1944, excluding parachute formations, independent tank brigades, and Dominion divisions, the British army mustered seven armoured divisions and twenty-three infantry divisions. Dupuy's sample, therefore, significantly underrepresents armoured divisions, the most powerful formations in the army. He also lists a mysterious 7th Infantry division as having fought two engagements in Italy between 17–22 October 1943. This division never fought in Italy. It had been broken up in 1939. In 1941 it was resurrected on paper as part of the British deception campaign in the Middle East, but was 'disbanded' again in June 1943.[39] Furthermore, he mistakenly lists the 50th division as having taken part in an engagement in Italy at Monte Grande on 16–17 October 1943. In reality the division, having participated in the con-

[37] S. Jary, *Eighteen Platoon* (Carshalton Beeches, Surrey, 1987), 16.

[38] Maj. J. S. Brown, 'Colonel Trevor N. Dupuy and the Mythos of the Wehrmacht Superiority: A Reconsideration', *Military Affairs*, 50 (1986), 16–20; Col. T. N. Dupuy, 'Mythos or Verity: The Quantified Judgement Model and German Combat Effectiveness', *Military Affairs*, 50 (1986), 204–10; Maj. J. S. Brown, 'The Wehrmacht Myth Revisited: A Challenge to Colonel Trevor N. Dupuy', *Military Affairs*, 51 (1987), 146–7; Col. T. N. Dupuy, 'A Response to the "Wehrmacht mythos" revisited', *Military Affairs*, 51 (1987), 196–7.

[39] Lieut.-Col. H. F. Olsen, *Orders of Battle Second World War 1939–45* (London, 1990), 51–2.

quest of Sicily, never landed on the mainland of Italy and was busy embarking to return home by mid-October.[40]

Dupuy's sample of German divisions that fought against the British is even more unrepresentative of the German army as a whole. In nineteen engagements that Dupuy analysed, British formations were opposed by Panzer or Panzer Grenadier divisions, but they were opposed by infantry or parachute divisions in only five engagements. (In the two remaining engagements they were opposed by smaller, combat-command-sized formations.) This suggests that the German army was a predominantly motorized and mechanized force. The reality was the reverse. The Germans concentrated their best troops and most modern and powerful equipment in a handful of Panzer and Panzer Grenadier divisions. The bulk of their army consisted of foot-marching infantry with far less lavish scales of equipment. By June 1944, the German army contained 222 infantry divisions, but only 52 Panzer or Panzer Grenadier divisions.[41] Dupuy has, therefore, pitted the best of the German army against a below-average sample of the British army. Any attempt to extrapolate conclusions from his findings about the relative combat capabilities of the two armies is therefore likely to be misleading and must be treated with considerable caution.

The third proviso is that the Germans were not entirely objective observers. When German officers wrote disparagingly of the poor morale and lack of operational and tactical acumen of their British opponents, they were not intent on providing later historians with impartial assessments; they were pursuing their own contemporary agenda. German soldiers were not military automata immune to hunger, loneliness and fear. Indeed, as the war proceeded, their commanders became increasingly worried about the declining morale of their own men. By late 1943 some German commanders in Italy were concerned about the growing numbers of their own men who went 'missing' from some of their infantry divisions 'in numbers that bore no relation to the intensity of the fighting'.[42] In mid-July 1944 Eberbach complained of growing signs of slackening morale and indiscipline amongst his troops.[43] By the time the commander of 276th Infantry division circulated his assessment of the performance of the British infantry in Normandy, the situation had worsened in the German army.[44] On 6 August all German regimental commanders in Normandy received a

---

[40] E. W. Clay, *The Path of the 50th* (Aldershot, 1950), 220–1.
[41] Ellis, *Brute Force*, Table 35.
[42] F. von Senger und Etterlin, *Neither Fear Nor Hope* (London, 1963), 183.
[43] LHCMA Dempsey MSS, 2 Army Intelligence summary no. 59, 2 Aug. 1944: Trans. of a letter from GOC Panzer Gruppe West to units under his command, 16 July 1944.
[44] LHCMA Dempsey MSS, 2 Army Intelligence summary no. 62, 5 Aug. 1994: Trans. of extracts from Divisional Daily Orders of 276 Infantry divn., 5 Aug. 1944.

message from the C-in-C West complaining that the ranks of the army included a number of 'uncontrolled, traitorous elements probably in the service of the enemy' who abandoned their weapons and ran away. He instructed his officers

to meet this contingency ruthlessly on the spot.

In such cases you must not shrink from using the utmost severity and harshness.

Every means is right if it serves to restore discipline forthwith as now ordered by the Führer for the East.

Summary shooting is to be envisaged for soldiers who cannot prove that it is through no fault of their own that they were found without weapons.[45]

By denigrating the morale and combat capability of the British, German officers hoped to raise the morale of their own troops. After 1945, it salved the pride of surviving German soldiers 'to encourage the theory and myth that, although superior as fighting men, they were beaten only by numerically superior forces and firepower'.[46] It was perhaps also in the interests of military commentators of the United States and Western Europe, areas whose forces later confronted the numerically formidable forces of the Warsaw Pact, to propagate the notion that small armies could defeat larger armies if only they were more skilful.

The final proviso which highlights the danger of overreliance upon German assessments of the British army's poor combat capability is that the same documents can be used to prove the very opposite. It is equally easy to use the same documents to find German observers heaping praise upon at least some facets of the British army's conduct of operations. This evidence will be explored in more detail in subsequent chapters. Two examples here must suffice. After fighting British and Commonwealth forces around Tobruk and at Sollum, the commander of 2nd battalion of the 104th Lorried Infantry regiment in 21st Panzer division reported that 'The English and Australians are tough and hard opponents as individual fighters, highly skilled in defence, unimaginative and inflexible in attack, cold-blooded and skilled in in-fighting, experienced in assault, and capable of standing hardships of all kinds'.[47] And in Normandy the Adjutant of 1st battalion, 25th Panzer Grenadier regiment of 12th SS Panzer division, noted the skill with which the British overran the forward positions of his battalion by plastering the German

---

[45]   PRO HW 5/554, CX/MSS/R.269, Reports and teleprints, 7–8 Aug. 1944: Message sent from C-in-C West to regimental commanders, 4 Aug. 1944, Despatched to regiments, 6 Aug. 1944.

[46]   Jary, *Eighteen Platoon*, 17.

[47]   AWM 3 DRL/6643/1/2Bii, GHQ, MEF, Daily Intelligence summary no. 612, 22 Jan. 1942: Report of 25 Aug. 1941, by 2nd Bn., 104th Lorried Infantry Regt. in reply to Divisional Questionnaire.

positions with artillery and bringing forward their infantry riding on their supporting tanks. By the time the Germans had emerged from their trenches the British infantry were already on top of them.[48]

This book will try to explain how these apparently contradictory assessments of the British army's combat capability can be reconciled and understood. The analysis will try to show not only how the army's development was constrained by the role it was accorded within British strategic policy, but it will also examine how the army worked at the operational and tactical levels of war.[49] The starting point of this book is that the combat capability of any army, that is its ability to generate and sustain fighting power, is composed of three elements, the conceptual, the material, and the moral.[50] This is reflected in the structure of the first four chapters of this book. They examine the doctrine of the army as it developed in the inter-war period, the recruiting and training of regimental officers and other ranks, their morale and discipline, and the design, and manufacture, of equipment and its transportation to the front. As many of the key decisions about these issues were taken in the inter-war period, the analysis of these factors will begin in the aftermath of the First World War. But combat capability not only depends upon how these elements interact with each other; it also depends upon how together they synergise with enemy forces. The second part of this book, therefore, analyses these interactions by looking at the campaign in France and Flanders in 1940 (Chapter 5), the post-Dunkirk reforms of the army at home (Chapter 6), the campaign in North Africa from December 1940 to July 1942 (Chapter 7), and, finally, the operations of 1st, 2nd, and 8th Armies from Alam Halfa to the Rhine crossing (Chapter 8).

[48] LHCMA Dempsey MSS, 2 Army Intelligence summary no. 38, 12 July 1944, Appendix A: Trans. of German document, 6 July 1944.

[49] In using these terms, I have very loosely followed the definitions employed in modern British doctrine. Strategic policy is the application of military resources to achieve political objectives. The operational level of war concerns the activities of corps and army headquarters in their conduct of large-scale military operations; the tactical level concerns the conduct of military operations at divisional level and below. See Joint Warfare Publications, *British Defence Doctrine* (London, 1997), sect. 1, pp. 8, 13.

[50] This definition is also taken from Joint Warfare Publications, *British Defence Doctrine*, sect. 6, p. 2. See also Col. C. Grant, 'The Use of History in the Development of Contemporary Doctrine', in J. Gooch (ed.), *The Origins of Contemporary Doctrine. Papers Presented at a Conference Sponsored by the Director General of Development and Doctrine at Larkhill, March 1996* (Camberley, 1996), 14–15.

CHAPTER ONE

'How Are You to Succeed without Causing Losses'?[1] Doctrine and Organization, 1919–1939

Politicians must bear some of the blame for the defeats that the British army suffered between 1940 and 1942. Their decisions about the priorities to be given to defence and other spending programmes, and the low priority they accorded the army compared to the navy and air force, left the army woefully unprepared in the physical sense for the kind of war it faced after September 1939.[2] But those defeats also stemmed from the army's own failures to develop appropriate concepts about how to fight the next war. The General Staff developed the idea of maintaining a small, professional and well-equipped mechanized and motorized army, able to win victories quickly and cheaply by substituting technology for manpower. But its doctrine was ill suited to exploit the advantages of such an organization to the utmost. Although it did develop a combined-arms doctrine, it remained committed to an autocratic command and control system that inhibited subordinate commanders from exercising their initiative and seizing the fleeting opportunities offered to them on the battlefield. The overriding importance of avoiding undue casualties also encouraged the framers of British doctrine to place the necessity of consolidating gains won on the battlefield before the need to exploit success. The army also developed organizational structures that sacrificed fire-power to mobility and divorced commanders from the fire-support weapons they required if they were to advance across the battlefield.

At a theoretical level the inter-war army recognized that doctrine was essential to ensure uniformity of thought and effort. Without doctrine, an organization that was so large would deform any commander's will. As Sir Philip Chetwode, GOC-in-C Aldershot Command, remarked in 1923, 'if an Army is to succeed, everyone in it must know the class of

[1] This question was posed by the CIGS, Sir George Milne. See PRO WO 279/74, Report on the Staff Conference held at the Staff College Camberley, 9–11 Jan. 1933.

[2] B. Bond, *British Military Policy Between the Two World Wars* (Oxford, 1980), *passim*; N. H. Gibbs, *Grand Strategy*, i. *Rearmament Policy* (London, 1976), *passim*; R. P. Shay, *British Rearmament in the Thirties. Politics and Profits* (Princeton, NJ, 1977), *passim*; G. Peden, *British Rearmament and the Treasury, 1932–39* (Edinburgh, 1979), *passim*.

action other people on their right and left, or in front of or behind them, will take under certain circumstances. It is fatal not to work to a common doctrine . . .'[3] Throughout the 1920s, successive CIGS, like the Earl of Cavan and Sir George Milne, insisted, to use Milne's phrase, that 'We must have one doctrine throughout the Army'.[4] The function of doctrine was to shape the actions of soldiers and to provide the basis for military education, training, and organization. The General Staff issued no less than four editions of its main doctrinal manual, the *Field Service Regulations*, between 1920 and 1935. Each edition was prepared under the auspices of the Director of Staff Duties at the War Office, although he usually delegated the preparation of a first draft to an officer outside the War Office. Major-General C. P. Deedes drafted the 1929 edition and Archibald Wavell prepared the 1935 edition.[5] The draft was circulated not only to the General Staff branches in the War Office, but also to the GOC-in-Cs of the home commands and the Staff College for comment. Each manual, therefore, represented a consensus of the General Staff's views.

The promulgation of the 'Ten Year Rule' in 1919 may have been posited on the assumption that the army had no need to prepare to fight a war in Europe for another decade, and it certainly had the effect of denying them the wherewithal to do so. But it did not prevent the General Staff from considering how they could fight a well-equipped, European army. *FSR* paid lip-service to the fact that the army might be engaged in imperial policing or wars against a second-class enemy such as the Afghans. But the whole tenor of the doctrine it promulgated was designed for a war against a first-class enemy. In the post-war era, when there was no one single obvious enemy to confront, it made sense to plan on a 'worst-case assumption', for if the army was prepared to fight a 'big' war, it could surely win a 'small' one.[6] The fact that *FSR* went through four editions, compared to the two editions of the German regulations, *Leadership and Battle with Combined Arms* (1921 and 1923) and *Troop Leadership* (1933), and the two editions of its French counterpart, *Instructions on the Tactical Employment of Large Units*, was itself proof that the British army was trying hard to understand the lessons of the First World War.

The British army reacted to the experiences of 1914–18 in exactly the

---

[3] LCHMA Liddell Hart MSS 15/8/56. Some Remarks on Training made by Lieut.-Gen. Sir Philip Chetwode to Aldershot Command, 21 Apr. 1923.

[4] PRO WO 279/55, Report on the Staff Exercise held by CIGS, 9–13 Apr. 1923; PRO WO 279/60, Report on the Staff Conference held at the Staff College Camberley, 16–19 Jan. 1928.

[5] PRO WO 279/70, Report on the Staff Conference held at the Staff College Camberley, 13–16 Jan. 1930.

[6] *FSR (1924)*, 1; T. R. Moreman, ' "Small Wars" and "Imperial Policing": The British Army and the Theory and Practice of Colonial Warfare in the British Empire, 1919–39', *Journal of Strategic Studies*, 19 (1996), 107–9.

same way as the Germans. It tried to assimilate the lessons of the First World War into its pre-war doctrine while simultaneously trying to predict how future developments in weapons technology might affect the conduct of war. British inter-war doctrine rested upon two fundamental assumptions. At the strategic level, it accepted that wars between great powers would be clashes involving the whole resources of every belligerent. Victory would, therefore, require the mobilization not merely of the armed forces, but the whole of society. Paradoxically, however, the General Staff showed a marked practical preference for limiting Britain's own commitment to a continental land war. The losses Britain suffered during the First World War convinced them that never again would the army be allowed to be as profligate with the lives of its men as it had been on the Western Front. In 1927, Milne concluded that 'in the war of the future we cannot depend on the man-power that we had in the last great war, nor will any nation stand the losses we went through again for another 100 years'.[7] '[C]ivilisation itself would go to pieces if a war similar to the last one were fought'.[8] Indeed, preserving 'civilisation' was now the function of war. At the Staff College in the 1920s, aspiring commanders were cautioned 'Finally, do not wear yourself away solely in order to wear away the enemy; remember that war is not an end in itself but a means to an end, namely, an economical victory which will secure a prosperous and contented peace.'[9]

Even before 1914 some senior officers had doubted the steadfastness of the urban-bred masses that filled the ranks of the army.[10] The war intensified their concerns. They now knew that they could not expect the automatic deference they had once enjoyed. The next generation of soldiers, better educated than their fathers and full of folk memories of the holocaust of the Western Front, were likely to be frankly sceptical of the military abilities of their leaders. They would not offer unquestioning obedience to their officers, a quality that senior officers believed was indispensable if troops were to be called on to endure heavy losses without flinching.[11] Furthermore, after 1930, senior officers knew that if their soldiers did disobey they no longer had the

[7] PRO WO 279/57, Report of the Staff Conference held at the Staff College Camberley, 17–20 Jan. 1927.

[8] LHCMA Milne MSS Box 3, Address to officers of the Mechanised Force by CIGS at Tidworth, 8 Sept. 1927.

[9] Staff College Camberley, Captain H. H. Dempsey MSS, Lecture to senior divn. by R. G. Finlayson, Jan. 1927: 'Grand Tactics of the Great War'.

[10] T. Travers, *The Killing Ground. The British Army and the Emergence of Modern Warfare 1900–1918* (London, 1987), 37–55; K. Surridge, ' "All you Soldiers are what we Call pro-Boer": The Military Critique of the South African War, 1899–1902', *History*, 82 (1997), 582–600.

[11] PRO WO 277/7, Brig. A. B. McPherson, *Discipline* (London, 1950), 4, 23; S. P. Mackenzie, *Politics and Military Morale. Current Affairs and Citizenship Education in the British Army 1914–50* (Oxford, 1992), 44–8.

right to shoot some to encourage the others.[12] In such circumstances, officers would have no option other than to study carefully the moods of their men and lead them by negotiation.[13] Casualty consciousness and the overriding need not to overtax their troops' morale was, therefore, deeply embedded in the thinking of senior British officers long before the Second World War.

Although they never entirely lost sight of the fact that in a great war Britain might be compelled to raise a much larger army, the General Staff's ideal in the 1920s and for much of the 1930s was to establish a small, highly mechanized professional army. Even before the cabinet had promulgated the 'Ten Year Rule' in 1919, the CIGS, Sir Henry Wilson, had accepted that in the immediate future there was no danger of another major European war. The army's main functions were, therefore, garrisoning the Empire and forming a small expeditionary force for colonial wars. However, Wilson also recognized that the international situation might worsen, and asked the government to re-establish the post-war army 'on a broader basis and one which will admit of considerable expansion in the future'.[14] Two schemes, one of which would have allowed the War Office to field fifty divisions and a second forty-one divisions, were prepared by July 1919.[15] But funding constraints, combined with a widespread loathing of any possibility of engaging in another costly continental land war, meant that both schemes were still-born. In 1921, faced by the prospect of further cuts in the funding of the regular army, both Wilson and his deputy preferred to reduce or even abolish the Territorial Army, even though it would threaten the War Office's ability to raise a larger force at the outset of the next great war.[16]

By the early 1920s the General Staff accepted that a relatively small but highly professional army, equipped with the most modern weapons, offered them the best way of avoiding a repetition of the stalemate and high casualties of the Western Front and the collapse of morale that it threatened. The threat of overwhelming air attack would, in any case, make the deployment of a mass army based upon the nation in arms, impossible.[17] 'We must', Milne insisted in 1929, 'never let the next war

[12] J. McHugh, 'The Labour Party and the Parliamentary Campaign to Abolish the Military Death Penalty, 1919–1930', *Historical Journal*, 42 (1999), 233–50.

[13] Brig. B. D. Fisher, 'The Training of the Regimental Officer', *Journal of the Royal United Services Institute*, 74 (1929), 242–3.

[14] *The Military Correspondence of Field-Marshall Sir Henry Wilson, 1918–22*, ed. K. Jeffrey (London, 1985), 121–2; PRO WO 106/316, Churchill to Cabinet and enc., 20 Aug. 1919.

[15] PRO WO 32/11356, DDSD to DDMO, Interim and post-bellum army, 4 Dec. 1918, and Harrington to Finance Member, 19 Dec. 1918; PRO WO 237/13, Report of Committee on organization of after-war army, July 1919.

[16] LHCMA Montgomery-Massingberd MSS 133/1, Chetwode to Montgomery-Massingberd, 20 July 1921.

[17] LHCMA, Milne MSS Box 3, Address to officers of the Mechanised Force by CIGS at Tidworth, 8 Sept. 1927.

reach the stage of the last one; mobility, activity and quickness from the beginning is the one thing that we have been aiming at.'[18] Far from ignoring the modern world and seeing the army as a refuge from it, senior General Staff officers eagerly embraced it. The only way to win wars quickly and cheaply, Milne decided in 1931, was through 'The scientific use and development of armaments for tactical purposes [which] is a problem which we, with our small resources in men and a small army, but with great resources in engineering and invention, must study very closely'.[19] Four years later, summing up a lecture on mechanization, one of Milne's successors, Sir Cyril Deverell, told the audience that, in the event of another great war,

we shall have to try in the first place to gain victory as quickly as possible. In other words, we must, if possible, avoid long static warfare; and in the second place we must avoid human casualties as much as it is in our power. As Colonel Martel has shown, mechanisation in its many forms applied in various ways holds out the only hope that an Army can achieve these results . . .[20]

It was hardly surprising, therefore, that in March 1939 most General Staff officers greeted the Chamberlain government's decision to double the size of the Territorial Army without enthusiasm. Chamberlain hoped that his gesture would deter Hitler from further aggression.[21] But if it failed, his decision threatened to commit a large British army to a continental war bereft of the very kind of modern equipment the General Staff believed to be essential if it was to avoid a repetition of the horrendous casualties of 1914–18.[22]

The second set of assumptions that underpinned British doctrine functioned at the operational level. *FSR* assumed that doctrine could be reduced to a set of principles, although no two editions of *FSR* listed them in exactly the same order. In 1929 Milne noted 'the much debated question of what may or may not constitute a principle of war'.[23] However, the four editions broadly agreed that the eight principles which underpinned all doctrine were: maintenance of the objective (the ultimate objective of the army was the destruction of the enemy's main force on the battlefield); offensive action (for victory could only be won by attacking the enemy); surprise (which was the most effective force-

[18] PRO WO 279/65, Report on the Staff Conference held at the Staff College Camberley, 14–17 Jan. 1929.
[19] PRO WO 279/74, Report on the Staff Conference held at the Staff College Camberley, 9–11 Jan. 1933.
[20] Col. G. Le Q. Martel, 'Mechanisation', *Journal of the Royal United Services Institute*, 82 (1937), 302.
[21] PRO PREM 1/296, H. J. [Wilson] to Hore-Belisha, 28 Mar. 1939.
[22] *Chief of Staff. The Diaries of Lieutenant-General Sir Henry Pownall, i. 1933–39*, ed. B. Bond (London, 1972), 196–7.
[23] Introd. by Sir G. Milne to Sir F. Maurice, *British Strategy. A Study of the Application of the Principles of War* (London, 1931), p. xvi.

multiplier); concentration (success depended upon concentrating a superior force at the decisive point); economy of effort (commanders had to ensure they made the most efficient use of their resources); security (commanders had to protect their own forces against enemy attacks); mobility (which conferred the ability to achieve surprise and to take offensive action); and co-operation (for only by working together could all arms exert their maximum effort).[24]

The leaders of the British General Staff were products of late nineteenth-century British society. They interpreted these principles in the light of the dominant social and cultural modes of discourse in that society and their own more recent professional experiences. In this period, their society had been transformed by the natural sciences, which were themselves rooted in the belief that human rationality could comprehend and ultimately control the natural world.[25] This encouraged soldiers to believe that they could develop doctrines which would reduce the chaos of the battlefield to order through the application of rational human analysis in just the same way that scientists and engineers had apparently brought order to the natural world. The first edition of FSR, published in 1909, tried to impose order on chaos by asserting that battles naturally fell into four phases. In the first stage the opposing armies manoeuvred against each other to seize key geographic points; in the second they sought to weaken each other through wearing-out operations; victory could only be gained by offensive action and so in the third phase one side mounted a decisive attack designed to break through the enemy's position; finally, the victor pursued the vanquished to destroy his army.[26] If the two sides were of roughly equal strength, victory would go to the army with the higher morale, 'a firmer determination in all ranks to conquer at any cost'.[27] As Tim Travers has argued, before 1914 the General Staff sought 'human solutions to modern firepower', in which high morale would suffice to enable attacking troops to cross the fire-swept zone.[28]

They did not find them, and the human cost of this doctrine was horrendous. The experience of 1914–18 did not undermine the conviction of senior officers that battles could be reduced to a series of discrete phases, each of which was susceptible to rational analysis and control. Unlike their German counterparts, they were unwilling to accept that the battlefield was inherently and inevitably chaotic and to

[24] FSR (1920), 14–15; FSR (1924), 2–4; FSR (1929), 6–9; FSR (1935), 24–5.
[25] D. Pick, War Machine. The Rationalisation of Slaughter in the Modern Age (London and New Haven, 1993), 165–6.
[26] FSR (1909), passim.
[27] FSR (1909), 131; M. Howard, 'Men against Fire: The Doctrine of the Offensive in 1914', in M. Howard, The Lessons of History (Oxford, 1993), 97–112.
[28] Travers, The Killing Ground, 48.

develop a doctrine that accepted that fact.[29] By 1918 the General Staff recognized that fire-power dominated the battlefield, but fire-power alone could not destroy an enemy who was properly dug-in. Armies, therefore, had to find some way of combining the ability to generate fire-power with the ability to manoeuvre across the battlefield. To achieve this goal, the General Staff recognized that they would have to practice combined-arms operations. This was a major departure from *FSR (1909)*, which had relegated all other arms to the role of mere auxiliaries to the infantry. But the heavy loses the infantry sustained between 1914–16 disabused commanders of this idea. They discovered that success depended upon the intelligent co-operation of all arms to over-whelm the defenders by weight of fire and enable the attacking infantry to manoeuvre without incurring unacceptably high losses.[30] The British army, therefore, did not lack a combined-arms doctrine after 1918.[31] The manuals taught that success could only be ensured by combined-arms operations because only thus could a force generate sufficient fire-power to restore mobility to the battlefield. Commanders at all levels from army down to platoon were enjoined to ensure that their plans were framed to allow for the fullest co-operation between all arms. In 1922, Cavan reminded senior officers that 'success in battle depends on efficient co-operation and we must not forget the lessons of the past'. Five years later, in 1927, Milne told another group that 'It is the co-operation of all necessary arms that wins battles'.[32] *FSR (1929)* put it bluntly when it insisted that 'The proper co-operation of all arms wins battles'. The 'fire of the defences is kept under subjugation by superior firepower', and 'It is by such superior firepower and not by men's bodies that success is won. Mere weight of numbers in the infantry assault will not of itself be effective and will result only in unnecessary casualties.'[33] Clearly, this was not a profoundly conservative doctrine intended to preserve the precedence of the traditional arms. Rather, together with the parallel quest to use mechanization to enhance mobility, it repre-

---

[29] M. Samuels, *Command or Control? Command, Training and Tactics in the British and German Armies, 1888–1918* (London, 1995), 3.

[30] For the extent of tactical developments on the Western Front, see Travers, *The Killing Ground, passim*; idem, *How the War Was Won. Command and Technology in the British Army on the Western Front, 1917–18* (London, 1992); P. Griffith, *Battle Tactics of the Western Front. The British Army's Art of Attack 1916–18* (London, 1994); idem (ed.), *British Fighting Methods in the Great War* (London, 1996); S. Bidwell and D. Graham, *Firepower. British Army Weapons and Theories of War, 1904–1945* (London, 1982), 98–111; R. Prior and T. Wilson, *Command on the Western Front. The Military Career of Sir Henry Rawlinson 1914–18* (Oxford, 1992).

[31] Cf. Murray, 'British Military Effectiveness', 111.

[32] PRO WO 279/54, Report on the Staff Exercise held by CIGS, 30 Oct.–3 Nov. 1922; PRO WO 279/59. War Office Exercise no. 2, Winchester, 9–12 May 1927. See also PRO WO 32/2382, Memorandum on Army Training, Collective Training period 1928, 26 Nov. 1928.

[33] *FSR (1929)*, 11–13, 108, 117. See also *FSR (1920)*, 22; *FSR (1924)*, 40–1; *FSR (1935)*, 7.

sented the distilled essence of the experience of 1914–18 and a concerted determination not to fight the next war in the same costly manner.[34]

Taken together, these doctrinal innovations might have helped to enable the British army to wage the same kind of rapid, mobile operations that the Germans practised between 1939 and 1941. However, another important element in British doctrine proved to be a major handicap to progress towards such developments. The British army was wedded to a command and control system that impeded the fullest possible development of 'mobility, activity and quickness' on the battle-field. It remained committed to a system of inflexible, autocratic command and control.[35] This was in part the product of a long historical tradition. In the middle of the Peninsular War one of Wellington's sub-ordinates remarked that 'at times his Lordship allows no troops to be moved, but in obedience to his own orders'.[36] But it was also derived from the experience of the First World War. The British knew that the battlefield was a chaotic environment and that it was essential to create order from chaos if they were to secure the degree of combined-arms co-operation they required. Operations between 1916 and 1918 had seemed to prove that co-operation could be achieved only by unity of control and careful planning to co-ordinate the work of supporting weapons with the movement of troops across the battlefield. Senior officers were, therefore, expected to prepare a 'master plan' to which each subordinate level of command was required to adhere unwaver-ingly. Co-operation, *FSR (1924)* asserted, 'can be ensured only by unity of control'.[37] Commanders had to be clear about their own objective, determined to succeed and to impress that determination upon their sub-ordinates by issuing clear orders.[38] The vital importance of ensuring that the master plan was a good one was underlined by the assertion that, once two forces had clashed, 'The commander of a force can have little influence on the course of the operations, once the attack had commenced, except through the medium of his reserves'.[39] Subordinates were required to do as they were told, not to act according to their own judgement according to the immediate situation facing them. British doctrine, therefore, persisted in attempting to bring the same regularity and order to the battlefield, through the application of the principles of war, as industrialists had brought to the modern factory.

[34] Cf. Bond, *British Military Policy*, 129.

[35] J. Kiszley, 'The British Army and Approaches to Warfare since 1945', *Journal of Strategic Studies*, 19 (1996), 194.

[36] R. Muir, *Tactics and the Experience of Battle in the Age of Napoleon* (London, 1998), 167.

[37] *FSR (1924)*, 4; *FSR (1920)*, 145–6.

[38] *FSR (1935)*, 26–7.

[39] *FSR (1924)*, 106.

A handful of senior officers, like Sir Jock Burnett-Stuart, GOC-in-C Egypt, recognized that in an age of machine-warfare this was no longer a realistic goal. In 1931 he told his officers that

The days of linear extensions with each man separated by a stated interval are over. The days of *all* regular diagrammatic fighting formations are over. The modern extended order consists of each unit and sub-unit having its own allotted avenue or area of approach and manoeuvre—and with a reasonable amount of give and take as regards the boundary lines. The attack against a modern enemy is no longer a matter of waves of men silting up to a final assault. It is a matter of infiltration, of intelligent co-operation, and of taking immediate advantage of opportunities which the action of neighbouring parties may open up.[40]

But officers like Burnett-Stuart were in a minority. *FSR* was the product of a bureaucratic culture that promised security and predictability to the individual, and confirmed the status and power of senior officers. These were obviously attractive benefits but such systems were apt to work well only in a stable and predictable environment. Battles were never stable and their course was rarely predictable.[41]

The German army's solution to these problems followed a different course. They rejected the idea that waging war was a 'scientific' discipline. They accepted that it was impossible to predict the course of a battle because no plan was likely to survive first contact with the enemy. Rather than rely upon a rigidly hierarchical system, in which all orders flowed down the chain of command from the top, they expected every subordinate to use his initiative. They pinned their faith instead in *Auftragstaktik*, ('mission command'). Senior commanders issued general directives but left their implementation to their subordinates, who were allowed a wide degree of latitude to interpret their orders provided they acted to secure their commander's *intention*. This was a doctrine that not only allowed but also actually required subordinate commanders to exercise the maximum amount of initiative within parameters that had been broadly defined by their superiors.[42] Junior leaders were taught that 'inaction was criminal: it was better to do something which might turn out to be wrong than to take no decision and remain inactive'.[43]

This had the potential for making an already chaotic situation even

---

[40] LHCMA Burnett-Stuart MSS 3, Burnett-Stuart, Training in Egypt, 1931.

[41] C. Handy, *Understanding Organisations* (London, 1993), 185–7; Capt. R. A. D. Applegate, 'Why Armies Lose in Battle: An Organic Approach to Military Analysis', *Journal of the Royal United Services Institute*, 132 (1987), 48.

[42] A copy of the 1933 edn. of the German army's *Truppenführung* can be found in PRO WO 287/124, German Army Field Regulations (T.F.), Part 1 (1933).

[43] PRO WO 287/226, Tactical and Technical Notes on the German Army no. 11, May 1939.

worse. But chaos was avoided, and combined-arms co-operation secured, because of the German army's commitment to a rigorous field-training programme. Soldiers at all levels were taught a series of drills to ensure that they had a common understanding of how to carry out frequently performed types of operation. The British, by contrast, shunned the adoption of tactical drills.[44] This may have been the product of a lingering class bias that persuaded senior officers that drills were pointless, because their soldiers were too lacking in intelligence to be able to function without close and constant supervision. But it was also the product of an attitude towards ideas, authority, and organization that pervaded much of the upper levels of British society, and not just the army. The General Staff's commitment to an autocratic command and control system clashed directly with the dominant liberal political culture in Britain that emphasized the importance of individuals exercising a wide degree of freedom of choice inside the boundaries of the institutions within which they existed. To be British was to be free to pursue individualism, to exercise freedom of religion, freedom of speech, and, critically in this context, to pursue ideas freely. Although senior officers in the British army were willing to accept the need for common doctrine on a theoretical level, they shared a pervasive British distaste for allowing their actions to be dictated by abstract ideas. Since the eighteenth century the British had defined their own national identity by contrasting themselves with their continental neighbours. One of the things that made them different from Frenchmen or Germans was their unwillingness to allow their actions to be governed by abstract reason. To the British, character was more important than intelligence, and improvisation in the face of difficulties had been of great benefit to the nation. By the early twentieth century, the British had developed a self-image that portrayed themselves as being god-fearing, tolerant, much given to compromise and committed to order, but also individualistic, independent and much habituated to muddling-through.[45] Senior officers were at one with many liberal intellectuals in their opposition to what one historian has called the 'enforced pursuit of collective ends, however noble'.[46] As Milne told a group of senior officers in 1927, 'The

[44] The only exception to this appears to have been Indian army units on the North-West frontier of India, which did adopt tactical drills in their efforts to combat hostile tribes on the Afghan border. They were, in turn, criticized by many British officers for pursuing a course of 'extreme formalism, comparable with the wars of stereotyped manoeuvre in Europe in the seventeenth and eighteenth centuries'. Moreman, ' "Small Wars" ', 117–18.

[45] R. Colls, 'Englishness and Political culture' in R. Colls and P. Dodd (eds.), *Englishness. Politics and Culture 1880–1920* (London, 1986), 31; S. Collini, *Public Moralists. Political Thought and Intellectual Life in Britain 1850–1930* (Oxford, 1991), 323–41; T. W. Heyck, 'Myths and Meanings of Intellectuals in Twentieth Century British National Identity', *Journal of British Studies*, 37 (1998), 192–9.

[46] J. Stephenson, 'Political Thought, Elites, and the State in Modern Britain', *Historical Journal*, 42 (1999), 263.

interpretation [of *FSR*] as you get on in the service, especially as regards senior officers of the General Staff, must be left to you to a great extent'.[47] What that meant in practice was that senior officers, particularly commanders of divisions and higher formations, were allowed wide latitude to interpret doctrine as they saw fit. Furthermore, the principle that officers who would lead men into battle were responsible for their training, not only made it possible for individual commanders to flout War Office directives wholesale, it also made it impossible to achieve a common level of training throughout the army.[48]

Just how deeply these ideas were embedded in the mental world of senior officers was illustrated by a report written in 1943 by Brigadier T. Ivor Moore. Even after several months spent commanding an Army Tank Brigade in Tunisia, he could still write that

A final point to clinch this argument is that to get the best out of any Army, it has to be led in accordance with its national characteristics. The GERMAN is at his best when fighting according to well known and practised drills, but when his plan is upset he finds it difficult to adapt himself to the changed conditions. We BRITISH, on the other hand, are better at doing what seems to us right according to the circumstances of a particular case. Our tactical handling of tanks or any other arm should, therefore, be based on [the] psychological fact that we are best 'taking the bowling as it comes'.[49]

Within this intellectual context it was, therefore, not surprising that most senior British officers were reluctant to follow their German counterparts and to recognize that doctrine was of little worth unless they adopted a common understanding of what it meant and actively sought some way to put it into practice. The advantage of the German system was that, by allowing the man on the spot to use his initiative, it promised to allow the German army to reap the full advantages of mechanization and motorization. The disadvantage of the British lack of system was that it did not.

To their credit, the British General Staff did recognize before 1939 that the combination of an autocratic command and control system and the need to generate superior fire-power to cover movements in the face of the enemy would retard the tempo of operations. They hoped that eventually scientific and engineering developments would provide commanders with rapid and flexible means of communications to link them with their subordinates. But as long as they did not, they accepted that subordinates would have to be allowed some degree of initiative. In

[47] PRO WO 279/57, Report on the Staff Conference. Other senior officers agreed with him: see LHCMA Liddell Hart MSS 15/478/56, 'Some Remarks on Training made by Lt. Gen. Sir Philip Chetwode to Aldershot Command'.
[48] PRO WO 279/57, Report on the Staff Conference.
[49] PRO WO 204/1894, Brig. T. Ivor Moore, Notes on the tactical teaching of 21st Tank bgd. for the information of British Troops in North African Battle School, 24 July 1943.

successive volumes of *FSR* they struggled with the need to strike a balance between ensuring that commanders fulfilled their role of securing the co-ordination of all arms and allowing subordinates the necessary degree of initiative required to take full advantage of fleeting opportunities. They tried to do so by telling commanders that their proper function was to allot definite tasks to their subordinates but to allow them to decide how to perform those tasks. Subordinates in turn were expected to show energy and determination and to accept responsibility. However, just where the dividing line lay between undue interference by senior commanders and undue licence on the part of their subordinates was left unclear. Granting a subordinate too much freedom could be as dangerous as granting him too little. Subordinates were expected to understand not only the meaning of their orders, but also their commanders' underlying intentions. But that did not imply British officers enjoyed the same latitude as their German opponents. In the British army, even if the circumstances in which the orders had been issued had changed, a subordinate did not have the unfettered liberty to disregard them and to adopt a new course provided it was consonant with his commander's intentions. The British officer was first required to report the changed circumstances to his superior and then await fresh orders. Only if there was not time to do so was he permitted to act on his own responsibility.[50] Ultimately everything was supposed to depend upon all concerned exercising 'A due sense of proportion'.[51]

This was a recipe for delay and lethargy. It was unsurprising that after the 1925 manoeuvres Cavan reported that, 'It was apparent from a number of the orders issued that the importance of giving a subordinate commander a definite task and leaving him to carry out that task, without undue interference from the higher authorities, is not fully appreciated.'[52] *FSR (1935)* tried to avoid this problem by permitting commanders to issue 'Operation instructions' when they felt it necessary 'to place a subordinate commander in a position in which he must act on his own judgement'. However, they were strictly enjoined to use them sparingly.

The emphasis that the army's inter-war doctrine placed on obedience to the letter of superior orders rather than the need to interpret them in the light of changing circumstances goes far towards explaining why British troops so often failed to react with the same swiftness as their enemies in 1940–5. However, it is not a complete explanation. Another reason why the British army was frequently so slow to exploit its successes was that its doctrine placed more emphasis on the overriding

[50] Ibid.; *FSR (1924)*, 10; *FSR (1935)*, 27–8.
[51] *FSR (1929)*, 5–6, 237–9.
[52] PRO WO 279/56, Report on Army Manoeuvres, 1925.

need to consolidate ground gained than it did on the necessity of exploit-ing enemy weaknesses and disorganization. *FSR* did recognize the pursuit of a defeated enemy as a definite stage of a successful battle. *FSR (1920)*, for example, insisted that when the enemy's main position had been occupied and he was retreating, the pursuit should be continued relentlessly. But it quickly vitiated the effect of that recommendation by cautioning against overconfidence, and insisted that a portion of the attacking troops should be left behind to prepare the captured position against counter-attack. The army's eventual solution to this conundrum was first propagated in *FSR (1929)*. Troops ordered to carry a well-prepared enemy position should be echeloned in depth. Each unit should be given a specific and limited objective and be relieved by fresh troops once it had secured it. A commander would thereby have sufficient forces to consolidate his gains whilst still being able to maintain the momentum of his attack.

This caution was the product of wartime experiences. On the Western Front British troops had frequently suffered heavy losses when they had pressed forward against what they believed was a beaten enemy only to become victims of the German defensive tactics of mounting an immediate counter-attack against troops that had become disorganized in the course of their own attack.[53] In a passage that formed the bedrock of British offensive doctrine during the Second World War, and revealed that commanders were concerned about the fragile morale of their troops long before the defeats of 1940–2 gave any real substance to their fears, *FSR (1929)* explained that

Troops engaged in close fighting under conditions of modern war are soon affected by physical and moral exhaustion; recovery from the former is ensured by a few hours sleep and suitable food; but recovery from the latter is a longer process. If troops, as is probable, are to be engaged with the enemy for long periods of time, it is important that their moral qualities should not be reduced to a point at which comparatively speedy recovery is impossible. The individual soldier should, therefore, not be engaged to the point of exhaustion, except in pursuit, and he should be made aware, as far as is possible, of the task which lies before him. Apart from providing every available means of support to infantry engaged in an attack, the allotment of a definite objective to units ensures that the demands likely to be made on their physical and moral powers receives due consideration.[54]

The often-noted unwillingness of British troops to exploit local success during the Second World War was not simply or solely a product of their poor morale, for, as Chapter 4 will demonstrate, their morale was not universally fragile. But it did reflect the fact that their doctrine

[53] LHCMA, Liddell Hart MSS 1/322/22, Gort to Liddell Hart, 30 Jan. 1925.
[54] *FSR (1929)*, 101.

taught them to place consolidation before exploitation and that their commanders had been taught before the war not to ask too much of them. In the late 1920s and in the 1930s the British developed a doctrine not of ruthless exploitation, but of rapid consolidation.[55]

If the British army remained wedded to these fundamental principles throughout the inter-war period, that is not to deny that successive editions of *FSR* did not incorporate a number of significant developments that distinguished each edition from its predecessor. These changes were the product of technological developments and experience gained in manoeuvres and Staff Exercises. The learning process began in the early 1920s. *FSR (1920)* had, for example, distinguished between only two types of offensive battle, an 'encounter attack' mounted against an unorganized defence and a 'deliberate attack', mounted against an opponent securely entrenched behind prepared defences.[56] This changed under Cavan. As CIGS his objective was to adjust the combined arms lessons of the First World War to the problems of mobile warfare. In 1922 and 1923 he held two major Staff Exercises to do this.[57] They indicated that, in view of the increasing danger that advancing columns would be spotted from the air, night operations would have to become more common if commanders wanted to retain an element of surprise. The 1924 manual, therefore, devoted more space to the encounter battle and included a whole new chapter on night operations.[58]

A concomitant of the manuals' increasing emphasis on mobile encounter battles was the need to secure the more rapid transmission of information and orders between commanders and their subordinates. Partly, this was a technical problem concerned with the maintenance of efficient means of communication. In 1918 some divisional commanders had developed a system of sending officers forward equipped with radios to send back up-to-the minute reports directly to their headquarters.[59] *FSR (1920)* ignored such innovations. It tried to impose the entirely unrealistic doctrine that hard-pressed subordinates, absorbed in fighting their own battles, must also remember to pass information back to their commanders.[60] Commanders of different arms at all levels were enjoined to maintain close personal contact with their colleagues and subordinates. But, at the same time, army commanders were required to

---

[55] *FSR (1935)*, 119; General Staff, *Infantry Section Leading (1938)*, 60–1.

[56] *FSR (1920)*, 158–61.

[57] PRO WO 279/54, Report on the Staff Exercises; PRO WO 279/55, Report on the Staff Exercise held by CIGS, 9–13 April 1923.

[58] *FSR (1924)*, 103–26, 199–211. The 1929 manual placed the same emphasis on night operations: *FSR (1929)*, 190–203.

[59] Montgomery, *Memoirs*, 36.

[60] *FSR (1920)*, 105.

place their headquarters sufficiently far to the rear 'as to be beyond the reach of distraction by local events'. This was a recommendation likely to ensure that they were out of touch with rapidly changing events at the front.[61]

There were several suggestions designed to deal with this problem. The 1924 edition of *FSR* ordered commanders to appoint liaison officers and to send them forward to collect information, rather than wait for their subordinates to send it back to them.[62] But the practical shortcomings of this system were highlighted in the 1925 manoeuvres. Neither of the opposing staffs had any experience of controlling mobile operations and issued overly long and prescriptive written orders. The opposing forces not only lost touch with each other, but their commanders also lost contact with their own troops. In 1922 the work of the Experimental Brigade at Aldershot had highlighted the need for mobile units to rely on wireless rather than on cable for their communications. Cavan was so anxious to force the pace of the development of better radios, and in particular sets which could operate from a moving vehicle, that in October 1922 he abolished cable communications in front of Corps headquarters except for the artillery. However, by September 1925, although one of the opposing HQs had been issued with a small number of experimental radios, they had not had enough time to train their operators, and communications collapsed.[63]

The 1929 edition of *FSR* for the first time, therefore, contained a whole chapter on communications and laid down the basic doctrine that remained in force for much of the Second World War. Authority rested with the General Staff. It was their task to inform the signal staff of their plans in sufficient time to allow the creation of an adequate communications system. The signallers were the servants of the staff. It was their task to create a communications network that could carry the required traffic. To ensure that it was not susceptible to a sudden collapse because of overdependence on a single form of communications, they were enjoined to utilize a mixture of cable, wireless, despatch riders, and aeroplanes. Divisional and lower commanders were required to reduce their dependence upon electronic means of communications by placing their Headquarters sufficiently close to the front line so that they could intervene personally if necessary. They were also told to send liaison officers to units on their flanks and their staff officers were expected to pay frequent personal visits to higher and lower headquarters.[64] These measures promised to hasten the speed of transmission of orders and

[61] *FSR (1920)*, 146–7.
[62] *FSR (1924)*, 61.
[63] LHCMA Kirke MSS 2/1/18, Lieut.-Gen. Sir P. Chetwode, Report on collective training, Aldershot Command, 14 Nov. 1925; PRO WO 279/56, Report on Army Manoeuvres, 1925.
[64] *FSR (1929)*, 256–66.

information. However, their effect was degraded by a continued insistence that orders continue to be transmitted in detail and in writing and that verbal orders should only be employed below division, and even then, if possible, confirmed in writing.[65]

Trying to secure better communications between the different levels of command was not the General Staff's only concern. Their acceptance that fire-power, not manpower, was the basis of the army's combat capability was reflected in the changing roles accorded to the three main teeth arms, the infantry, the artillery, and the tanks. This can most clearly be seen in the function of the infantry, the most manpower-intensive of all the teeth arms. In *FSR (1920)* it was noted that 'infantry is the arm which in the end wins battles'. By 1929 they had been downgraded to being the arm that 'confirm[s] victory'. Infantry remained the most adaptable of all arms of the service because it could operate over any terrain by both day and night. But it was also extremely vulnerable to well-armed enemy infantry and, if it was to advance without undue casualties, tank and artillery support was essential to suppress enemy fire.[66]

The task of artillery in providing the necessary fire-support to enable the infantry to close with the enemy remained constant throughout the 1920s. The General Staff never accepted the French doctrine that artillery conquered and the infantry merely occupied its gains. The gunners' task was 'to assist the other arms in breaking down opposition, and to afford all possible support to the infantry, with whom the eventual decision rests'.[67] The time necessary to amass huge stockpiles of shells for bombardments on the Western Front had been a significant factor in slowing the tempo of operations in 1915–17. But by 1918 better artillery techniques meant that prolonged preliminary bombardments, which forfeited surprise, were no longer necessary. The Royal Artillery had perfected techniques for firing off the map so that they could put down effective fire-support without the need for preliminary ranging. They had also recognized that their main function was not to kill the enemy before the infantry assault, but to produce suppressing fire during the assault so that the enemy's defending weapons, particularly his artillery and machine-guns, were neutralized while the attacking infantry crossed the fire-swept zone. Building on this experience, and in accordance with the quest for 'quickness', the 1929 manual suggested that the best way for the gunners 'to gain fire superiority' was to centralize the control of all available artillery at divisional level and

---

[65] Ibid. 238.

[66] *FSR (1920)*, 22; *FSR (1929)*, 11–12.

[67] *FSR (1920)*, 24; *FSR (1924)*, 15; Col. L. C. L. Oldfield, 'Artillery and the Lessons we have Learnt with regard to the Late War', *Journal of the Royal United Services Institute*, 67 (1922), 580.

to employ short and intense bombardments as they were more likely to neutralize the defenders than those which were longer but less intense.[68]

The newest of the teeth arms was the tank. In May 1919 the General Staff decided that it wanted 'an after war army with a good proportion of tanks in it'.[69] In November 1919, the Army Council agreed to establish a post-war Tank Corps in the new year. They also decided that the army needed two types of tank units, an armoured force for exploiting success and a separate type of unit to offer close support for the infantry.[70] But technological problems had to be considered. First World War vintage tanks had suffered from numerous shortcomings. They were slow, vulnerable to artillery fire, mechanically unreliable, placed a heavy strain on the BEF's logistical system, and their crews quickly became exhausted because of the high temperatures, petrol fumes, and noise they experienced in the fighting compartments. Nor could they cross swamps, wide streams, deep sunken roads, or thick woods, and their crews' field of vision was very narrow.[71] The first two post-war editions of FSR conceded these weaknesses, emphasizing their vulnerabilities and arguing that only if they operated in proper conjunction with infantry and artillery, and only if they were used in large numbers, could they deliver a devastating surprise attack.[72]

It was not until 1923 that the post-war army had a real opportunity to practise mobile operations with tanks on any scale.[73] These manoeuvres saw the employment of the first Vickers Medium Tanks. As the troops facing them had no dedicated anti-tank weapons, they dominated the battlefield. In the eyes of the enthusiasts of the RTC, the manoeuvres proved that tanks should not be tied to marching infantry, but, accompanied perhaps by lorried infantry, they should push ahead of the marching troops or attack the enemy's flank.[74] Corps level manoeuvres in 1925 seemed to point to a similar lesson.[75] A gap opened up between the RTC and mainstream thinkers in the General Staff that in many

[68] FSR (1929), 14–16, 121–3.

[69] PRO WO 32/5685, DCIGS to MGO, 6 May 1919.

[70] PRO WO 163/24. Minutes of the Proceedings of the Army Council, Precis 1003, Future organisation of the machine gun corps, signals corps, and tank corps, and 258 meeting of the Army Council, 28 Nov. 1919.

[71] J. P. Harris, Men, Ideas and Tanks. British Military Thought and Armoured Forces, 1903–1939 (Manchester, 1995), 112–13, 126–31, 159–66, 180–6; D. J. Childs, 'British Tanks 1915–1918, Manufacture and Employment', Ph.D. thesis (Glasgow, 1996), passim.

[72] FSR (1920), 31–2 185–6; FSR (1924), 21–2, 122–3.

[73] PRO AIR 5/1382, Moreland to Secretary, WO, 30 Sept. 1922; LHCMA Montgomery-Massingberd MSS 133/1, 2, Chetwode to Montgomery-Massingberd, 21 May and 6 Sept. 1921; LHCMA Kirke MSS I/14, 'The Experimental Brigade': Lecture by Col. W. M. St. G. Kirke [c.1922]; Lieut.-Col. W. D. Croft, 'The Influence of Tanks upon Tactics', Journal of the Royal United Services Institute, 67 (1922), 52.

[74] Lieut.-Gen. Sir G. Le Q. Martel, An Outspoken Soldier. His Views and Memoirs (London, 1949), 49–50.

[75] PRO WO 279/56, Report on Army Manoeuvres, 1925.

ways mirrored and continued the argument that had developed in 1918 between the exponents of 'mechanical' and 'traditional' forms of war.[76] The RTC believed that they should be allotted an independent operational mission. The latter argued that tanks would be effective only if they were properly incorporated into the combined arms battle. The infantry's first-line transport had to be mechanized and the army had to develop 'a mechanicalised formation comprising all arms and possessing its own powers of reconnaissance and protection'.[77] Much to the ire of the spokesmen of the RTC, when Milne decided to establish the Experimental Mechanised Force in 1926, he adhered to the latter school of thought. He tried to organize it as a balanced all-arms force, or at least as balanced as the prevailing shortage of resources would allow.[78] By 1928 the work of the Experimental Mechanised Force had convinced the General Staff that it was indeed desirable to give the tanks an independent operational mission and to form an armoured force with the task of operating 'as an independent formation over most country other than mountains and swamps'.[79] The experiments showed that tanks could not operate alone. They needed infantry, both to overcome hostile anti-tank weapons and to open passages for them through defiles. But even if the infantry was carried in six-wheeled lorries, intimate co-operation was virtually impossible because of the differing cross-country speeds of tanks and lorries.[80] In the short term, until the infantry could be given their own small armoured vehicles, Milne and other senior General Staff officers reluctantly agreed that the only solution was to separate the infantry and tanks and to commit the former to co-operation with the latter only for particular operations. Even then, such an amalgam would only be possible, they believed, at divisional not brigade level.[81] This was a fateful decision. It meant that, although British doctrine postulated that battlefield success depended on combined-arms co-operation, by the end of the 1920s the British had virtually abandoned the attempt to create permanent, all-arms formations incorporating a balance of tanks, infantry, and supporting arms.

These developments were reflected in the third post-war edition of *FSR*. It was the first manual to refer explicitly to 'Armoured units'.

[76] This distinction was first highlighted by Travers in his book *How the War Was Won*, 32–49.

[77] LHCMA, Kirke MSS 2/1/18, Lieut.-Gen. Sir P. Chetwode, Report on collective training, Aldershot Command, 14 Nov. 1925.

[78] PRO WO 32/2821, Milne to Secretary of State, 8 Feb. 1926; PRO WO 32/2820, DDSD to DSD, May 1926, and Col. G. M. Lindsay to DDSD, 14 May 1926; Milne to DSD, 1 June 1926; DSD to CIGS, 11 June 1926; PRO WO 279/59, War Office Exercise no. 2 (1927), 9–12 May 1927; Harris, *Men, Ideas and Tanks*, 211–13.

[79] PRO WO 279/60, Report on the Staff Conference.

[80] PRO WO 279/65, Report of the Staff Conference.

[81] Ibid.; PRO WO 32/2382, Memorandum on Army Training. Collective Training period 1928, 26 Nov. 1928.

Thanks to the work of the Experimental Mechanised Force, it contained a far more detailed analysis of their role, strengths, and weaknesses than its predecessors. Armoured units could be used either to pierce the enemy's front or in a wide turning movement against his headquarters and rear services. If they were to succeed in frontal attacks, they had to be used *en masse*, needed friendly artillery to neutralize the enemy's artillery, and required infantry to suppress his anti-tank guns and to consolidate ground gained.[82] The General Staff issued two further manuals on the employment of armoured formations, *Mechanised and Armoured Formations (1929)* and *Modern Formations (1931)*. These envisaged an army composed of four basic, brigade-sized building blocks: infantry brigades, cavalry brigades, light armoured brigades, and mixed armoured brigades. (The latter were to be composed of a mixture of light and medium tanks.) Combined arms co-operation would be secured at the divisional level either in the shape of an infantry division or a mobile division. The former, depending on the terrain, might consist entirely of infantry troops and supporting arms or it might have a mixed armoured brigade attached to it. Mobile divisions might consist of either a cavalry brigade or an infantry brigade in buses and two mixed tank brigades. Both types of division would require mechanized engineers, artillery, and either cavalry or light tanks for reconnaissance.[83]

It is therefore quite erroneous to conclude that the army waited until the establishment of the Kirke Committee in 1932 to learn the 'lessons' of the First World War.[84] It had abandoned its pre-1914 quest for a 'human-centred' solution to the problem of overcoming the fire-power of the modern battlefield over a decade before the committee was established. It had enthusiastically embraced a technological solution and was experimenting with ways to give it effect. Milne established the Kirke Committee after he read Sir James Edmonds's official history of the opening of the Somme. However, the work done in the 1920s shows that it would be unfair to conclude from this that the General Staff had suddenly been aroused by Edmonds's work from a state of mental torpor to a sudden recognition that something had been wrong with the way in which the army had fought the war. Milne's comment, that 'I cannot help feeling that we must never allow it [the conduct of operations] to degenerate into what happened in the years 1915, 1916 and

[82] *FSR (1929)*, 16–17, 124–5.

[83] Harris, *Men, Ideas and Tanks*, 224; J. P. Harris, 'British Armour 1918–40: Doctrine and Development', in J. P. Harris and P. Toase (eds.), *Armoured Warfare* (London, 1990), 37–9; LHCMA Liddell Hart MSS 15/8/81, *Modern Formations* (1931).

[84] Cf. Bond and W. Murray, 'British Military Effectiveness, 1918–39', in A. R. Millett and W. Murray (eds.), *Military Effectiveness, ii. The Interwar Period* (London, 1988), 121; Bidwell and Graham, *Firepower*, 187; J. A. English, *The Canadian Army and the Normandy Campaign. A Study in the Failure in High Command* (New York, 1991), 24–5.

1917', did no more than echo what he and his predecessors and been saying since the armistice.[85]

None the less, the work of the committee did serve to crystallize much of the thinking since 1918 and to push it a step further in some directions. The committee was asked to analyse the lessons of the war and discover if they were being properly applied in the army's manuals and training regime. In an introductory note to its report, Kirke acknowledged that this was nothing new because the issues he and his colleagues had considered 'have formed the subject of close study by every General Staff for fourteen years'.[86] The committee's report did not demand a fundamental reassessment of the army's tactical and operational doctrine. Rather, it endorsed the doctrine that mobility could be restored to the battlefield only by combined arms action designed to generate superior fire-power. The crucial problem which it highlighted and to which *FSR* did not offer a solution, was how to convert a 'break-in' into a 'break-through.' Kirke recommended a combination of solutions. These included greater use of surprise, effected by the employment of smoke and night attacks; the greater use of tanks; and conferring greater mobility and fire-power on the infantry by lightening the load carried by each man and giving battalions their own organic indirect fire support in the shape of mortars.

The committee also recognized that the creation of a more flexible and mobile army would demand changes in organization, staff procedures, and communications. Existing divisions had twelve infantry battalions but only sufficient organic artillery to support two of them in an attack. When confronted by a stubborn enemy, divisional commanders had to appeal to corps or army commanders for more fire-support, producing an inevitable slowing-down in the tempo of operations. The committee recommended that the number of infantry battalions per division be reduced to nine and that each division be given sufficient organic artillery to conduct most assault operations without having to ask for outside fire-support. The men liberated could be used to form tank battalions and corps and army artillery units. They could be allocated to divisions when particular operations demanded it. This smaller and handier division would be more mobile and have proportionately much more fire-power behind it. But the committee also recognized that changes in organization alone would not hasten the tempo of operations. Greater mobility would also require a command and control system better suited to mobile warfare. Headquarters, therefore, had to be close behind the front. Commanders needed armoured

[85] PRO WO 32/3155, CIGS to DSD, 6 June 1932.
[86] PRO WO 33/1297, Report of the Committee on the Lessons of the Great War, 13 Oct. 1932.

command vehicles and more liaison officers. *FSR* had to make it plain
that it was the duty of higher commanders to send forward for information and employ verbal, not written, orders. Wireless had to be used for
all communications forward of brigade. And to make the system work,
younger and more aggressive commanders with the mental capacity to
control fast-moving operations were essential.

However, for all its apparent radicalism, the report represented a
major missed opportunity. The committee, in accordance with British
thinking since 1918, opted for technological and organizational innovations as the best way to hasten the tempo of operations. It was not prepared to break with the past and abandon the doctrine of autocratic
control. Like *FSR*, it preferred a philosophy of command and control
that seemed to promise stability and security and affirmed the superior
status of senior officers. It paid lip-service to the need to allow subordinates to use their initiative, but its ideal remained 'the continuous
control from above which constitutes the difference between generalship
and a mere dog fight, between reinforcing success and hammering away
at failure in the manner so adversely commented upon in the Official
History'.[87] Liddell Hart and historians who have followed his lead
believe that the report was a damp squib because its most important
conclusions were suppressed. Milne's successor as CIGS, Sir Archibald
Montgomery-Massingberd, was sensitive about some of the criticisms
which had been levelled at him for his conduct of operations during the
war.[88] In fact, a comparison of the committee's original report and the
published version that appeared in April 1933 shows that censorship
was confined to only two areas. The published version was bereft of
most of the specific criticisms of the conduct of particular operations
during the Great War, and it did not contain a series of criticisms that the
committee had levelled against those politicians in charge of the conduct
of the war. It is debatable whether these omissions materially detracted
from a document intended to improve the army's future operational and
tactical performance. The citing of numerous historical examples might
only have served to clutter a text designed to give clear guidance to busy
officers. Criticisms of politicians would hardly have won the army
friends in high places at a time when it badly needed them.[89]

The Kirke report was not shelved. It did lead to changes in both
doctrine and organization. Several members of the Committee who
rose to powerful positions within the army in the 1930s carried its
recommendations forward. Kirke became Director General of the Terri-

[87] PRO WO 33/1297, Report of the Committee on the Lessons of the Great War, 13 Oct.
1932.

[88] B. H. Liddell Hart, *The Memoirs of Captain Liddell Hart* (London, 1965), i, 213.

[89] A copy of the published version can be found in PRO WO 33/1305, 'Notes of certain
lessons of the Great War', 6 Apr. 1933.

torial Army and C-in-C Home Forces. A. E. McNamara served as DMT, B. D. Fisher became commandant of Sandhurst, C. C. Armitage became commandant of the Staff College, and W. H. Bartholomew became CGS India and GOC-in-C Northern Command. Furthermore, the discussions of a General Staff conference held in January 1933, which was attended by the Military Members of the Army Council, the heads of the General Staff Directorates, the GOC-in-Cs of the home commands, the commanders of the regular and Territorial divisions in Britain, and the commandants of the army's major schools, revealed widespread support for most of its conclusions.[90]

The conference agreed that the section of FSR dealing with how to mount an attack and effect a breakthrough had to be rewritten in the light of the committee's report and its influence can clearly be discerned in the last pre-war edition of FSR. Drafted by Wavell, it appeared in 1935. It included all of Kirke's strictures concerning the need for the greater use of night operations—although in this respect it added little to FSR (1929). It accepted the need for commanders to send forward for information and to remain in close personal contact with events at the front. To do this, it recommended a new departure. Headquarters of divisions should be divided into a rear echelon consisting of those officers not required for the immediate conduct of operations, and a smaller forward HQ composed only of those staff officers the commander needed to assist him in the tactical conduct of the battle. It also agreed that within the division wireless, supplemented by cable and despatch riders, should be the main means of communication. It accepted the need to secure surprise, but had little to say about how to do so. Combined-arms co-operation remained of paramount importance and centralized command of the artillery was again recommended. But it also followed Kirke in asserting that the main function of the commander was the management of his subordinates through ensuring that they adhered to his master plan. Orders remained something subordinates were expected to obey to the letter and to depart from only if the circumstances in which they had been issued had radically altered.[91]

The section in FSR (1935) devoted to tanks clearly showed the influence of the doctrinal debates of the late 1920s. The task of breaking through prepared positions was allotted to infantry divisions, supported by Army Tank battalions. The latter were equipped with slow-moving heavy Infantry tanks that were especially designed to co-operate with infantry and artillery. Only after they had broken through and created a gap in the enemy's defences could the Mobile division come into its

[90] PRO WO 279/74, Report on the Staff Conference held at the Staff College Camberley, 9 to 11 Jan 1933.

[91] Wavell's edition was issued in two vols., FSR (1935) and FSR, iii. Operations: Higher Formations (1935).

own.[92] The Mobile division, built around a Tank brigade equipped with a mixture of light and cruiser tanks, was designed to pass through the gap and, taking advantage of the speed and wide radius of action of its tanks, take the enemy by surprise and 'strike a blow not only at the flanks of an enemy but also at his headquarters and rear services'. By 1939 the Mobile division, Army Tank battalions, and mechanized cavalry regiments had also acquired the extra function of counter-attacking an enemy armoured penetration.[93] By creating a rigid distinction between Infantry tanks and cruisers and by allotting different functions to each of them, *FSR(1935)* codified a bifurcation in British armoured doctrine and unintentionally impeded combined-arms co-operation. It was to bedevil armoured operations for much of the war.

In 1922 the Aldershot Experimental Brigade had underlined the helplessness of infantry confronted by tanks, but Wavell's volume was the first edition of *FSR* to devote sustained attention to anti-tank doctrine.[94] It suggested two possible solutions. Troops should deploy behind physical obstacles in so-called tank-proof localities and infantry should be issued with their own anti-tank weapons. Tanks could be stopped by natural obstacles such as woods and rivers or by man-made obstacles such as minefields. However, both types of obstacles had to be covered by fire, for otherwise they could be removed or bridged. Protection against tanks in regions with good communications would be more difficult. Anti-tank weapons would have to be issued not merely to front-line troops but also to those on the lines of communications, who would have to establish themselves in all-round defended localities. Experience after 1939 demonstrated the essential soundness of this doctrine. What was lacking until 1942 was the equipment to put it into practice.

The major shortcoming in *FSR(1935)* was that, like its predecessors, it had little to say about air power and the need to integrate the air and land battle. It did recognize the need to achieve at least local air superiority. But, as in earlier editions, it did not explain how that could be done beyond hinting that air attacks against the enemy's communications centres might force his aircraft into the sky where they could be destroyed. It deprecated the employment of aircraft in close air support missions because of the heavy losses they would probably incur. Both points were reiterated in 1938 in a separate manual, *The Employment of Air Forces with the Army in the Field*. It listed the need to secure air superiority as an additional duty of the Air Component of the Field Force, but placed it on an equal footing with reconnaissance, bombing

[92] *FSR (1935)*, 4; *FSR, iii. Operations. Higher Formations (1935)*, 46–7.
[93] *FSR (1935)*, 82–4; General Staff, *ATM No. 21. Individual Training Period 1938/39* (London, 1938); General Staff, *Notes on Defence. Provisional. MPT no. 15* (London, 1939).
[94] LHCMA Kirke MSS 2/1/3, Kirke, 'The Experimental Brigade' [c.1922].

military objectives behind the front, and carrying out low-flying attacks on enemy ground forces.[95]

It was not entirely the fault of the General Staff that combined-arms doctrine was not extended to co-operation between ground and air forces. The RAF was itself not a willing partner. Anxious to justify its own existence as a separate service, the RAF was reluctant between the wars to embrace a mission that did nothing to promote the cause of an independent air force. In 1917–18 the RAF's close air support operations had been successful in spreading alarm and despondency amongst German troops, but the RAF's own post-war analysis dwelt instead upon the heavy losses their own aircraft had suffered. The result was that by 1939 the RAF had neither pilots trained for this mission nor aircraft designed to perform it. An Air Component was tasked to co-operate with the BEF, but its fighters were intended to carry out air superiority missions and its light and medium bombers to perform deep interdiction operations against the enemy army's lines of communication.[96] This was in sharp contrast to the German Luftwaffe. The latter was committed to winning air superiority as a primary goal. But it had also developed a close air support doctrine and by 1939 it had created specialist dive-bomber units and a command and control system to put that doctrine into practice.[97]

The army's doctrine of employing machinery rather than manpower was given concrete expression in its organization and equipment. In January 1927 Milne decided that battles in the future would be won at least cost if the army made the maximum possible use of mechanical devices. 'You will not get in the Army of the future infantry battalions of 1,000 men. To make up for the firepower of reduced numbers you have got to have mechanical fire producers.'[98] The need to produce formations which were highly mobile and could generate superior fire-power but were economical in the manpower they required were three of the major factors that determined how the army organized its resources. The fourth was flexibility. In view of the many different theatres of war and

---

[95] General Staff, *The Employment of Air Forces with the Army in the Field* (London, 1938), *passim*; *FSR (1935)*, 16–17.

[96] R. R. Muller, 'Close Air Support: The German, British and American Experiences, 1918–1941', in W. Murray and A. R. Millett (eds.), *Military Innovation in the Interwar Period* (Cambridge, 1996), 152, 163–4, 165–8. On the perceived advantages of interdiction, see the lecture given by Air VM H. R. M. Brooke-Popham, the first commandant of the RAF Staff College, at London University in 1926, 'Air Warfare', in Sir G. Aston (ed.), *The Study of War* (London, 1927) 155–7; and Col. P. S. Meilinger, 'John C. Slessor and the Genesis of Air Interdiction', *Journal of the Royal United Services Institute*, 140 (1995), 43–8.

[97] J. S. Corum, 'The Luftwaffe's Army Support Doctrine, 1918–1941', *Journal of Military History*, 59 (1995), 53–76; idem, 'From Bi-Plane to Blitzkrieg: The Development of German Air Doctrine between the Wars', *War in History*, 3 (1996), 85–101.

[98] PRO WO 279/57, Report on the Staff Conference.

opponents which the army might have to fight, its organization and equipment 'must be suited to the average rather than exceptional conditions' and be sufficiently flexible so that it could be modified to suit particular needs.[99] Their goal, as Chetwode defined it in 1921, was 'to evolve a much harder hitting, quicker moving and, above all, a quicker deploying division than we ever had before. If we don't we shall be beaten by those who do.'[100]

In the inter-war period the General Staff struggled to balance the demands of mobility against fire-power. The 1914 model Infantry division had produced mobility at the expense of fire-power. By 1918 the division that had evolved on the Western Front had sacrificed a good deal of mobility, but gained enormously in fire-power. It was lavishly equipped with artillery, trench mortars, machine-guns, and light automatics, but with only three-quarters of the infantry battalions of its predecessor.[101] Battalion and brigade commanders had enough direct and indirect fire weapons under their own immediate control so that, under conditions of semi-mobile warfare, they could often fight their own way forward without the time-consuming need to ask divisional and corps commanders for fire-support.[102] In the immediate aftermath of the war, a committee led by a former DSD, Major-General Sir W. D. Bird recommended retaining an organization based upon the 1918 model division. Had these recommendations been accepted, the postwar division would have been lavishly equipped with fire-support weapons. The 1914 model division had one artillery piece for every 169 bayonets. The Bird Committee recommended a ratio of one gun or mortar for every 87 infantrymen. However, the committee's recommendations founded on three obstacles. The Treasury rejected them as being hopelessly expensive. They violated the requirements of flexibility because they required large numbers of specialist units such as trench mortar batteries, whereas the immediate need of the peacetime army was to re-create large numbers of identical infantry battalions to support the Cardwell system and to garrison the empire. Finally, the sheer size of the 'Bird' division threatened to impede the army's prime goal, to restore mobility to the battlefield. Fully equipped it would occupy over sixteen miles of road-space and threatened to be dangerously immobile.[103]

---

[99] *FSR*, i. *Organisation and Administration, 1930* (repr. with Amendments, nos. 1–11; London, 1939), 1–3.

[100] LHCMA Montgomery-Massingberd MSS 122/3, Chetwode to Montgomery-Massingberd, 12 Jan. 1921.

[101] General Staff, *Field Service Pocket Book 1914* (London, 1914), 6, 10.

[102] Griffith, *Battle Tactics*, 115; CCC Bonham-Carter MSS BHXT 11/1, Bonham-Carter to Milne, 16 Mar. 1928.

[103] PRO WO 237/13/933, Recommendations of committee on army matters, 1900–20, Reorganisation of field army: Maj.-Gen. W. D. Bird, Report 1, Infantry Divns., 21 Mar. 1919;

The General Staff therefore turned to some practical experiments for a better solution. Sir Henry Wilson, the CIGS from 1918 to 1922, hoped the Aldershot Experimental Brigade would 'decide what the division of the future is to consist of'.[104] By the time it was disbanded at the end of 1922, it had indicated that the answer to the question of how to resolve the competing demands of economy, flexibility, fire-power, and mobility was to equip battalions and divisions only with those supporting weapons that they constantly needed. Pursuit of the principle of the economy of force suggested weapons needed only occasionally by divisions, such as tanks, heavy, medium, and anti-aircraft artillery, should be organized as Corps or Army Troops. The army conducted numerous further experiments and debates to discover the precise forms of organization for infantry and armoured formations in the inter-war period, but this remained the essential doctrine that underlay British organization until the outbreak of war and beyond.[105]

Experimentation gave way to wholesale reform in the mid-1930s. As early as 1921 Montgomery-Massingberd had accepted that the days of the horse-drawn army were numbered. In 1926, as chairman of the Cavalry Committee, he had favoured the partial mechanization of the cavalry when vehicles with an adequate cross-country capability became available.[106] In September 1934, following Kirke's recommendations, Montgomery-Massingberd inaugurated the most far-reaching programme of modernization, motorization, and reorganization undertaken by the army between the wars. The programme was continued by his successor, Sir Cyril Deverell.[107] The final outcome was the 1938 model Infantry division and infantry battalion, the Mobile division, later renamed the Armoured division, and the Motor division. Together they were the basic organizations with which the army went to war.

A comparison of the 1938 model Infantry division and its nearest German counterpart, the thirty-five First Wave infantry divisions, suggests that in their effort to restore mobility to the battlefield, the British adopted a form of organization that did not synergise with their doctrine that battles were won by securing mobility through the

LHCMA Montgomery-Massingberd MSS 122/3, 5, Chetwode to Montgomery-Massingberd, 12, 26 Jan. 1921.

[104] LHCMA Montgomery-Massingberd MSS 122/1, Chetwode to Montgomery-Massingberd, 30 Dec. 1920.

[105] FSR, i. Organisation & Administration. (1930), 4–5; PRO AIR 5/1382, Moreland to Secretary, War Office, 30 Sept. 1922.

[106] LHCMA Montgomery-Massingberd MSS 133/1, Montgomery-Massingberd to Chetwode, 16 Aug. 1921; 157/2, Final Report of the Cavalry committee, 4 Jan. 1927.

[107] PRO WO 32/2847, CIGS to Military Members of the Army Council, 15 Oct. 1934; Col. G. N. Macready, 'The Trend of Organisation in the Army', Journal of the Royal United Services Institute, 80 (1935), 8–10; PRO WO 32/4612, Montgomery-Massingberd to Secretary of State and enc., The Future organisation of the British Army, 9 Sept. 1935; Lieut.-Gen. Sir G. N. Macready, In the Wake of the Great (London, 1965), 89–93.

generation of overwhelming fire-power. The British division could undoubtedly be more mobile than its German equivalent, but it was also a form of organization that left British commanders dangerously dependent on fire-support weapons that they themselves did not control.[108] The most obvious disparity between the two types of division was that the British division was completely motorized and each British Corps included a RASC troop-carrying company capable of lifting the marching troops of an entire brigade. By contrast, the German division still contained nearly 5,000 horses and there was no pool of lorries at its disposal to lift its infantry.[109] British infantry formations, therefore, had a clear advantage in physical mobility. Both divisions were triangular formations, consisting of three brigades (British) or regiments (German), each of which possessed three battalions. The British battalions were built around the Bren light machine-gun and each British division possessed 432 Brens, compared to the 378 light machine-guns in each German division. However, the Germans' inferiority in this respect was more than compensated for by the fact that each of their divisions also possessed 138 heavy machine-guns. British divisions had no heavy machine-guns. In the British army these weapons were concentrated into separate machine gun battalions, which were organized as corps troops and outside the direct control of the divisional commander. The Germans also had more medium mortars (54 to 18) and the British division possessed only 48 2-pdr. anti-tank guns, 27 fewer than a German division. Furthermore, the British weapons were organized into separate Royal Artillery anti-tank regiments, and it was not until after the outbreak of war that the British aped the Germans and allotted an anti-tank company to each brigade.[110] German divisions also had their own organic light anti-aircraft artillery, whereas British LAA was organized as corps troops. This left front line units potentially vulnerable to attack by enemy close air support aircraft unless the RAF had established air superiority.

The difficulty that British infantry experienced during the Second World War in practising fire and movement tactics owed much to faulty

[108] Details of British and German organisations are taken from PRO WO 32/4119, Deverell to GOC-in-Cs, 22 Oct. 1937; M. Cooper, *The German Army 1933–1945* (London, 1978), 162, 560; PRO WO 33/1510, *ATM no. 20A. Developments in organisation and equipment*, 6 July 1938; PRO WO 163/69/CCAC221, DCIGS, Composition of the full field force of 6 regular and 26 Territorial divns., 29 Apr. 1939. The U.S. army adopted a broadly similar form of organization to the British. See R. Weigley, *Eisenhower's Lieutenants. The Campaign of France and Germany 1944–45* (Bloomington, Ind., 1981), 25–8.

[109] PRO WO 163/69/CCAC221 DCIGS, Composition of the full field force of 6 regular and 26 Territorial divns., 29 Apr. 1939.

[110] LHCMA Burnett-Stuart MSS 3, Burnett-Stuart, Southern Command, Annual Report on training of the Regular Army, 1936–7, Nov. 1937; Bidwell and Graham, *Firepower*, 193–5; PRO WO 260/24, Bayley to Wilton, 24 July 1939.

pre-war doctrine and organization. The 1938 model infantry battalion, with some comparatively minor modifications, remained largely unchanged until 1943. Composed of 780 all-ranks, it consisted of a HQ company and four rifle companies. It had two serious weaknesses, its size and its lack of effective organic indirect fire-support weapons. Because it was so small, unit cohesion was likely to come under considerable strain after it had suffered even a comparatively small number of casualties. The fact that each platoon had a 2-in. mortar was used as a reason for allotting only two 3-in. mortars to the battalion's mortar platoon. The former was really good only for producing smokescreens. This meant that the battalion commander lacked sufficient indirect fire-support under his own command and this placed him at a considerable disadvantage compared to his German counterpart, who had six 81mm. mortars.

British pre-war infantry doctrine, embodied in two manuals, *Infantry Training(1937)* and *Infantry Section Leading (1938)*, insisted that the only way in which infantry could make headway against an enemy in prepared defences was if it took full advantage of the fire of supporting weapons. So essential was it that they did this that they were forbidden to stop to fire their own weapons unless enemy fire became so persistent that it compelled them to go to ground.[111] The notion that it was the task of the infantry to manoeuvre and the task of supporting arms to provide the covering fire they required was reflected in the composition of the most basic building block of infantry battalions, the infantry section. In the 1938 model battalion, each section consisted of just eight men, armed with a Bren gun and seven rifles. This placed them at a serious disadvantage compared to the Germans. German sections consisted of thirteen men, similarly equipped with rifles and a light machine-gun. But their greater size enabled a German section commander to practise fire and movement tactics within his section. He could divide it into a fire-support sub-section built around the light machine-gun and an assault sub-section composed of the rest of his men. British sections were so small that they could either act as fire units or manoeuvre units. They could not do both simultaneously.[112]

The pursuit of the principle of the economy of force, combined with the determination of senior British commanders to control the actions of their subordinates by retaining control of as many fire-power assets as possible, meant that British infantry units had too little organic fire-support. They had no option, therefore, but to rely on artillery and tanks to provide them with the fire-support they required to manoeuve across

[111] General Staff, *Infantry Training (Training and War) 1937* (London, 1937), *passim*, and *Infantry Section Leading (1938)* (London, 1939), *passim*.

[112] Maj. G. F. Ellenberger, 'The Infantry Section—French, German and British', *Journal of the Royal United Services Institute*, 83 (1938), 539–51.

the battlefield. But the way in which the army organized those supporting arms only served to impede the close collaboration upon which
successful combined arms operations depended. British divisions
possessed three field artillery regiments equipped with a total of 72 25-
pdr. gun/howitzers. German divisions had less artillery in their field
regiments (36 light and 12 heavy field howitzers). But this apparent
numerical inferiority was compensated for by the fact that the Germans
supplemented their divisional artillery by devolving control of a further
two dozen guns down to infantry regimental commanders, the equivalent of British brigade commanders. Each regimental commander
possessed his own gun company, equipped with eight artillery pieces and
this enabled him to lay on a quick fire-plan using assets under his own
immediate control.[113]

When his British counterpart wanted artillery support, he had to go
through the time-consuming business of requesting it from the divisional
artillery. This was made even more difficult on the eve of war. Until
1939 each British division possessed nine batteries, so one battery could
be earmarked to support each of the division's nine battalions. But in
May 1939 field regiments were reorganized into two larger batteries.
The advantage claimed for the new organization was that it would facilitate mobility. The disadvantage was that it made close co-operation
between the gunners and the infantry they were supporting more
difficult. It was made even more difficult because the British also
organized a large proportion of their artillery entirely outside their
divisional structure. Corps and Army artillery was supposed to be provided on the basis of two field regiments and two medium regiments for
every three divisions.[114] The upshot was that a British battalion or
brigade commander might enjoy the advantage of considerably heavier
artillery support than his German counterpart. But whether he actually
received it, and how quickly it could be delivered, depended upon how
well his communications with his supporting gunners were working. If
they were not, the construction of a suitable fire-plan could take a great
deal of time and significantly retard the tempo of operations.

The fact that each regular infantry division of the British army,
although not their Territorial counterparts in 1939, boasted a mechanized cavalry regiment might suggest that the British division enjoyed a
major advantage compared to its German counterpart, which had no
tanks of its own. However, the function of British mechanized cavalry

---

[113] PRO WO 193/846, Periodical Notes on the German Army, German Infantry in the
Attack, Jan. 1941.
[114] PRO WO 260/24, DSD to GOC-in-C Aldershot, 18 May 1939; PRO WO 277/5,
Pemberton, *Artillery Tactics and Equipment*, 10–11; LHCMA Liddell Hart MSS 15/8/107,
General Staff, *Notes on the New Organisation of the Field and Royal Horse Artillery and their
Tactical Handling. MTP No. 5* (London, 1938).

regiments, equipped with light tanks and carriers, was reconnaissance
and protection, not infantry support.[115] That mission was the task of
quite separate Army Tank brigades, equipped with heavier and slower
Infantry tanks. According to the last pre-war Field Force Conspectus,
Army Tank brigades, organized as Corps troops, were to be provided in
the ratio of five brigades (each of three battalions) to twenty-two
infantry divisions. Training pamphlets issued in 1938 and 1939 made it
plain that their success in action would depend upon the extent to which
they could co-operate closely with infantry and their supporting
gunners. 'Infantry' tanks could destroy enemy machine guns, but they
depended upon the gunners and infantry to neutralize enemy anti-tank
guns and to occupy the ground they had gained. However, by placing
the tanks outside the divisional organization, the General Staff made
achieving that co-operation difficult because they deprived the three
arms of the opportunity to live and train together.[116]

The main role of the infantry and their supporting heavy tanks was to
break into the enemy's defensive position. It was the function of the
Mobile division, supported by the six Territorial Army Motor divisions
that the General Staff decided to create in 1938, to transform the 'break-
in' into a 'break-through'. The motor divisions, more than anything else,
exemplified the General Staff's determination to place mobility before
fire-power. Their task was to carry out the rapid consolidation of
ground captured by the Mobile divisions. To that extent, their function
matched that of the German army's motorized and light divisions. But
there the similarities ended. German motorized divisions were organized
on a triangular basis and equipped in much the same way as First Wave
Infantry divisions. Light divisions were smaller but possessed their own
tank battalion. In contrast, British motor divisions possessed sufficient
transport to carry all of their infantry, but were otherwise much weaker
than normal infantry divisions. They had only two infantry brigades,
two artillery regiments, and no tanks.[117]

The Mobile division was created by combining the Tank Brigade with
the Cavalry division and by mechanizing the cavalry. In Montgomery-
Massingberd's original plan, the cavalry would have been given a
mixture of light tanks and trucks, so that some regiments would be able
to perform the duties of motorized infantry. However, the cavalry themselves objected that this would waste their skills in reconnaissance and

---

[115] General Staff, *Notes on the Organisation, Training and Employment of a Mechanised Divisional Cavalry Regiment. MTP No. 12* (London, 1939).

[116] LHCMA Liddell Hart MSS 15/8/110, General Staff, *Notes on the Tactical Handling of Army Tank Battalions. MTP No. 8* (London, 1938), and *Tactical Handling of Army Tank Battalions. MTP No. 22, Part III: Employment* (London, 1939).

[117] Cooper, *German Army*, 560–1; LHCMA Liddell Hart MSS 15/8/136, *The Motor Division (Including the Motor Cycle Battalion)* (London, 1939).

shock action, so in 1938 the General Staff agreed to place all of them in light tanks. This was a mistake, but not because the cavalry had no aptitude or liking for mechanization. The few die-hards who publicly regretted the end of horsed cavalry were outnumbered by a much larger group of professional officers who accepted that the days of horsed cavalry were over and that they had to learn new skills.[118] The real fault was that by deciding to put all of the cavalry into light tanks the General Staff had forfeited the opportunity to make the Mobile division— renamed the 1st Armoured division in April 1939—a balanced all-arms formation. Instead they created a 'tank-heavy' division with too few infantry and supporting arms. It had six cavalry light tank regiments in its two mechanized cavalry brigades, and three medium regiments in its Tank Brigade. But it had only two motorized infantry battalions and two artillery regiments.[119] The mechanized cavalry were designed to reconnoitre, not to fight, and the infantry were intended to protect the tanks when they were resting and replenishing. They were not, according to Burnett-Stuart who was responsible for overseeing the division's early training, 'to be put on to a position by Tanks and told to hold it, and they are not meant to fight side by side with your tanks in the forefront'.[120]

This organization of the Mobile division, therefore, stood outside the mainstream of official doctrine. While the rest of the army was, at least on paper, pursuing a doctrine that insisted that only combined-arms co-operation could win battles, the Mobile division, dominated by the RTC, was committed to a machine-age vision that tanks by themselves could win battles. At almost exactly the same time German theorists of tank warfare had concluded that tanks working on their own or merely in conjunction with infantry would never be a decisive weapon. They quite correctly believed that the key to success lay in combining tanks and supporting arms in the same divisional organization under a single commander.[121] It was not until 1942 and after a series of defeats in North Africa, that the British evolved a similarly well-balanced organization.

[118] PRO WO 32/4195, Minutes of an informal Army Council meeting, 22 Oct. 1937; LHCMA Liddell Hart MSS 11/1937/82, Talk with Maj.-Gen. C. C. Armitage, 1 Nov. 1937; R. H. Larson, The British Army and the Theory of Armoured Warfare, 1918–40 (Newark, NJ, 1984), 27–31; IWM Dept. of Sound Records, Accession no. 000893/03: Col. G. W. Draffen, 32–3; 000/968/02: Col. Sir Douglas Scott, 2–4.

[119] B. H. Liddell Hart, Europe in Arms (London, 1937), 236; Harris, Men, Ideas and Tanks, 262–3; PRO WO 32/2826, DSD to Bovenschen, 2 Oct. 1936; Anon., 'Army Notes', Journal of the Royal United Services Institute, 82 (1937), 886.

[120] LHCMA Burnett-Stuart MSS, Burnett-Stuart, Conference, 8 Sept. 1937.

[121] Maj.-Gen. F. W. von Mellenthin, Panzer Battles. A Study in the Employment of Armour in the Second World War (Okla., 1956), pp. xv–xvi; Gen. H. Guderian, Panzer Leader (London, 1974), 29; Cooper, German Army, 146–7.

After 1918 senior British officers knew that never again would society allow them to expend their soldiers' lives in the same profligate way that they had on the Western Front. They, therefore, shunned a return to the slow-moving attritional warfare of the Western Front. They embraced mechanization because they hoped that it would enable them to restore mobility to the battlefield, pave the way to cheaper victories, and allow them to extract the maximum fighting power from every man in their small army. Their doctrine emphasized combined arms operations and postulated that victory would ultimately depend upon high morale, mobility, and, above all, the ability to generate superior fire-power. However, although by the late 1930s they were rapidly modernizing their equipment and organization, they failed to modernize in one crucial area and in doing so threw away many of the advantages they might have reaped. The British never embraced the rigidities of the French army's *bataille conduite* (methodical battle) within which all units advanced according to a carefully prescribed timetable and which shunned encounter battles at all costs.[122] However, the need to generate superior fire-power by co-ordinating the assets of several different layers of command, each progressively more remote from the front line, threatened to reduce the tempo of their operations to something close to those of the French. It ensured that troops could not manoeuvre more rapidly than the artillery could lay on fire-support. Nor could front line units operate with much confidence beyond the range of its guns. Above all, by placing authority in the hands of senior commanders remote from the scene of the action, and by severely constraining the initiative of their subordinates, the British adhered to a command and control system that promised to negate many of the advantages of mechanization. It had worked well enough in 1918, but it was incapable of responding quickly to a rapidly changing situation and they therefore left themselves dangerously vulnerable to an enemy who was capable of operating at a more rapid tempo.

A revised version of *FSR* was under preparation when the war began in 1939 but it was never published. The 1935 edition, therefore, had to guide commanders through a period when the organization and equipment of the army underwent their most radical changes since 1918. In the four years before 1939 the horse was supplanted by the internal combustion engine and many of the First World War vintage weapons that the army possessed were replaced by the new generation of equipment with which it was to fight the opening battles of the Second World War. However, the army's basic doctrine did not change to reflect these

---

[122] R. A. Doughty, 'The French Armed Forces, 1918–1940' in A. R. Millett and W. Murray (eds.), *Military Effectiveness, ii. The Interwar Period* (London, 1988), 54–5; R. A. Doughty, *The Seeds of Disaster. The Development of French Army Doctrine, 1919–1939* (Hamden, Conn., 1985), 8–10.

developments. It was accepted that modern, motorized divisions could deploy much more rapidly than could their horse-drawn predecessors. But, beyond issuing some strictures encouraging commanders to employ greater forethought, no serious consideration was given as to whether these changes might require a fundamental reassessment of the army's doctrine for command and control.[123] Rather than innovate at a fundamental doctrinal level, new weapons were incorporated into existing doctrine. The mechanized cavalry regiments allotted to regular infantry divisions were, for example, given exactly the same reconnaissance and protective functions as their horsed cavalry predecessors.[124]

Some senior officers did realize that there was a growing gap between their doctrine and the operational possibilities opening up to their troops as new equipment began to reach them in the late 1930s. In October 1937 Lord Gort, who became CIGS two months later, privately admitted that 'At the moment we have no definite policy and we talk gaily of the attack in terms of 1918 slightly furbished up but not really in accordance with mechanized warfare and its increased pace'.[125] He recognized that an army facing a mechanized opponent was likely to be subjected to vigorous attacks by tanks and aircraft. But his recipe to fight such a battle was a mixture of vagueness, utopianism, and quiet despair. Commanders of mechanized forces would have to react to new situations and issue orders with much greater rapidity than in the past. They had to prepare definite plans before the battle and subordinates had to be taught to act on verbal orders. During his brief period as Commandant at Camberley, Gort had tried to train students to issue orders using map tracings instead of enumerating a long list of different points in writing.[126] The army did need more direct air support but, given the RAF's commitment to strategic air operations, it was unlikely to receive it.[127] Nevertheless, beyond appointing Sir Edmund Ironside as Inspector General of Overseas Forces with responsibility for the higher training of the army in May 1939, Gort did little to improve matters. Ironside was painfully aware of how far apart doctrine and technology had drifted, but as he assumed his duties only in July, he had no opportunity to have any appreciable impact before the war began.[128]

The British failed to foresee that the Germans might outmanoeuvre them because they did not understand that German doctrine was essen-

---

[123] General Staff, *ATM no. 21. Individual Training Period 1938–39* (London, 1939).

[124] LHCMA Liddell Hart MSS 15/8/106, General Staff, *Notes on Mechanized Cavalry Units. MTP No. 4* (London, 1938).

[125] LHCMA Liddell Hart MSS 1/322/50, Gort to Liddell Hart, 24 Oct. 1937.

[126] LHCMA Liddell Hart MSS 11/1936/81, Notes on talk with Gort and others at Staff College, 5 Oct. 1936.

[127] LHCMA Liddell Hart MSS 1/332/48, 52, Gort to Liddell Hart, 20, 31 Oct. 1937.

[128] *The Ironside Diaries 1937–40*, ed. Colonel R. Macleod and D. Kelly (London, 1962), 60, 74–5, 87–8.

tially different from their own. The German army intended to defeat its enemies by practising a doctrine that was designed to shatter their moral and physical cohesion. They practised a doctrine that actually *required* leaders at all levels to use their initiative to the utmost. The British were so locked into their own system that they failed to recognize the advantages of giving subordinates wider latitude to use their own initiative. Indeed, they believed that such latitude was a positive handicap to success. Visiting the battlefield of Tannenberg in 1935, Sir John Dill, who became the CIGS in 1940, asked his host 'how the Germans had achieved such success despite the notorious disobedience of the junior officers'.[129]

Dill's comment suggested two things, that senior British officers were afraid to let their subordinates use their initiative and that he had only a limited understanding of the essence of military intelligence. Successive editions of *FSR* devoted considerable space to the importance of collecting accurate information about the enemy's order of battle, dispositions, and capabilities.[130] What they did not do was to require intelligence officers or commanders to analyse the intellectual framework within which enemy commanders operated. The British failed to recognize that German doctrine was in many respects fundamentally different from their own. This was so because they brought to the study of the German army cultural stereotypes that suggested that the Germans were imbued with a determination to plan everything down to the last detail. They were convinced that the Germans were incapable of improvising if anything went wrong with their plan. Visiting German manoeuvres in 1937, Ironside reflected that 'They are probably more industrious than we are, but I am sure that they require all their rules to be there . . . They shrink from improvisation.'[131] A British officer who witnessed a German battalion on a training exercise in Upper Silesia in May 1939 believed that German officers and NCOs lacked imagination because, when confronted by a tactical problem, nearly all of them opted for the same solution.[132] What he failed to see was that this actually demonstrated that the German army possessed the inestimable advantage that its junior leaders had imbued a common understanding of their tactical doctrine.

This failure to grasp that the basic ethos of foreign armies might differ from that of the British was a reflection of two things. It highlighted a major fault in the training regime of the inter-war army. Exercises were conducted on the assumption that enemy forces would be organized and

---

[129] von Senger und Etterlin, *Neither Fear Nor Hope*, 219.
[130] *FSR (1920)*, 104–16; *FSR (1924)*, 51–63 ; *FSR (1929)*, 48–57 ; *FSR (1935)*, 61–75.
[131] *The Ironside Diaries*, ed. Macleod and Kelly, 31.
[132] PRO WO 287/226, MI3b, Tactical and Technical notes on the German army no 11 [n.d.].

equipped, and would operate, in the same way as the British. The serious study of foreign armies and military ideas was for a long time not encouraged at the Staff College. In 1932 one graduate complained that the syllabus consisted of 'Schemes of purely frontal attacks and no light given on foreign armies and ideas'.[133] It was not until Gort served, briefly, as Commandant at the Staff College in 1936 that budding senior officers were required to study foreign armies and to make them the basis for training schemes.[134]

The second point highlighted by the failure of senior British officers to understand that the ethos of other armies might be fundamentally different from their own was that the British also possessed a stereotypical view of themselves which was the antithesis of their image of the Germans. Just as they believed that the Germans would be lost without their drills, so they believed that they could best flourish in an army without them. Their most fundamental concept of what it meant to be British was bound up with the idea that they belonged to a historically free people capable of making choices and that it was this freedom that had put the 'great' into Great Britain. Battles, they believed, were in any case too unpredictable to be reduced to a series of drills. Attempting to do so was positively dangerous because it would produce stereotyped tactics.[135] It was no accident that the British army's doctrinal manuals stated general principles but did not provide concrete examples to show how those principles should be put into practice. This omission was deliberate, because it was designed to enable each individual commander to decide how to apply them in the light of the particular circumstances he confronted. Indeed, senior British officers credited themselves with a rare ability to do so. While he was being trained as an officer cadet at 168 OCTU in the winter of 1939–40, David Hunt was taught that

the Germans were fiendishly clever and worked out schemes of the utmost ingenuity based on full and accurate information provided by a superhumanly efficient intelligence service. But, my instructors would insist, the moment their plans began to run into difficulties they were at a sad loss. The British, I was told, were always at their best in these circumstances; but the Germans were quite unable to improvise . . .[136]

Hunt's service as an intelligence officer in North Africa and Italy convinced him that the very opposite was the case. He learnt that 'the pre-

---

[133] LHCMA Liddell Hart MSS 11/1932/1, Diary entry, 12 Aug. 1932.

[134] LHCMA Liddell Hart MSS 11/1936/81, Notes on talk with Gort and others at the Staff College, 5 Oct. 1936.

[135] LHCMA Liddell Hart MSS, 15/3/115, General Staff, *ATM no. 22 April 1939* (London, 1939).

[136] Sir D. Hunt, *A Don at War* (London, 1966), 41.

eminent German characteristic was brilliance at improvisation', and that German commanders showed 'enormous initiative'.

Reliance on the notion that when it came to a crisis the British army would always be able to improvise a successful solution to any problem was a mainstay of the General Staff's doctrinal thinking. It conferred the great advantage that it allowed them to close their eyes to the numerous illogicalities and gaps in their doctrine. It allowed them to ignore the fact that, although they wanted to organize and equip their army for mobile and mechanized operations, they remained wedded to an autocratic command and control system that threatened to forfeit many of the potential advantages of motorization and mechanization. It allowed them blithely to assume that the RAF would be there when required to support them, when all the signs were that the RAF's commitment to strategic bombing suggested that they would not. It encouraged them to persist in assuming that, come the next major war, their political masters would have provided them with the weapons and equipment they required to fight a mechanized and motorized war, when they were manifestly reluctant to do so. Its drawback, as they were to discover in 1940, was—to extend Brigadier Moore's metaphor—that Germans did not play cricket.

CHAPTER TWO

Regimental Officers and the Rank and File

The combat capability of the British army did not merely depend upon the appropriateness of its doctrine and organization to fulfil the missions it had to undertake. It also depended upon the quality and quantity of its equipment and its ability to attract sufficient men of the requisite quality and to train them to perform the tasks it had to undertake. The difficulty that many British units experienced in matching their German opponents' ability to act with swiftness and decision on the battlefield was not simply a product of Britain's hierarchic class structure. That played a part, but it also resulted from a combination of other, quite different, factors. The privates and subalterns of 1939 were the sergeants and battalion commanders of 1944. However, the pre-war regular and Territorial armies could not recruit enough men of the required quality to fill their establishments, and they failed to train them adequately to provide a cadre for the expanded wartime army. Initially, the wartime army, swelled by conscripts, had less difficulty in filling its establishments. But, until 1942, it failed to make the optimum use of this bounty because it lacked an appropriate personnel selection system. When it did establish such a system, it used it in conformity with its doctrine that prescribed that battles were won by machinery to shift the best men into the technologically intensive arms of the service, and left the worst in the infantry. However, underlying all of these factors were the values that the army inculcated into every one of its soldiers during basic training. Parade-ground drill was employed to teach recruits that obedience came before everything; comparatively little emphasis was placed on producing soldiers capable of achieving an intelligent appreciation of their part in a battle. Indeed, it sometimes seemed as though the army was working hard to squeeze the initiative out of those men who were intelligent and might otherwise have employed it had they been required to do so. This was not a product of the British class system; it was a function of the army's fundamental doctrine, itself based upon the fear that unless soldiers were taught to place obedience before all other virtues, once in battle their morale would collapse.

The inter-war regular army was handicapped because it could not find enough good quality volunteers to fill its establishment. By April 1937 it was 11 per cent below its establishment.[1] Resorting to conscription was politically impossible. In January 1937, a public opinion poll had shown that the public was overwhelmingly opposed to its reintroduction.[2] The quality of the men presenting themselves also left much to be desired. Three-quarters of recruits for the rank and file were unskilled, urban labourers.[3] Many of them were rejected before they enlisted or during their basic training because they could not meet the army's not particularly stringent medical requirements.[4] The establishment of universal primary education did mean that recruits were better educated than they had been in the nineteenth century.[5] Even so, by the late 1930s men who could scarcely read or write were still enlisted.[6] Confronted by a serious shortage of men, the CIGS, Sir Cyril Deverell, decided that 'I have no objection to any man who is not an imbecile being enlisted, i.e. I do not consider rejection on educational grounds alone should be a sine qua non, but I should not proclaim it loudly.'[7]

The notion that the officer corps was a refuge for the sons of the landed classes was largely a myth. Even before 1914 officer cadets from the gentlemanly and landed classes were a minority of all new officers. It was, however, becoming self-replicating, as large numbers of sons were following their fathers by acquiring a commission. Both trends accelerated in the inter-war period.[8] But like the rank and file, the officer corps was also short of recruits. The army needed about 650 new officers each year, but by 1937 it could only recruit about 550 per annum.[9] According to Colonel M. A. Wingfield, a General Staff officer responsible for the oversight of officer cadet training, in 1924, it wanted young men who were 'physically sound, of a high standard in character,

---

[1] PRO WO 287/38, Statistical Review of officers and other ranks of the Regular Army, Regular Army Reserve, Supplementary Reserve, Territorial Army, for the Financial Year 1936–7, May 1937.

[2] *The Gallup International Public Opinion Polls. Great Britain, 1937–1975, i. 1937–64*, ed. G. H. Gallup (New York, 1976), 1.

[3] K. Jeffery, 'The Post-War Army' in I. F. W. Beckett and K. Simpson (eds.), *A Nation in Arms. A Social Study of the British Army in the First World War* (Manchester, 1985), 223.

[4] PRO WO 32/4643, Maj. W. A. S. Turner to Maj. C. W. Baker, 6 Apr. 1936; PRO WO 279/65, Report on the Staff Conference held at the Staff College Camberley, 14–17 Jan. 1929.

[5] Maj. S. M. Noakes, 'The New Leadership', *Journal of the Royal United Services Institute*, 81 (1936), 589.

[6] PRO WO 32/4354, Director of Recruiting and Organization to GOCs-in-C, 8 Sept. 1938, and to GOC-in-C Southern Command, 21 Dec. 1938.

[7] PRO WO 32/4354, Karslake to CIGS, 24 Sept. 1937, and minute by Deverell, 11 Oct. 1937.

[8] K. Simpson, 'The Officers', in I. Beckett and K. Simpson (eds.), *A Nation in Arms. A Social Study of the British Army in the First World War* (Manchester, 1985), 91.

[9] PRO WO 163/456 Committee on the Supply of Officers, Mar. 1937.

with powers of leadership, with the best education to be had, and, as in other professions, containing a due proportion of the best brains in the country'.[10] It sought them from amongst public school graduates. This was not an entirely dysfunctional policy. Boys who had attended them usually left having been imbued with the 'high standard in character' that the army thought was so desirable, a combination of self-restraint, perseverance in the face of adversity, and courage in the face of danger. Team games taught boys not only how to channel their aggression and to work as part of a team, but also made them physically fit, taught them how to make decisions quickly and to disregard their personal safety.[11] This was an ideology that was well suited to men facing a dangerous and uncertain future, and there could be fewer more dangerous and uncertain futures than those facing an officer on the battlefield.[12] It also was another reason why the General Staff did not feel the need to impose a universal understanding of its doctrine on the army. Wingfield wanted officers with 'character' because he believed that they would be able to react appropriately to whatever new challenges presented themselves on the battlefield.

There were many reasons for the shortfall in recruiting. The demographic slump caused by the First World War meant that the available pool of young men of military age shrank in the mid-1930s. Service in the ranks still carried a social stigma in the eyes of respectable working class families.[13] The infantry bore a double stigma. Not only did it evoke memories of the slaughter of 1914–18, but neither did it teach men a trade that they could use when they left the army.[14] Men who wanted to join the services preferred the navy and RAF, both of which had comparatively little difficulty in finding recruits.[15] They offered better prospects and pay, training in a trade, and less possibility of being sent on an unpopular overseas posting to India.[16]

Reliance upon the middle and upper classes and the public schools to fill the ranks of the officer corps was not inevitable. By 1917–18 the wartime regimental officer corps contained a great number of former

[10] Col. M. A. Wingfield, 'The Supply and Training of Officers for the Army', *Journal of the Royal United Services Institute*, 69 (1924), 432.

[11] G. D. Sheffield, 'Officer–Men Relations, Morale and Discipline in the British Army, 1902–1922', Ph.D. thesis (London, 1994), 122, 129–31.

[12] S. Collini, 'The idea of "Character" in Victorian Political Thought', *Transactions of the Royal Historical Society*, 35 (1985), 29–50.

[13] PRO WO 32/2984, Knox to Army Council, 4 Oct. 1935.

[14] PRO WO 279/65, Report on the Staff Conference; C. N. Barclay, *The London Scottish in the Second World War* (London, 1952), 4; Lt Col. G. McM. Robertson, 'The Army as a Career', *Journal of the Royal United Services Institute*, 76 (1931), 39.

[15] PRO WO 32/2827, Shute to CIGS, 27 Oct. 1930; Maj.-Gen. G. H. Barker, 'Army Recruiting', *Journal of the Royal United Services Institute*, 83 (1937), 75.

[16] LHCMA Bartholomew MSS 2/3/16, Chetwode to Bartholomew, 7 Mar. 1936; PRO WO 32/4195, Informal Army Council, 5 July 1937.

rankers who had been commissioned after proving their worth on the battlefield and who did not come from privileged backgrounds. In 1923 a committee chaired by the former Secretary of State for War, Lord Haldane, believed that it was no longer either desirable or necessary to draw officers from only one class. The high standard of education available in many grammar and secondary schools meant that it would be safe to admit boys from them. Indeed, if the army did not make officership more clearly a career open to talent quickly, the public would be convinced that the army was a 'hopelessly conservative institution'.[17] To this end Haldane recommended that the military cadet colleges offer a small number of free cadetships to rankers. However, their impact was limited. By the 1930s, only about 5 per cent of officers were ex-rankers, and many of them joined unfashionable regiments like the RASC.[18] There were numerous other obstacles to improving recruiting. Some schoolmasters warned their pupils that their brains would be wasted in the army, the cost of entering the army was too high, and pay and allowances were too low. Regimental life in peacetime was dull and promotion by seniority in the lower ranks and the limited opportunity for young, able, and ambitious officers to receive accelerated promotion was disheartening.[19] Many officers who had commanded battalions or brigades during the First World War reverted to their permanent peacetime rank, several levels below their wartime rank. Those who remained in the service blocked the promotion of their juniors, as only a handful of especially meritorious officers were offered accelerated promotion.[20] The rest had to wait until a vacancy occurred in the rank above them in their own regiment. In the early 1930s, many officers were in their midforties or older, and verging on middle age, when they took command of their units as Lieutenant-Colonels.[21] It was not surprising that junior officers 'live on in hopes of either another war or a recurrence of the Black Plague'.[22]

None of these problems was addressed seriously until the late 1930s, when Leslie Hore-Belisha, the Secretary of State for War between 1937–9, attempted to make the army a more attractive career for both officers and other ranks. The Haldane Committee had recommended greater use of accelerated promotion for the meritorious and time promotion for all officers up to the rank of major irrespective of their

[17] PRO WO 32/4353, Report of the Committee on Education and Training of Officers, 28 June 1923. See Sheffield, 'Officer–men relations', 330–2.
[18] Sheffield, 'Officer-Men Relations', 330–2.
[19] PRO WO 163/456, Committee on the supply of officers, Mar. 1937.
[20] PRO WO 32/3734, Boyd to Adjutant-General, 7 May 1928.
[21] Capt. J. R. Kennedy, *This, Our Army* (London, 1935), 85–7.
[22] Lieut. R. D. Foster, 'Promotion by Merit in the Army', *Journal of the Royal United Services Institute*, 25 (1925), 685.

seniority in their regiment. But its proposals became bogged down in a series of investigations about how to devise a fair and equitable scheme.[23] Some officers shunned the very idea for fear that promotion by merit would undermine *espirit de corps* and cause massive discontent amongst those passed over when 'the "meritorious" trampled, as it were, over the bodies of their fallen comrades'.[24] In was not until August 1938 that Hore-Belisha broke this impasse by lowering the retirement ages for all officers and introducing time promotion for those up to the rank of major.[25] He also succeeded in attracting a better class of recruit, like J. E. Bowman, a grammar-school boy, into the rank and file. But Bowman himself noted that many of his fellow recruits 'looked as if they had been transferred from a Dr Barnado's soup kitchen in the late nine-teenth century'.[26] Recruiting reached an inter-war peak in 1938–9, but that was partly the result of the lowering of medical standards, and by January 1939 the Regular Army was still 20,000 men below its estab-lishment of 201,000.[27]

It was an eloquent testimony to the regular army's inability to tap the talent of the entire nation until the eve of war that one recruiting officer, having spent some time in the summer of 1939 interviewing a batch of conscripted Militiamen—men who were drawn from a real cross section of the community—wrote that 'Compared with them the average regular recruits are milk with the cream skimmed off'.[28] The contrast with the Reichswehr was striking. The latter had little difficulty in recruiting up to its manpower ceiling of 100,000 men. In the early 1920s the German military authorities deliberately attempted to recruit a higher quality of men into the rank and file. They wanted soldiers who, after appropriate training, would be able to step up at least one level in rank when the limitations of the Treaty of Versailles were removed. They therefore increased levels of pay, relaxed the army's rigid disci-plinary regime, and drastically improved the living standards of the rank and file. These measures helped to improve the army's already high

[23] PRO WO 32/3737, Report of Lord Plumer's committee on the promotion of officers in the army, Précis no. 1209 for the Army Council, Mar. 1925; minutes of the Army Council, 15 May 1925.

[24] Lt.-Col. B. Smith (rtd.), 'Promotion by Rejection in the Army', *Journal of the Royal United Services Institute*, 71 (1926), 54.

[25] PRO WO 163/608, Committee on the conditions of service of officers in the Royal Navy, the Army, and the Royal Air Force, July 1938; Anon., 'Army Notes', *Journal of the Royal United Services Institute*, 83 (1938), 878–80.

[26] J. E. Bowman, *Three Stripes and a Gun* (Braunton, 1987), 18–19, 22.

[27] PRO WO 163/50/AC(41) 42, Paper by the Adjutant-General on use of manpower in the Army, 1941; PRO WO 163/93/ECAC/P(44)12, Joint Secretaries, Plans for the transition peri-od, Brief for the Secretary of State prepared by the Army post-war planning committee, 8 Feb. 1944.

[28] Maj. B. T. Reynolds, 'Interviewing for the New Militia', *Journal of the Royal United Services Institute*, 84 (1939), 510.

status in German society and by 1928 the Reichswehr had fifteen applications for every post.[29]

If the regular army was theoretically designed to provide the leadership cadre of an expanded wartime army, the Territorials were to provide its manpower and structure. In January 1920 Churchill, then Secretary of State for War, told the Territorial Associations that in another great war the army would not attempt to raise another 'New Army' on the Kitchener model. Instead, in peacetime it would maintain fourteen Territorial divisions, each consisting of men enlisted for general service and they would form the sole basis of the expansion of the wartime army.[30] On general mobilization each Territorial division would throw off cadres for a second, and if necessary a third, line.[31] However, as the possibility of another great war receded, the Territorials became the victims of governments determined to reduce estimates, and a War Office that preferred to see the cuts fall upon the part-time Territorials rather than the regulars.[32] As an economy measure Territorial units were, therefore, permitted to recruit only up to 60 per cent of their wartime establishment.[33] In fact they failed to do even that, and by April 1937 the Territorial Army had reached less than 80 per cent of its shrunken peacetime establishment.[34] Its value as an immediate reserve was, therefore, limited. On the outbreak of war, not only would most units have to reject some of their existing men on medical grounds; they would have to throw off a cadre to train a second line; and they would have to recruit and train about half their establishment strength before they were ready to take the field.[35]

The rank and file of most Territorial units were drawn from the working class, and in many parts of the country it was increasingly difficult to recruit what one Territorial CO called 'the better class of black-coated man', who often became good NCOs.[36] Only a handful of 'class units', such as the London Scottish and the Honourable Artillery Company, were able to attract well-educated recruits.[37] There were many reasons

[29] J. S. Corum, *The Roots of Blitzkrieg. Hans von Seeckt and German Military Reform* (Lawrence, Kan, 1992), 69–70.

[30] Anon., 'Military Notes', *Journal of the Royal United Services Institute*, 65 (1920), 421; PRO WO 32/11358, Churchill to CIGS, 23 Jan. 1920.

[31] PRO WO 32/11356, DDSD to DDMO, Interim and post-bellum army, 4 Dec. 1918; PRO WO 237/13, Report of a Committee on Organization of post-bellum army, 1919.

[32] P. Dennis, *The Territorial Army 1907–1940* (London, 1987), 38–181.

[33] Anon., 'Military Notes', 421.

[34] PRO WO 287/38, Statistical Review.

[35] PRO WO 33/1308, Supplementary Report on the Staff Conference held at Camberley, 9–11 Jan. 1933.

[36] PRO WO 33/1376, Report on the Staff Conference held at the Staff College Camberley, 7–10 Jan. 1935.

[37] Barclay, *The London Scottish*, 11–13; Lt.-Col. Lord Birdwood, *The Worcestershire Regiment, 1922–1950* (Aldershot, 1952), 155; PRO WO 279/70, Report on the Staff Conference, Comments by Lt.-Col. M. Cuthbertson.

for the shortfall in numbers and the poor quality of many recruits. The Territorials had to compete with a growing range of other leisure activities for the spare time of its members. For much of the inter-war period there was no obvious and pressing threat to national security. Government neglect of the force did little to encourage men to enlist or to remain in it, as it left the Territorials themselves and the general public with the impression that they did not have an important role to play in national defence.[38] Even in the late 1930s, Territorial field force formations were starved of new equipment.[39] But underlying all of these reasons was the fact that the generation reaching maturity in the 1930s was 'the sons of the infantrymen of the last war, the men of the Somme and Passchendaele'.[40]

Equally serious was the shortage of officers. By 1934 the Territorials were approximately 1,000 officers below even their shrunken peacetime establishment and the educational standards of those men who were applying for commissions fell below that of the regulars.[41] The expense of serving as an officer ensured that commissions in the Territorials remained the preserve of the middle and upper classes. The consequences of the shortage of officers and their sometimes low quality were revealed when recruits who enlisted in 1938 complained that 'The successful planning and management of the training of individual units obviously needs under present conditions a degree of intelligence, initiative and executive ability which seems unfortunately to be lacking in most of the officers in whose hands the matter rests'.[42] But, in fairness, many Territorial officers did not know how to train their men because, with so few recruits presenting themselves until the eve of the war, they had been given too little practice in the art of command. 'It is difficult to train leaders', one Territorial battalion commander remarked in 1930, 'without giving them the material over which to exercise command.'[43]

The quantity and quality of Territorial recruits did improve in 1938–9. Hore-Belisha's steps to popularize the Territorials were partly responsible, but it probably owed more to the increasingly obvious threat from Germany.[44] In the opinion of one regular officer who served

[38] CCC Bonham Carter MSS BHCT11/1, Bonham Carter, Report on the Territorial Army by the DGTA, October 1935.
[39] LHCMA Bartholomew MSS 2/4/6, Montgomery-Massingberd to Bartholomew, 6 Feb. 1936.
[40] Liddell Hart, *Europe in Arms*, 66.
[41] PRO WO 279/70, Report on the Staff conference, Comments by Col. C. G. Ling; PRO WO279/75 Report on the Staff Conference held at the Staff College Camberley, 8–12 Jan. 1934, Comments by Maj.-Gen. J. K. Dick-Cunyngham.
[42] PRO WO 32/4610, War Office to GOC-in-Cs and enc., Memorandum on the Territorial Army, 24 June 1938.
[43] PRO WO 279/70, Report on the Staff Conference, Comments by Lieut.-Col. M. Cuthbertson.
[44] CCC Hore-Belisha MSS HOBE 5/21, Liddell Hart, Progress achieved during the two

with them, most Territorial junior officers and other ranks 'were what the regulars would have given their eye-teeth for as peacetime recruits'.[45] But on the debit side, the growth in recruiting only further emphasized the shortage of instructors, training equipment and accommodation from which the force suffered.[46]

During basic training, soldiers learnt that obedience was the single most important military virtue. Recruits were taught close-order drill because the army believed it was the quickest way to teach 'instant, unhesitating, and exact obedience of orders'.[47] Some officers were lyrical in advocating close order drill, insisting that

in the united effort to produce drill so good that it becomes a thing of beauty, a source of mutual satisfaction, an expression of military pride, and, in short, a form of disciplined self-expression: a military work of art . . . It has, indeed, the spirit of the morris dance, and it has survived the morris dance just because it has continued to be a natural expression of real feelings.[48]

A recruit, who tried to excuse a mistake on the parade ground by saying 'Sorry, sarge, I thought you said . . .' and received the utterly crushing reply 'Oh, you thought, did you! Now who the hell gave you permission to think? You ain't got time to think in the army, mate', was left in no doubt that obedience came before the exercise of intelligence or initiative.[49] The system usually worked. One gentleman ranker who passed through the Guards said of his basic training at the depot that 'while I was there I soon became most disinclined to think after the first three weeks, and from that time onwards until my recruit training ended I became an automaton.'[50]

This was entirely in conformity with the army's basic doctrine with its emphasis on control from the top. But it was also the product of a concern that permeated much of the officer corps when they contemplated how their soldiers might behave under fire. Many regimental officers, like their pre-1914 counterparts, feared that intelligent men, particularly urban-dwellers, were not as well suited as their less-educated country cousins to withstand the psychological and physical stresses of the

months Oct.–Nov. 1937, 28 Mar. 1938; R. J. Minney, *The Private Papers of Hore-Belisha* (London, 1960), 47–9.

[45] Brig. S. Bidwell, 'After the Wall Came Tumbling Down: A Historical Perspective', *Journal of the Royal United Services Institute*, 135 (1990), 60.

[46] Dennis, *The Territorial Army*, 154–5, 160–2, 164; PRO WO 32/4610, War Office to GOC-in-Cs and enc. Memorandum on the Territorial Army, 26 June 1938.

[47] General Staff, War Office, *Infantry Training, i. Training* (London, 1932), 11.

[48] Maj. M. K. Wardle, 'A Defence of Close Order Drill: A Reply to "Modern Infantry Discipline"', *Journal of the Royal United Services Institute*, 79 (1934), 717.

[49] S. Mays, *Fall Out the Officers* (London, 1969), 62.

[50] LHCMA Liddell Hart MSS 1/40/6, Maj.-Gen. M. G. H. Barker and enc., to Liddell Hart [c.Jan. 1937].

battlefield. Giving evidence to the War Office Committee on shell-shock in 1922, Lieutenant-Colonel E. Hewlett, formerly Inspector General of Infantry Training, asserted that 'A battalion of real countrymen (less intelligent) will stick out a situation which a battalion of townsmen (greater intelligence) will not'.[51] Officers like Hewlett preferred an authoritarian style of leadership. They feared that reliance upon the initiative and intelligence of individuals and small groups might discourage soldiers from automatically deferring to them and would not sustain unit cohesion in the heat of combat.[52]

However, there was some recognition that modern fire-power would force troops to disperse on the battlefield or risk annihilation. Individual soldiers would, therefore, rarely be under the direct command of their officers and even private soldiers would sometimes have to act on their own initiative. The 1934 *Training Regulations* explained that

The conditions of modern warfare necessitate considerable decentralisation of responsibility to junior leaders and individuals. The soldier must therefore be intelligent, adaptable, and capable of acting on his own initiative. These qualities are developed by educational training, which though it includes instruction and study not purely military in character, is an integral part of military training.[53]

This confronted the army with a serious conundrum that it never really solved, namely how to inculcate unquestioning obedience and at the same time encourage ordinary soldiers to exercise intelligent initiative. They attempted to achieve this through educational training. It was intended, according to Milne

to give the soldier at the beginning of his service the ability to learn, and subsequently encouraging him to work by himself. This principle of the individual learning and acting for himself is the basis of modern education, and is particularly applicable to the Army, which aims at the creation of initiative as well as mental development. In all military training the aim should be similar—instruction followed by individual performance without over-supervision.[54]

In practice, however, the army habitually placed obedience before initiative. This was demonstrated by the structure of recruit training. In 1932 recruits underwent 420 hours of training at the depot before being posted to their regiment. Nearly a quarter of that time (104 hours) was devoted to formal drill, compared to only 75 hours to education training.[55]

[51] [Cmd. 1734] *Report of the War Office Committee on Enquiry into 'Shell-Shock', Parliamentary Papers*, XII, 1922, 18.
[52] LHCMA Liddell Hart MSS, 1/340, Gurney to Liddell Hart, 11 Nov. 1934.
[53] War Office, *Training Regulations 1934* (London, 1934), 4.
[54] PRO WO 32/2382, Milne to Birdwood, 26 Nov. 1928, and enc., Memo on Army Training, Collective Training period 1928.
[55] General Staff, *Infantry Training*, i. *Training* 39–40.

Hewlett was probably representative of the majority of officers, but some others, like Archibald Wavell, did think that instilling an instinct for blind obedience into recruits at the expense of almost everything else, was counter-productive. 'Barrack square psychology' would not win battles he insisted in 1933, for in action 'where two or three are gathered together, there shall be courage and enterprise in them' and excessive amounts of parade-ground drill stifled enterprise. He was critical of training methods that taught recruits how to march across a parade-ground, but not how to move across country by day or night.[56] But sceptics like Wavell were only able to bring about a very slight change in emphasis. In 1937 the time devoted to formal drill in recruit training was reduced to 94 hours, and the time freed was given over to elementary fieldcraft.[57]

The practical consequences of these modest reforms were limited. It was axiomatic throughout the army that each officer was responsible for training the troops he would lead in battle, and the training regulations gave him wide latitude to interpret the principles incorporated in the official manuals.[58] Many senior officers were genuinely perplexed about the proper relationship between teaching obedience and encouraging initiative. Sir John Dill opined that 'Parade drill may be an archaic survival but something of the kind is necessary'.[59] Troops needed both discipline *and* initiative. The upshot was that some unit commanders, like Lieutenant-Colonel J. McMilling or Lieutenant-Colonel Harold Franklyn, did develop battalion training programmes that gave NCOs real responsibility and required private soldiers to act on their own initiative. But they were in a minority. Most COs, anxious to stand well in the eyes of their superiors, emphasized physical fitness, weapons training, and games in their training programmes. Success at any of these could easily be measured against the performance of other units.[60] The high proportion of officers to other ranks in the British army also meant that the officers 'tended to wet nurse the men mentally with the result that the rank and file never thought for themselves and all including warrant officers and NCOs lacked initiative'.[61]

[56] Brig. A. P. Wavell, 'The Training of the Army for War', *Journal of the Royal United Services Institute*, 78 (1933), 256.

[57] General Staff, *Manual of Elementary Drill (All Arms), 1935* (London, 1940), 3; General Staff, *Infantry Training. (Training and War) 1937* (London, 1937), 212.

[58] PRO WO 279/65, Report on the Staff Conference; General Staff, *Training Regulations (1934)* 5–6.

[59] LHCMA Liddell Hart MSS 1/238/12, Dill to Liddell Hart, 15 May 1932.

[60] Lt.-Col. J. McMilling, 'Individual Training', *Journal of the Royal United Services Institute*, 75 (1930), 794–80; idem, 'The Training of the Infantry Soldier', *Journal of the Royal United Services Institute*, 74 (1929), 515–19; Brig. G. Taylor, *Infantry Colonel* (Upton-upon-Severn, Worcs., 1990), 16–17.

[61] J. Prendergast, *Prender's Progress. A Soldier in India 1931–47* (London, 1979), 56; Taylor, *Infantry Colonel*, 16.

Junior officers experienced a similar training regime. The Royal Military Academy at Sandhurst and the Royal Military College at Woolwich produced young officers who were physically fit, who could perform polished drill, and who felt themselves to be members of an élite. 'Life at Sandhurst', according to a cadet who graduated in 1929, 'was tough but it was exhilarating and the cadets were a dedicated corps d'elite.'[62] The constant hustling to which the cadets were subjected ensured that they could work satisfactorily under pressure.[63] What the colleges did very imperfectly was to encourage cadets to use their initiative and think for themselves, or to train them in leadership skills and as tacticians.[64] It was only when they arrived at their regiment that young officers began to learn how to lead men, usually under the benign tutelage of their platoon or troop sergeant.[65] The purely educational content of the syllabus was increased in the 1920s at the expense of military training but, even so, a cadet who passed through Sandhurst in 1935 recorded that 'Independent thinking is frowned on as heresy—no divergence from official view allowed'.[66] The initiative and intellectual curiosity that was supposed to be imparted by the educational syllabus was largely nullified by too much time spent on the parade ground. A Staff Sergeant curtly informed a cadet who tried to express an opinion that 'You are not allowed to think, Sir!'[67] Out of a total of 1,350 training hours, no less than 515 hours were spent 'producing the private soldier cadet'.[68] This was a dysfunctional approach to training. It ill-fitted officers to deal with the unexpected calls which were going to be made on them on the battlefield.[69]

A comparison with the education that German officer cadets received showed that the tactical training of British cadets was woefully inadequate. German officer cadets were already fully trained private soldiers before they were posted to their cadet college. Whereas the British colleges barely taught platoon tactics, German cadets 'learned everything an infantry battalion commander had to know in any kind of pre-combat or combat situation. At the end of our training we would theoretically be able to command an infantry battalion in combat.'[70]

---

[62] D. Niven, *The Moon's a Balloon* (London, 1971), 63.

[63] P. Carrington, *Reflect on Things Past. The Memoirs of Lord Carrington* (London, 1989), 21–2; see also M. Carver, *Out of Step. The Memoirs of Field Marshal Lord Carver* (London, 1989) 22; Niven, *The Moon's a Balloon*, 58.

[64] PRO WO 32/2374, Milne to all GOC-in-C, 27 Nov. 1926.

[65] IWM Dept. of Sound Records, Accession nos. 000834/08: Brig. R. N. Harding-Newman; 000857/02: Maj.-Gen. P. R. C. Hobart, 12.

[66] LHCMA Liddell Hart MSS 11/1935/121, Talk with B. F. Ewart, 27 Dec. 1935.

[67] LHCMA Liddell Hart MSS 11/1937/27, From the distinguished father (who was himself there before the War) of a boy at Sandhurst, 14 Nov. 1937.

[68] LHCMA Liddell Hart MSS 11/1935/121, Talk with B. F. Ewart, 27 Dec. 1935.

[69] Applegate, 'Why Armies Lose in Battle', 48.

[70] S. Knappe with T. Brusaw, *Soldat. Reflections of a German Soldier, 1936–1949* (Shrewsbury, 1993), 104; Corum, *The Roots of Blitzkrieg*, 79–84.

This conferred two advantages on the German army. It produced junior officers able, with a minimum of further training, to accept command responsibilities and step into the shoes of their superiors if the latter became casualties. And by centralizing tactical training it produced an officer corps with a common understanding of the army's tactical doctrine.

The British forfeited both advantages by relying on a system of post-graduate training to meet these needs. After receiving their commissions, young gunner, engineer, tank, and signals officers went to their arm of service school to begin to learn the technical aspects of their profession.[71] However, neither the infantry nor the cavalry had its own junior officer's tactical school. Junior officers in these arms were posted to their regimental depot, where they spent nine months learning (or in reality relearning) drill and the interior economy of their unit, and being reproved for every minor error in dress and deportment. Infantry officers did spend three months at the School of Musketry at Hythe, but there they were taught to become musketry instructors, not tactical leaders.[72] The army thus lost the opportunity to imbue young officers of the different arms of the service with a common understanding of its tactical doctrine at the outset of their careers.

All junior officers were expected to pass promotion examinations to enable them to command troops at one or two levels above their existing rank. Lieutenants seeking promotion to captain were thus expected to answer questions concerned with the deployment of a reinforced company, and captains seeking promotion to major had to understand how to command a reinforced battalion. By 1936 the test had been made stiffer. Captains were expected to discuss the tactics of a mixed force of brigade size and lieutenants seeking promotion to captain were expected to be able to write orders for a mixed force of battalion strength.[73] In theory this should have been excellent preparation for the test that many of these officers were to face after 1939. But in practice it was vitiated by four factors. First, the tactical training of junior officers was decentralized, being left in the hands of their unit commander. The quality of the training they received, therefore, varied enormously. Some commanders were enthusiastic and well-educated instructors, who were willing to allow their subordinates to exercise real initiative

[71] Wingfield, 'The Supply and Training of Officers for the Army', 437; IWM Dept. of Sound Records, Accession nos. 000954: Brig. W. R. Smijth-Windham, 4–6; 000944/03. Maj. A. H. Austin, 5.

[72] LHCMA Liddell Hart MSS 15/8/284. *Small Arms School, Hythe, June 1922. Memorandum 2. Training Junior Leaders as Instructors* (London, 1922); PRO WO 279/70, Report on the Staff Conference; IWM Dept. of Sound Records, Accession no. 000968/02: Col. Sir Douglas Scott, 6.

[73] LHCMA Liddell Hart MSS 15/8/97, War Office, Examination of Army Officers for Promotion, Paper set Oct. 1936.

and organized programmes of regular discussions, lectures, TEWTs, and field exercises.[74] Others were poor teachers and succeeded only in boring their officers, so that their professional development suffered accordingly. Secondly, many units at home were so under-strength that subalterns had hardly any men to command and they 'could not be taught self-reliance, responsibility, or even the tactical ability to handle men and use the ground'.[75] Thirdly, some units on small foreign stations were isolated from other arms of the service and any kind of combined arms training was virtually impossible. Finally, some commanders were reluctant to devolve day-to-day responsibilities onto their senior NCOs, and officers thus spent too much time in routine administration and weapons training, whereas they would have been better employed undergoing more extensive tactical training.[76]

A few senior officers recognized that the system was failing to imbue junior officers with a common understanding of the army's tactical doctrine. The former wanted to create a 'College of Tactics' and require all captains to graduate from it before being promoted to major.[77] In 1937 Deverell rejected the idea because 'I have a strong prejudice against Young Officer's courses. If a young officer can not learn his job in his own unit, there is something wrong with the unit. He should learn it there. Schools are to produce instructors, not to teach the elements.'[78]

Nothing was done until March 1939, when, encouraged by Gort and the DCIGS, Sir Ronald Adam, Hore-Belisha agreed to establish a tactical school. All captains would be required to pass a ten-week course at the school before taking their promotion examination for major, which would ensure the dissemination of a common understanding of tactical doctrine throughout all arms of the service.[79] But this came too late to have any impact on the tactical competence of junior officers before the war.

Slightly more senior officers, those who aspired to command their units, did have to attend a special school, the Senior Officers' School. Established on a permanent peacetime footing in 1920–1, the school had two branches, one at Sheerness and the other at Belgaum in India. The

---

[74] Lt.-Col. W. N. Nicholson, 'The Training of an Infantry Battalion', *Journal of the Royal United Services Institute*, 74 (1929), 49–54.

[75] PRO WO 279/70, Report on the Staff Conference, Col. Hewlett, GSO1, 2nd divn., Aldershot.

[76] Capt. H. C. Westmorland, 'The Training of the Army', *Journal of the Royal United Services Institute*, 75 (1930), 584–6.

[77] Col. H. R. Sandilands, 'The Case for the Senior Officers' School', *Journal of the Royal United Services Institute*, 73 (1928), 235–8.

[78] LHCMA Alanbrooke MSS 11/3, Alanbrooke biography, notes by Mrs C. Long, 31 July 1937.

[79] LHCMA Liddell Hart MSS 11/1937/79, Talk with Maj.-Gen. Sir R. Adam, 25 Oct. 1937; Anon., 'Army Notes', *Journal of the Royal United Services Institute*, 84 (1939), 205, 429–30.

fact that it was necessary was a cause for concern to many senior officers because this indicated that many existing COs were incapable of training their own subordinates.[80] It had two functions, to prepare majors for unit command and to spread a common understanding of tactical doctrine throughout the army. It met with only limited success.[81] The course, which lasted for only three months, was too short. Many of the students were already in their forties, perhaps having commanded a battalion during the First World War, and were not receptive to new ideas. Finally, it failed to detect those men who were temperamentally incapable of functioning effectively under the stresses that would be imposed on them on the battlefield. The consequences of this were seen in the case of the commander of a regular battalion in 9th Infantry brigade holding part of the line on the Escaut in Belgium in May 1940. He 'was apparently a careful diligent man who never delegated anything to anyone' with the result that he had nervous breakdown and 'was carried off on a stretcher'.[82]

It is easy to exaggerate the extent to which regimental officers saw the army as a refuge from the real world. Alan Adair, who rose to command the Guards Armoured division in the Second World War, did remain in the Grenadier Guards after 1918 because he was in no hurry to run his family's estates.[83] Similarly, when George Taylor joined the West Yorkshire Regiment in 1929 he found his seniors reluctant to speak of their First World War experiences and that 'The great majority of my brother officers had little interest in war. To the young, it was something remote that would not happen in their time, though they would not be averse to taking part in a small "North-West Frontier" type of war.'[84] But the significance of the oft-cited reluctance of cavalry officers to give up their horses in favour of tanks and armoured cars can be exaggerated. Some senior regimental officers did resent mechanization. But many embraced it out of an acceptance that it was inevitable and that it was essential if their regiments were to retain their individual corporate identities. Lieutenant-Colonel Blakiston-Houston, the commanding officer of 12th Lancers who were mechanized in 1928, summed up their attitude. 'We've been given this role and it's a very important role. And you're damm well going to do it. I won't have you bloody well bellyaching.'[85]

[80] PRO WO 279/57, Report on the Staff Conference.
[81] Fisher, 'The Training of the Regimental Officer', 252.
[82] M. Henniker, *An Image of War* (London, 1987), 35.
[83] *A Guard's General. The Memoirs of Major General Sir Alan Adair*, ed. O. Lindsay (London, 1986), 84.
[84] Taylor, *Infantry Colonel*, 13.
[85] IWM, Dept. of Sound Records, Accession nos. 000892/06: Col. G. J. Kidston-Montgomerie of Southannan, 8; 000985/04: Col. T. B. A. Evans-Lombe, 19–20. I am most

Certainly, it is apparent that the system of promotion examinations was designed to ensure that junior officers could not ignore the world around them. Papers in military organization, military law, and regimental organization emphasized the extent to which they were expected to be competent at the 'house-keeping' aspects of their job. This was an important role which all officers had to master, because, by ensuring that their men had sufficient supplies of food, drink, and shelter and warmth, and that they were fairly treated by the army's bureaucracy, officers could sustain unit morale. But the wider world was not neglected. They were also required to pass examinations in 'Imperial Military Geography'—what today would be called 'strategic studies' and military history—taught in such a way as to 'illustrate the principles laid down in official manuals by actual events that have taken place in war'.[86] It was a measure of the zeal and ambition of many young officers that by the late 1920s large numbers of them were also competing for the limited number of Staff College places that were available. In 1929, for example, 409 British service officers competed for Camberley and Quetta, but there were only places for 56.[87] Again, the entrance examinations required candidates not only to master the technicalities of their profession, but also to display a wide understanding of political, economic, and strategic issues as they pertained to imperial defence. Even the majority of candidates who failed the examination had learnt something of value from the experience, for in the opinion of one examiner who marked nearly 600 papers in 1926, only about one in six of the candidates had not prepared himself seriously for the examination.[88]

The battalion and brigade commanders of the expanded wartime army were supposed to be provided from the ranks of the 'middle piece officers', of the pre-war regular army, that is senior captains and majors. That some of them failed to perform successfully was not because they lacked professional ambition, regarded soldiering as an agreeable pastime, and looked upon the army as a refuge from the industrial world. They failed because the army had not created a system to ensure that they received the appropriate training to succeed.

The training of Territorial regimental officers was even more haphazard and theoretical than that of the regulars. In the late 1930s some

grateful to my former student, Jeremy Barnett, for discussing these issues with me and for allowing me to read his MA thesis on the mechanization of the British regular cavalry in the late 1930s.

[86] War Office, *King's Regulations for the Army and Army Reserve 1928* (London, 1928), 482; Maj. D. H. Cole, *Imperial Military Geography. General Characteristics of the Empire in Relation to Defence* (London, 1939), was a popular textbook which went through numerous revisions before 1939; War Office, *Training Regulations 1934*, 111–12.

[87] PRO WO 279/70, Report on the Staff Conference.

[88] CCC Bonham-Carter MSS BHCT 9/3, C. Bonham-Carter, 'Autobiography, 1921–39'.

Territorial officers began to attend short courses at Sandhurst, but most could only spare enough time to attend three or four weekend camps each year in addition to weekly evening drills.[89] Junior officers were expected to pass an examination to judge their competence within three years of being commissioned. However, as the practical part of the examination was set by their own adjutant, who was himself the officer responsible for training them, it was rarely a stiff test of their competence. Promotion, as in the regular army, was by seniority within regimental establishments.[90] But unlike their regular counterparts, who were at least in theory trained to assume appointments two ranks above their current job, Territorial officers were trained to carry out only their existing appointment. The result, according to another Territorial battalion commander, was that 'the average Territorial officer, though first rate at remembering any lessons he has learnt, is more incapable of thinking for himself under strange conditions and surroundings than the average regular officer'.[91]

However, the greatest weakness in the training of the Territorial officer cadre was that aspiring battalion commanders, unlike their regular counterparts, were not required to attend the Senior Officers School before commanding their unit.[92] The only training most senior Territorial officers received in combined arms operations took the form of TEWTs, so that they rarely had 'the actual chance of seeing the co-operation of all arms'.[93] The consequence, according to Deverell in December 1936, was that 'There are too many [CO's] who through no fault of their own have had no tactical experience and who are not able to train their units'.[94]

In September 1939 the British Army appeared to be a formidable force of 53,287 officers and 839,410 other ranks. The reality was that it was neither a homogenous nor a fully trained fighting force. The Regular Army mustered 224,000 all ranks. They were supported by the Regular Army Reserve of 131,100 men. However, only 3,700 of them, men who had left the colours in the preceding year, were fully trained. The rest had been in civilian life for up to thirteen years and needed considerable retraining to become familiar with the latest equipment and forms of organization. The Supplementary Reserve consisted of 42,600 men.

[89] PRO WO 279/65, Report on the Staff Conference, Comments by Brig. R. M. Luckock.

[90] War Office, *Regulations for the Territorial Army (Including the Territorial Army Reserve) and for County Associations 1936* (London, 1936), 34–5, 50.

[91] PRO WO279/75, Report on the Staff Conference, Comment by Lieut.-Col. W. H. Brooke.

[92] PRO WO279/75, Report on the Staff Conference, Comment by Maj.-Gen. J. K. Dick-Cunyngham.

[93] PRO WO 279/70, Report on the Staff Conference, Comments by Maj. R. H. Lorrie.

[94] LHCMA Liddell Hart MSS 1/232/16, Deverell to Liddell Hart, 29 Dec. 1936.

Many of them were mechanical transport drivers and tradesmen whose civilian occupations supposedly fitted them to take their place in the army immediately on mobilization. But only half of them had done any annual military training. The introduction of conscription in April 1939 brought 34,500 Militiamen into the army. Although many of them proved to be excellent soldiers and went on to become NCOs and officers, by September they had only just completed their basic training.[95] The largest reserve organization was the Territorial Army, which consisted of nearly 18,900 officers and 419,200 other ranks, supported by a reserve of about 7,750 officers and 13,000 other ranks. Like the Militiamen, the other ranks were keen to learn and often better educated and more intelligent than pre-war regular recruits. Nevertheless, keenness and intelligence alone could not transform civilians into soldiers. They required between eighteen months and two years of training before they were capable of meeting the Germans on anything like an equal footing.[96]

In September 1939, all male British subjects between the ages of eighteen to forty-one became liable for call-up. Between September 1939 and June 1941 the army nearly tripled in size. By June 1941 it numbered 2.2 million men. Thereafter this breakneck rate of expansion slowed and it reached its wartime maximum of 2.9 million men in June 1945.[97] At least until 1942, the army was not short of men. It also benefited from the fact that the population from which it recruited displayed a high degree of consensus in favour of the war. Only 1.2 per cent of the 5 million men called up by the armed services registered as conscientious objectors.[98] However, conscription did not mean that the army was now able to draw its recruits from a complete cross-section of British society. Men who volunteered to enlist before they were called up were allowed to opt for the service of their choice, and even conscripts were permitted to express a preference between the three services. Except in the summer of 1940, the army attracted few volunteers and throughout the war more conscripts opted for the RAF and the navy than they required.[99] They, therefore, were able to pick the most physically and mentally able recruits and the army had to make do with what remained.[100]

There is ample anecdotal evidence to suggest that the military authorities were unhappy with the quality of the men they received. In 1945 a large draft of RAF and naval personnel were compulsorily trans-

[95] PRO WO 277/12, *Manpower Problems* (London, n.d.), 9.
[96] Reynolds, 'Interviewing for the New Militia', 510.
[97] PRO WO 277/12, Piggott, *Manpower Problems*, 80.
[98] R. Barker, *Conscience, Government and War* (London, 1982), 121.
[99] W. K. Hancock and M. M. Gowing, *British War Economy* (London, 1949), 58–9.
[100] H. R. Moran, *In My Fashion. An Autobiography of the Last Ten Years* (London, 1945), 96; PRO WO 32/10942, Status of infantry soldiers, Minutes of a meeting, 9 Mar. 1945.

ferred to the army. Their new instructors were immediately struck by both their physical fitness and their keenness.[101] There is also some statistical evidence to suggest that a considerable number of the men the army did receive were not sufficiently physically fit to serve in the front line, were poorly educated, or were of below average intelligence. Comprehensive statistics exist for only the period after mid-1942, but they show that from then until the end of the war more than 20 per cent of recruits were not physically 'A1', and that a considerable number of men lacked the mental stability to become effective front line soldiers. In the course of the war, military psychiatrists in Britain examined over 225,000 soldiers referred to them by medical officers and recommended some form of psychiatric treatment or medical downgrading for 80 per cent of those they examined.[102] In the second half of 1941 the army was discharging about 1,300 men each month who had broken down during training because they were psycho-neurotics.[103] Of the 710,000 recruits who passed through the General Service Corps scheme after July 1942, interviewing officers identified only 6 per cent who seemed to have the potential to become officers and the same number who had the potential to become NCOs.[104] By July 1944 the latter figure had dropped to only 4.2 per cent.[105]

Statistics also suggest that the army received a large number of ill-educated and unintelligent men. Again comprehensive statistics only exist for the second half of the war, but they suggest that just 6 per cent of all recruits had a University degree or comparable professional qualification, a quarter had received some secondary education, half had received only an elementary education, and a quarter were educationally retarded or illiterate.[106] After September 1943 little more than a quarter of soldiers were placed in the top two of the six categories used to measure the intelligence levels of recruits, and nearly 30 per cent were of below average intelligence.[107] However, these figures may exaggerate the deficiencies of the army's intake measured across the whole of the war. The education of the young conscripts who enlisted after 1942 was likely to have been seriously disrupted by the war. Men who had enlisted before 1942 were more likely to have received a higher quality of educa-

---

[101] PRO WO 32/10943, Col. J. G. W. Davies to DPS, 3 Apr. 1945.
[102] Brig. J. R. Rees, *The Shaping of Psychiatry by War* (New York, 1945), 46. These figures relate merely to outpatient work and excluded men who had been in battle and were suffering from battle exhaustion.
[103] PRO WO 32/4726/MAC19, Detection of psycho-neurosis by medical boards, Jan. 1942.
[104] PRO WO 277/19, Col. B. Ungerson, *Personnel Selection* (London, 1953), 48.
[105] PRO WO 163/53/AC/G(44)32, War Office Progress Report, July 1944, 23 Aug. 1944.
[106] PRO WO 163/490, Personnel Selection, 1947, Statistics relating to men who have undergone General Service Procedure at Primary Training Units: Distribution by Medical Category, 2 July 1942–19 Apr. 1947; PRO WO 277/19. Ungerson, *Personnel Selection*, 47–8.
[107] PRO WO 163/490, Personnel Selection, 1947.

tion. The fact that only 6 per cent of recruits were graduates or had equivalent qualifications and that half of all recruits had only an elementary education must be set against the fact that less than 2 per cent of the relevant age group in the population went to university in the inter-war period and that only 15 per cent had attended a secondary school.[108] The army, therefore, attracted at least its fair share, if not more, of the better-educated part of the population.

To ascribe the wartime army's problems simply to the fact that it failed to attract sufficient men of high intelligence and good education, is misleading and over-simplistic. In view of the antipathy of officers like Lieutenant-Colonel Hewlett to intelligent and better-educated recruits, there is no guarantee that every commanding officer would have welcomed a larger influx of them in any case. More to the point, it also overlooks the fact that for a long time the army failed to make the most appropriate use of the men that it did receive. The army's doctrine prescribed that it fight using the maximum quantity of machinery and the minimum number of men in the front line. This was reflected in the way in which the military authorities allocated manpower. In September 1939 approximately four out of ten soldiers were placed in what was generally (and mistakenly) regarded as the least skilled arm of service, the infantry. By October 1941, the proportion of infantry had fallen to three out of ten soldiers, and although the proportion of troops allocated to the RAC had halved, their actual numbers had risen from 54,500 to 82,000. The proportion of troops involved in supplying and maintaining equipment of all kinds and providing base facilities (the RAOC, RASC, and Pioneer Corps) had more than doubled.[109] The army now recognized over 500 separate trades or highly skilled jobs and, given the wholesale introduction of mechanical transport and wireless, even the infantry had a growing demand for men with mechanical skills.[110] By October 1941, out of a total establishment of 2,317,500 men, more than a quarter (632,000) were classified as tradesmen.[111]

One of the disadvantages of reliance upon the voluntary system before 1939 was that there was no way for the authorities to direct recruits to where they were most needed. Some regiments and corps were relatively popular and could maintain themselves at a reasonable strength. Others were not, but the compulsory transfer of men from one corps to another was contrary to the Army Act. If men were turned away from a particular corps, they did not usually join another one and were lost to

---

[108]   R. McKibbin, *Classes and Cultures. England 1918 to 1951* (Oxford, 1998), 248, 260.

[109]   These figures are derived from PRO WO 163/50/AC/P(41)62, Paper by the Adjutant-General on use of manpower in the army, Oct. 1941.

[110]   PRO WO 277/19, Ungerson, *Personnel Selection*, 4.

[111]   PRO WO 163/50/AC/P(41)62, Paper by the Adjutant-General on use of manpower in the army, Oct. 1941.

the army. Any kind of scientific personnel selection was impossible. This was significant, because the First World War had highlighted the importance of proper medical screening for recruits to ensure that men who were psychologically unstable were not sent to combat units because they had an increased likelihood of becoming psychological casualties.[112] In the first half of the war the army suffered from the growing problem that too many men were assigned to the wrong job. Before 1942, recruits were posted to a particular arm of service after only the most cursory investigation into their own skills, aptitudes, and wishes. The result was that many men had subsequently to be posted to a different arm or even discharged because they were unfit.[113] Large numbers of men broke down under training. They either lacked the intelligence to absorb what they were being taught or they were too neurotic to be able to adjust to the demands the army made upon them.[114]

The solution to this problem was provided by the importation into the army of industrial psychologists. When he served as DCIGS in 1939, Sir Ronald Adam had read accounts of how the US army and some British businesses used scientific personnel selection systems to fit the man to the job.[115] When he returned from Dunkirk to become GOC Northern Command, he encouraged the Corps psychiatrist to carry out personnel selection experiments in some of his training units. They demonstrated that the Ministry of Labour were misallocating manpower on a large scale.[116] In September 1941, a committee under Sir William Beveridge reported that the army was failing to make the best use of the skills of its men. This was partly because it did not have a complete job description of the whole variety of military occupations and partly because it had insufficient knowledge of the aptitudes and skills of its men.[117] When he returned to the War Office in June 1941, this time as Adjutant General,

[112] *Report of the War Office Committee* (Cmd. 1734); T. Bogacz, 'War Neurosis and Cultural Change in England, 1914–22. The Work of the War Office Committee of Enquiry into "Shell-Shock"', *Journal of Contemporary History*, 24 (1989), 244–5, 248.

[113] PRO WO 32/4726/MAC16, National Service Act, Medical Advisory Committee, Errors in grading by civilian medical boards, May 1941.

[114] Brig. J. R. Rees, 'The Development of Psychiatry in the British Army', *Military Neuropsychiatry. Proceedings of the Association, December 15–16 1944, New York* (Baltimore, Md., 1946), 50; A. P. Thorner, 'The Treatment of Psychoneurosis in the British Army', *International Journal of Psychoanalysis*, 27 (1946), 54.

[115] PRO WO 163/50/AC/P(41)62, Paper by the Adjutant-General on use of manpower in the army.

[116] LHCMA Adam MSS ADAM 3/13, Gen. Sir R. Adam, 'Various Administrative Aspects of the War', TS narrative, 1960; PRO WO 32/4726, Horden Committee on the examination of recruits by civilian medical boards, Apr. 1941; PRO WO 32/9814. Adam to PUS, WO, 28 May 1941.

[117] PRO WO 277/12, Piggott, *Manpower Problems*, 27–8; PRO WO 163/85/ECAC/P(41)76, Joint Secretaries, Employment of tradesmen in the services, 18 Sept., 1941; G. Natzio, 'British Army Servicemen and Women 1939–45: Their Selection, Care and Management', *Journal of the Royal United Services Institute*, 138 (1993), 36–7.

Adam began to institutionalize these lessons. He established the Directorate of Personnel Selection. Its tasks were to develop an analysis of the physical and mental attributes needed to perform all of the jobs in the army and to devise and implement intelligence and aptitude tests for recruits and serving soldiers whose units were converted to other arms.[118] After July 1942, all recruits spent their first six weeks in the army in the newly created General Service Corps. They underwent basic infantry training at a Primary Training Centre and took aptitude and intelligence tests to discover their real potential. Only then were they posted to a Corps Training Centre to receive training peculiar to their new arm of service. Corps Training lasted for between sixteen weeks for the infantry and a maximum of thirty weeks for a signaller. Finally, they were then either posted to a unit or sent to one of three Reserve Divisions created in December 1942 where they received five weeks of section, platoon, and company training. This culminated in a strenuous three-day exercise before they were sent on an overseas draft.[119]

The army never conducted any systematic testing to assess the success of Adam's system, but selective testing suggested that it did reduce failures in training.[120] The scheme enabled the army to identify potential tradesmen as soon as they enlisted. Anecdotal evidence also indicated that the tests were a reasonably accurate predictor of the ability of individuals to withstand the stresses of combat. This was not evident at first. In July 1942, when the 5th Grenadier Guards underwent a series of psychological selection tests, there was much merriment when the RSM was placed in the lowest of three grades and 'all concerned considered the whole process to be a waste of time'. But by May 1943, when the battalion had seen extensive active service in Tunisia, the troops' attitude to the tests had changed. According to Sergeant Danger, 'It was now apparent that those men with low scores were beginning to crack up under stress, while those with higher scores were quite on top of things'.[121]

[118] PRO WO 163/AC/P(41)53, WO Progress Report, July 1941, 28 Aug. 1941; PRO WO 32/9814, Minute, Selection of personnel, Progress report, 29 July 1941; PRO WO 277/19, Ungerson, *Personnel Selection*, 12–13, 28–36; PRO WO 163/50/ACP(41)40, Selection tests for the army, 13 June 1941; /ACM(41)8, Minutes of the Army Council, 17 June 1941; C. S. Myers, 'The Selection of Army Personnel', *Occupational Psychology*, 18 (1943), 1–5.

[119] PRO WO 163/AC/G(42)16, WO Progress Report, Apr. 1942, 19 May 1942; PRO WO 163/86/ECAC/P(41)106, Adjutant-General, Common reception centres and basic training and selection of army class intake, 26 Nov. 1941; PRO WO 32/11519, DMT to all GOC-in-Cs Home Commands and C-in-C Home Forces, 22 Apr. 1942; PRO WO 163/88/ECAC/P(42)58, Adjutant-General, Selection of Army class intakes and introduction of common primary training, 4 May 1942; PRO WO 163/88, Minutes of 58 meeting of the Executive committee of the Army Council, 8 May 1942; PRO WO 204/1895, Notes taken by Army liaison officer at dictation of Maj.-Gen. Hayman-Joyce, Collective training carried out by 48 Reserve division in England, Apr. 1944.

[120] PRO WO 277/19, Ungerson, *Personnel Selection*, 48–9.

[121] IWM E. P. Danger MSS 82/37/1, 'Diary of a Guardsman', i.

Selection tests also improved morale. They signalled to the recruits that they were 'valued for their private abilities and personal peculiarities'.[122] As one officer wrote in 1943:

Although their tests at first sight seem gibberish, one point stands out—the men themselves believe in it. Previously, if a man fancied himself as a clerk, nothing would persuade him that he really ought to be a mechanic, but if D.P.S. tells him so he seems willing to admit that he must have been wrong.

This has, of course, an enormous psychological effect in making men contented and keen at their work.[123]

Most soldiers eventually reached their own private accommodation with the demands that the army placed upon them. Those who failed to do so were usually referred to one of the army's psychiatrists. The increasingly pressing shortage of manpower confronting the army after 1941 made the military authorities receptive to the psychiatrists' promise that they could find a suitable niche for most men. The psychiatrists mediated between the army and the individual. They owed two loyalties, as doctors to their patients, and as officers who were part of the chain of command to the army. They did not attempt to cure their patients, for they had too little time to do so; rather they attempted to achieve what one doctor described as 'a social management of psychoneurotics'.[124] The cornerstone of this system was the power given to psychiatrists to recommend men for a change of employment.

But despite the introduction of Selection Testing, serious shortcomings remained in the ways in which the army allocated and trained its personnel and these undoubtedly contributed to degrading its combat capability. Selection Testing did not ensure a perfect fit between the aptitudes of the individual soldier and the needs of the army. No force went overseas in which every man had gone through the selection procedures. Nor could the system alter the fact that the army simply did not receive enough recruits of sufficiently high intelligence to fill all of the available jobs.[125] When the aptitudes of the individual and the needs of the army clashed, the latter inevitably triumphed. By the second half of 1943, the infantry was so short of men that Ronald Gladman, who was conscripted in June 1943, remembered that when he was undergoing his intelligence tests 'It had been made clear, however, that

[122] T. Harrison, 'The British Soldier: Changing Attitudes', *British Journal of Psychology*, 35 (1944–5), 34–9. PRO CAB 98/29, War Cabinet, Ministerial Committee on the work of psychologists and psychiatrists in the services, Report by the expert committee, PPM(45)1, 31 Jan. 1945.

[123] PRO WO 153/52/AC/G(43)10, War Office Committee on Morale in the Army. Fourth Quarterly Report, Nov. 1942–Jan. 1943, 7 April 1943.

[124] Thorner, 'The Treatment of Psychoneurosis', 57.

[125] Rees, *Shaping of Psychistry*, 60; PRO WO 205/1c, Minutes of the C-in-C's conference held at GHQ, 13 Aug. 1942.

at this stage of the war everyone would be posted to the infantry no matter what trade had been followed in civilian life'.[126] Nor was the system infallible, as was demonstrated by the case of a private in 2nd battalion Essex regiment who was called up in April 1943 and found guilty of cowardice in France in September 1944. In Britain he had been categorized as of average intelligence and emotional stability. But when he was examined closely by the Corps Psychiatrist in France he was found to be emotionally immature, suffering from a nervous condition that preceded his enlistment, and was of below average intelligence.[127]

But the most serious problem was the way in which manpower was allocated to the infantry. In an infantry division only about 4,500 men actually served as front line infantrymen. Their significance as the ultimate cutting edge of the army was out of all proportion to their numbers, for if they were unwilling or unable to advance in the face of the enemy, the entire army stalled. Adam hoped that Selection Testing would ensure that 'the circumstances in which the infantry had in the past, on occasion, received in effect the rejects from other arms of the Service, were unlikely to be repeated in the future'.[128] He was disappointed. The RAF and the navy and technical units in the army still took the most intelligent and skilled men. The infantry continued to be left with the residue.[129] As one divisional commander reported in May 1943, 'The men we get in the infantry are to a great extent those not required by the RAF or with insufficient brains for technical employment'.[130] A draft destined for 2/5th Queens regiment in 56th division in Italy in October 1944 contained a typical cross-section of the kinds of men posted to the infantry after the other arms had creamed off the better-educated and the most skilled. They included men who variously described themselves as farm labourers, labourers, a stable lad, a press operator, a woollen piecer, a messenger, a handyman in a factory, a core-maker, a scaffolder's mate, a nurseryman and gardener, a plumber's mate, a dyeing hand, and a painter.[131] When large numbers of anti-aircraft gunners were transferred to the infantry in Italy in mid-1944, the officers responsible for retraining them commented

---

[126] IWM 92/1/1, Ronald Gladman MSS, TS Memoirs, 9.

[127] PRO WO 71/911, Proceedings of a Field General Court Martial of Pte. B, 1944.

[128] PRO WO 163/88, Minutes of 58 meeting of the Executive Committee of the Army Council, 8 May 1942.

[129] PRO WO 277/19, Ungerson, *Personnel Selection*, 43; PRO WO 193/25, AG1A to COs of armoured regts. and tank bns., 18 Dec. 1941; PRO WO 199/461, Minutes of a meeting held in room 220, War Office, at 3 p.m. Tues. 5 Jan. 1943, to consider the build-up of forces for offensive operations, 5 Jan. 1943.

[130] PRO WO 231/10, Maj.-Gen. Freeman-Attwood to GHQ, 1 Army, 30 May 1943.

[131] PRO WO 71/940, Proceedings of Field General Court Martial on Cpl. A and thirty others of 2/5th Battalion the Queens Royal Regt. charged with mutiny, 1944.

favourably that they were of far higher quality than the men the infantry usually received.[132]

In 1943 a Director of Infantry was appointed at the War Office to give the infantry a voice on a par with the other teeth arms. He lobbied strenuously to secure better recruits for the infantry. But, as the DSD noted with resignation in November 1944, Britain's manpower was fully mobilized 'and it is proving extremely difficult to maintain even our existing standards'.[133] The policy of posting the worst men to the infantry was contrary to its real needs. Infantrymen had to be fitter, to possess more initiative, endurance, and leadership skills than other arms because their job was more arduous, dangerous, and continuous. According to Sir William Slim, the commander of 14th Army,

In modern war the Infantryman no longer stands shoulder to shoulder with his comrades and acts mechanically on a word of command. He fights as a highly-skilled individual. Any Infantry-man who is capable of going out on a long-distance patrol must have acquired a variety of knowledge, a quickness of perception, and a skill in the handling of his own weapons which is required of no other fighting man.[134]

A study conducted amongst American infantrymen after the Korean War suggested that aggressive infantry soldiers were distinguished from their less aggressive comrades by, amongst other traits, their better health, their greater social maturity, and their higher intelligence.[135] One of the fundamental factors that degraded the combat capability of the British infantry during World War Two was that the army's manpower allocation policy ensured that it lacked a sufficient number of these men. By 1944, according to one experienced battalion commander, 'the average platoon includes three or four heroes, three or four irreconcilables and the rest respond in direct relationship to the quality of their leaders'. It was, he concluded, 'uneconomical of men's lives not to provide them with adequate leaders. This appears to be fully recognized in the German army where my experience is that the standard of junior leadership is still high.'[136] A War Office observer who took part in the invasion of Sicily supported his conclusions. He concluded that

every platoon can be analysed as follows: six gutful men who will go anywhere and do anything, twelve 'sheep' who will follow a short distance behind if they

---

[132] PRO WO 193/981, Director of Military Training's tour of the Mediterranean Theatre, Aug.–Sept. 1944.

[133] PRO WO 32/10942, Memorandum by the Director of Infantry on extra pay for the Infantry during the present war [c.20 Nov. 1944].

[134] PRO WO 32/10942, Slim to Leese, 1 Apr. 1945.

[135] M. Janowitz and R. W. Little, *Sociology and the Military Establishment* (London and Beverly Hills, Calif., 1974), 74–5.

[136] PRO WO 231/14, Col. T. N. Glazebrook to Directorate of Military Training, 4 Jan. 1944.

are well led, and from four to six ineffective men who have not got what it takes in them ever to be really effective soldiers.[137]

By neglecting to send the best men to the infantry, the army's personnel selection policy reflected and reinforced its commitment to fighting a war of material. Its personnel selection policy was entirely in conformity with its doctrine that prescribed that battles would be won at least cost using the maximum of machinery and the minimum of manpower. But it overlooked the fact that even a machinery-intensive army could not dispense entirely with well-trained infantry. It also ensured that its combat effectiveness depended to an unnecessarily high degree upon the quality of leadership provided by the regimental officer corps.

Both during the war and subsequently, much of the blame for the army's apparently low combat capability was laid at the door of the regimental officer corps. When the war was going badly in 1942, politicians, particularly on the left, were quick to blame the government for failing to create an officer corps based upon merit rather than on class privilege. During the debate on the vote of censure following the fall of Tobruk, one MP insisted that 'The fact of the matter is that the British Army is ridden with class prejudice. You have got to change it, and you will have to change it.'[138] After nearly two months of serving with 49th Infantry division in Normandy in 1944, Lieutenant-Colonel A. E. Warhurst, a War Office Liaison officer wrote of the typical infantryman that 'His heart is not in the fighting as an individual. He prefers to have his mates alongside him in battle; he expects to be commanded by a resolute leader. He deserves the best young leader he can be given.'[139] Warhurst believed that the quality of the regimental officer corps in Normandy was variable. At the start of the campaign most were well trained and resolute, but the quality of their replacements varied greatly.[140] Looking back on the campaign Liddell Hart placed much of the blame for the army's slow progress in Normandy not on the generals but on the regimental officers.[141]

In April 1942 Brigadier Gerald Templer, soon to take command of 47th division, presented to an audience of junior officers a scenario which encapsulated the essence of their job. 'You are advancing peacefully with your platoon along a quiet lane. Suddenly all hell is let loose.

---

[137] PRO WO 231/14, Lieut.-Col. L. Wigram to Directorate of Military Training, Current Reports from Overseas No. 15, Section 1. Infantry Tactics in Sicily, 16 Aug. 1943.

[138] Churchill, *The Second World War*, iv, 359.

[139] PRO WO 232/21. Lieut.-Col. A. E. Warhurst, Notes from Theatres of War, 20 Aug. 1944.

[140] LHCMA Liddell Hart MSS 1/56/6, Belchem to Liddell Hart, 7 Aug. 1952.

[141] LHCMA Liddell Hart MSS 11/1944/45b, Liddell Hart, Lessons of Normandy, Feb. 1952.

You look up, and your platoon sergeant's guts are hanging on a tree beside you. The platoon is turning to run—it is then, gentlemen, that you must grip those men.'[142]

The regular officer corps numbered approximately 14,000 men. The Territorials could muster less than 19,000 officers. Nearly a quarter of a million men were commissioned between 1939 and 1945.[143] The vast majority of regimental officers during the Second World War had, therefore, been civilians in 1939 and the wartime officer corps was composed overwhelmingly of amateur soldiers.

Until 1942, there seemed to be ample evidence to support the charge that class bias was undermining the efficiency of the officer corps. New entrants were effectively restricted to the same social groups from which the pre-war regular and Territorial officer corps had been drawn. Senior regular officers remained convinced that men of middle- and upper-class backgrounds were much more likely to possess powers of natural leadership than men from the lower middle or working classes. 'I am quite sure', Dill wrote in November 1939, 'that the men will follow & work better for some young lad who is a gentleman than they will for a more experienced W[arrant] O[fficer]. It has always been so.'[144] As Secretary of State for War in 1940, Anthony Eden agreed that leadership qualities were most likely to be found in young men who had received the education of an English gentleman. In October 1940, he rejected the option of following the RAF's example and granting commissions to Polish officers on the grounds that 'The officer in the Royal Air Force Squadron is first a technician and a commander only second; the Army officer must be a leader first and a technician second'.[145]

Early in the war the only selection procedure for OCTU candidates consisted of a short interview with a divisional or district commander, combined with a commanding officer's report on the suitability of each candidate for a commission.[146] However, by 1941 most candidates were selected by Command Interview Boards. They were created in September 1940 to prevent commanding officers from retaining potential officers as NCOs.[147] Each board consisted of a permanent president and two field officers drafted in for the day. The system failed on three counts. The failure rate of candidates sent to OCTUs reached 50 per

---

[142] N. Craig, *The Broken Plume. A Platoon Commander's Story, 1940–45* (London, 1982), 33.

[143] PRO WO 277/12, Piggott, *Manpower Problems*, 81.

[144] LHCMA Montgomery-Massingberd MSS 160, Dill to Montgomery-Massingberd, 18 Nov. 1939.

[145] PRO WO 163/48/ACM(AE023), Minutes of the Army Council, 10 Oct. 1940.

[146] ACI No. 1160. Officer training—Men serving in the ranks, 13 Mar. 1940; PRO WO 163/48/ACM(OS)11, Minutes of the Proceedings of the Army Council, 8 Mar. 1940.

[147] PRO WO 163/48/ACM(AE)15, Minutes of the Proceedings of the Army Council, 6 Aug. 1940.

cent.[148] Too many men who were commissioned subsequently suffered nervous breakdowns.[149] Finally, the system threatened morale because many men who had been rejected did not feel that they had been given a fair chance to put their own case and blamed their failure on the social snobbery of the selectors.[150] By mid-1941, the Secretary of State for War was receiving as many as thirty Parliamentary Questions each week that were critical of the system.[151]

Beginning in April 1942 the War Office, therefore, introduced a new system of selecting candidates for OCTU, the WOSB. It was loosely modelled upon the German system. Each WOSB consisted of a permanent president, a number of experienced regimental officers, a psychologist, and a psychiatrist. The WOSB system represented the abandonment of the idea that leadership was socially inherited and assumed that it was a varying relationship between personality and social situation. The WOSBs tried to identify candidates with the potential to become junior officers by testing their intelligence and by placing groups of applicants in mildly stressful situations while observers noted which of them emerged as effective leaders.[152] Between 1942 and 1945 over 100,000 candidates passed through the WOSBs.

The WOSB system did have a positive impact on the morale of other ranks. This was attested by the increasing number of them willing to put themselves forward for commissions and by the fact that both successful and unsuccessful candidates believed that the system had treated them fairly.[153] It also produced some limited democratization of the social background of the officer corps by enabling more men with only limited formal education to gain commissions. Even so, measured across the whole the war, only 21 per cent of officers had been educated at elementary schools, whereas 34 per cent had been educated at public schools.[154] Whether WOSB cadets became better officers was debatable. Those responsible for training them thought so. In December 1943, the Director of Military Training, Major-General J. A. C. Whitaker, was convinced that 'First rate leaders can come from any social class, pro-

[148] PRO WO 163/89/EAC/P(42)132, Adjutant-General, The officer situation, 28 Sept. 1942.
[149] C. Berg, 'Clinical Notes on the Analysis of a War Neurosis', *The British Journal of Medical Psychology*, 19 (1941–3), 156.
[150] PRO WO 277/36, Lt.-Col. W. L. Gibb, *Training in the Army* (London, 1961), 250; PRO WO 216/61, Capt. P. M. Studd, Main points of a memorandum on selection for commission, 28 Jan. 1941.
[151] B. S. Morris, 'Officer Selection in the British Army, 1942–45', *Occupational Psychology*, 23 (1949), 220.
[152] Col. F. I. de la P. Garforth, 'WOSBs (OCTU)', *Occupational Psychology*, 19 (1945), 97–106; LHCMA ADAM 8, Gen. Sir R. Adam, 'Various Administrative Aspects of the War', 1960; PRO WO 277/19, Ungerson, *Personnel Selection*, 56–60; PRO WO 32/10466, Minutes of a conference held at Horse Guards 10 Apr. 1942 to discuss officer production.
[153] Morris, 'Officer Selection', 221–6.
[154] PRO WO 277/16, Lt.-Col. J. Sparrow, *Morale* (London, 1949), 21.

vided they possess the right qualities, and are fully trained'.[155] But when commanding officers in both the Mediterranean and 21st Army Group were questioned in 1943–4, they could find little to choose between the products of the WOSBs and earlier systems of granting commissions.

This suggests that whatever the faults of the regimental officer corps, class bias was not the major cause of them. Whitaker had inadvertently pointed to the real reason, when he insisted that men from any social class could become effective leaders provided 'they are fully trained'. The most important factor that degraded the combat capability of the regimental officer corps was not the social class that it drew its recruits from; it was the defective training that it gave its acolytes. Like the pre-war cadet colleges, the OCTUs placed too little emphasis on producing leaders and too much, in Adam's words, 'on training the cadet to be the perfect private soldier'.[156] One wartime-commissioned officer believed that 'the cadets were treated like peacetime recruits, i.e. they were assumed to be unwilling and stupid learners who required to be driven to work'.[157] Junior officers in the wartime army, like their pre-war regular colleagues, were not expected to learn more than the most basic rudiments of tactics and man-management at OCTU. In any case training in leadership skills could only be largely theoretical, for there were no men for the cadets to lead.[158] In September 1939 the Royal Artillery OCTU syllabus required cadets to spend only 5 percent of their time learning tactics.[159] H. T. Bone thought that 'The standard of elementary tactics instruction [at 167th OCTU] is not a patch on that at Hythe Small Arms School'.[160] Cadets wasted a good deal of time relearning the formal drill they had already learnt during basic training.[161]

Wartime commissioned officers, therefore, like their peacetime predecessors, required a great deal of training after they joined their unit. But that was not always easy, because the wholesale dilution of the regular officer corps meant that most units had few regulars who could teach them.[162] In the early years of the war divisional and corps commanders established their own tactical schools. But as no two schools taught according to exactly the same syllabus, this did little to develop a

[155] PRO WO 231/8, DMT, General Lessons from the Italian Campaign, 18 Dec. 1943.

[156] PRO 205/1c, Minutes of the C-in-C's Conference held at GHQ, 14 May 1942.

[157] PRO WO 216/61, Training of Officers, Report of a meeting called by the Secretary of State for War, 29 Jan. 1941.

[158] General Staff, ATM No. 49 (London, 1944).

[159] PRO WO 287/112, Officer cadet training unit, General instructions for the guidance of regimental commanders on mobilisation, 9 June 1939.

[160] IWM Bone MSS 87/31/1, Diary entry, 24 Jan. 1941.

[161] B. Johnston, Someone Who Was. Reflections on a Life of Happiness and Fun (London, 1993), 70.

[162] PRO WO 163/48, Minutes of the Army Council, 18 Dec. 1939; PRO WO 163/52/AC/ G(43)10, War Office Committee on Morale in the Army, Fourth Quarterly Report, Nov. 1942–Jan. 1943, 7 Apr. 1943.

common understanding of tactical doctrine.[163] The infantry was particularly badly affected because until the establishment of the School of Infantry, it alone of all of the combat arms had 'no establishment for ensuring common doctrine and keeping abreast of modern developments'.[164] It was not until mid-1942 that the War Office stepped in to try to produce a greater element of uniformity in what was taught and increased the amount of time each OCTU devoted to teaching tactics.[165]

By 1944, most British troops were well trained in minor tactics. However, the experience of real combat taught them that a mastery of weapons and minor tactics was not enough. Effective leadership was the key to success and regimental officers did not fail to provide it. They shared the hardships of their men, led from the front, and suffered correspondingly higher casualties. Troops who had been repeatedly shelled and shot at, who were hungry, thirsty, tired, and very frightened, needed firm leadership if they were to continue to advance in the face of enemy fire. In the attack the single most important role of junior officers was, by their personal example, to give their men the momentum to go forwards and—a much more difficult task—to give them a renewed forward momentum if they had gone to ground before they had reached their objective.[166] Experienced platoon and company commanders soon recognized that in a big battle they had little control over how their sub-unit was used and that their main task was to lead by their personal example. According to Norman Craig they 'had to feign a casual and cheerful optimism to create the illusion of normality and make it seem as if there was nothing in the least strange about the outrageous things one was asked to do.'[167]

Lieutenant Tom Flanagan discovered how important leading from the front was when his platoon was ordered to clear a farm believed to be occupied by the Germans. His men crawled forward at night to within sight of the farm buildings, and there the foremost section remained, refusing to go any further. 'My training and later my experience as a training officer never considered this facet of battle—a reluctance to go forward as planned.' Flanagan adopted the only course of action that seemed open to him. Crawling forward past his men,

---

[163] PRO WO 32/10466, Joint Committee on instruction of officers and schools, Syllabuses of some Home Forces Schools [c.4 May 1942].

[164] PRO WO 216/82, Report of a joint committee on instruction of officers and schools, 17 May 1942.

[165] Army Bureau of Current Affairs, *War. He Leads, the Others Follow* (London, 1943); PRO WO 277/36, Gibb, *Training*, 252–6; PRO WO 163/89/ECAC/P(42)132, Adjutant-General, The officer situation, 28 Sept. 1942; PRO WO 216/82, Report of a joint committee on instruction of officers and schools, 17 May 1942.

[166] P. Cochrane, *Charlie Company. In Service with C Company 2nd Queen's Own Cameron Highlanders 1940–44* (London, 1979), 56–7.

[167] Craig, *Broken Plume*, 75.

I whispered to each in turn to prepare to move once I reached the gate. As I crawled my mind was accepting the fact that a lot of these lads were just that— they were lads, twenty years old perhaps, but still young, and in spite of all their previous battle experience —maybe because of it, had reached an 'end of tether' stage. There was a need to remove any fears that might be building up over the past hour or so on empty stomachs. They needed '. . . the Officer' to lead them. I learned that in a five minute crawl on the verge without a word being spoken to me.[168]

Officers who saw battle as a stepping-stone towards their own advancement were bitterly resented by their own men, who feared that they would sacrifice them to further their own ambition. Successful regimental officers had to possess a combination of technical military skills, a strong personality, and the physical and moral courage to earn the respect and trust of those serving under them.[169]

The price of leading from the front was high. In all of the teeth arms, officers suffered a higher proportion of casualties than the other ranks they led. In North West Europe officers suffered 26.5 casualties per 1,000 men per month, compared to other ranks who suffered 19.6 casualties per 1,000 men per month.[170] The most dangerous job in the army was commanding a rifle platoon or rifle company. In North West Europe between June and November 1944, about one-third of rifle platoon and company commanders became casualties each month. Nearly 70 per cent of officer casualties took place when units were attacking and 40 per cent of them took place when the attacking troops were within less than 500 yards of the enemy. This meant that by the end of the North West European campaign only one rifle company commander in the whole of 3rd Division who had landed in Normandy on 6th June 1944 was still alive and unwounded.[171] After battalions had been in combat for only a short period, many of their original officers were bound to become casualties. Command of platoons therefore devolved upon their NCOs but, in the opinion of many unit commanders, not enough of them were up to the task. By 1944 many of those who possessed real leadership qualities had probably already been commissioned or had joined the commandos or parachute regiment;

[168] IWM Capt. T. H. Flanagan MSS 87/19/1, 'Tom's War, 15 February to 8 May 1945'.

[169] P. Fielden, *Swings and Roundabouts* ([n.pl.]1991), 32–3; Jary, *Eighteen Platoon*, 8, 34; P. Roach, *The Eight-Fifteen to War. The Memoirs of a Desert Rat* (London, 1982), 76; I. C. Hamerton, *Achtung Minen! The Making of a Flail Tank Troop Commander* (Lewes, Sussex, 1991), 153.

[170] LHCMA, Maj.-Gen. Sir F. de Guingand MSS IV/4/3. Anon., *The Administrative History of the Operations of 21 Army Group on the Continent of Europe, 6 June 1944 to 8 May 1945* (Germany, 1945), Appendix M. See also PRO WO 291/1331, Operational Research in North West Europe, No. 2 Operational Research Section, 21 Army Group, Report no. 19, Infantry Casualties n.d.; PRO CAB 106/1024, Dept. of Scientific Adviser to the Army Council, Military Operations Research Unit, Report no. 23. Battle Study, Operation Goodwood n.d.

[171] IWM Lieut.-Col. E. Jones MSS 94/4/1, TS Memoirs.

those who had not often lacked sufficient training.[172] A vicious spiral could then set in. The remaining officers found themselves doing jobs that might have been done by capable NCOs and suffered consequently higher casualties.[173]

Unit commanders also needed to be able to feign the same casual attitude towards the physical dangers of the battlefield. If they could do so they quickly earned the respect of their men.[174] Eighteen per cent of rifle battalion commanders were killed or wounded each month. But they also needed a much higher degree of tactical skill than their subordinates because the decisions and choices facing them were more complex. They needed to be able to think quickly and calmly under intense stress, to see the essentials of any tactical problem and be able to make life-and-death decisions on the basis of incomplete and contradictory information.[175] Not surprisingly, such men needed what one platoon commander called 'rough and vibrant stamina'.[176] Training exercises could only produce a pale imitation of the stress of real war, and men who were found to lack these qualities in action were soon replaced. At the end of its first battle in Normandy, the commander of 11th Armoured Division dismissed one of his brigadiers, one of his infantry battalion commanders, and his motor battalion commander.[177] The influence that a good unit commander exercised could be measured by what happened when they became casualties themselves, for their demise was often followed by a marked increase in the incidence of psychological casualties in their unit.[178]

During the First World War, competent and lucky officers were able to rise rapidly to command through successful service in the field. During the opening years of the Second World War, the fact that most of the army was in Britain made it more difficult for senior officers to identify subordinates who were incapable of commanding troops in the field and promoting able junior officers who were. Unable to be guided by the acid test of active service, when in doubt the military authorities gave command of field force units to regular officers.[179]

---

[172] PRO WO 231/14, Col. T. N. Glazebrook to Directorate of Military Training, 4 Jan. 1944; PRO 231/850, Director of Military Training to officers responsible for future military training, 18 Dec. 1943; LHCMA Liddell Hart MSS 1/56/6, Belchem to Liddell Hart, 7 Aug. 1952.

[173] PRO 260/50, Report on Director of Military Training's visit to Mediterranean Theatre, 24 Nov. 1943; PRO WO 193/981, Director of Military Training's tour of the Mediterranean Theatre, Aug.–Sept. 1944.

[174] J. Hillier, *The Long Road to Victory. War Diary of an Infantry Despatch Rider 1940–46* (Trowbridge, Wilts, 1995), 99.   [175] Taylor, *Infantry Colonel*, 38.

[176] IWM Bone MSS 87/31/1, Bone to his mother, 23 July 1944.

[177] Maj.-Gen. G. P. Roberts, *From the Desert to the Baltic* (London, 1987), 164, 167.

[178] PRO WO 177/321, Maj. D. J. Watterson, Monthly report for June 1944 by psychiatrist attached to 2 Army, 7 July 1944.

[179] IWM 86/4/1, Lt.-Col. A. T. A. Browne, 'Destiny. Portrait of a man in Two World Wars',

Between September 1939 and October 1941, only 133 regular Lieutenant-Colonels were removed from their commands. In contrast a quarter of all Territorial unit commanders (265 Lieutenant-Colonels) were dismissed.[180] By September 1941 only 18 Territorial officers were commanding brigades in the field force, 181 were commanding units and 19 were GSO1s. Unsurprisingly, this wholesale clear-out of senior Territorial officers caused considerable resentment amongst the Territorials.[181] However, in the light of the very inadequate training that they had received before 1939, it was both inevitable and salutary.

The defeats of 1940–2 quickly gave currency to the idea that the army was led by too many elderly 'Blimpish' colonels.[182] The Army Council reacted by reducing the age of field force unit commanders, convinced that only young men would be able to cope with the rigours of mechanized warfare. In September 1941 the average age of Lieutenant-Colonels commanding field force units in the major teeth arms was only slightly below what it had been a decade earlier.[183] Out of 774 such officers, only 110 were below the age of forty-one and 276 were forty-six or older. The Military Members of the Army Council decided that no officer over the age of forty-five would be appointed to command a field force unit and that by September 1943 that age limit would be reduced to forty-three. No officer was to be allowed to remain in command of a field force unit after he reached the age of fifty, unless he had very special qualifications. By October 1942 the average age of officers promoted to Lieutenant-Colonel had fallen to forty-two in the RA, to forty-one in the RE, RCS, Guards, and line infantry, and to thirty-eight in the RAC. Each of them had an average of sixteen years' service. In 1943 Montgomery decreed that for command of an armoured regiment, the preferred age on appointment should be between thirty and thirty-five.[184] To the extent that it was possible, success on the battlefield also brought its rewards. In 1942 officers serving in the Middle East were about nine months younger than their counterparts in Britain when they were promoted to Lieutenant-Colonel.[185]

TS memoirs; PRO WO 163/49/ACM(OS)23. Memo by the Adjutant-General to the Secretary of State, 27 Feb. 1940; PRO WO 163/49/ACM(OS)16, Minutes of the Proceedings of the Army Council, 29 Mar. 1940.

[180] PRO WO 163/86/ECAC/P(41)94, Military Secretary, Age limits for the appointment of officers to command and their retention in command and employment, 30 Oct. 1941.

[181] Ibid.; PRO WO 163/50/AC/P(41)61, P. J. Grigg, Age limit for the retention of officers, 6 Nov. 1941; *Hansard 385 HC Deb.* 5s., cols. 679–80, 1963–4, 24 Nov., 16 Dec. 1942.

[182] PRO WO 259/64, WO Press Conference, 18 Mar. 1942.

[183] PRO WO 163/86/ECAC/P(41)90), Annex, Statement of ages of regimentally employed officers of RAC, RA, Infantry, and Recce. Corps *c.*10 Sept. 1941 (excluding POWs, missing, officers of the Quartermaster Class).

[184] Maj.-Gen. D. Belchem, *All in the Day's March* (London, 1978), 118.

[185] PRO WO 365/149, Average age of officers on promotion, Oct. 1942 and return of

The army's personnel policy and system of individual training significantly degraded its combat capability, although not in those ways that are most frequently cited. The blame for many of the faults of the wartime army have been laid at the door of the inter-war regular officer corps, for it was they who dominated the middle ranks of the wartime army. But they were not at fault because they were a conservative and rural élite who saw the army as a refuge from the industrial world and knew nothing of mechanized warfare. It was the system, not the individuals who were at fault. In peacetime the army failed to provide them with the training appropriate to their wartime functions. In wartime it filled the rank and file of the infantry with the residue of recruits after the other two services and the army's own technical units had taken the cream. This was entirely in conformity with the army's basic doctrine that prescribed that battles would be won at least cost using the maximum of machinery and the minimum of manpower. But it overlooked the fact that even a machinery-intensive army could not dispense entirely with well-trained infantry. In both peace and war it failed to teach a common understanding of its tactical doctrine. The German army avoided each of these pitfalls. German junior officers received a thorough tactical training before they were commissioned and therefore found it comparatively easy to step up in rank during combat. In the German army each arm of service was allocated an equal proportion of the best recruits.[186] In view of the fact that the British infantry rank and file tended to get the least intelligent recruits, leadership in the infantry was vitally important in the effort to maintain its combat capability. In 1942 the War Office circulated a German assessment of the quality of British regimental officers. It conceded that they were 'brave and self-sacrificing' and had received a good theoretical training, but criticized them for their lack of practical experience of battlefield leadership.[187] It was a measure of the extent to which the reforms of 1942 had improved matters that two years later the 12th SS Panzer Grenadier Division remarked on the 'outstanding battle leadership' of the units of 49th Division who were opposing them.[188]

number of officers promoted (Distinguishing between Middle East and elsewhere) and showing average age on promotion, and at date of commission, Nov. 1942.

[186] M. Van Creveld, *Fighting Power. German and US Army Performance 1939–45* (London, 1983), 66–7.

[187] LHCMA 15/8/166, General Staff, *ATM no.* 44 (London, 1942), Appendix B, 'As the Germans see us.'

[188] K. Meyer, *Grenadiers* (Winnipeg, Man., 1994), 133.

CHAPTER THREE
Weapons and Equipment

In 1918 the British army possessed a full outfit of the equipment it required to fight slow-moving set-piece battles against another major European army. After 1919 the General Staff built on the experience of the First World War to develop a doctrine that sought the restoration of mobility to the battlefield by combined arms co-operation and the generation of overwhelming fire-power. To translate this doctrine into reality, the army needed a new generation of weapons that combined mobility and the ability to generate sustained fire-power. Ideally they had to be reliable, cheap, easy to mass-produce, and supported by a maintenance system that could repair damaged equipment expeditiously. They also had to be available in adequate quantities. But if at the level of doctrine the General Staff could spend a good deal of effort in considering how to fight a first-class enemy, the reality of inter-war soldiering was very different. After 1918 the army's immediate task was not preparing to fight another continental war, it was upholding Britain's imperial authority. The majority of soldiers were employed in policing and defending the frontiers of the empire. This was a task that placed a premium on mobility and tested the capacity of the army's logistics system to sustain forces far from their bases. The ability to generate overwhelming fire-power was of only secondary importance. The British army had learnt in the nineteenth century that 'small wars' were 'campaigns against nature rather than against hostile armies'.[1] Weapons that consumed too much ammunition could defeat their own purpose because they overstrained the available transport facilities. And in operations to restore internal order weapons that could easily be fired indiscriminately might cause excessive casualties and thus actually increase antagonism to British rule. In the opinion of Major-General Sir Charles Gwynn, a leading expert on imperial policing and a former commandant of the Staff College at Camberley, 'in dealing with mobs, it is the weapons which are easy to control and have the quality of selectiveness which are most suitable. Great destructive power is seldom required . . .'.[2] The upshot was that, although in 1939 the army did possess some weapons, like the Infantry tank, that were well suited to

[1] Col. C. E. Callwell, *Small Wars. Their Principles and Practice* (2nd edn., London, 1914), 57.
[2] Maj.-Gen. Sir C. W. Gwynn, *Imperial Policing* (London, 1934), 14–15, 20, 30–2.

the needs of a European war, various of its other weapons were not. One of the greatest handicaps under which the army laboured after 1939 was that much of its equipment had been designed primarily to meet the demands of colonial warfare and gave priority to mobility over fire-power. This fact was brought home to one War Office weapons expert who had experience of fighting on the North West Frontier of India in the summer of 1942. After spending several weeks watching the fighting on the Gazala line that culminated in the fall of Tobruk in June 1942, he blamed the 8th Army's setbacks in part on 'The little mortars, L.M.G.s, and other grenades, so excellent for our pre-war conditions in Palestine etc.', because they lacked the ability to generate the sustained fire-power of their German counterparts.[3] It was fortunate, therefore, that by late 1942, the army could compensate itself for these disadvantages to a considerable extent because of the efficiency of its logistical 'tail'. What it lacked in quality, it could make up for in quantity.

The design and development of weapons and equipment between the wars was impeded by three factors. First, the army, with large stockpiles of World War One vintage weapons, soon discovered that 'any suggestion for buying anything new created alarm and despondency in the Finance Branch and the Treasury.'[4] Between 1926–34 the army never had more than £1m per annum for new equipment.[5] The second factor was the rapid rate of technological progress. This made it difficult for the military authorities to decide the right moment to stop experimenting and to go into production. As the DSD, Major-General Cameron, explained in 1927:

We have got to strike a happy mean, and while making certain that we have got the vehicle we want before we adopt it, yet not waiting too long for perfection before going to production. And if we go to production now with the machines we have got, we may find ourselves, a year afterwards, wishing that we had adopted another kind. Therefore, with the present rate of progress in invention we shall have to be careful before we put a lot of our capital into machines.[6]

Cameron was right to be cautious, as is shown by a comparison of the capabilities of the motor vehicles the army was experimenting with in the late 1920s and the vehicles it actually went to war with in 1939. In 1928 the army was carrying out trials with a mixture of half-tracks and

---

[3] PRO WO 163/183, Visit by Lieut.-Col. H. A. Livock (SD5, War Office) to operations area, Western Desert, 4–28 June 1942, 3 Aug. 1942.

[4] LHCMA Kirke MSS 2/1/3, Kirke, 'The Experimental Brigade'.

[5] WO 279/54, Report on the Staff Exercise held by CIGS, 30 Oct.–3 Nov. 1922, Statement by the Master-General of the Ordnance as to the development of new weapons since the war; Macready, 'The Trend of Organization in the Army', 1–20.

[6] PRO WO 279/57, Statement by Maj.-Gen. A. R. Cameron, Report on the Staff Conference held at the Staff College Camberley, 17–20 Jan. 1927.

six-wheeled lorries that had an average road speed of 15 m.p.h. and a range of less than seventy miles.[7] In 1933 it began to experiment with lighter four-wheeled trucks, and in 1939 it was equipped with a mixture of 15- and 30-cwt. four-wheel trucks, 3-ton lorries and artillery tractors, all based on commercial designs, with a range of between 160–250 miles, a maximum road speed of between 40 and 45 m.p.h., and with many interchangeable parts to facilitate maintenance.[8]

The third impediment was the army's clumsy system of overseeing the design and development process. Following the abolition of the Ministry of Munitions after the First World War this task reverted to the control of the War Office.[9] Henceforth the DMO&I predicted the types of warfare for which provision had to be made and provided evidence concerning the weapons possessed by potential enemies. The DSD prepared specifications for the armoured fighting vehicles, small arms, and gun tractors that the army needed. But the task of overseeing their development was divided between the MGO and the QMG. The MGO was responsible for developing artillery and other warlike stores and the QMG for developing supply and transport vehicles. Thus there was not a single authority responsible for the design and development of weapons and equipment.[10] The situation worsened after 1939. Following the establishment of the Ministry of Supply in 1939, the War Office lost control over the design and production of its own weapons. Henceforth, it could only pass on user opinions to the Ministry and hope that they were acted upon. The result, according to the ACIGS in July 1942, was that 'In the past the procedure had been rather that a weapon had been invented or produced haphazard and the Army had then utilised it as best they could'.[11]

The army was further handicapped by the late start of its rearmament programme and the crippling losses of equipment it suffered at Dunkirk. Together they meant that, until late 1942, the need to get almost any weapons into the hands of the troops took priority over the production of the best possible weapons. Once the process of mass-producing an item of equipment had begun, major design changes could be carried out only at the cost of stopping production while new tools and jigs were

[7] LHCMA Liddell Hart MSS 11/1928/2, Memorandum about armoured and non-armoured vehicles [c.Jan. 1928].

[8] The Tank Museum, *Data Book of Wheeled Vehicles. Army Transport 1939–45* (London, 1983), 38–49; Anon, 'Army Notes', *Journal of the Royal United Services Institute*, 78 (1933), 428; PRO WO 32/2840, Creedy to GOCs-in-C, 6 Apr. 1937; PRO WO 32/4118, Deverell to GOCs-in-C., 28 July 1937.

[9] *Winston S. Churchill, iv. Companion pt 2, Documents July 1919–March 1921*, ed. M. Gilbert, (London, 1977), 939.

[10] PRO WO 277/8, Anon., 'Fighting, Support, and Transport Vehicles, and the War Office Organization for their Provision.'(London [1948]), 49–52, 81–2.

[11] PRO WO 163/183, Record of the first meeting of the General Staff Committee on weapons and equipment held in the War Office, 17 July 1942.

assembled. In November 1940 Churchill insisted that 'At this stage in tank production numbers count above everything else. It is better to have any serviceable tank than none at all.'[12] The troops often received what the Ministry of Supply could most easily mass-produce, rather than the weapons they actually wanted.[13]

This last point can be illustrated by examining the rifles, machine-guns, and mortars and hand-held anti-tank weapons issued to the infantry. After spending some days with the 50th Division in Normandy, a New Zealand military observer, Brigadier James Hargest, noted that every time they encountered German resistance they called for artillery support. He believed this meant that 'The old trouble of not relying on their own weapons is prevalent among infantry here', something he thought was the result of a combination of low morale, tiredness, and poor training.[14] The real reasons were twofold. Most infantry weapons were ill designed for the job they were required to do, and British doctrine prescribed that higher commanders situated behind the front line controlled most support weapons.

The army's standard rifle, the Short Lee Enfield, was originally adopted in 1903.[15] It was a robust weapon that, in the hands of a well-trained marksman, could hit a small target at a considerable distance. But because it was a bolt-action weapon, it was capable of firing a maximum of only 15 rounds per minute. In view of the General Staff's commitment to generating overwhelming firepower, it might be thought that they would have tried to replace it with a weapon capable of a higher rate of fire. In November 1926 the War Office did issue a specification for an automatic (that is, a self-loading) rifle.[16] None of the designs submitted quite met all of its requirements, but the most promising could fire between two-and-a-half and three times faster than the Lee Enfield.[17] However, it was not adopted. This was partly because the Treasury insisted that the large numbers of World War One vintage Lee Enfields must not be scrapped. But it was also because the General

[12] PRO WO 277/8, Anon., 'Fighting, Support, and Transport Vehicles', 38; M. M. Postan, D. Hay, and J. D. Scott, *Design and Development of Weapons. Studies in Industrial Organisation* (London, 1964), 322.

[13] See, e.g., the criticisms of Brig. A. G. Kenchington in CCC Lewin MSS RLEW 2/1, Kenchington, Notes for History, n.d.

[14] PRO CAB 106/1060, Report from Normandy, 1944, 6 June–10 July, by Brig. James Hargest.

[15] PRO WO 279/60, Statement by Col. S. C. Peck, Director of Mechanization, Report on the Staff Conference; PRO WO 279/65, Statements by Brig. B. D. Fisher and Lt.-Gen. Sir W. Gillman, Report on the Staff Conference; PRO WO 32/2827, Milne to DSD, 10 Sept. 1930; General Staff, *ATM No. 18* (London, 1937).

[16] PRO WO 279/54, Statement by the Master-General of the Ordnance as to the development of new weapons since the war, Report on the Staff Exercise; PRO WO 32/2374, PUS WO, to arms manufactuers, 4 Nov. 1926.

[17] LHCMA Liddell Hart MSS 15/3/62–67, *The Times*, 11 Sept. 1930.

Staff feared they would actually retard the army's mobility by placing an extra burden on its logistical system. Automatic rifles—and, even more so, sub-machine-guns, weapons they derisively dismissed as 'gangster-guns'—would encourage troops to blaze away indiscriminately, and waste their limited supplies of ammunition. Rather than let that happen, the General Staff preferred infantrymen who were expert shots, able to hit a small target at a considerable distance, rather than mere 'lead pumpers'. They knew that riflemen would only be presented with 'indefinite and fleeting targets at ranges within 600 yards'.[18] Their commitment to 'scientifically accurate shooting' flew in the face of one of the main lessons of the First World War, that rifle fire over ranges of about 300 yards was a waste of ammunition.[19] But rather than accept that their goal was unattainable, and that the infantry would be better equipped with rapid-fire weapons that could suppress the enemy rather than kill him, they placed mobility before fire-power and opted for weapons they hoped would produce more accurate fire.[20]

The Germans followed the opposite course. They also rejected semi-automatic assault rifles in the early 1920s, for they, too, had large stocks of World War One vintage rifles and continued to use them until 1945.[21] However, German infantry had used sub-machine-guns during the First World War, and German manufacturers continued to develop them in the inter-war period. Following the experience of the Spanish Civil War, they adopted the MP38 1938. Weighing only 9 pounds, it had a rate of fire of 500 rounds per minute and could easily be mass-produced.[22] The British were so impressed by its performance that in January 1941 they belatedly decided to produce their own modified version, the Sten gun. The first Stens were produced in June 1941.[23] They were cheap and easy to mass-produce, but their lack of an adequate safety-catch sometimes made them dangerous to their owners. Tests showed that under battle-field conditions, at ranges of below 300 yards, and in the hands of semi-

[18] War Office, *Small Arms Training, i, Pamphlet No. 1. Annual course—Regular Army. Cavalry Regiments (Horsed) and Infantry (Rifle) Battalions. 1938* (London: War Office, 1938); LHCMA Liddell Hart MSS 15/3/57, *The Times*, 9 Aug. 1937; LHCMA Liddell Hart MSS 15/3/62–67, 'Memo Weapon Training (Rifle and light gun) Annual Course—Regular Infantry and Cavalry, Small Arms School, Hythe, Kent, June 1922' (Small Arms School, 1922); Gilbert (ed.), *Churchill. Companion, v. pt 1*, 344–5.

[19] Lt.-Col. R. L. Sherbrooke, 'The New Infantry Weapons', *Journal of the Royal United Services Institute*, 83 (1938), 136–44; LHCMA Liddell Hart MSS 15/3/57, *Morning Post*, 20 Apr. 1931.

[20] General Staff, *Infantry Training. Training and War* (1937), 3.

[21] Corum, *The Roots of Blitzkrieg*, 104; PRO WO 208/3003, War Department, Washington, German Infantry Weapons, Prepared by Military Intelligence Service, 25 May 1943.

[22] I. V. Hogg, *The Encyclopaedia of Infantry Weapons of World War II* (London, 1977), 63–4.

[23] PRO WO 106/1775, Report of the Bartholomew Committee [*c.*2 July 1940]; Hogg, *Infantry Weapons*, 52–3.

skilled troops, they were better weapons than the Lee Enfield. Faced by
fleeting targets, the Stens' rapid rate of fire meant that their users were
far more likely to hit their target than were rifle-armed infantry.[24]

During the First World War, the infantry had been armed with two
direct-fire automatic weapons, the Lewis automatic rifle and the belt-fed
Vickers medium machine-gun. Both were heavy weapons, useful on the
defensive but because of their weight liable to slow the rate of the
infantry's advance.[25] By 1930 Milne, in an effort to simplify the organization and training of the infantry, wanted a single general purpose
machine gun, lighter than the Lewis but capable of the same accurate,
sustained, and long-range fire as the Vickers.[26] In 1935 the War Office
adopted a Czech-designed weapon, redesigned to take the British
.303-in. cartridge and christened the Bren gun.[27] But the Bren fell short
of Milne's specifications. It was about 10 pounds lighter than the Lewis.
However, even when mounted on a tripod, it was no match for
the Vickers in producing sustained fire-power.[28] Vickers guns were
therefore retained, although they were relegated to separate machine-
gun battalions.

The poor performance of rifles and Sten guns in the hands of wartime
conscripts, plus the fact that in action most platoons were below
strength, meant that in practice rifle sections relied upon their Bren
gun to generate fire-power.[29] The main task of riflemen was to carry
ammunition for their section's Bren.[30] Experiments conducted in 1944
revealed the inadequacies of the army's small arms. They demonstrated
that infantry armed with rifles, Stens and Bren guns needed to be able to
fire at or, in the case of rifles, beyond their normal maximum rate of fire
if they were to generate sufficient fire-power to neutralize enemy troops
in slit trenches or pill boxes.[31] They also demonstrated that the army's

[24]   PRO WO 291/473, Army Operational Research Group, Memorandum no. 128, A comparison of rifle, bren, and sten guns [c. May 1944].

[25]   PRO AIR 5/1382, Lt.-Gen. Sir T. L. N. Moreland, Interim Report on Experimental
Brigade, 1922, Equipment of the Infantry Soldier, 30 Sept. 1922; Croft, 'The Influence of
Tanks upon Tactics', 42; PRO WO 279/60, Statement by Maj.-Gen. Sir W. Thomson, Report
on the Staff Conference.

[26]   PRO WO 32/2827, Milne to DSD, 10 Sept. 1930; Milne to DSD, 18 Sept. 1930.

[27]   PRO WO 279/54, Statement by the Master-General of the Ordnance as to the develop-
ment of new weapons since the war; CCC Bonham-Carter MSS BHCT 9/3,Bonham-Carter,
'Autobiography, 1921–39'; Macready, In the Wake of the Great, 93–4; War Office, 'The Bren
Light Machine Gun', Journal of the Royal United Services Institute, 81 (1936), 102–8.

[28]   PRO WO 106/1775, Lieut.-Col. A. Cazenove to Alexander, 12 June 1940; A. M. Low,
Modern Armaments (London, 1939), 46.

[29]   PRO WO 231/16, 152nd Infantry Bde, Discussion of lessons learned during the year from
El Alamein to Messina, 6 Nov. 1943.

[30]   PRO WO 204/1895, School of Infantry, Infantry Training Conference Apr. 1944, Points
raised by delegates, Agenda for discussion to be held at 14.15 hrs, 23 Apr. 1944.

[31]   PRO WO 291/471, Army Operational Research Group, Memorandum no. 123, Weight
of small arms fire needed for various targets, 7 May 1944.

obsession with conserving ammunition was misconceived. Bren gunners were more likely to hit men in the open if they disregarded their training and fired complete magazines as rapidly as possible instead of firing in short bursts.[32]

British infantrymen were at a serious disadvantage compared to German infantry, because the latter were equipped with a genuine general-purpose machine gun, the MG-34. Although it was slightly heavier than the Bren, it was belt-fed. That meant that it had a much higher rate of fire and that, when fitted with a tripod, it could also fulfil the role of a medium machine-gun.[33] The Bren may have been robust and simpler to maintain than either the MG-34, or its successor, the MG-42, which had an even higher rate of fire, but the psychological effect of their high rate of fire was considerable.[34] The German weapons were capable of firing long, sustained bursts of fire. They could, therefore, pin the British to the ground even if they did not hit them.[35] As one British infantryman recalled, 'The machine-gun's chilling, unmistakable sound—almost like cloth being ripped—always sent a shiver through me, even when it was not firing in my general direction'.[36]

The First World War had demonstrated that infantry needed their own indirect fire weapons so that they could neutralize or destroy hostile machine-guns without waiting for artillery support. The army developed a variety of mortars, and after 1918 many battalion commanders wanted to keep the light Stokes trench mortar as a form of pocket artillery. But the General Staff disliked this, as their retention complicated training in the infantry battalions. In the 1920s close support was instead provided by giving each division a brigade of light 3.7-in. howitzers under the control of the Royal Artillery.[37] But the infantry continued to lobby for their own weapon, and in 1933 the War Office adopted a new 3-in. mortar transported in a small tracked carrier.[38] First delivered in 1936, early versions malfunctioned in wet weather, and

[32] PRO WO 291/473, Army Operational Research Group, Memorandum no. 125, Interim Report on the performance of bullet weapons [c. May 1944].

[33] Corum, *The Roots of Blitzkrieg*, 104; Hogg, *Infantry Weapons*, 85–6; PRO WO 208/3003, War Dept., Washington, German Infantry Weapons, Prepared by Military Intelligence Service, 25 May 1943; PRO WO 291/473, Army Operational Research Group, Memorandum no. 125, Interim Report on the performance of bullet weapons [c. May 1944].

[34] PRO WO 291/474, Army Operational Research Group, Memorandum no. 126, The rate of fire of the L.M.G. [c. April 1944]; PRO WO 205/998, G(Operations) Infantry, 21 Army Group, to G(SD), Infantry Notes no. 6, 17 Sept. 1944; Cochrane, *Charlie Company*, 8.

[35] Jary, *Eighteen Platoon*, 53.

[36] S. Whitehouse and G. B. Bennett, *Fear is the Foe. A Footslogger from Normandy to the Rhine* (London, 1995), 153.

[37] PRO AIR 5/1382, Appendix F, Interim Report on Experimental Bde. 1922, Value of light trench mortar, whether organized on a battalion or brigade basis, 30 Sept. 1922.

[38] PRO WO 279/54, Report on the Staff Exercise; PRO WO 279/60, Statement by Col. H. Karslake, Report on the Staff Conference; PRO WO 32/2400B, CIGS to GOCs-in-C, 31 Oct. 1933.

were too heavy for the infantry to manhandle. Consequently, in July 1937 the Army Council decided to issue no more than two per battalion, and to develop a lighter weapon for company commanders.[39] The result was that the army went to war with two mortars, the 2-in. mortar, a platoon weapon that weighed only 10.5 pounds with a range of 500 yards, and the much heavier 3-in. mortar with a range of 1,600 yards. Few infantrymen had much to say in favour of the 2-in. mortar. In theory a platoon of six 3-in. mortars could place more high explosives on a target in one minute than a troop of four 25-pdr. field guns.[40] But its German equivalent, the 81mm. mortar, had a longer range and a faster rate of fire.[41] Apart from the Stuka dive-bomber, German mortars made the most serious psychological impression on the British infantry.[42] In Tunisia, over 40 per cent of all psychiatric casualties were caused by exposure to mortar fire, the equivalent of those caused by bombing and shelling combined.[43] The Germans, by contrast, were little concerned by British mortar fire.[44] In Normandy the Germans retained their superiority in mortaring by employing large, multi-barrel mortars, the Nebelwerfers. The noise of their approaching bombs sounded like a tube-train approaching from a tunnel and struck terror into those on the receiving end.[45]

The most inadequate of all of the weapons that were issued to the British infantry was the Boys anti-tank rifle. Not only was it too heavy to be easily manhandled, but even in 1940 it was effective only at short ranges against light tanks and armoured cars.[46] It quickly lost the confidence of those required to use it.[47] After Dunkirk troops were taught either to withhold their fire until hostile medium tanks were only 30 yards distant or to fire it against their vulnerable suspension. Expecting such accuracy or stoicism to be habitual was unrealistic.[48] During the

[39] PRO WO 32/4195, Informal Army Council meeting, 27 July 1937; Sherbrooke, 'The new infantry weapons', 141.

[40] PRO WO 277/5, Pemberton, *Artillery Tactics*, 140.

[41] Hogg, *Infantry Weapons*, 104, 110; PRO WO 106/2223, Notes from Theatres of War, Cyrenaica, Nov. 1941–Jan. 1942, May 1942; PRO WO 291/1370. Operational Research Memorandum no. 5, The comparative accuracy and range and line of British 3-in. and German 81 mm. mortars under field conditions, 28 Aug. 1943.

[42] PRO WO 231/10, GOC 78 Divn. to HQ, 1 Army, 24 May 1943.

[43] PRO WO 201/527, Extracts from the report of a War Office observer in North Africa, May 1943.

[44] PRO WO 232/14, Lieut.-Gen. K. Anderson to AFHQ and Director of Research, WO, 16 June 1943.

[45] Lecture by Sydney Jary, author of *Eighteen Platoon*, King's College London, 16 Mar. 1994.

[46] PRO WO 106/1775, Report of the Bartholomew Committee [c. 2 July 1940]; DAFV to commanders, armoured units, BEF [c. 12 June 1940].

[47] T. Bishop, *One Young Soldier. The Memoirs of a Cavalryman* (Norwich, 1993), 59.

[48] PRO WO 201/2588, Middle East Training Memorandum no. 3, Tank hunting platoons, 8 Oct. 1940.

CRUSADER offensive, 8th Army's staff could not find a single example of the Boys anti-tank rifle being used successfully against German armour.[49] In 1943 it was finally replaced by an improved weapon, the PIAT (Projector, Infantry, Anti-Tank). In theory its hollow charge projectile could penetrate 100mm. of armour at 100 yards. But trials carried out in early 1944 confirmed contrary field experience in Sicily. Even a skilled man scored less than 60 per cent hits at 100 yards, and because of faulty fuses only three-quarters of hits actually detonated. Even so, during the opening weeks of the Normandy campaign, when much of the fighting was semi-static, PIATs accounted for 7 per cent of all German tanks destroyed by British troops, which compared favourably to the 6 per cent destroyed by aircraft rockets.[50] But when the Germans responded to hollow charge weapons by fitting light armoured skirts to their tanks which detonated the charge before it made contact with the tank's armour, the PIAT lost much of its effectiveness.

There is no evidence that, even if more money had been available for weapons development before 1939, the army would have chosen to go down a different path and develop infantry weapons capable of generating greater fire-power. The inescapable conclusion is that during the war the British infantry had to pay the price for doctrinal decisions taken before 1939 that placed a premium on mobility at the expense of fire-power. In the opinion of one weapons training expert, who spent most of June 1942 personally observing the fighting that led to the fall of Tobruk: 'No matter what the skill of the soldier or the subtlety of the plan, we cannot overcome a superior weight of more modern weapons'.[51] The tactical consequences were plain. Because the infantry were not issued with weapons able to generate greater fire-power than their German equivalents, they had no option other than to rely upon artillery to provide fire-support. As a battalion commander in 21st Panzer Division noted in August 1941: 'If his [the British] infantry fire is answered from our side he immediately concentrates his artillery fire on individual weapons. We can only gain superiority in infantry fire if support is given by systematic counter-battery fire.'[52]

In the 1920s British doctrine stipulated that the main role of field artillery was to assist the infantry to close with the enemy. It did so by

---

[49] PRO WO 106/2255, Lessons from operations, Cyrenaica no 6, Notes on the employment of infantry [c. Dec. 1941].

[50] PRO WO 291/1331, Operational Research in North West Europe, No. 2 ORS, 21 Army Group, Report no. 17, Analysis of German tank casualties in France 6 June–31 Aug. 1944; PRO WO 163/183, General Staff, General Staff Policy committee paper on infantry weapons [c. Sept. 1942].

[51] PRO WO 163/183, Visit by Lieut.-Col. H. A. Livstock.

[52] AWM 3 DRL/6643/1/2Bii, Part ii, Appendix B to GSI, GHQ MEF, Daily Intelligence summary no. 6123, 22 Jan. 1942, Report of 25 Aug. 1941 by 2nd Bn., 104 Lorried Infantry Regt. in reply to Divn. Questionnaire.

providing covering fire, by repelling enemy attacks, by neutralizing hostile batteries, by assisting in the destruction of enemy defences, and, in emergencies, by destroying hostile tanks. To fulfil these functions, it had to be sufficiently mobile to keep pace with the infantry.[53] In 1922 the General Staff decided that it wanted a single weapon to replace the 13-pdr. gun of the Royal Horse Artillery and the 18-pdr. gun and the 4.5-in. howitzers of the field artillery.[54] Homogeneous units would be easier to organize and supply. In 1934 they issued a specification for a gun/howitzer, weighing no more than 30 cwt., with a range of at least 12,000 yards, compared to the 7,000 yards of the 4.5-in howitzer and the 11,000 yards of the latest mark of 18-pdr. The extra range was essential if batteries were not to be continually changing their locations and if they were to be able to outrange German field artillery. They also specified that the new weapon had to be able to protect itself against tank attacks in an emergency.[55] The result was that the 25-pdr. gun/howitzer was adopted in the autumn of 1937.[56]

It proved to be a reliable and robust weapon. It was an effective man-killer against troops in the open and could also neutralize troops behind cover. But the quest for mobility meant that it sacrificed shell-weight to range. Its German equivalent, the 105mm. gun/howitzer, threw a heavier shell weighing just over 32 pounds, but had a maximum range of only 11,675 yards. The 25-pdr. could throw a shell weighing 25 pounds to a range of 13,400 yards. However, when the Germans modified their gun in 1941, the British lost even that advantage.[57] Furthermore, the British had bought range at the expense of shell-power. The high explosive content of the shell was only 7 per cent. This was adequate when it was filled with high grade explosives, but by 1941–2 shortages of TNT meant that shells were filled with lower grade amatol, which considerably reduced its blast effect.[58] A 25-pdr. concentration against well-dug-in troops could do little more than force them to keep their heads down and, if prolonged, subject them to considerable psychological trauma. It was unlikely to kill many of them. It was, therefore, essential

[53] General Staff, *FSR (1920)*, 27; General Staff, *FSR Vol. 2 (1935)*, 9.

[54] PRO AIR 5/1382. Lt.-Gen Sir T. N. Moreland, Interim Report on the Experimental Bde. Appendix B, Rearming of horse artillery, 30 Sept. 1922; PRO WO 279/54, Statement by the Master-General of the Ordnance, Report on the Staff Exercise held by CIGS, 30 Oct.– 3 Nov. 1922; I. V. Hogg, *British and American Artillery of World War Two* (London, 1978), 25–8; PRO WO 279/60, Statement by the Director of Artillery, Report on the Staff Conference.

[55] Hogg, *British and American Artillery*, 26.

[56] Macready, *In the Wake of the Great*, 95; PRO WO 32/4451, DSD to CIGS, 26 July 1935, and PUS, War Office, to Treasury Inter-Service Committee, 5 May 1936; Hogg, *British and American Artillery*, 28.

[57] PRO WO 277/5, Pemberton, *Artillery Tactics*, 12.

[58] PRO WO 163/183, General Staff, General Staff Policy on Field, Medium, and Heavy Artillery, 31 July 1942.

for British infantry to keep close behind a 25-pdr. barrage to ensure that they arrived on top of the enemy's defences before they had time to recover from the psychological shock of the shelling.[59]

The 25-pdr. had a chequered history as an anti-tank weapon. In France in 1940, it proved capable of stopping German light and medium tanks in close country.[60] Even in the desert in 1941 it did score some successes against hostile armour.[61] But its solid AP shot was only effective at ranges below 1,200 yards. By early 1942, after some painful experiences when tanks executed frontal charges against 25-pdr. regiments and were repulsed, the Germans had developed a drill to overcome them. They stayed out of range and employed the longer-range, high-explosive fire of their Mark IV close-support tanks armed with 75mm. howitzers to destroy the British field guns. Only then did they commit their medium tanks and infantry to a final, and usually successful, charge.[62]

The 25-pdr. could, therefore, kill hostile troops in the open and neutralize them behind cover. But something heavier was needed to kill them. However, little work was done on developing new medium or heavy artillery until 1936. Then the General Staff discovered that the German army was developing medium guns with a range of up to 16,500 yards and they recognized the need for similar weapons. The Director of Artillery vetoed redesigning the 25-pdr. to match this. It would have required a complete redesign and delayed production by two years.[63] He opted instead to improve the range and mobility of existing First World War vintage 60-pdr. guns and howitzers, by fitting them with pneumatic tyres and new barrels.[64] It was only in August 1939 that the War Office approved production of a 5.5-in. gun/howitzer able to fire a 90lb. shell a distance of 16,000 yards. At the same time, the Director of Artillery was designing a 4.5-in. gun/howitzer to fire a shell weighing 55lb. up to 20,500 yards. However, neither weapon had gone into production by September 1939, and the army went to war equipped with First World War vintage weapons.[65] The first modern 4.5-in. guns were not issued to units until 1941, and the first 5.5-in. guns did not see

[59] PRO WO 106/2223, Notes from Theatres of War no. 4, Cyrenaica, Nov. 1941–Jan. 1942, May 1942.

[60] R. Holding, *Since I Bore Arms* (Cirencester, Glous., 1987), 118.

[61] PRO WO 201/357, Report by Commander, 4 Indian divn. on operations in the Western Desert, 15–18 June 1941.

[62] Lieut.-Gen. Sir F. Tuker, *Approach to Battle. A Commentary. Eighth Army 1941 to May 1943* (London, 1963), 15; PRO WO 163/183, General Staff, General Staff Policy on Field, Medium, and Heavy Artillery, 31 July 1942.

[63] PRO WO 32/4451, Re-armament of the field artillery with 25-pdr. equipment [c.1936].

[64] PRO WO 279/54, Statement by the Master-General of the Ordnance, Report on the Staff Exercise; PRO WO 279/60, Statement by the Director of Artillery.

[65] D. Smurthwaite, *"Against All Odds". The British Army of 1939–40* (London, 1990), 29–30.

service until May 1942.[66] The lack of modern medium artillery was a major handicap for the army before 1942, especially as the Germans already possessed medium artillery that was capable of comparable, and in some cases better, performance than the new British weapons.[67] Experience in 1940 showed that the First World War vintage 9.2-in. howitzers that the army had hoped to use for long-range counter-battery work were hopelessly immobile. Development work therefore began on a modern 7.2-in. howitzer. However, it did not enter service until 1942. It was able to fire a 200lb. shell a distance of over 19,000 yards, and heavy regiments were then formed consisting of three batteries of these guns and one battery of First World War vintage 6-in. guns.[68]

Four factors underpinned this lackadaisical approach. First, it was assumed that heavy and medium artillery would probably be too slow to fit easily into the army's quest for mobility. Secondly, until the final collapse of the Geneva Disarmament Conference, it seemed likely that international law would ban the development of medium and heavy artillery and so there seemed little point in developing new weapons. Thirdly, air power promised to fulfil the functions once carried out by such weapons more effectively.[69] Finally, when these factors were taken into account, it must have seemed more cost-effective to spend the army's tiny weapon's development budget on other items of higher priority. Pre-war procurement decisions were a major constraint on how the army employed its artillery during the war. Historians who have been critical of the army's inability to employ massed artillery in North Africa before October 1942 have overlooked one salient fact. The pre-war army's determination to restore mobility to the battlefield had led it to neglect the development of modern medium and heavy artillery. It was only when such weapons were available in sufficient quantity, in the second half of the war, that it was possible for the gunners to employ massed concentrations.

Despite its shortcomings, the artillery was one of the few British arms of service for which German troops felt real fear and respect.[70] Even so, on the eve of the Normandy landing, Montgomery was under no illusions about its technological defects. Its field guns had an adequate range even though its HE shells were incapable of killing large numbers of men behind cover. The range of its medium guns was too short for effective counter-battery work. It did have time fuses for its HE shells,

---

[66] Hogg, *British and American Artillery*, 42, 47.

[67] Maj.-Gen. I. S. O. Playfair, *The Mediterranean and Middle East, iii. British Fortunes Reach their Lowest Ebb (September 1941 to September 1942)* (London, 1960), 431.

[68] PRO WO 163/183, General Staff, General Staff Policy on Field, Medium, and Heavy Artillery, 31 July 1942; PRO WO 277/5, Pemberton, *Artillery Tactics*, 37.

[69] Macready, *In the Wake of the Great*, 92.

[70] *The Rommel Papers* ed. B. H. Liddell Hart (London, 1953), 185.

but they were unreliable and so predicted shooting in an unregistered fire plan was sometimes dangerously inaccurate.[71] Given these defects, it was hardly surprising that the British had to use large quantities of artillery to compensate for the qualitative defects of their weapons.

By the inter-war period the army had considerable experience of developing rifles and machine-guns. But specialized anti-tank weapons were a novelty. During 1918 the Royal Artillery had sometimes deployed 18-pdr. field guns in an anti-tank role. This was not only a wasteful use of such weapons, but, as they were under the control of the Royal Artillery, the infantry and cavalry were worried lest they would be suddenly withdrawn for some other task. They wanted a weapon under their own control that was small, mobile, and could be operated by a handful of men. In 1919–20 the Tank Corps experimented with anti-tank mines designed to blow-off tank tracks and make them easy prey to artillery. These were effective, but difficult to transport and to lay.[72] Early experiments with anti-tank machine-guns were unsuccessful, and, as an interim measure, Cavan decreed in April 1923 that the 3.7-in. howitzers of the divisional light artillery brigade would assume the dual role of providing both close support and anti-tank defence for the infantry.[73] This was an unsatisfactory solution, for the brigade's main role was silencing enemy machine-guns.[74] Finally in 1934 the General Staff agreed to adopt a 2-pdr. high-velocity quick-firing gun for both the Royal Artillery's anti-tank regiments and the tanks of the Tank Corps.[75]

By 1941–2, after repeated failures in North Africa, the 2-pdr. had acquired a poor reputation. But when it entered service in 1938, it was probably the best anti-tank weapon in the world. Whereas its German equivalent, the 37mm. anti-tank gun could only penetrate 27mm. of armour at 30 degrees at a range of 1,000 yards, the 2-pdr. could penetrate 40mm. of armour at the same range.[76] The General Staff had

---

[71] IWM Montgomery MSS BLM 117/10, Address by C-in-C 21 Army Group to senior officers of the Royal Artillery, Larkhill, 30 April 1944; PRO WO 277/5, Pemberton, *Artillery Tactics*, 170; PRO WO 210/527, Extracts from the Report of a War Office observer in North Africa, May 1943.

[72] Martel, *Outspoken Soldier*, 28; Lt.-Col. J. C. Dundas, 'Anti-Tank', *Journal of the Royal United Services Institute*, 67 (1922), 110.

[73] PRO WO 279/55, Statement by CIGS, Report on the Staff Exercise held by CIGS, 9–13 Apr. 1923.

[74] PRO WO 32/2371, CIGS to CGS, Australia, 27 Jan. 1926; PRO WO 279/59, War Office Exercise no. 2 (1929), Winchester, 9–12 May 1927; PRO WO 279/60, Statements by Cols. H. Karslake and J. Blaikston-Houston, Report on the Staff Conference; PRO WO 279/65, Statement by Col. C. P. Heywood, Report on the Staff Conference.

[75] Postan, Hay, and Scott, *Design and Development of Weapons*, 315.

[76] PRO WO 277/5, Pemberton, *Artillery Tactics*, 16; B. T. White, *Tanks and Other Armoured Vehicles of World War Two* (London, 1972), 153–4; PRO WO 106/1775, Report of the Bartholomew Committee [c. 2 July 1940]; PRO WO 32/9642, Martel to Dewing and

adopted the 2-pdr. with war in Western Europe in mind. They assumed that tank actions would take place on the move and at ranges of 800 yards or less.[77] The gun proved successful in the close country of Belgium and Northern France in 1940, because anti-tank gunners were usually able to conceal themselves and to open fire at comparatively short ranges. But that was not possible in the desert. The phasing-out by the Germans of their Panzer Is and IIs and the effective up-armouring of their Mark IIIs and IVs—something which the British were unaware of until March 1942—meant that by 1941–2 anti-tank gunners required the utmost tactical skill, not to say courage, if they were to engage German armour. To do so effectively, they had to be dug-in and facing obliquely across the front of the troops they were protecting so that they could engage enemy tanks from the flank and preferably at ranges of 300–500 yards or even less.[78] This put them at a serious disadvantage, because by mid-1941 German Mark IVs armed with a low-velocity 75mm. gun could stand off and successfully engage them at ranges of up to 4,000 yards.[79]

The 2-pdr. remained in front-line service for about a year after it had become obsolete. In late 1940, knowing that the Germans had captured many 2-pdrs. at Dunkirk, and would presumably be able to up-armour their own tanks in the light of tests with them, the General Staff wanted to hasten the production of a more powerful weapon. In 1938 they had ordered a pilot model of a 6-pdr. anti-tank gun, but its development was assigned a low priority. The design of the gun was not agreed until April 1940 and the carriage was not ready for production until early 1941.[80] The reason reflected production realities. To have put the weapon into immediate mass production would have meant sacrificing the 1941 output of 600 2-pdrs. for only 100 6-pdrs. The Ministry of Supply and the War Office reluctantly decided that the need to get any weapon into the hands of the troops was more pressing than getting the best possible weapon to them. It was, therefore, not until early 1942 that the 6-pdr. began to reach the troops.[81] It was an immediate success. Not only did it have better penetration than the 2-pdr.—it could pierce the frontal

enc., 9 July 1940; PRO WO 199/3186, Report on the organisation and equipment of 1 Armoured Divn., 26 June 1940; PRO WO 201/2586, Middle East Training Pamphlet no. 10, Lessons of Cyrenaica Campaign, Dec. 1940–Feb. 1941.

[77] IWM Dept. of Sound Records, Accession no. 000858/05, Maj.-Gen. F. W. Gordon Hall.

[78] PRO WO 201/2590, CGS, GHQ, MEF to 8, 9, and 10 Armies, 19 Aug. 1942; F. H. Hinsley et al., *British Intelligence in the Second World War. Its Influence on Strategy and Operations* (London, 1981), ii, 297.

[79] PRO WO 277/5, Pemberton, *Artillery Tactics*, 88; Tuker, *Approach to Battle*, 13–14; LHCMA Hobart MSS 15/11/10, DAFV to ACIGS, 24 Aug. 1941.

[80] PRO WO 277/5, Pemberton, *Artillery Tactics*, 16; Martel, *Outspoken Soldier*, 132; PRO WO 32/4684, Director of Artillery to Superintendent of Design, 13 and 25 April 1938.

[81] PRO WO 277/32, Lieut.-Col. French, Rearmament, ii.

armour of a Panzer III or IV at 1,000 yards[82]—but also it was more accurate.[83] Herbert Lumsden, who commanded 1st Armoured division during the Gazala fighting, thought that one 6-pdr. was worth two 2-pdrs. and the Germans rated it as superior to their own 50mm. anti-tank guns.[84] But it was not until mid-1943 that every infantry battalion had an anti-tank platoon of four 6-pdrs.

In April 1941, eight months before the 6-pdr. began to come off the production line, design work began on the next generation of anti-tank guns, the 17-pdr. The General Staff specified that it should be able to penetrate 125mm. of armour at 600 yards. By August a wooden mock-up was ready and orders were placed for 500 without even waiting for a pilot model to be produced.[85] First employed in small numbers in Tunisia, it had a slightly better performance than even the German 88mm.[86] In 1944–5 both the 6-pdr. and 17-pdr. were effective against the latest marks of German tanks, the Mark V (Panther) and the Mark VI (Tiger), although at different ranges and not always with a head-on shot. The performance of both British guns was significantly increased when they were issued with discarding sabot ammunition, consisting of a tungsten carbide core enclosed in a light metal casing. It improved their penetration by up to 50 per cent.[87] The Germans themselves confirmed the vulnerability of their own tanks, and by July 1944 were recommending that in the attack Panthers should lead but that they should be accompanied by Mark IVs to protect their vulnerable flanks.[88]

The British have been much criticized for their unwillingness to ape the Germans, who made excellent use of their 88mm. Anti-Aircraft gun in an anti-tank role, and do the same with their own 3.7-in. AA

---

[82] PRO WO 216/24, Lucas to Greaves, 31 Oct. 1942.

[83] PRO WO 32/101365, Army Operational Research Group, Middle East. Accuracy of fire from tank guns, 30 Mar. 1943.

[84] PRO WO 106/2235, Report of a Court of Enquiry, ii, Statement by Maj.-Gen. Lumsden commanding 1 Armoured divn. from 12 Feb. 1942; PRO CAB 146/15, Enemy Documents Section, Appreciation no. 9, Part IV, Appendix 9.

[85] PRO WO 277/5, Pemberton, *Artillery Tactics*, 126–7.

[86] PRO 201/527, Extracts from the Report of a War Office Observer in North Africa, May 1943; LHCMA Alanbrooke MSS 14/50/15a, Anderson to Brooke, 25 Dec. 1942; PRO WO 216/24, S. Redman to Rickets, Minute 38B, Performance against homogenous plate at 30 degrees angle of attack, 5 Apr. 1943.

[87] LHCMA Dempsey MSS, 2 Army Intelligence summary nos. 6: Appendix E, Panther Tank, 9 June 1944; 38: 12 July 1944; PRO WO 205/401, Lieut.-Col. A. E. Warhurst to Main HQ, 21 Army Group, 1 and 30 July 1944; PRO WO 163/183, Anti-tank artillery: General Staff policy, Memorandum by ACIGS(W) and DRA, 1 June 1944; PRO WO 205/404, OC 65th Anti-Tank Regiment to GSO1(L), Main HQ, 21 Army Group, 20 June 1944; IWM Maj.-Gen. R. Briggs MSS IWM 66/76/1, Notebook no. 2, 10–12 Aug. 1944; PRO WO 277/5, Pemberton, *Artillery Tactics*, 211; PRO WO 163/183, Anti-tank artillery: General Staff policy. Memorandum by ACIGS(W) and DRA, 1 June 1944.

[88] LHCMA Dempsey MSS, 2 Army Intelligence summary nos. 20: 24 June 1944; 57: 31 July 1944.

gun.[89] In fact a handful were employed as anti-tank weapons during the Gazala fighting in the summer of 1942 and the Germans themselves admitted their effectiveness.[90] But there were good reasons why greater use was not made of them in this role. The 88mm. gun was fitted with an optical sight that meant it could be used both as an anti-tank and an anti-aircraft weapon. However, the 3.7-in. gun was a more sophisticated design. It lacked an optical sight because it had been designed as an anti-aircraft gun to work off range data provided by radar. Critics of Auchinleck's reluctance to use them in a ground role in 1942 also overlooked the fact that there were too few of them in the Middle East to fulfil their prime function, anti-aircraft defence, at a time when the British lacked air superiority and were still suffering from the traumas of being exposed to air attacks in Norway, France and Greece. Finally, weighing nearly 9 tons, compared to the 2.5 tons of the 88mm., the 3.7-in. gun was too slow and immobile to be used as an anti-tank weapon in highly mobile operations.[91]

The ideal tank needed to be adequately armoured, to be mechanically reliable, and to carry a gun capable of engaging hostile tanks and 'soft' (that is, unarmoured) targets successfully. British tanks were frequently and vociferously criticized for lagging behind German designs in all three fields.[92] In June 1944 Sir P. J. Grigg, the Secretary of State for War, privately warned Montgomery that an officer in the Guards Armoured division, Major William Anstruther-Gray, the Conservative MP for North Lanark, was threatening to ask questions in the Commons about the poor performance of British tanks.[93] Montgomery was so concerned that official reports of the apparent inferiority of British tanks would undermine morale that he forbade their circulation.[94] 'If we are not careful, there will be a danger of the troops developing a "Tiger" and "Panther" complex—when every tank becomes one of these types: compared to the old days when every gun was an 88mm.'[95] In the Commons Grigg denied that British tanks were not up to their German counter-

[89] Tuker, *Approach to Battle*, 14; Barnett, *The Desert Generals*, 109.

[90] PRO CAB 146/15, Enemy Documents Section, Appreciation no. 9, Part IV, Appendix 9.

[91] P. Griffith, 'British armoured warfare in the Western Desert, 1940–43', in J. P. Harris and F. N. Toase (eds.), *Armoured Warfare* (London, 1990), 77; PRO WO 163/183, Minutes of 17th meeting of the Organisation and Weapons Policy Committee, 15 Dec. 1942; PRO WO 204/7955, de Guingand to X and XXX Corps and CRA 8 Army, 19 Feb. 1943; LHCMA Hobart MSS 15/11/15, Pile to Hobart, 4 Feb. 1942; PRO WO 106/2223, Notes from Theatres of War no. 6, Cyrenaica, Jan.–June 1942, Oct. 1942.

[92] See e.g. *Hansard 385 HC Deb. 55*, col. 567, Mr Stokes, 25 July 1944; Postan, Hay, and Scott, *Design and Development of Weapons*, 322.

[93] PRO WO 205/5b, Montgomery to de Guingand, 24 June 1944.

[94] CCC Grigg MSS, PJGG 9/8/11, Montgomery to Grigg, 25 June 1944.

[95] PRO WO 205/5b, Montgomery to de Guingand, 24 June 1944.

parts, but such criticisms have continued to be repeated by modern authors.[96]

The Royal Armoured Corps was the victim of decisions taken about tank design and procurement nearly a decade before the war. By 1931 the General Staff had decided that the work of the Experimental Mechanised Force showed that the army needed three kinds of tanks: a medium tank, armed with a machine-gun and a small anti-tank gun, to destroy the enemy by fire and shock action; a light tank armed with machine-guns to perform reconnaissance missions and to co-operate with the mediums to destroy enemy anti-tank guns; and a close support tank, armed with a gun capable of firing HE and smoke shells to provide close fire-support for tank attacks.[97] These did not seem to be unattainable objectives. Throughout the 1920s Britain had remained in the forefront of tank design. However, in 1932, alarmed at its cost, the Director of Mechanisation ordered all development work to stop on a replacement for the army's existing medium tank. When rearmament proper began in 1936–7, the army did have a satisfactory light tank. What it lacked was the necessary design-team to produce a satisfactory medium tank and the powerful purpose-built engine to power it.[98] This gave the Germans a lead in medium tank design that they never lost.[99]

Rather than try to catch up the German lead, and produce a medium tank that could operate both as a close support weapon for the infantry and fulfil independent operational missions, the British opted to produce two different types of tank. The Kirke Committee had shown the need to provide tanks to work with the infantry, and in 1934 the Army Council agreed that every infantry division required a battalion of 'Infantry' tanks. This resulted in two tanks, the A11, which had 60mm. armour, weighed 10 tons, possessed a crew of two and was armed only with a machine-gun, and its more formidable successor, the A12. The latter had even thicker armour, was armed with a machine-gun and 2-pdr. anti-tank gun and was operated by a crew of four. The 'Matilda', as it was christened, proved to be a formidable fighting machine in France and the Western Desert in 1940–1. Its armour was proof against any of the standard Italian or German anti-tank guns.[100] It came as an

[96] IWM Montgomery MSS BLM 114/30, Grigg to Montgomery, 28 Mar. 1945 and enc.; Horne and Montgomery, *The Lonely Leader*, 176–8.

[97] LHCMA Liddell Hart MSS 15/8/81, General Staff, *Modern Formations (1931). Provisional.*

[98] PRO WO 32/4441, CIGS to Secretary of State, 9 Oct. 1936.

[99] J. P. Harris, 'British Armour and Rearmament in the 1930s', *Journal of Strategic Studies*, 11 no. 2 (1988), 220–44.

[100] Brig. R. M. P. Carver, 'Tank and Anti-Tank', *Journal of the Royal United Services Institute*, 91 (1946), 40–1; IWM Dept. of Sound Records, Accession no. 000944/03: Maj. A. H. Austin; PRO WO 32/9642, Martel to Dewing, 21 May 1940; H. von Luck, *Panzer Commander. The Memoirs of Colonel Hans von Luck* (New York, 1989), 41.

unpleasant surprise to the Italians when it successfully spearheaded the opening of Operation COMPASS. However, by the opening of BATTLEAXE the Germans had taken its measure and a handful of dug-in 88mm. blunted the British offensive almost before it had begun. The Matilda's other serious disadvantage was its very limited radius of action and mechanical unreliability. Matildas could only manage about forty miles between refills, which limited their tactical adaptability.[101] Within three days of going into action against the Italians in December 1940, 7th RTR had lost half of its Matildas, many through mechanical break-downs.[102] Before CRUSADER the 1st Army Tank Brigade decided that the only way to ensure the reliability of their Infantry tanks was not to drive them, which placed a serious restriction on their ability to train between battles.[103] The Matilda's successor, the Valentine, possessed armour that was thicker than any opposing German tank, and was more mechanically reliable than the Matilda, but it was just as slow and no better armed.

The second type of tank the British began to develop in the late 1930s was the lighter, cruiser tank. The first of these, the A9, entered service in 1939. It was the first of a series of unsatisfactory designs, being followed by the A10, the A13 (Covenanter), and the A15 (Crusader) Each was fast, armed with the 2-pdr. gun, lightly armoured, and mechanically unreliable. The British were well aware of all of these faults; many of them were the product of over-hasty design and development; correcting them proved to be more difficult.[104] The A9s, 10s, and 13s employed by 7th Armoured division against the Italians in 1940–1 withstood the fire of Italian anti-tank guns without difficulty, but easily succumbed to the German 50mm. tank and anti-tank guns.[105] Because these machines were underpowered, the British found it difficult to follow the German example and significantly increase the thickness of their armour.[106] Britain's late start in rearmament meant that these tanks were developed too quickly and issued to the troops when they were still suffering from serious mechanical defects. In France, large numbers of cruisers had to

[101] PRO WO 201/2586, Middle East Training Pamphlet no. 10, Lessons of Cyrenaica campaign, Dec. 1940–Feb. 1941.

[102] PRO WO 201/2505, Wavell to CIGS, 2 Jan. 1941.

[103] PRO WO 201/479, Lessons from operations in Cyrenaica no. 8, Co-operation of infantry and army tanks, 27 Dec. 1941.

[104] Postan, Hay, and Scott, *Design and Development of Weapons*, 312–13; D. Fletcher, *Mechanised Force. British Tanks Between the Wars* (London, 1991), 118–24; PRO WO 199/3186, HQ, 1 Armoured divn. to Brigs. Morgan, Crocker, and McCreery, 26 June 1940; PRO WO 106/1775, Minutes of a meeting held by the DAFV, 28 June 1940.

[105] LHCMA O'More Creagh MSS, Creagh, Points of general interest arising out of the operations, 9–15 Dec. 1940; PRO WO 106/2223, Notes from Theatres of War ,no. 1, Cyrenaica, Nov. 1941, 19 Feb. 1942.

[106] D. Fletcher, *The Great Tank Scandal. British Armour in the Second World War, pt 1* (London, 1989), 109.

be abandoned by their crews because they broke down.[107] By May 1941 the CIGS believed that the breakdown rate of cruisers in North Africa 'had been deplorably high', and Wavell admitted that 'Technical breakdowns are still too numerous'.[108]

By the end of CRUSADER, 8th Army's tank regiments were in no doubt that their cruisers were not only mechanically inadequate, but that they were also out-gunned by German tanks. (In reality, however, German anti-tank guns caused most of their losses.)[109] Hitherto, up-gunning British tanks had been prevented because of a basic design parameter. Throughout the inter-war period, knowing that tanks could not undertake long-distance movements by road without frequent breakdowns, the War Office had specified that all tanks had to be capable of being transported by rail. This imposed a maximum width of 9 feet, which in turn limited the size of gun that could be fitted into the turret.[110] This restriction was not lifted until March 1942, when the War Office accepted that new tanks need no longer be bound by this limitation provided sufficient road transporters could be found to move them.[111] The Germans did not suffer from a similar handicap because of the wider gauge of the continental railway system. Thus, having captured a number of Matildas at Dunkirk, they were able to up-gun their Mark IIIs to carry a larger and more effective 50mm. gun. This was the first in a series of improvements to the armaments of their Mark IIIs and IVs which in 1942 saw the former fitted with a long 50mm. gun and the latter with a long 75mm. This gave the Germans an advantage, for not only did these weapons have equal or better penetrative capability than the British 2-pdr., they could also fire high-explosive shells to destroy soft targets, something the 2-pdr. could not do.[112]

It was the lack of a HE capability for the 2-pdr. that represented the most serious disadvantage British tank crews confronted in the first half of the war. It meant that when faced by German anti-tank guns they had two choices. They would wait until their own field guns had destroyed them, or they could charge them in the usually vain hope that they could overrun them before they themselves had been blown to pieces. The

[107] LHCMA Bridgeman MSS 2/6, Bridgeman, 'The campaign of the BEF, May 1940'; Brig. A. B. Beauman, *Then a Soldier* (London, 1960); 135; PRO WO 199/3186, HQ, 1 Armoured divn. to Brigs. Morgan, Crocker, and McCreery, 26 June 1940.

[108] PRO WO 163/50/ACM(41)6, Minutes of the Army Council, 1 May 1941; W. S. Churchill, *The Second World War*, iii. *The Grand Alliance* (London, 1950), 304.

[109] PRO WO 201/527, BGGS, 8 Army, to 13th and 30th Corps, 7 Jan. 1942; LHCMA Pyman MSS 3/1, 7 Armoured divn., An account of the operations in Libya, 18 Nov.–27 Dec. 1941, 31 Jan. 1942.

[110] Brig. O. E. Chapman, 'The Influence of the Late War on Tank Design', *Journal of the Royal United Services Institute*, 96 (1951), 51.

[111] Postan, Hay, and Scott, *Design and Development of Weapons*, 336.

[112] Playfair, *The Mediterranean and Middle East*, ii. *The Germans Come to Help their Ally (1941)* (London, 1956), 342, and iii. 440–1.

seriousness of the anti-tank threat to British tanks is highlighted by the fact that in North Africa anti-tank guns accounted for a higher proportion of British tank losses (40 per cent) than did hostile tanks (38 per cent).[113] Each British tank regiment did have a small number of close support tanks, but their mortars were not the equal of the short-barrelled 75mm. howitzer fitted to the German Mark IV. The latter, with a range of 4,000 yards, could stand off and bombard British anti-tank guns with HE shells in safety. British close-support tanks, with a range of only 1,000 yards, were vulnerable to German anti-tank fire, and in any case lacked the HE shells and range-finders necessary to engage hostile anti-tank guns successfully.[114]

By late 1942 there was widespread dissatisfaction with every British-designed tank in service. One of the RAC's spokesman at the War Office, the Major-General AFV, concluded that the 'Crusader's name is still mud owing to his unreliability and lack of hitting power even with the 6-pdr with its present ammunition' and 'Valentine, though he has done good work, is now definitely obsolete. Everything that shoots goes through his armour and his 2-pdr is effective neither as an anti-tank nor as an anti-personnel weapon. The 6-pdr Valentine is a bastard.'[115] Senior officers saw their only salvation in adopting American vehicles, and until the end of the war the British relied heavily upon American designs.[116] Auchinleck had employed 300 Stuart/Honey light tanks during CRUSADER. Although they were more mechanically reliable than any British cruiser, they were too lightly armoured and under-gunned to match the German mediums, and they only had a range of 40 miles.[117] But the next American medium tank issued to the 8th Army, the Grant tank, which first saw action in May 1942, was a major improvement on any previous tank deployed by the British. It was slower and less manoeuvrable than German mediums were, and difficult to conceal in hull-down positions because its main armament was mounted in a side-sponson. However, its frontal armour gave it good protection against any German tank gun except the handful of long-75mms., and its own 75mm. gun was superior to the short-barrelled 50mm. mounted on most German tanks.[118] It was also the first tank in British hands to mount a

[113] PRO WO 291/1186, Army Operational Research Group, Internal Memorandum no. 16, The comparative performance of German anti-tank weapons during World War II, May 1950.
[114] PRO WO 201/357, Lieut.-Gen. Beresford Pierce to GHQ MEF, 6 Aug. 1941; LHCMA Liddell Hart MSS 1/153/84, Carver to Liddell Hart, n.d.
[115] PRO WO 236/36, Maj.-Gen. AFV to DAFV, War Office [c.late 1942].
[116] LHCMA Alanbrooke MSS 14/50/10a, 15a, Anderson to Brooke, 14, 25 Dec. 1942; LHCMA Hobart MSS 15/11/5, Martel to Hobart, Feb. 1943.
[117] LHCMA Alanbrooke MSS 6/D/4d/h, Auchinleck to Churchill, 12 Jan. 1942; PRO 106/2223, Notes from Theatres of War no. 1 Cyrenaica, Nov. 1941, 19 Feb. 1942.
[118] *The Rommel Papers*, ed. Liddell Hart, 196–7; Carver, 'Tank and Anti-tank', 44–5; PRO CAB 146/15, Enemy Documents Section, Appreciation no. 9, Part IV, Appendix 9. PRO WO 106/2223, Notes from Theatres of War no. 6. Cyrenaica, Jan.–June 1942, Oct. 1942.

dual-purpose anti-tank/anti-personnel gun, so that at last the RAC had a weapon with which they could engage hostile tanks and anti-tank guns.[119]

The Sherman, first used by the British at Alamein, had all of the Grant's advantages, plus the fact that its 75mm. gun was mounted in the turret. It could engage hostile anti-tank guns from the safety of hull-down position at ranges of up to 2,700 yards.[120] In late 1942, its crews believed that it was superior in all-round performance to either the German Mark III or Mark IV.[121] However, its comparatively light armour meant that it was vulnerable to hostile anti-tank weapons of 50mm. calibre and above, and it was dangerously prone to catch fire when hit. Investigations in 1943 suggested that this was probably the result of ammunition stored in the turret igniting when the tank was hit and henceforth it was fitted with armoured ammunition bins.[122] But because the bins were poorly designed many crews continued to store shells outside them, and to suffer the horrendous consequences when their tank was hit.[123]

The only British-built cruiser that saw widespread service in the final two years of the war and was a match for the Sherman was the Cromwell. It was issued to armoured reconnaissance regiments in North West Europe and was the main battle tank of the 7th Armoured division. After seeing the success of the 75mm.-armed Shermans at Alamein in engaging hostile anti-tank guns, Montgomery had strongly urged that the Cromwell, which initially had been fitted with the 6-pdr., should be re-equipped with a dual-purpose 75mm. gun.[124] It became the first British-built cruiser so equipped. It was also the first British cruiser that enjoyed a reputation for mechanical reliability.[125]

It was not until August 1942 that the General Staff tacitly admitted that the bifurcation in tank design between cruiser and infantry tanks had been a mistake. In order to facilitate production and maintenance in

[119] PRO CAB 146/15, Enemy Documents Section, Appreciation no. 9, Part IV, Appendix 9. DAK's report on fighting, May–July 1942, 10 Aug. 1942.

[120] *The Rommel Papers*, ed. Liddell Hart, 309; Carver, 'Tank and Anti-Tank', 45; PRO WO 201/2156, 8 Army Intelligence summary no. 462, Appendix A, Trans. Report issued by HQ 90th Army Corps, 11 Dec. 1942; PRO WO 201/2592, GHQ, MEF to 8 and 9 Armies, May 1943.

[121] PRO WO 291/1299, Capt. D. H. Parkinson to Scientific Adviser to Army Council, 15 July 1943.

[122] PRO WO 32/101365, Army Operational Research Group Middle East, Operational Research Memorandum no. 6, The distribution and effect of AP shot and HE in Churchill tank casualties, 25 Aug. 1943.

[123] PRO WO 204/7957, Brig. Richardson to BGS, 8 Army, 25 Dec. 1943; PRO WO 291/1331, Operational Research in North West Europe, Report no. 12, Analysis of 75mm. Sherman tank casualties, 6 June–10 July 1944; Hamerton, *Achtung Minen!*, 68.

[124] LHCMA Alanbrooke MSS 6/2/21, Montgomery to Brooke, 28 Dec. 1942.

[125] PRO WO 205/404, Lieut.-Col. A. H. Pepys to GSO1(L), Main HQ, 21 Army Group, 19 June 1944.

the field, they now wanted a single chassis for both their main cruiser and infantry tank.[126] Montgomery wished to take the logical next step and develop a single 'capital' tank to perform both roles. While waiting for a suitable design to be developed, he urged that both armoured brigades (normally allotted to armoured divisions) and army tank brigades (normally employed to support infantry divisions) be equipped with Shermans. They would then be tactically interchangeable.[127] However, he was overruled, probably because there were insufficient Shermans available, and production of the Churchill, the final mark of Infantry tank, was well under way. Early marks of the Churchill suffered from the same reliability problems which had plagued all British-designed tanks in the early years of the war.[128] However, once these had been overcome, the Churchill proved to be an effective infantry support weapon. Not only was it immune to anything other than a 75mm. or 88mm. shell or a hollow charge weapon, it was less likely than the Sherman to incinerate its crew when it was hit. Furthermore, its ability to traverse broken ground and steep slopes meant that in Tunisia, for example, 'the Churchill has accomplished marvels and has supported the infantry onto positions which in the past might never have been attempted'.[129]

Although the Sherman, Cromwell, and Churchill were improvements on the vehicles issued to the RAC before 1942, the RAC's tanks remained under-gunned and under-armoured compared to their German counterparts in the last two years of the war. Within a few days of landing in Normandy, the 7th Armoured division had recognized the superior gun power and armoured protection of the Panther and Tiger compared to their Cromwells and 75mm.-armed Shermans.[130] While German tanks could destroy their British opponents at ranges of up to 1,500 yards, the British had to approach dangerously close to the former, and preferably from a flank, to be able to do them significant damage.[131] To a large extent this was the result of factors entirely beyond the control of the army. Both the need to transport them over-

[126] PRO WO 193/25, Kennedy to DAFV, 19 Aug. 1942.

[127] *Montgomery and the Eighth Army. A Selection from the Diaries and Correspondence and Other Papers of Field Marshal the Viscount Montgomery of Alamein, August 1942 to December 1943*, ed. S. Brooks (London, 1991), 118, 274; IWM Montgomery MSS BLM 129/2, Montgomery, 'Future design of the capital tank', 24 Oct. 1944.

[128] PRO WO 193/25, Maj. Hussey to Secretary, Joint Planning Staff, 22 June 1942.

[129] PRO WO 201/527, Extracts from the report of a War Office observer in North Africa, May 1943; PRO WO 32/101365, Army Operational Research Group Middle East, Operational Research Memorandum no. 6, The distribution and effect of AP shot and HE; 25 Aug. 1943; P. Gudgin, *With Churchills to War. 48ᵗʰ Battalion Royal Tank Regiment at War 1939–45* (Stroud, 1996), 111.

[130] PRO WO 205/404, Lieut.-Col. A. H. Pepys to GSO1(L), Main HQ, 21 Army Group, 19 June 1944.

[131] IWM Bucknall MSS 80/33/1/folder 11, Bucknall to 2 Army, 16 June 1944.

seas and the expectation that once they arrived in a theatre of war they would have to cross numerous hastily constructed military bridges limited the total weight of British tanks. This meant that it was not practical to consider building a tank with a total weight of more than about 40 tons.[132] But the RAC's inferiority in gun power was at least partly the product of choice, rather than of necessity. It reflected how the General Staff saw the tactical role of cruiser tanks in armoured divisions. Before 1942 they believed that their main role was to fight hostile tanks and that to do so they needed a gun with an optimal anti-tank capability.[133] However, experience showed that they were more likely to engage hostile anti-tank guns, infantry, and motor transport. Throughout the war, it was the anti-tank gun, rather than the tank, which was the main enemy of the tank. Thirty per cent of British tanks were destroyed by anti-tank guns, compared to 25 per cent by hostile tanks and 22 per cent by mines. (The remaining losses were caused by self-propelled guns or hand-held hollow charge weapons).[134] To engage soft targets they needed a gun capable of firing HE shells.[135] In Tunisia, for example, tanks fired only a quarter of their ammunition at hostile tanks, and senior commanders and tank officers were insistent that they needed a weapon with a better HE shell.[136] In July 1942 the General Staff decided to sacrifice armoured protection to mechanical reliability, a dual-purpose gun, and a range of at least 100 miles.[137] Henceforth, they intended to rely upon anti-tank guns to destroy hostile tanks.[138] The Ministry of Supply agreed. In January 1943 they admitted that, faced by the German long 75mm. and 88mm. guns, they could not produce a tank capable of withstanding anti-tank fire at normal battle ranges. In February 1943, the General Staff therefore abandoned work 'on the development of a tank carrying sufficient armour to take on guns at close range'.[139]

Producing a dual-purpose gun capable of firing an effective HE and AP round that could be fitted into a tank weighing no more than 40

---

[132] PRO WO 277/32, Lt.-Col. French, 'Rearmament', ii; PRO WO 163/183, Record of 1 meeting of the General Staff Committee on weapons and equipment held at the War Office, 17 July 1942.

[133] PRO WO 163/183, General Staff policy on AFVs, 12 July 1942.

[134] PRO WO 291/1186, Army Operational Research Group, Internal Memorandum no. 16, The comparative performance of German anti-tank weapons during World War II, May 1950.

[135] PRO WO 193/25, SD1, Note on tank policy, 31 July 1942.

[136] PRO WO 231/10, RAC report, North Africa, 29 May 1943; PRO WO 193/26, Alexander to DRAC, War Office, 18 May 1943.

[137] PRO WO 193/25, SD1, Note on tank policy, 31 July 1942.

[138] PRO WO 163/183, General Staff policy on AFVs, 12 July 1942, and Minutes 5 meeting of the General Staff committee on organisation and weapons policy, 5 Aug. 1942.

[139] PRO WO 216/24, R. B. Tippets (Ministry of Supply) to Churchill, 22 Jan. 1943; PRO WO 232/36, Note on a meeting held in DCIGS's room, 22 Feb. 1943, to consider tank policy.

tons, proved to be an insuperable problem before the end of the war.[140] The British, therefore, compromised. To be fully effective, a HE round had to be fired at a muzzle velocity of no more than 1,500 ft./sec. But an effective AP round had to be fired at no less than 2,600 ft./sec.[141] In 1942 the General Staff believed that the 6-pdr. would be adequate to counter any German tank they might encounter.[142] Officers with actual combat experience disagreed and wanted something bigger.[143] As a stop gap, thanks to the insistence of the new DRAC Major-General Raymond Briggs, who had commanded 1st Armoured division in North Africa, armoured units that landed in Normandy in 1944 were equipped with a proportion of Shermans fitted with the 17-pdr.[144] Only these 'Fireflies' carried a weapon of comparable armoured piercing capability to the Panther and Tiger. The remainder of their Shermans, and all of their Cromwells and Churchills, were fitted with either the 75mm. dual purpose gun or the 6-pdr., which by 1944 had a small HE shell.[145]

Until 1942 the British fought with tanks that were so mechanically unreliable that they often undermined their doctrinal commitment to mobile operations, that were sometimes adequately armoured, but sometimes not, and that were equipped with a gun that had a diminishing ability to destroy enemy tanks and almost no ability to damage soft targets. In the middle of the war they did succeed in introducing better vehicles with better guns. But by July 1943, the DRAC believed that existing designs of cruiser and infantry tanks had almost reached the limits of their development because their suspension systems could not carry any more weight. However, the development of completely new designs would take between 18–24 months, an option precluded because Churchill and the Chiefs of Staff had by then agreed that no weapons should be developed which were not likely to be in service when they expected the war to end, by December 1944.[146]

The Germans had quite different design priorities. Their Panthers and Tigers were initially designed as mobile anti-tank weapons to defeat the Russian T-34 tank. Their tanks could carry thicker armour than British

[140] It was not one that the Germans solved. The Panther weighed nearly 45 tons and the Tiger I over 54 tons.
[141] PRO WO 291/1299, Capt. D. H. Parkinson to Scientific Adviser to the Army Council, 15 July 1943.
[142] PRO WO 163/183, General Staff policy on AFVs, 12 July 1942.
[143] Roberts, *From the Desert to the Baltic*, 108; IWM Montgomery MSS 117/2, Montgomery to Nye, 28 Aug. 1943.
[144] D. Fletcher, *The Universal Tank. British Armour in the Second World War Part 2* (London, 1993), 84–5.
[145] PRO WO 193/26, Alexander to DRAC, War Office, 18 May 1943; PRO WO 216/24, S. Redman to Rickets, 5 Apr. 1943.
[146] PRO WO 163/183, Minutes of 28 meeting of the General Staff committee on organisation and weapons policy, 29 July 1943; PRO WO 163/183, Lieut.-Gen. Sir R. Weeks, General Staff policy on tanks, 16 Aug. 1943.

tanks because they did not have to be shipped overseas in large numbers and they could carry bigger guns because of the wider gauge of the European railway system. This meant that in Normandy whereas the Germans had to hit a Sherman with only 1.63 shells to knock it out, the British had to hit a Tiger with 4.2 shells and a Panther with 2.55 shells to put them out of action.[147] But the Germans bought protection and gun power at the expense of range and mechanical reliability. The Tiger, and to a lesser extent the Panther, had a very limited range—the former could only manage about 40 miles between refills.[148] In 1944–5 German Panzer units were very vulnerable when their logistical support was interrupted. It was not coincidental that three-quarters of the 223 German tanks examined by the operational research section attached to 21 Army Group in Normandy between 8 and 31 August had been abandoned or destroyed by their own crews.[149] Most had broken down or run out of fuel. By contrast, during the pursuit from the Seine to Brussels between 28 August and 7 September, Montgomery's Sherman- and Cromwell-equipped armoured brigades each travelled an average of 317 miles but lost fewer than six tanks per day per brigade to mechanical breakdowns.[150]

It would, therefore, be wrong to conclude that British tanks were consistently inferior to the Germans in all respects. There were occasions when the British sprang technical surprises on the Germans, although they were few and short-lived. In May 1940 the Matilda's armour came as an unpleasant shock to Rommel's 7th Panzer division. At Alamein the commander of DAK, von Thoma, admitted that 'the quality and the number of these [Shermans] we had produced had astounded him'.[151] The Germans believed that the bocage was impenetrable to tanks, so they were badly surprised in July 1944 when the Churchill's of 6th Guards Tank brigade were able to cross it *en masse* in support of 15th (Scottish) Infantry Division during operation BLUECOAT.[152] The British were unique in that they also developed a whole family of specialized armour. By February 1943, the British had realized that when they landed in Northern France they would be confronted by large numbers of natural and man-made obstacles. They therefore

[147] PRO WO 291/1331, Operational Research in North West Europe, Report no. 17, Analysis of German tank casualties in France 6 June–31 Aug. 1944.

[148] P. Gudgin, *Armoured Firepower. The Development of Tank Armament 1939–45* (Stroud, 1997), 90.

[149] PRO WO 291/1331, ORS in N. W. Europe, Report no. 17, Analysis of German tank casualties in France 6 June–31 Aug. 1944.

[150] PRO WO 291/1331, ORS in N. W. Europe, Report no. 18, Tank casualties during the exploitation phase after crossing the Seine.

[151] PRO WO 201/2155, 8 Army Intelligence summary no. 357, Appendix A, 5 Nov. 1942.

[152] LHCMA Dempsey MSS, 2 Army Intelligence summary no. 46, 20 July 1944, Trans. of enemy doc.

developed specialized armour to clear minefields, destroy concrete fortifications and bridge water obstacles.[153] Organized under the command of 79th Armoured division, which was formed in March 1943, these vehicles played a prominent and generally successful role in every major operation between D-Day and the end of the war in Europe.[154] The arrival of the 79th Armoured division's amphibious tanks on the D-Day beaches at practically the same time as the assaulting infantry caught the Germans by surprise.[155] The division's Crocodile tanks (Churchill tanks equipped with flame-throwers) were particularly detested by the Germans who tended to surrender readily when they made an appearance.[156]

However, this should not obscure the fact that many items of equipment in the British army's inventory were ill designed or inadequate for the task they were required to fulfil. Determined never again to repeat the human cost of the First World War, the inter-war army hoped that machinery would be a substitute for manpower and enable them to restore mobility to the battlefield. But they developed a series of designs for small arms, artillery, and tanks that emphasized mobility at the expense of fire-power. This proved to be a misjudgement for which the wartime army had to pay a heavy price. It soon became apparent that there could be no mobility unless the enemy's fire was first suppressed by overwhelming fire-power. It meant, therefore, that what the British army lacked in the quality of its weapons, it had to make up for in their quantity. It consequently depended heavily upon the ability of British industry to deliver sufficient quantities of equipment and munitions. However, in the aftermath of the First World War the army's defence industrial base had shrunk massively, and the commitment of successive governments to 'limited liability' meant that its expansion in the late 1930s was very slow. Between 1934 and 1939 the government allocated only 22 per cent of the money it found for rearmament to the army, and much of that was spent on anti-aircraft equipment rather than on the field army.[157] Consequently, in September 1939 the QMG held sufficient equipment for the four regular divisions of the BEF, but, apart from clothing, personal equipment, and rifles, he had almost nothing for the remaining twenty-eight divisions of the army's thirty-two division programme. Gort's troops went into action short of their full complement of tanks, modern field artillery, radios, heavy-gun tractors, light anti-

[153] PRO WO 232/36, Maj.-Gen. A. R. Godwin-Austen to DCIGS, 26 Feb. 1943.
[154] D. Fletcher, *Vanguard of Victory. The 79th Armoured Division* (London, 1984), *passim*.
[155] PRO WO 232/25, Special Tactical Study no. 30, German views of the Normandy landing, 28 Nov. 1944.
[156] PRO WO 204/7580, DMT, News and views on training, 10 Dec. 1944.
[157] M. M. Postan, *British War Production* (London, 1952), 28.

aircraft ammunition, anti-tank guns, mortars, and Bren gun carriers.[158] At Dunkirk most of the army's personnel was saved, but sufficient equipment for between eight and ten divisions was abandoned. Immediately after the evacuation there was sufficient modern equipment in Britain for only a single division, enough ammunition for no more than one day's intensive fighting, and only fifty modern tanks.[159]

On 19 June 1940, the Cabinet Defence Committee agreed quality had to give way to quantity and that their aim was to get the maximum number of weapons into the hands of the troops as quickly as possible.[160] In March 1941, the War Cabinet fixed the size of the field army at fifty-nine divisions. The German army then totalled 203 divisions. To redress this imbalance, equipment would have to be a substitute for manpower. 'We cannot hope', Churchill had written in October 1940, 'to compete with the enemy in numbers of men, and must therefore rely upon an exceptional proportion of armoured fighting vehicles.'[161] The British army was to have a ratio of one armoured division or its equivalent to three infantry divisions. This compared to the German army, which had a ratio of only one panzer division to every eight and a half infantry divisions.[162] These decisions had fateful consequences. They meant that until 1942 troops in the field frequently had to make do with obsolescent equipment. The case of the 6-pdr. anti-tank gun has already been considered.[163] Similarly, because industry was already tooled-up to produce more infantry tanks than cruisers, it was allowed to continue to do so in 1941, despite the fact that they were quite unsuitable equipment for the army's burgeoning number of armoured divisions.[164] The tank supply situation was further worsened because of the teething problems suffered by the new generation of Mark V and VI cruisers. By January 1941 even the best-equipped armoured division in Britain, 1st Armoured, had only 70 per cent of its establishment of tanks, and many of those were obsolescent light tanks.[165]

Home Forces was the victim of Britain's slow start in rearmament and the low priority given to the army compared to the RAF and navy for

---

[158] PRO CAB 106/268, Equipment notes, 1940–51; PRO WO 259/59, Gort to Stanley, 21 Mar. 1940; *Chief of Staff*, ed. Bond, i, 294; LHCMA Bridgeman MSS 3/6/2, Bridgeman to DCGS, 8 Apr. 1940; PRO WO 163/48/ACM(OS) 19, Minutes of the Army Council, 8 Apr. 1940; PRO WO 259/59, Gort to Stanley, 11 Apr. 1940.

[159] PRO WO 277/31, Anon., 'Rearmament', i.

[160] *The Churchill War Papers, ii. Never Surrender, May–December 1940*, ed. M. Gilbert, (London, 1994), 376.

[161] Ibid. 948.

[162] Cooper, *The German Army 1933–1945*, 275.

[163] PRO WO 277/32, French, 'Rearmament', ii.

[164] J. R. M. Butler, *Grand Strategy* (London, 1957), ii, 481–2.

[165] PRO WO 199/597, Maj.-Gen. Burrows to Brooke, 4 Jan. 1941.

equipment. Despite the fact that in 1941 British industry produced 3,400 field and medium guns, 8,750 tank and anti-tank guns, 4,800 tanks and 182,100 wheeled vehicles, until late 1942 Home Forces remained short of equipment of all kinds.[166] In June 1941, after visiting units and formations in South Eastern Command which would bear the initial brunt of any invasion, Lieutenant-General C. Liddell, the Inspector General of Training, reported sadly that 'a most disquieting and depressing impression is created by the general lack of equipment which still obtains'.[167] It was not until October 1941 that infantry divisions' holdings of field guns, Bren guns, medium machine-guns, sub-machine-guns, and 3-in. mortars exceeded 90 per cent of their war establishments. Even nine months later, none of the fifteen Higher Establishment infantry divisions in Home Forces was fully equipped. Three of them had only two of their three field regiments and all lacked their full complement of Bren guns, light anti-aircraft guns, and anti-tank guns. The nine Lower Establishment divisions, created specifically to economize on scarce artillery and transport, were in an even worse position.[168] Only in September 1942 did GHQ Home Forces believe that it was within sight of receiving its full allocation of equipment and that most deficiencies would have disappeared by the spring of 1943.[169]

Formations overseas did a little better, as they were given priority for supplies and equipment. In October 1941, the Chiefs of Staff decided that Home Forces would retain only 35 per cent of equipment produced in Britain. The rest was to be sent abroad.[170] But even so, units actually in contact with the enemy were frequently without adequate quantities of essential equipment in the first half of the war. At the start of operation COMPASS, O'Connor's force had only a single regiment of medium artillery and, as it was without any first-line transport, the regiment could not operate at more than 20 miles from a railhead.[171] Tanks were in such short supply in North Africa that in March 1941 one armoured regiment of 2nd Armoured division had to be equipped with captured Italian medium tanks. During BATTLEAXE, Wavell only had enough tanks to equip four of the 7th Armoured division's six armoured regiments and its 4th Armoured Brigade was equipped with slow-moving Infantry tanks, which were quite unsuitable for work with an armoured division. In general, at least until Alamein, the army both at home and

---

[166] PRO WO 163/87/ECAC/P(42)8, Director General of Army Requirements, Army Requirements in 1942 and 1943, 16 Jan. 1942.

[167] PRO WO 216/62, IG Training to CIGS, 4 July 1941.

[168] PRO WO 163/50/AC/P(41)63, War Office Progress Report, Oct. 1941, 23 Dec. 1941; PRO WO 193/979, Field Forces in the UK, Iceland (C), and Faroes, 1 July 1942; PRO WO 260/43, DSD to Brooke, 11 Nov. 1941.

[169] PRO WO 199/451, BGGS(SD) to DCGS, Home Forces, 8 Sept. 1942.

[170] PRO WO 277/31. Anon., 'Rearmament', i.

[171] PRO WO 277/5, Pemberton, *Artillery Tactics*, 43–4.

overseas faced a constant problem with shortages of key items of vital equipment and munitions, shortages that went some way towards explaining the series of defeats it suffered.[172] It must also be emphasized that the period of relative abundance it enjoyed from Alamein onwards owed a great deal to the arrival of supplies from North America. Over the course of the war more than half of the tanks used by the British army were produced in the USA.[173] It was even more dependent upon North American supplies for motor vehicles. Thirty-eight per cent of the motor transport it employed came from Canada, 20 per cent from the USA and only 42 per cent was home produced.[174]

However, if defeat was, therefore, sometimes the consequence of lack of equipment in the first half of the war, victory was not always the result of an abundance of equipment in the second half. Even in the period of relative plenty beginning in the autumn of 1942, essential items were still sometimes lacking. By mid-1943 motor transport was in such short supply that a number of formations in the Mediterranean theatre were grounded.[175] In November 1943, after several weeks operating in the close country of Italy, the 7th Armoured division asked in vain for a larger supply of White half-tracks in order to improve co-operation between its armoured regiments and lorried infantry battalions.[176] By the spring of 1944 it was apparent that production of field and medium artillery ammunition was lagging behind demand. In March, Alexander had to order his commanders to ration its use.[177] The situation worsened in the autumn of 1944, by when expenditure of 25-pdr. ammunition in France and Italy was exceeding production by 1.5 million rounds per month. In the winter of 1944–5 priority in allocation was given to 21 Army Group, and forces in Italy had again to economize in order to create a stockpile sufficient for their needs during the forthcoming spring offensive.[178] In November 1944, Montgomery also rationed expenditure in quiet periods in order to stockpile supplies for his next offensive.[179] The heavy artillery preparations that

[172] Macready, *In the Wake of the Great*, 128.
[173] Postan, *British War Production*, 247.
[174] PRO WO 277/8, Anon., 'Fighting, Support, and Transport Vehicles', 46
[175] Ibid. 24–5.
[176] PRO WO 232/17. Maj.-Gen. G. W. E. J. Erskine, 7 Armoured Division, Report on operations, 20 Nov. 1943.
[177] Brig. C. J. C. Molony, *The Mediterranean and Middle East, vi Victory in the Mediterranean, pt 1. 1 April to 4 June 1944* (London, 1984), 29–30; LHCMA Alanbrooke MSS 14/65, Alexander to Brooke, 22 Mar. 1944.
[178] Molony, *The Mediterranean and Middle East, vi Victory in the Mediterranean, pt 2. June to October 1944* (London, 1987), 378–9; Maj.-Gen. Sir W. Jackson, *The Mediterranean and Middle East, vi Victory in the Mediterranean, pt 3. November 1944 to May 1945* (London, 1988), 30–1.
[179] Maj. L. E. Ellis and Lieut.-Col. A. E. Warhurst, *Victory in the West, ii* (London, 1994), 134.

characterized British tactics in 1942–5 were, therefore, often only made possible by applying strict economy in quieter periods.

In many respects, therefore, the British army was equipped with weapons that were inferior to those of their enemies and until late 1942 they often lacked sufficient quantities of essential items. However, the British enjoyed one compensating advantage, their superior ability to provide their troops in the field with supplies and ordnance stores. This fact was fundamental to understanding how the British army was able to generate superior fire-power between 1942 and 1945. Its success in doing so has too often been taken for granted and passed over in silence as if it were inevitable. It was not; it was the result of a deliberate commitment of resources and ingenuity, combined with a willingness to improvise on the basis of existing doctrine.

Once supplies and munitions had been produced, they had to be transported to the troops that needed them. The army's logistical demands were prodigious. By 1944, an armoured division in North West Europe required 1,000 gallons of petrol to move just one mile. An infantry division consumed 1,300 tons of food each month.[180] Throughout the war, the army relied upon railways for logistical maintenance between its bases and a point near to the front line. Railways remained an essential element in British logistics throughout the war. Beginning in December 1940, for example, the British took great pains to extend the Egyptian coast railway from Mersa Matruth, itself 200 miles from the army's main base at Alexandria. By March 1942, it had reached Capuzzo.[181] In the winter of 1944–5, before the Rhine crossing, great effort was put into repairing the French and Belgian railway systems that had been so carefully bombed by the allied air forces. Railways had a far superior load carrying capacity to that of lorries. A single 10-ton railway wagon could carry 1,960 gallons of petrol in 4-gallon tins, compared to only 640 gallons carried by a 3-ton lorry.[182] In their reliance upon railways as the foundation of their logistical system, the British were no different from the Germans.

However, the British did rely to a far greater extent than the Germans upon motor transport for their logistics support forward from their railheads. This was the result of a deliberate choice made after 1919. The British army was not simply forced into mechanization because of a

---

[180] Anon., *Taurus Pursuant. A History of the 11ᵗʰ Armoured Division* (Germany, 1945), 119; Anon., *Team Spirit. The Administration of the 53ʳᵈ Welch Division during Operation "Overlord" June 1944 to May 1945* (Germany, 1945), 22.

[181] PRO WO 277/10, Lt.-Col. J. A. H. Carter and Maj. D. N. Kann, *Maintenance in the Field*, 2 vols. (London, 1960), i, 223.

[182] General Staff, 'Field Service Pocket Book. Pamphlet no. 9 1939. Supply and Replenishment of Material in the Field' (London, 1941), 11.

growing shortage of horses in the civilian economy between the wars.[183] The army interpreted mobility as meaning motorization, and motor transport offered the prospect of increasing the tempo of operations and thereby avoiding a repetition of trench warfare. Senior officers may have been fond of horses, but they recognized that their days were numbered and that mechanical traction could restore mobility to the army in a way that horses never could. Major-General Sir Louis Jackson, the Director of Trench Warfare and Supplies in 1915–18, has been cited as an outstanding example of a dyed-in-the-wool reactionary because in 1919 he dismissed the tank as 'a freak'. However, the remainder of his lecture was a powerful plea that the army should study ways of organizing its transport on a caterpillar-tracked basis, so that whole divisions could operate independent of all roads.[184] Jackson was not a lone voice. In 1921 the DCIGS, Sir Philip Chetwode, himself a cavalryman, made the development of cross-country mechanical transport for the artillery, divisional ammunition column, and eventually for the infantry, a priority.[185]

Progress towards this goal was retarded by several factors, of which shortage of finance at home was only one, albeit an important one. Under the Cardwell system, units in Britain had to be interchangeable with those in India. In 1921 the General Staff in India was as eager as their British counterparts to replace the horse with mechanical vehicles. As Montgomery-Massingberd, then DCGS in Delhi wrote, 'Horses are bound soon to be a thing of the past, firstly because the supply will not be sufficient, and secondly because in modern warfare they cannot hope to exist for long, nor can we afford the enormous road space they require.'[186] But the Indian government's reluctance to find the necessary funds was a major stumbling block until 1935 when the Army Council finally decided that 'we ought not to allow the Indian tail to wag the British dog.'[187]

The pace of mechanization was also determined by the available technology. Ideally, mechanized transport had to be mechanically

---

[183] Anon., 'Military Notes', *Journal of the Royal United Services Institute*, 68 (1923), 341; Institution of the Royal Army Service Corps, *The Story of the Royal Army Service Corps 1939–1945* (London, 1955), 21.

[184] Maj.-Gen. Sir L. C. Jackson, 'Possibilities of the Next War', *Journal of the Royal United Services Institute*, 65 (1920), 71–89.

[185] LHCMA Montgomery-Massingberd MSS 122/3, Chetwode to Montgomery-Massingberd, 12 Jan 1921; LHCMA Montgomery-Massingberd MSS 123/17, Chetwode to Montgomery-Massingberd, 15 Feb. 1921; LHCMA Montgomery-Massingberd MSS 133/1, Chetwode to Montgomery-Massingberd, 20 July 1921.

[186] LHCMA Montgomery-Massingberd MSS 133/1, Montgomery-Massingberd to Chetwode, 16 Aug. 1921.

[187] PRO WO 32/2840, QMG to CIGS, 30 May 1935, and Army HQ, Simla, to War Office, 4 May 1936; PRO WO 279/57, Statement by Maj.-Gen. A. Cameron, Report on the Staff Conference.

reliable and simple to maintain, to possess at least the same cross-country capability as horsed traction, and the vehicles adopted had to be suitable for rapid mass production in wartime. Cost alone made it impossible for the army to maintain the massive stockpiles of vehicles it would need following mobilization. This meant that suitable vehicles had to be based upon designs that were in civilian production.[188] It was not until 1934 that some of these obstacles had been overcome. In 1918 wheeled vehicles were largely road-bound because they were fitted with small-section, high-pressure tyres. Between 1923 and 1935 the army experimented with a variety of tracked and half-tracked vehicles in an effort to find something with a suitable cross-country performance.[189] But such vehicles had an inherent drawback. As there was little civilian demand for them, production of large numbers quickly in wartime would be expensive, as it would be difficult to convert existing civilian factories to make them.

These experiments with tracked and half-tracked vehicles ended when it became apparent that wheeled vehicles had been developed that were cheap to mass-produce, easy to maintain, and had adequate cross-country performance. Working in conjunction with civilian manu-facturers, in the late 1920s the RASC developed wheeled vehicles fitted with large-cross-section, low-pressure pneumatic tyres whose cross-country performance was almost as good as half-tracked vehicles.[190] In 1934 Montgomery-Massingberd ordered the wholesale mechanization of the artillery and first-line transport of the infantry on this basis. Beginning in 1936 each infantry platoon was issued with a 15-cwt. four-wheeled truck fitted with low-pressure pneumatic tyres and able to carry all of its weapons, equipment, packs, and greatcoats. As it was based on an existing commercial design, it could be easily and cheaply mass-produced. Sufficient reserve companies of motor transport were also to be provided to lift one infantry brigade in every division.[191] By late 1938 the British army had only 5,200 horses in service, compared to the 28,700 it had possessed on the eve of the First World War.[192]

The decision to rely upon modified civilian designs did have some drawbacks. Most of the vehicles were mechanically reliable, but many of

[188] PRO WO 279/57, Statement by Maj.-Gen. A. R. Cameron; PRO WO 32/4120, 'Mechanization (Wheeled Vehicles)', lecture, MGO 6, Feb. 1937.

[189] PRO WO 32/2382, Milne to Birdwood, 7 Jan. 1929; PRO WO 279/65, Statement by Maj.-Gen S. C. Peck, Director of Mechanization, Report on the Staff Conference.

[190] PRO WO 32/2382, Milne to Birdwood, 7 Jan. 1929; IWM Dept. of Sound Records, Accession no. 000991/03: Visc. Bridgeman.

[191] PRO WO 279/75, Statement by CIGS, Report on the Staff Conference; Col. G. N. Macready, 'The Trend of Organization in the Army', *Journal of the Royal United Services Institute*, 80 (1935), 1–20; LHCMA Lindsay's papers, Liddell Hart MSS 15/12/8, Heywood to GOC Southern Command, 7 Dec. 1934; Anon., 'Army Notes', *Journal of the Royal United Services Institute*, 80 (1935), 435.

[192] Anon., 'Army Notes', *Journal of the Royal United Services Institute*, 83 (1938), 439.

them had only two-wheeled drive and their speed and load-carrying capacity compared unfavourably with many of the American-manufactured vehicles the army received under Lend-Lease.[193] This was the consequence of a tax regime that encouraged civilian manufacturers in Britain to produce light trucks with small engines.[194] The Americans did not suffer from similar constraints and they were able to produce an excellent all-round vehicle, the two-and-a-half ton lorry, that British commanders thought superior to anything they possessed.[195] American maintenance problems were also eased because, unlike the British, they used the same vehicle as a load carrier and a prime mover for their artillery.[196] Industrial constraints also handicapped the army in other ways. Armoured units in the desert suffered because the Ministry of Supply, in an effort to maximize the output of vehicles, failed to produce enough spare parts.[197] In January 1942, for example, the Support Group of 1st Armoured division had to abandon many of its trucks near Benghazi because they had not been issued with sufficient spares to repair them.[198] The delivery of supplies of petrol and water was immensely hampered because they were carried in flimsy kerosene tins with the result that a great deal of their contents was lost through leakage. The far sturdier German 'jerricans' were much coveted by British troops.[199]

During the Second World War, the British army relied entirely upon motor transport both within divisions and to bridge the gap between divisional depots and railheads. Between 1940 and 1944 the army received over 1 million wheeled vehicles of all types.[200] By October 1943, each infantry division in Italy possessed 3,745 motor vehicles of all kinds, including 951 motor cycles.[201] This conferred both benefits and drawbacks. It provided the British with an extra margin of tactical and strategic mobility that the German army did not enjoy. However, it also meant that the British had to devote a high proportion of their best men to maintaining their arsenal of vehicles and equipment. In 1935 the DSD calculated that every motor vehicle added to the army's inventory

---

[193] Postan, Hay, and Scott, *Design and Development of Weapons*, 277–78.

[194] PRO WO 277/8, Anon., 'Fighting, Support, and Transport Vehicles', 79.

[195] PRO WO 204/7952, Leese to Main HQ, 8 Army, 20 Sept. 1943; PRO WO 204/7975, Leese to Main HQ, 8 Army, 30 Sept. 1943.

[196] D. R. Beaver, '"Deuce and a Half": Selecting US Army Trucks, 1920–45', in J. A. Lynn (ed.), *Feeding Mars. Logistics in Western Warfare from the Middle Ages to the Present* (Boulder, Colo., 1993), 251–70.

[197] IWM Dept. of Sound Records, Accession no. 000866/08: Maj.-Gen. G. W. Richards.

[198] PRO WO 106/220, Report by Maj.-Gen. Messervy on operations by 1 Armoured divn. in Western Cyrenaica, 24 Feb. 1942.

[199] Tuker, *Approach to Battle*, 17; PRO WO 277/11, Carter and Kann, *Maintenance in the Field*, ii, 87.

[200] PRO WO 277/8, Anon., 'Fighting, Support, and Transport Vehicles', 46.

[201] PRO WO 204/7592, Main HQ, 8 Army, to XXX Corps, 5 Oct. 1943.

required one and a half drivers and one mechanic to be added to the maintenance echelon. Consequently, whereas 74 per cent of soldiers in 1914 had been in fighting echelons, the number had now dropped to 58 per cent.[202] The relationship between men in fighting units and those in supply units—the 'teeth to tail' ratio'—was a constant irritant to Churchill. In March 1940 he 'poked fun at the vast requirements in the back areas of the B.E.F. He said that our Expeditionary Force, instead of being a steel-capped spear was becoming a pin on the end of an enormous scaffold pole—and other observations in the same vein.'[203] By January 1941 the General Staff calculated that each division of approximately 18,000 in the Middle East needed a 'divisional slice' of 41,000 men, when account was taken of the supply and maintenance units required to keep it in the field. The best figures they had for the German army suggested that they required only 30,000 men to keep one of their divisions in the field. The General Staff's justification for this was twofold. Not only did the British have to sustain their forces in often under-developed countries at the end of lengthy sea-lanes, but that it was the inevitable product of mechanization.[204]

It was, therefore essential to make the most economical use of maintenance personnel. This became even more urgent in late 1941, as complaints mounted about large-scale waste of skilled mechanics at home and as troops in the field were comparing their own repair and recovery organization unfavourably with the Germans'.[205] The problem was compounded because responsibility for repairs was divided. As the largest user of motor transport, the RASC was responsible for repairing its own breakdowns, while the RAOC repaired vehicles belonging to all other arms of the service. By late 1941 workshops in Britain and North Africa were seriously overloaded with a backlog of repairs, even though only a fraction of the army was in action.[206] In February 1942, the War Office therefore agreed to optimize the available skilled labour by merging the RASC's and RAOC's repair organizations together with some RE personnel into a new corps, the REME. It was officially established in October 1942.[207] First-line maintenance personnel, however, remained

---

[202] Macready, 'The trend of organization in the Army', 16.

[203] PRO CAB 65/56/WM (40)69, War Cabinet, Confidential Notes, 15 Mar. 1940.

[204] PRO WO 216/1, Memorandum, The need for administrative services as an integral part of the Field Army, 21 Jan. 1941.

[205] PRO WO 106/2223, Notes from theatres of war no. 2, Cyrenaica, Nov.–Dec. 1941, 7 Mar. 1942; PRO WO 106/220, Report by Maj.-Gen. Messervy on operations by 1 Armoured divn. in Western Cyrenaica, 24 Feb. 1942; PRO WO 199/3186, HQ 1 Armoured divn. to Brigs. Morgan, Crocker, and McCreery, 26 June 1940; PRO WO 201/352, Operations Western Desert, Dec. 1940, Lessons from, 18 Jan. 1940.

[206] PRO WO 163/85/ECAC/P(41)83 PUS, Corps of mechanical engineers, 10 Oct. 1941.

[207] PRO WO 277/32, French, 'Rearmament', ii; Brig. B. B. Kennett and Col. J. A. Tateman, *Craftsmen of the Army. The Story of the Royal Electrical and Mechanical Engineers* (London, 1970), 148–53.

part of their own unit and were not transferred to the REME.[208] But even this did little to check the growth of the tail compared to the teeth. In Normandy service and administrative duties absorbed 44 per cent of the army.

This was entirely consonant with the priority the army gave to logistics. Montgomery was not peculiar amongst British generals in allowing his operational plans to be subordinated to logistical practicalities.[209] Even before 1914 British staff officers had been taught to afford primacy to questions of supply and transport.[210] The experience of the war on the Western Front only reinforced the lesson that a properly organized administrative infrastructure was the first essential for success in battle.[211] Sir Archibald Wavell gave a flavour of the importance that senior British officers afforded logistics in a lecture he delivered in 1939. A successful general, he insisted, must have

what the French call *les sens du praticable*, and we call common sense, knowledge of what is and what is not possible. It must be based on a really sound knowledge of the "mechanism of war", i.e. topography, movement, and supply. These are the real foundations of military knowledge, not strategy and tactics as most people think.[212]

Before 1939 British logistical doctrine was based on pack trains. Once supplies and ordnance stores had been landed by sea at an overseas base, they were moved forward by rail to a railhead where they were loaded onto motor supply columns. These carried them forward to delivery points, from where they were distributed to units. The system was intended to operate as a conveyor belt to obviate the need to build up large supply dumps dangerously close to the front line where they might easily be captured. The main drawback of this system was that it tied troops closely to their railhead. Each motor supply column was designed to work over a distance of no more than forty miles between the railhead and the delivery point, although for brief periods it might be possible to double that distance.[213]

[208] PRO WO 163/91/ECAC/P(43)70, Adjutant-General, REME, Absorption of regimental maintenance tradesmen of all arms (phase II), 2 June 1943.

[209] FM Visc. Montgomery of Alamein, *El Alamein to the River Sangro* (London, 1948), 63–6, 126–9.

[210] Sir E. B. Hamley's, *The Operations of War Explained and Illustrated* (London, rev. edn., 1907), was a standard textbook employed at the Staff College before 1914. Three of its first four chapters were concerned with logistics.

[211] I. Brown, 'The Evolution of the British Army's Logistical and Administrative Infrastructure and its Influence on GHQ's Operational and Strategic Decision-Making on the Western Front, 1914–1918', Ph.D thesis (London, 1996), *passim*.

[212] Sir A. Wavell, *Generals and Generalship* (London, 1941), 8.

[213] Lieut.-Gen. W. G. Lindsell, *Military Organisation and Administration* (22nd edn., Aldershot, 1939), 89–91, 96; General Staff, *Field Service Pocket Book. Pamphlet No. 9 1939. Supply and Replenishment of Material in the Field* (London, 1941); General Staff, *Field Service*

Early in the war British operations were characterized by large-scale logistical failures. Operations in Norway were seriously hampered because the landings were mounted before a proper administrative reconnaissance had been conducted of the base areas that commanders had chosen. Units were loaded into different ships with the result that when operational plans were changed at the last minute, men were landed at one place and their transport and stores at another.[214] In France the BEF had ample time to create a logistical infrastructure in accordance with accepted pre-war doctrine. Many of its base facilities were established south of the Somme and in the west of France between Nantes–Rennes and Brest, to minimize the possibility of destruction by German air attacks. By 10 May 1940, the BEF had amassed reserves of supplies and petrol for sixty days and ammunition for forty-five days. However, apart from stocks held by units and seven days' worth of supplies held in field supply depots north of the Somme, most of these supplies were held in the base depots south of the river. This was not a problem during the advance to the Dyle. The *Luftwaffe* concentrated its air attacks on the major road and rail junctions behind the BEF, but the QMG moved supplies forward using minor stations as railheads.[215] However, by 21 May communications across the Somme had been severed, thus cutting the BEF off from its main supply bases. By 1 June most units were living off their own stocks and what they could scrounge from abandoned trucks or trains or loot from civilians.[216] Some formations did this on a grand scale. Montgomery's 3rd division rounded up several herds of cattle to supplement their rations while some units of 42nd division were issued with tinned lobster requisitioned from a shop in Lille.[217] In part, the BEF was defeated because its logistical system, like its C3I system, was insufficiently flexible to respond to the pace of the German offensive.

British generals have sometimes been accused of affording too much attention to the constraints of logistics and thereby letting slip fleeting chances on the battlefield. However, the outstanding fact about British logistics between 1941 and the end of the war was the willingness of senior officers to abandon the pre-war manuals and improvise success-

Regulations, i. Organisation and Administration. 1930. Reprinted with Amendments (nos. 1–11) 1939 (London, 1939), 154–5.

[214] PRO WO 231/1, DMT to C-in-C Home Forces *et al.*, 7 June 1940.

[215] PRO CAB 65/2/WM72(39), Minutes of the War Cabinet, 6 Nov. 1939; PRO WO 197/112, Lt.-Gen. W. G. Lindsell, Movement and maintenance in the BEF, 3 Sept. 1939–31 May 1940, 23 June 1940; PRO WO 197/113, DQMG(A), Short historical summary of the maintenance situation of the BEF in France [*c.*June 1940]; Beauman, *Then a Soldier*, 114–20; PRO WO 277/10, Carter and Kann, *Maintenance in the Field*, i, 25–50.

[216] PRO WO 197/111. DQMG to Pownall, 17 June 1940; Anon., *The Story of the Royal Army Service Corps 1939–1945* (London, 1955), 72–4.

[217] A. Bryant, *The Turn of the Tide 1939–42* (London, 1957), 117.

fully. The system of supply outlined above was designed to be utilized in temperate climates and in countries with a developed railway and road infrastructure. But long experience of fighting outside Europe and across terrain that lacked both roads and railways had taught the British that improvisation had to be the order of the day and that was exactly what they did in North Africa, where they developed logistical flexibility and improvisation to a high art.[218] The sheer distances involved, combined with wildly fluctuating demands for different kinds of stores and supplies, made reliance upon regular resupply by pack trains from railheads impossible. Before the war Hobart, when he commanded the 7th Armoured division, improvised a new logistical doctrine. It involved the establishment of a series of large dumps, eventually referred to as Field Maintenance Centres, in the forward areas. Each was designed to support a single Corps and was linked to the forward troops by a series of motor convoys.[219] They were first employed successfully during Operation COMPASS. At the start of CRUSADER some FMCs were even secretly established in front of the start lines before the offensive began.[220] The system was so flexible that it became the basis of the army's maintenance doctrine for the remainder of the war. In Normandy, for example, each corps had its own FMC.[221] A further element of flexibility was introduced in the summer of 1941 when the hitherto rigid distinction between RASC transport companies, each devoted to the carriage of either petrol, ammunition, or supplies, was abolished. Henceforth, most transport companies were organized on a general-purpose basis.[222]

Throughout the war, logistics imposed constraints on the operational freedom of commanders. The 'stop–go' nature of much of the fighting in North Africa in 1941–3, where offensives were followed by lengthy pauses, was forced on commanders by the need to prepare the maintenance facilities that they required to sustain their troops in what was, quite literally, a desert. The disaster that overtook 2nd Armoured Division in Cyrenaica in April 1941 was in part caused by the fact that it had no railhead and could not be provided with sufficient motor transport to enable it to build up a sufficient reserve of supplies some 350 miles from the nearest base.[223] After Alamein 1st Armoured Division at the head of the pursuit trying to outflank and cut off the remnants of Rommel's forces, became immobilized in the desert for lack of petrol.

[218] Lindsell, *Military Organisation and Administration*, 98–101.

[219] IWM Dept. of Sound Records, Accession no. 000877/03: FM Lord Carver.

[220] Roberts, *From the Desert to the Baltic*, 56; PRO WO 201/352, Operations Western Desert, Dec. 1940. Lessons from, 18 Jan. 1941; PRO WO 106/2223, Notes from theatres of war no. 4. Cyrenaica, Nov. 1941–Jan. 1942, May 1942.

[221] Maj. L. F. Ellis, *Victory in the West*, i. *The Battle for Normandy* (London, 1962), 85–6.

[222] PRO WO 163/85/ECAC 51, QMG and VCIGS, Re-organisation of RASC Transport units, 7 July 1941; Anon., *Story of the Royal Army Service Corps*, 116–17.

[223] Anon., *Story of the Royal Army Service Corps*, 128–9.

Its supply vehicles were literally bogged down in a desert quagmire created by three days of heavy rain. A larger proportion of four-wheeled drive vehicles might have made a considerable difference. Rommel's remaining troops were able to continue their own retreat by the simple expedient of keeping to the only metalled road.[224] Even so, the distance that 8th Army advanced, 778 miles from Alamein to Agedabia, at an average of 39 miles per day, between 4 and 23 November, was a remarkable performance.[225] It was made possible only because Montgomery was prepared to ground one of his corps and to use its motor transport to support his remaining troops. Even so, the rate of advance was retarded by poor traffic control that left vital maintenance convoys stuck in traffic jams.[226] Similarly, in the early days of the Normandy campaign, follow-up formations arrived on average two days behind schedule. If the infantry brigade of 7th Armoured Division, 49th Infantry Division and 33rd Armoured Brigade had arrived on schedule in early June, XXX Corps might have been able to secure Villers Bocage by the middle of the month before the arrival of the German Panzers that eventually barred its way.[227] The Germans sometimes suspected that Montgomery had unlimited quantities of artillery ammunition. That was not so. Offensive operations in Normandy were delayed because the planners had under-estimated the requirements of field and medium artillery ammunition, whereas the amount of anti-aircraft ammunition landed was far beyond the army's requirements. One reason why GOODWOOD was preceded by attacks by heavy bombers was that 2nd Army lacked sufficient field artillery ammunition to support its tanks.[228]

The army's commitment to motorization combined with the logistics staff's willingness to improvise meant that they were, temporarily and on occasions, able to break free from the umbilical cord of the railway. Without this willingness to throw away the rule book and improvise on a grand scale, offensive operations in the desert, 21 Army Group's pursuit from the Seine to southern Holland in August and September 1944, or 2nd Army's 200-mile advance from the Rhine to the Elbe in April 1945 without the benefit of railway logistics, would have been impossible. However, there were limits to the army's willingness to improvise and gamble with its logistics. The unexpected slowness with which the allies had expanded their bridgehead in Normandy in June and July 1944 gave them plenty of time to build up supply dumps. But,

---

[224] PRO WO 277/11, Carter and Kann, *Maintenance in the Field*, ii, 76.

[225] Ibid. ii, 89.

[226] PRO WO 201/2596, Middle East Training Memorandum no. 8, Lessons from Operations, Oct.–Nov. 1942.

[227] Ellis, *Victory in the West*, i, 264–5.

[228] PRO WO 277/11, Carter and Kann, *Maintenance in the Field*, ii, 287–8; N. Hamilton, *Monty. Master of the Battlefield 1942–44* (London, 1983), 682–4, 733.

in late August this advantage was lost due to the unexpected speed of their advance. Twenty-one Army Group had not anticipated that the German army would collapse so quickly. They predicted that the Germans would fight a delaying action on the Seine and so give them time to bring forward their supply dumps for the subsequent pursuit. But the British crossed the Seine more quickly than anticipated, advancing some 300 miles between 26 August and 3 September. At this pace, it was impossible for them to repair the railways or to use motor transport to carry out large-scale dumping of supplies behind the continuously advancing front line. Second Army was only able to supply two of its three corps by grounding the third and using all of its transport to supply the remaining two, each of which advanced an average forty miles per day, or twice the expected rate. Montgomery halted Horrocks's XXX Corps in Brussels because

My transport is based on operating 150 miles from my ports and at present I am over 300 miles from Bayeux. In order to save transport I have cut down my intake into France to 6000 tons a day which is half what I consume and I cannot go on like this.[229]

Horrocks, however, later claimed he had sufficient petrol to continue his advance for another two days. Had he done so might have been able to seize a crossing over the Rhine.[230] But whether he could have continued from there without a lengthy pause is doubtful.

In April 1941 the CIGS, Sir John Dill, wrote to one of his predecessors that

The efficiency of the Bosch (or is it Bosche?) takes some standing up to. I don't think the Bosche soldier is anything but good & on the whole rather ordinary, but he has the most up-to-date equipment & masses of it. If only we had his tools we could do so much more.[231]

After 1918 British doctrine sought to restore mobility to the battlefield by enhancing the army's ability to generate overwhelming fire-power. However, many of the weapons it eventually adopted sacrificed fire-power to mobility. British troops, therefore, possessed small arms that were in some respects inferior to those issued to the German army. As one British platoon commander remembered, 'it was my experience that German infantry and armour had far superior firepower to ours. Their

---

[229] Ellis and Warhurst, *Victory in the West*, ii, 17.

[230] PRO WO 205/998, Immediate Report no. 86, Some Q. problems in the advance of Second Army from Falaise to Brussels, 26 Aug.–3 Sept. 1944; Sir B. Horrocks with E. Belfield and Maj.-Gen. H. Essame, *Corps Commander* (London, 1977), 79–80; Ellis and Warhurst, *Victory in the West*, ii, 3.

[231] LHCMA Montgomery-Massingberd MSS 160/17, Dill to Montgomery-Massingberd, 15 Apr. 1941.

guns and mortars could produce a devastating display.'[232] The infantry, therefore, had to rely on the gunners because their own weapons were not good enough. The development of British tanks and anti-tank guns was the victim of political decisions taken about the strategic role of the army between the wars and the fact that proper development work had to be cut short after Dunkirk by the overwhelming need to get any weapons into the hands of the troops quickly. The same factors also contributed to the fact that it was not until late 1942 that adequate quantities of supplies and equipment finally reached formations in the field. Even after 1942 there were occasions when industry could not meet all of the army's demands and, in at least two crucial respects, the supply of tanks and motor transport, it would not have been able to meet them at all had it not been for supplies from North America.

The significance of the British army's willingness to commit so many men and resources to its logistical system can be highlighted if it is contrasted with German practice. The image of the German army of 1939 as a highly mobile motorized and mechanized force is misleading. Like the British, the Germans tried to rely upon rail communications to bring the bulk of their supplies forward. But, unlike the British, experience in Russia and North Africa was to demonstrate that at crucial moments they could not cut loose from the railways. In 1939 the German motor industry was incapable of meeting the army's needs, with the result that only sixteen of its 103 divisions were fully motorized. Although the remaining divisions each had over 900 vehicles, their troops marched on foot and their supplies were carried in horse-drawn carts. Each infantry division required between 4, 000 and 6,000 horses to pull the carts that transported its supplies from the railhead to the troops.[233]

Behind the propaganda myth, the Germans had produced a semi-modern army, well suited to fulfil the limited objectives of Bismarck and von Moltke, but lacking in the operational reach to fulfil Hitler's totalitarian objectives.[234] Since the eighteenth century the British army had become habituated to operating overseas far from its bases. Experience had taught it the penalties of neglecting its logistical preparations. In the Second World War, the Germans, by contrast, accorded far less effort to logistical preparations because they were habituated to fighting continental wars across short distances supported by good communications. British generals, and in particular Montgomery, have been frequently criticized because of their habit of waiting until their logistical arrange-

[232] Jary, *Eighteen Platoon*, 17.

[233] R. L. DiNardo and A. Bay, 'Horse Drawn Transport in the German Army', *Journal of Contemporary History*, 23 (1988), 129–42; M. van Creveld, *Supplying War. Logistics from Wallenstein to Patton* (Cambridge, 1977), 142–44.

[234] L. H. Aldington, *The Blitzkrieg Era and the German General Staff 1865–1941* (New Brunswick, NJ, 1971), p. xv.

ment were in perfect order before taking the offensive. German generals, and in particular Rommel, have conversely been accorded high praise for their willingness to take risks with their logistics. These criticisms fly in the face of all logic. The German system worked across the short distances involved in fighting in France and Poland and against enemies with an inferior operational doctrine, lacking sufficient air support and handicapped by serious strategic errors. But in Russia, North Africa, and finally in Normandy, the German effort foundered. This was in part because their reach exceeded their logistical grasp. Time and again in North Africa Rommel was able to achieve tactical successes, but lack of transport meant that he could not transform them into operational victories.[235] British offensives may have proceeded at a more stately pace and on occasions the logistical system, even in 1944–5, could not meet all demands placed upon it.[236] But after 1941 major British operations rarely failed because of breakdowns in logistics.

[235] Van Creveld, *Supplying War*, 142–201; Aldington, *The Blitzkrieg Era*, 159–76.
[236] Ellis and Warhurst, *Victory in the West*, ii, 134; PRO WO 204/7955, BGS XIII Corps to 8 Indian divn. and 6 AGRA, 18 Feb. 1944.

CHAPTER FOUR

Discipline and Morale

Senior officers during the war and historians subsequently have made too much of the apparently poor morale of the British army. The latter have sometimes been too willing to generalize about poor morale from an excessively narrow range of evidence, just as some of the former were apt to fix on supposedly poor morale as an excuse for their own failures.[1] With the abolition of the death penalty for most offences committed on active service in 1930, senior officers could no longer rely ultimately on coercion to ensure that their men fought and, if necessary, died. Few of the conscripts enlisted after 1939 had much relish for soldiering or fighting, and few were motivated by a highly developed ideological commitment to the political cause of eradicating Nazism. But lack of enthusiasm should not be confused with poor morale. The great majority of soldiers regarded the war as an unpleasant but necessary job that had to be completed so that they could then return to their everyday civilian lives. The stresses of battle did sometimes produce an incidence of psychiatric casualties and desertions that worried senior commanders. When Adam visited Italy in January 1945 he found many of them 'obsessed with [the] problem of desertion'.[2] But the British Army never even came close to experiencing the wide-scale refusal of its men to take the offensive that overcame the French Army in the spring of 1917. Morale was sustained by many factors. Basic training did succeed in indoctrinating soldiers with the idea that the army was a structured hierarchy that had a right to extract obedience from them. The military bureaucracy was usually able to meet most of their basic human needs for food, clothing, and shelter. The military hierarchy also went to considerable lengths to ensure that regimental officers recognized that ensuring this was one of their essential functions. The regimental system played a significant part in mediating between the ordinary soldier and the army as a whole by providing the former with a sense that he belonged to a caring community. Even so, wartime conscripts constructed the meaning of the regiment in a different way from

---

[1] French, '"Tommy is no soldier"', 155–7; D. French, 'Discipline and the Death Penalty in the British Army in the Second World War', *Journal of Contemporary History*, 33 (1998), 538–40.
[2] LHCMA Adam MSS ADAM 3/13, Report by the Adjutant-General on his tour overseas Jan.–Feb. 1945, 1 Mar. 1945.

regular officers. For the former what was important was that they knew and were respected by the men with whom they worked most closely. For many of them, abstractions like the reputation of their regiment were only a secondary concern. In action, primary group cohesion was a major factor in convincing troops to remain on the battlefield, by persuading the individual soldier that he was not facing mortal danger alone and by exploiting his masculine pride. When primary group cohesion crumbled because of heavy casualties, morale suffered accordingly. What the army did not succeed in doing was imbuing the great majority of its soldiers with ideological fervour and with the desire to close with their enemies and kill them at close quarters.

During the inter-war period regimental officers had a wide range of rewards and sanctions that they could use to command obedience. They controlled the promotion of all other ranks in their units up to the rank of RSM. NCOs were expected to avoid using 'harsh or intemperate language towards the men', but were themselves expected to command obedience and 'to lose no opportunity of enforcing discipline'.[3] Unit commanders could inflict summary punishments of a fine or up to 28 days' detention or field punishment. In the case of more serious offences, soldiers could be tried by a court martial which could inflict long prison terms or even the death penalty, although the latter sanction was seriously curtailed in 1930 when it was abolished for all offences on active service except mutiny and treachery.[4]

However, it would be wrong to conclude that soldiers obeyed simply because they were compelled to do so. The army also offered a range of tangible and less tangible rewards. The military hierarchy legitimized the subordination of the other ranks by creating a sense of corporate loyalty to the regimental system, and by striking a tacit bargain between officers and other ranks based upon reciprocal obligations. Since the early 1880s each regiment had, in theory, drawn its recruits from one particular part of the country. This allowed the army to exploit local and regional loyalties to sustain unit morale.[5] However, many regiments had to accept recruits from outside their own district. In 1923, for example, whereas the Cameron Highlanders contained 85 per cent of Scotsmen (making them the most 'Scottish' of all the Scottish regiments), the Highland Light Infantry contained only 54 per cent of Scotsmen, and the Welsh Regiment only 38 per cent of Welshmen.[6] 'County or clan spirit'

[3] Anon., *Standing Orders of the King's Royal Rifle Corps 1930* (Aldershot, 1930), 22.
[4] French, 'Discipline and the Death Penalty', 531–45.
[5] PRO WO 33/1488, Report of the Committee on the Cardwell System, Aug. 1937; J. Keegan, 'Regimental Ideology', in G. Best and A. Wheatcroft (eds.), *War, Economy and the Military Mind* (London, 1976), 11–15.
[6] IWM Maj.-Gen. D. N. Wimberley MSS, IMM PP/MCR/182, 'Scottish Soldier: The Memoirs of Major-General Douglas Wimberley', vol. 1; Jeffery, 'The Post-War Army', 218.

was, therefore, not ready-made and the army had to work hard to create it and to establish a cultural hegemony over its recruits.[7] They did so by emphasizing the overwhelming significance of the regiment in the life of the soldier. The process began the moment the recruit arrived at his unit. Every recruit underwent a period of basic training designed to transform civilians into soldiers by socializing them into a new community. On entering their depot, recruits were stripped of their civilian clothing, given a bath, issued with a uniform, an army number, and a bed in a barrack block. These changes were only an outward manifestation of the psychological transformation that they underwent. Every recruit was made to feel that he had become a member of a unique corporate body. Each could take a legitimate pride in it and must do nothing to bring disgrace upon it.[8] In 1932 the *Infantry Training* manual emphasized that

Strict and unvarying maintenance of infantry organization in all circumstances is the surest guarantee of espirit de corps. On and off parade the man should work and play as a member of his section, platoon, or company, and not as an individual. Competitions in work and games between units and sub-units stimulate pride in the unit and loyalty to it.[9]

Corporate pride was developed in the minds of each recruit by visits to regimental museums and lessons in regimental history, and was brought alive by regimental ceremonial parades.[10] The rank and file were given, often for the first time in their lives, a sense that they 'belonged to something of consequence'.[11]

Most regular recruits were from working-class backgrounds and their education and civilian lives had already prepared them for what the army expected of them. Elementary schools had taught them the need for obedience and punctuality. Men like A. R. Gaskin, who enlisted in the King's Shropshire Light Infantry in 1933, found that the new life did not come hard to him, as his father, a stoker in a gas works and a former soldier himself, had imposed strict discipline at home.[12] Better-educated recruits, like Tim Bishop, who enlisted in the Life Guards in 1934, found

[7] PRO WO 33/1488, Report of the Committee on the Cardwell System, Aug. 1937.

[8] Recruits in the 13/18 Hussars were taught that 'The past is the heritage which nothing can take from you, but the present and the future are in your hands, see that you are worthy of these great traditions.' 'J. P. R.', *A Short History of the 13th Hussars* (Aldershot, 1923), 63; *A Guards General*, ed. Lindsay, 56–7.

[9] General Staff, War Office, *Infantry Training, i. Training (1932)* (London, 1932), 12.

[10] Most regiments had their own brief regimental histories that they issued to recruits to 'enable them to realise the spirit of their forebears so that they may emulate their deeds when opportunity occurs'. See Brig. C. A. L. Graham, *The Story of the Royal Regiment of Artillery* (Woolwich, 1939), p. i.

[11] Mays, *Fall Out the Officers*, 24, 40–1, 63, 68; Maj. R. L. Sherbrooke, 'Regimental Depots', *Journal of the Royal United Services Institute*, 77 (1932), 574–5

[12] IWM A. R. Gaskin MSS, 87/44/1, 'The little bit of green or the light infantryman', TS memoirs; S. Sokoloff, 'Soldiers or Civilians? The Impact of Army Service in World War II on Birmingham Men', *Oral History*, 25 (1997), 63.

basic training a more unpleasant experience. But even he admitted that the system persuaded recruits to identify with their regiment by producing a deep sense of camaraderie.[13]

The army also created a nexus of reciprocal obligations between officers and other ranks. There was a wide social gulf between them, but across that gap there were clearly defined reciprocal responsibilities. Other ranks were expected to behave deferentially towards their officers and to exhibit 'a cheerful and unhesitating obedience to orders'.[14] In return officers were obliged to provide paternal leadership by ensuring that their men benefited from the army's bureaucracy and did not simply feel themselves to be its defenceless victims.[15] The goal of every commanding officer was to ensure a high standard of morale, discipline and leadership in the belief that in peacetime they would produce contented soldiers and in action they would at least delay, if not entirely prevent, the collapse of their troops' morale.[16] Provided both parties carried out their parts of this bargain, 'there was', in the opinion of one soldier who served in the ranks of a cavalry regiment in the 1920s 'friendship as well as discipline, and both were sure and certain'.[17]

The result was soldiers who were loyal, hierarchically minded and well disciplined. However, this system had two potentially serious weaknesses. It depended upon a sufficient supply of paternal officers and the willingness and ability of the military authorities to support the system by persisting with a manning and reinforcement policy that sustained the regimental system. This was easy enough in the inter-war period, but neither of these requirements could be met consistently after 1939. Following the outbreak of war and the progressive collapse of the regimental system, the psychological needs of the individual took second place to the bureaucratic demands of the larger army. Secondly, although the authorities' insistence on rigid obedience to superior orders was in conformity with its management doctrine, it was not well suited to the demands of the front line. British observers of the German army in the mid-1930s were struck not only by 'the comparative freedom of its discipline, its increased appeal to the spirit, and decrease of the punitive element', but also by the insistence that every private soldier had to exhibit leadership qualities.[18] The British regular army followed a different path, because it feared that if the rank and file were taught to exercise their intelligence and initiative they would question orders and

[13] Bishop, *One Young Soldier*, 6–7, 10–13.
[14] General Staff, WO, *Infantry Training, i. Training (1932)*, 11.
[15] Ibid. 21.
[16] Sheffield, 'Officer–Men Relations', *passim*; Bidwell, 'After the Wall came Tumbling Down', 59.
[17] Mays, *Fall Out the Officers*, 91–2.
[18] Liddell Hart, *Europe in Arms*, 64; Maj.-Gen. Sir K. Strong, *Intelligence at the Top: The Recollections of an Intelligence Offier* (London, 1968), 42–3.

break down under the stress of battle. In fact, the experience of war demonstrated that it was the least intelligent who were usually the first to break down and that the dispersion which was necessary on the battlefield required even the lowest ranks to exercise their intelligence and initiative.[19]

The rapid expansion of the army during the Second World War presented the military authorities with three fundamental problems. Many recruits were suspicious of the army, did not want to join it, and did not want to fight. Less than a quarter of all wartime recruits actually volunteered to join the army. Their fathers and uncles who had fought in the First World War had taught them the army would, by turns, exploit them, ignore their needs, and possibly needlessly sacrifice them.[20] Peter Cochrane remembered that 'As a schoolboy in the thirties I had absorbed the conventional wisdom that the regular army was officered by a coterie of elderly Blimps with a leaven of frivolous young men whose only occupations were riding or shooting.'[21] Compared to prewar recruits, wartime recruits were often older and brought with them a well-developed sense of their roles in civilian life in relation to family, friends, and occupation.[22] Following the establishment of the General Service Corps in July 1942, all recruits were asked about their eagerness to enter combat. Of 710,000 recruits, only 5 per cent fell into the top category ('Markedly suited by disposition and personality to a combatant role') and 3 per cent were categorized as having a poor combatant temperament.[23] The rest fell between these two extremes.

Many recruits brought little ideological commitment with them to the war when they enlisted. Although an ill-defined Germanophobia was commonplace in Britain before 1939, many of recruits had little idea of the causes for which they were fighting.[24] In early 1940, the CO of an Infantry Training Centre asked his recruits to answer three questions: with whom was Britain at war? Which countries were Britain's allies? Why was Britain at war? 'Some of the answers were rather astonishing and showed that the individuals concerned had few, if any, ideas on the subject.'[25] By 1942, little had altered. The COs of two Primary Training Centres thought that the great majority of their recruits 'lack enthusiasm and interest in the war and betray ignorance of the issues involved in it'.

[19] Janowitz and Little, *Sociology and the Military Establishment*, 57–9.
[20] Fraser, *And We Shall Shock Them*, 98.
[21] Cochrane, *Charlie Company*, 16.
[22] PRO WO 199/1649, Minutes of a conference held by GOC-in-C, Southern Command, 7 Aug. 1940.
[23] PRO WO 277/19. Ungerson, *Personnel Selection*, 48; PRO WO 32/11519, DMT to all GOC-in-Cs Home Commands and C-in-C Home Forces, 22 Apr. 1942.
[24] S. Dyson, *Tank Twins. East End Brothers in Arms 1943–45* (London, 1994), 132.
[25] General Staff, *ATM No. 31* (London, 1940).

Trained soldiers often showed a similar lack of interest in the progress of the war.[26]

The army's task during basic training was to impose a whole new set of occupational and personal relationships and roles on these men, to break down their resistance to fighting, and to inculcate them with some ideas about why they were being asked to fight. Wartime conscripts were put through the same basic training regime as pre-war regulars. They assumed their new status as soldiers when they were issued with their battledress uniform.[27] There then followed a period, usually lasting about three months, of drill, musketry, physical training, route marches, discipline, learning how to read a map, and taking part in elementary exercises. Len Waller's first month of recruit training at Chelsea barracks in early 1940 conformed to the stereotype of what basic training was supposed to be. It was designed to turn

sloppy civilians into soldiers. It wasn't done by kindness, either. Every day we were marched and yelled at up and down the barrack square. We were cursed, humiliated, degraded and worked until we were fit to drop. At the end of each day's training we were allowed to relax by sitting astride our beds polishing and burnishing a bewildering array of equipment.[28]

Richard Whitefield had a similar experience when he joined 39th Signals Training Regiment, RA, at Scarborough in December 1939.

We spent four weeks in A Battery, chased from pillar to post by the sergeant and bombardier in charge of the squad. One of their objects seemed to be to make us forget that we had ever been civilians and turn us into automatons ready to obey without question and to a certain degree they succeeded.[29]

Most recruits found basic training physically demanding, but after a few weeks began to enjoy a new sense of physical well being as well as becoming bonded to their comrades through their shared hardships.[30] But the extent to which the army succeeded in persuading recruits to shed their civilian personae and to identify with the army is questionable. The bonding that basic training was intended to create between a recruit and his regiment did not always extend much beyond the platoon or company. Norman Craig believed that the hardships of basic training quickly created strong bonds of comradeship between the men who shared his barrack hut but that 'Outside this little self-protective union of friends was the jungle, the anarchy, the sauve qui peut of selfish indi-

[26] PRO WO 163/52/AC/G(43)10, WO Committee on Morale in the Army, Fourth Quarterly Report, Nov. 1942–Jan. 1943, 7 Apr. 1943.

[27] IWM H. T. Bone MSS 87/31/1, Diary entry, Jan. 1940.

[28] IWM Len Waller MSS 87/42/1, 'How did we ever win?', TS memoirs.

[29] R. Whitefield, The Eyes and Ears of the Regiment. 67th Field Regiment RA, 1939–1946 (Upton on Severn, Worcs, 1995), 2.

[30] P. Hennessey, Young Man in a Tank (Camberley, 1995), 12.

vidualism where the instinct for survival was epitomised in the immortal army principle, "Fuck you Jack, I'm all right." '[31]

Such feelings manifested themselves in everyday occurrences like incidences of petty theft and the near-universal tendency of units on active service to hoard scarce items of equipment for their own benefit, but to the detriment of the army as a whole.[32] In September 1942 a survey of letters written by soldiers suggested that

the ordinary soldier does not fully identify himself with the Army; he looks with detachment upon it and those who control it, and thinks of those in authority, whether political or military, as his governors rather than as his leaders. The morale and fighting spirit of the Army as a whole would be enhanced if the ordinary soldier could be reassured that differentiation due to social tradition and the subordination involved in military discipline do not imply a fundamental conflict of interests.[33]

There was, according to a War Office report of December 1942, 'a regrettable tendency to think of officers, "the authorities", and "the Army" as an impersonal "They"—a body of a different caste, a large part of whose function consists in badgering the soldier about, for reasons which he does not understand.'[34] One reason for this disenchantment was because the army's disciplinary code continued to punish even the smallest infringement. Ronald Gladman discovered that 'Thirteen metal studs must always be fixed in each boot; just one missing could result in a charge and possibly confined to camp and fatigues'.[35]

This was not inevitable. The social distance between officers and other ranks in most Territorial units before 1939 was rarely as wide as it was amongst the regulars. Relations between officers and men had rested upon a more informal basis. In the North Somerset Yeomanry, many of the senior NCOs were successful businessmen who 'Between them . . . could have bought out the impecunious squirearchy, from which the officers were mainly recruited, without feeling it'.[36] In 1934 Major-General R. J. T. Hildyard, GOC of 43rd (Wessex) Territorial Division explained that

[31] Craig, *Broken Plume*, 18.

[32] Hillier, *The Long Road to Victory*, 31; PRO WO 163/161/MC/M(43)8, Material for Army Bureau of Current Affairs Articles, Broadcast: ATM and ACI to deal with scrounging by units, 27 Aug. 1943.

[33] PRO WO 163/51/AC/G(42)32, War Office Committee on Morale in the Army, Second Quarterly Report, May–July 1942.

[34] PRO WO 163/51/AC/G(42)41. War Office Committee on Morale in the Army. Third Quarterly Report, Aug.–Oct. 1942, 28 Dec. 1942.

[35] IWM 92/1/1, R. Gladman MSS, TS memoirs, 8.

[36] J. Verney, *Going to the Wars. A Journey in Various Directions* (London, 1957), 30; Sheffield, 'Officer–Men Relations', 333; PRO WO 279/70, Report on the Staff Conference held at the Staff College Camberley, 13–16 Jan. 1930, Comments by Maj.-Gen. C. P. Deedes.

The peace time discipline, though based on different sanctions to those of the Regular Army, is of a very high standard, and a competent and tactful officer invariably commands the unquestioning obedience and loyalty of his men. It is a discipline of camaraderie, which is the opposite of rigid discipline.[37]

Some Territorial units carried this kind of discipline with them to France in 1940.[38] But it became much less prevalent following the Army Council's decision in March 1940 to begin to replace Territorial commanders with regulars.[39] The latter introduced a much higher standard of unit administration, but also a much more rigid disciplinary code. The rank and file of the wartime army were no more encouraged to use their initiative than were the pre-war regulars. The lesson that recruits learnt was not to think about orders, but to obey them.[40] After joining the Royal Artillery in 1943 James Sims thought that 'If you had any spirit at all the RA seemed determined to break it. Their attitude has been summed up as follows: If it moves—salute it! If it stands still— blanco it! If it is too heavy to lift—paint it!'[41] The tactical consequences were that the army produced rank-and-file soldiers who were good followers, but poor leaders. As Peter Carrington, a young Guards officer, later wrote, 'Where manoeuvre is required, so is speed and imagination and initiative. I never thought that our system was perfect for breeding those qualities. Individuals possessed them—splendidly. But the system itself was differently designed.'[42]

The army's ideal was exemplified by a training pamphlet issued in January 1944 which insisted that 'The battalion commander must be able to control his battalion as a conductor controls his orchestra, bringing one part or another into play to give a harmonious effect to the whole.'[43] But he was to be the leader of a disciplined classical orchestra, not that of a jazz band that welcomed improvisation. Good leadership at the regimental level was, therefore, all-important. 'Our success', one divisional commander concluded, 'depends entirely upon good leadership by off[ice]rs and NCOs. If they become casualties the remainder do not know what to do in many instances . . .'.[44] And as most battalions, after a short time in action, could probably only muster twenty of their complement of thirty-six officers, men frequently were left leaderless on

[37] PRO WO279/75, Report on the Staff Conference, Comment by Maj.-Gen. Hildyard.
[38] Holding, *Since I Bore Arms*, 19.
[39] PRO WO 163/49/ACM(OF)16, Minutes of the Proceedings of the Army Council, 29 Mar. 1940.
[40] Hennessey, *Young Man in a Tank*, 12.
[41] J. Sims, *Arnhem Spearhead. A Private Soldier's Story* (London, 1978), 1.
[42] Carrington, *Reflect on Things Past*, 39.
[43] General Staff, *Infantry Training. Part 1. The Infantry Battalion (1944)* (London, 1944), 31.
[44] PRO WO 231/10, Maj.-Gen. Freeman-Attwood, Lessons from Operations in the North African Campaign, 46 Divn., 30 May 1943.

the battlefield.[45] The army, provided with an influx of recruits of much higher quality than they had received between the wars, wasted this potential asset by its stubborn adherence to its pre-war disciplinary regime.

In 1941–2 the army in Britain did experience a real crisis of morale. However, this did not mean that the fears entertained by senior officers before the war that the morale of wartime conscripts would crumble were justified or about to come true. Confidence in victory remained high. The crisis was focused on the army itself and 'the whole of the "existing system" '.[46] Many soldiers felt that they were powerless cogs in a vast, impersonal bureaucratic machine. They saw little meaning in their daily activities, which appeared to be far removed from fighting Hitler. 'Bull', petty punishments for minor infringements of regulations, and endless fatigues, concluded Tom Harrison, 'set in motion that mixture of cynicism and subterranean anger which makes for becoming "browned off".'[47] Morale was strained by news of the seemingly endless series of defeats which the army was suffering abroad, defeats which helped to undermine the troops' confidence in themselves, their leaders, and the quality of their training. At heart they remained civilians who had been called upon to complete a dangerous and arduous job and who were determined to return to civilian life just as soon as they had done so.[48]

Administrative shortcomings, such as low pay and inadequate leave, together with the strains of being separated from family and friends and press criticism of the army and its leadership, compounded the problem and created a worrying incidence of men going AWOL or deserting.[49] Most deserters had been law-abiding citizens before they enlisted and it was the demands placed upon them by the army that transformed them into criminals.[50] They retained family responsibilities and sometimes officers failed to fulfil their paternal responsibilities by granting compassionate leave to men with serious family problems. This pointed to a wider failure of the army in the early years of the war. There were many good regimental officers; men like Captain Pennock of the 8th Middlesex, 'an excellent officer, down to earth with a good sense of

---

[45] PRO WO 231/14, Lieut.-Col. T. N. Grazebrook, Memorandum, 4 Jan. 1944.

[46] PRO WO 259/62, Morale Report—Feb. 1942; PRO WO 163/51/AC/G(42)20, Adjutant-General, Morale Committee, Report, Feb.–May 1942, 12 June 1942.

[47] Harrison, 'The British Soldier', 35; J. M. Lee Harvey, D-Day Dodger (London, 1979), 20–1.

[48] Sokoloff, 'Soldiers or Civilians?', 59.

[49] PRO WO 277/7, McPherson, Discipline , 21–2; R. H. Ahrenfeldt, Psychiatry in the British Army in the Second World War (London, 1958), 273.

[50] PRO WO 277/7, McPherson, Discipline, 49–50.

humour'.[51] Officers like Pennock earned the respect of their men. They knew their own jobs, they shared the discomforts of their men, they sheltered them from the more unreasonable demands placed upon them by higher authority, they took a personal interest in their problems, and they took them into their confidence as far as possible by explaining to them the reasons for troublesome orders and apparently needless restrictions on their liberties.[52] But the wartime army found it difficult to infuse its temporary officers with the same paternal ethos as the regulars usually possessed. There were growing complaints about the suitability of men chosen for commissions and their lack of man-management skills. Some regular officers thought this was the inevitable consequence of abandoning the pre-war practice of recruiting from the traditional officer-producing classes.[53] However, as the problem existed in the Brigade of Guards, that still recruited its officers from that source, that explanation is defective.[54] The real reason was that the army's burgeoning demand for junior officers meant that the latter received no more than the most rudimentary training at OCTU before being commissioned.

In 1939 an aspiring infantry subaltern spent four months at OCTU but in November 1940, the course was reduced by a month.[55] Persistent and noisy public criticisms of the military authorities against a background of defeat in the first half of 1942, compelled the War Office to act. Some of their measures, such as the introduction of more realistic training, 'scientific' personnel selection, and the WOSB system of officer selection, have already been examined. Others included improved pay and leave arrangements for men in Britain.[56] The establishment of the Army Catering Corps in March 1941 did something to improve the quality of food served in army messes, and by mid-1943 most troops in the UK were content with their rations.[57] Pay remained a source of discontent, but otherwise the troops gave these reforms a positive welcome.[58]

But the most significant individual measure was that gradually the

---

[51] IWM Codling MSS 88/4/1, E. A. Codling untitled TS, 14.

[52] PRO WO 193/981, 'The Army in Winter', 1941.

[53] PRO WO 163/52/AC/G(43)27, WO Committee on Morale in the Army, May–July 1943.

[54] PRO WO 163/52/AC/G(43)10, WO Committee on Morale in the Army, Fourth Quarterly Report, Nov. 1942–Jan. 1943, 7 Apr. 1943.

[55] PRO WO 163/85/ECAC/P(41)87, Adjutant-General, Supply of officers and OCTU candidates, 20 Oct. 1941.

[56] PRO WO 277/16, Sparrow, *Morale*, 6; PRO WO 163/AC/G(42)53, War Office Progress Report, Feb 1942, 16 Mar. 1942.

[57] PRO WO 163/52/AC/G(43)27, WO Committee on Morale in the Army, May–July 1943.

[58] PRO WO 163/51/AC/G(42)20, Adjutant-General, Morale Committee, Report, Feb.–May 1942, 12 June 1942; PRO WO 163/51/AC/G(42)41, WO Committee on Morale in the Army, Second Quarterly Report, Aug.–Oct. 1942; PRO WO 163/52/AC/G(43)10, WO Committee on Morale in the Army, Fourth Quarterly Report, Nov. 1942–Jan. 1943, 7 Apr. 1943.

wartime officer corps learnt their jobs and their standards of man-management improved. The passage of time meant that the poorly trained teenage second lieutenants of 1939–40 had become mature captains of twenty-three or twenty-four by 1944, who had learnt the skills of man-management by dint of constant practice.[59] By 1942 psychiatrists were lecturing to OCTU cadets and regimental officers on man-management and the crucial role they had to play to maintain morale.[60] In November 1942 the Army Council ordered units to establish a 'Request hour' and all officers were enjoined to take special care to help men with domestic problems. This was followed in the next quarter by a gratifying drop in the rate of men going AWOL.[61] By mid-1943 the army at home had surmounted its morale crisis.[62] Many commanders at home believed that 'the Army is "on the map" and knows it' and that morale had not been higher since 1939.[63] However, these improvements were not uniform across the army. Officer–other rank relations tended to be best in the teeth arms, and in units on active service, because officers had perforce very often to share the physical hardships of their men. They were worst in static support units, where they could more easily avoid doing so.[64] As late as December 1943, a private in the Black Watch believed that 'There is certainly an outward show of cohesion in the average army unit, but in some respects this is superficial, liable to be affected by the strain of battle or the insidious and disintegrating influence of the defeatist'.[65] Furthermore the military authorities failed to break down entirely the sense of alienation between the army and many ordinary soldiers. In January 1944, the Army Council received a report that many soldiers felt 'an attitude of antagonism to an impersonal "they", variously identified with the "War Office", "the authorities" and (by the rank and file) with "the officers" or even "the Army" generally, which militates against solidarity, co-operation and espirit de corps in the Army as a whole.'[66]

[59] Maj. Robert Kiln, *D.-Day to Arnhem with Hertfordshire's Gunners* (Welwyn, 1993), 15.

[60] PRO CAB 98/29, War Cabinet, Ministerial Committee on the work of psychologists, 31 Jan. 1945.

[61] PRO WO 163/51/AC/G(42)41, WO Committee on Morale in the Army, Second Quarterly Report, Aug.–Oct. 1942; PRO WO 163/52/AC/G(43)10, WO Committee on Morale in the Army, Fourth Quarterly Report, Nov. 1942–Jan. 1943, 7 Apr. 1943.

[62] PRO WO 163/52/AC/G(43)17, WO Committee on Morale in the Army, Fifth Quarterly Report, Feb.–Apr. 1943.

[63] PRO WO 163/52/AC/G(43)27, WO Committee on Morale in the Army, May–July 1943.

[64] PRO WO 163/161/MC/M(43)1, Minutes of the Morale Committee of the Executive Committee of the Army Council, 15 Jan. 1943; PRO WO 163/52/AC/G(43)27, WO Committee on Morale in the Army, May–July 1943.

[65] PRO WO 163/161/MC/P(43)1, Essay on morale in the army by a private in the Black Watch, Dec. 1943.

[66] PRO WO 163/53/AC/G(44)4, WO Committee on Morale in the Army, Seventh Annual Report, Aug.–Oct. 1943, 11 Jan. 1944.

Nor was the army any more successful at indoctrinating its soldiers with an understanding of the issues at stake in the war. Indoctrination smacked too much of politics, and *King's Regulations* forbade serving soldiers from taking part in any political activities.[67] Furthermore, the army had to take its lead from the government. The latter propagated the idea that the war was a conflict between two groups. One was composed of decent, peace-loving, and democratic Britons committed to defending their way of life based upon equality, democracy, justice, and the rule of law.[68] The other consisted of a German state in which democracy was dead, that had twice tried to secure world domination in the space of a generation, and was inhabited by people portrayed as Vandals, Goths, and Huns.[69] But portraying the whole German nation as innately aggressive echoed too closely the coarse propaganda of the First World War. It had only a limited appeal because 'Reared on the cynicism following the First World War we would not allow ourselves any patriotic fervour', as one soldier wrote.[70] Asked by Gallup in January 1942 how the Germans should be treated after the war, 41 per cent of respondents wanted to prevent Germany from ever making war again, 18 per cent wanted to shoot the Nazis but to leave the rest of the German people in peace, 16 per cent wanted to punish the German people but not extract vengeance, and 7 per cent wanted to 'invite the Germans to our democratic world.' Only 11 per cent wanted to exterminate them.[71]

It was only in 1941 that the War Office belatedly realized that the morale of the German soldier was based to a large extent upon 'a set of convictions that have been seared into his mind by unscrupulous and skilful propaganda'. Unit commanders were now instructed to lecture their men about the issues for which they were fighting.[72] But after listening to such lectures, one soldier concluded that 'Getting the English worked up enough to defend democracy was an uphill task, as the average soldier appeared to have only three basic interests: football, beer and crumpet'.[73] Many soldiers, in default of more effective official guidance, had great difficulty in explaining why they were at war. Those who came from a working-class background had been inculcated with a

[67] War Office, *King's Regulations 1928* (London, 1928), 166.
[68] D. Morgan and M. Evans, *The Battle for Britain. Citizenship and Ideology in the Second World War* (London, 1993), 5, 18–23; I. McLaine, *Ministry of Morale. Home Front Morale and the Ministry of Information in World War II* (London, 1979), 150–2.
[69] A. Osley, *Persuading the People. Government Publicity in the Second World War* (London, 1995), 19–22.
[70] Roach, *The 8.15 to War*, 57.
[71] *Gallup International Public Opinion Polls*, ed. Gallup, i, 53.
[72] General Staff, *ATM No. 38* (London, 1941); Mackenzie, *Politics and Military Morale*, 91–3.
[73] Sims, *Arnhem Spearhead*, 22.

fatalistic attitude which was summed up by one soldier who wrote of the '"Well we are all in this together for the duration, so let's make the best of it" attitude'.[74] Winning the war was an unpleasant task they had to fulfil. Returning home to his family and familiar surroundings was the most important war aim of nearly every soldier.[75]

The military authorities did try hard to dehumanize German soldiers, and thus make it easier for their own men to kill them, but again they had only limited success. The Germans were portrayed as being courageous, professional, and disciplined, but infused with a docility that made them too ready to swallow the lies of Nazi propagandists and ignore the laws of war.[76] During basic training the army attempted to diffuse the taboos against killing German soldiers by telling recruits that unless they killed Germans, they would be killed by them.[77] During bayonet training 'What is aimed at in the instruction is "blood, hate, fire and brimstone". It is "guts and gristle" instruction, with nothing peacetime or "pansy" about it.'[78]

Some soldiers did internalize these ideas. But, for many of them, the ideas that they took into the front line were little more than a faint echo of official propaganda. An officer who served with 3rd Division in North West Europe believed that

The division was not fighting for some ideal, some hare-brained theory of racial supremacy, such as can inspire German divisions. The British are better at practice than theory, and the division fought well for no better reason than that the Germans had finally to be defeated at their own game of war: the alternative was to acknowledge them masters of Europe, if not of the world.[79]

The army thus sent men into battle who had been trained to place obedience before the intelligent use of their own initiative. They had little innate relish for fighting, they often felt little identification with 'the army' as an institution, they had only hazy notions of the causes for which they were fighting, and they had not been primed to kill because they believed that their enemies were sub-humans fit only for extermination. Given these disadvantages it was surprising that they fought as well as they did.

[74] IWM 89/13/1, G. H. C. Abrams, MSS, 'A Male Nurse in War and Peace', TS memoirs; McKibbin, *Classes and Culture*, 131.
[75] Roach, *The 8.15 to War*, 26–7; PRO WO 163/53/AC/G(44)22, WO Committee on Morale, Eighth Quarterly Report, Nov. 1943–Jan. 1944.
[76] General Staff, *ATM No. 41* (London, 1941); Army Bureau of Current Affairs, *War. No. 29. The British Soldier* (London, 1942); ABCA, *War no. 50. Mediterranean Journey* (London, 1943).
[77] General Staff, *ATM No. 35* (London, 1940).
[78] Ibid.
[79] N. Scarfe, *Assault Division. A History of the 3rd Division from the Invasion of Normandy to the Surrender of Germany* (London, 1947), 18.

Front-line troops inhabited a world characterized by lethal uncertainty. They confronted deafening noise, danger, and discomfort. They were isolated from their families and familiar civilian surroundings. They had little understanding of what was happening around them. One private recalled that at Alamein

Everyone was shouting, screaming, swearing, shouting for their father, shouting for their mother, I didn't know whether to look at the ground or at the sky, someone said look at the ground for the spider-mines, someone said look at the sky for the flashes, shells were coming all ways, the man next to me got hit through the shoulder, he fell down, I looked at him and said Christ and then ran on, I didn't know whether to be sick or dirty my trousers.[80]

Weapons did not only kill people; they also inflicted psychological harm.[81] In the early years of the war, Stuka dive-bombers were particularly loathed because there was nothing the individual soldier could do to combat them except cower in a slit trench.[82] In North Africa the morale of infantry units was repeatedly eroded in 1941–2 because they lacked their own anti-tank weapons which were effective against German tanks, a problem only solved in 1943 when each battalion was issued with half a dozen 6-pdr. anti-tank guns. The Germans' dual purpose 88-mm. anti-tank/anti-aircraft gun was especially disliked because its high muzzle velocity meant that troops had little warning before the shell arrived.[83] Armoured units in North Africa in 1941–2 and in North West Europe in 1944–5 were depressed by the apparent ease with which their own tanks could be 'brewed-up' by German tanks and anti-tank guns. They lived in constant fear of being burnt to death in their tanks.[84] Throughout the war the British were intimidated by the rapid rate of fire of German light machine-guns and the unpredictable lethality of their mortars.[85]

Most soldiers found battle to be the most traumatic experience of their lives. Confronted by multiple threats to their survival, they faced a series of choices. They could flee. In theory the military authorities could employ force to make men stay and fight and there were some instances

[80] N. McCallum, *Journey with a Pistol* (London, 1959), 50.

[81] PRO WO 222/124, The moral effect of weapons, Investigations into reactions of a group of 300 wounded men in North Africa, 1943.

[82] Holding, *Since I Bore Arms*, 129.

[83] R. M. Wingfield, *The Only Way Out. An Infantryman's Autobiography of the North-West European Campaign August 1944–February 1945* (London, 1955), 27.

[84] PRO WO 236/1, Erskine to Latham, 8 Oct. 1949; PRO WO 291/1299, Operational Research Memorandum no. 4, Report on Tour of Armoured Formations in North Africa, Apr.–June 1943.

[85] Holding, *Since I Bore Arms*, 74; PRO WO 163/183, Visit by Lieut.-Col. H. A. Livstock to operations area, Western Desert, 4–28 June 1942, 3 Aug. 1942; PRO WO 291/1331, Operational Research in North West Europe, Report no. 11, The Location of Enemy Mortars; F. A. E. Crew, *The Army Medical Services: Campaigns* (London, 1956), ii, 510; PRO WO 201/527, Extracts from the Report of a War Office Observer in North Africa, May 1943.

of officers threatening their own men with their revolvers.[86] Many regular officers believed there was a close link between the incidence of psychiatric casualties, a unit's morale, and discipline and leadership. This view had been strongly endorsed by the Report of the War Office Committee on Enquiry into Shell Shock, which was published in 1922. However, beyond trying to maintain the regimental system and the ethos of paternal officership, the inter-war army did little to establish prophylactic measures against future incidences of 'shell-shock'. Senior officers like Lord Horne, who had commanded 1st Army on the Western Front, dismissed it as the product of the static nature and intense bombardments of the Western Front and were confident that it would not recur in the mobile warfare of the future.[87] By 1942 the military authorities realized that this was over-optimistic. Soldiers needed specific training to help them overcome their fears, and some men were incapable of doing so and ought not to be sent to the front line. From 1942 the army employed psychologists to weed out men who they believed were mentally unfit for combat. They taught soldiers that feeling afraid was normal and that, even though men felt fear, they could overcome it.[88] Through Battle School drills they also tried to reduce the disruptive impact of fear by exposing men to simulated battle conditions.

The willingness of soldiers to continue serving in the front line varied between individuals and within the same man over time. But at some point the morale of most front-line soldiers was likely to be eroded by the traumatic events they experienced on the battlefield. The vulnerability and coping capacity of individual soldiers varied according to the acuteness and persistence of such traumatic events, and the individual's degree of exposure to them. Unfit, poorly trained troops who were physically exhausted, badly led, and poorly supplied with ammunition and food were more likely to succumb than well-trained, well-led, fit, well-supplied troops who had been rested.[89] R. M. Wingfield, who fought as an infantryman in North West Europe in 1944, believed that 'no normal man is not scared by the thought of action. Any man who won't admit that he's scared is either a liar or a B[loody] F[ool].'[90] Before 1914, the dominant image of manhood was that real men were strong, determined, heroic, honest, and could control their fears. The First World War did little to undermine these beliefs amongst soldiers who

---

[86] Whitefield, *The Eyes and Ears of the Regiment*, 48–9; Whitehouse and Bennett, *Fear is the Foe*, 153; Bowman, *Three Stripes and a Gun*, 79–80.

[87] *Report of the War Office Committee on Enquiry into 'Shell-Shock'*.

[88] LHCMA Adam MSS, ADAM 3/4/6. Adam to Corps, District, Divn. and Area Commanders, Dec. 1943.

[89] Lieut.-Col. I. Palmer, 'Battle Stress and its Treatment', *Journal of the Royal United Services Institute*, 143, (1998), 65–6.   [90] Wingfield, *The Only Way Out*, 45.

were brought up in the 1910s and 1920s. Their greatest fear was that they would be unable to control their fears.[91] Their ingrained sense of masculine self-respect made them fight 'because we were afraid to show that we were afraid'.[92]

However, familiarity with the imminent prospect of death did not breed contempt. After two months of fighting in Normandy, Steven Dyson thought that he and his comrades 'still felt the usual collywobbles before the off'.[93] After a few weeks in the line soldiers acquired useful skills which aided their survival. Men going into battle for the first time were usually most disconcerted and frightened by the noise.[94] Lieutenant E. Jones, who landed in France on D-Day, thought that by mid-July 'You got very expert on enemy gun-fire. You would almost sub-consciously note the thud of the discharge and gauge the flight of the shell in order to decide whether to dive for cover or not.'[95] Some men also began to experience a sense of exhilaration that they had con-fronted the threat of death and had overcome their fears. Many, how-ever, began to develop a fatalistic attitude towards the loss of comrades and friends and their own chances of survival.[96] Most men found that, after serving in the front line for anything between several weeks and about six months, and seeing their friends killed or wounded, their own nerves began to become frayed.[97] Physical exhaustion, brought about by heavy manual labour, lack of sleep, inadequate washing facilities, and poor or inadequate food, also contributed to the sapping of their psychological resilience.[98] After seven months in action in Sicily and Italy, J. M. Lee Harvey discovered that

I had learnt to be a fatalist and to accept the fact that if a bullet or a shell had my number on, then there was nothing that could be done about it. I had become numb to the real sense of danger and supposed that this was due to all the lucky breaks I had experienced since coming abroad.[99]

Near misses from shells or mortar bombs were liable to leave men temporarily deaf and stunned. In September 1944 1st/6th Queens were subjected to a heavy bombardment, and, although no one was hurt, the

[91] A. Bowlby, *Recollections of Rifleman Bowlby*, 20; Hillier, *The Long Road to Victory*, 91; Roy Cawston, *Before I Forget. Some Recollections of a Sharpshooter 1939–1945* (Bristol, 1993), 45.

[92] P. Ross, *All Valiant Dust. An Irishman Abroad* (Dublin, 1992), 76; Craig, *Broken Plume*, 75.   [93] Dyson, *Tank Twins*, 88.

[94] Cochrane, *Charlie Company*, 22.

[95] IWM 94/4/1, Lieut.-Col. E. Jones, TS memoirs.

[96] IWM E. P. Danger MSS 82/37/1, 'Diary of a Guardsman', TS memoirs, i; McCallum, *Journey with a Pistol*, 68–9.

[97] M. Lindsay, *So Few Got Through* (London, 1946), 216; Whitehouse and Bennett, *Fear is the Foe*, 125–6; Hamerton, *Achtung Minen*, 172–3.

[98] IWM Eric A. Codling MSS 88/4/1, TS memoirs, 43.

[99] Harvey, *D-Day Dodger*, 106–7.

psychological damage was so great that in the opinion of one member of the battalion 'A counter-attack within the next hour would have been a complete success'.[100] Front-line soldiers discovered that being forced to remain inactive and cowering in their slit trenches, unable to retaliate when they were shelled, was especially demoralizing, particularly if they were alone.[101] Watchful officers tried to prolong the militarily useful careers of men who had been in combat for several months by giving them short breaks out of the front line where, for two or three days, they could feel safe, wash, sleep, and eat their fill. But on returning to the front they confronted the same stresses. A breakdown was usually finally precipitated by some overwhelmingly traumatic event. An anti-aircraft gunner stationed at Manston aerodrome for several weeks in August 1940 was finally reduced to a state of nervous collapse by a bomb falling nearby. 'After the explosion of that bomb I seemed to lose complete control of myself. The explosion seemed to do something. I felt dizzy and lost control.'[102]

Officially, the army labelled men who had reached their own psychological breaking point as suffering from 'battle exhaustion'. Their comrades called them 'bomb happy'.[103] Such men reacted in one of two ways. They either absented themselves from the battlefield or suffered a nervous collapse. On five occasions during the war, in North Africa in the summer of 1942, in the Italian mountains during the winters of 1943–4 and 1944–5, in the Anzio beachhead in early 1944, and in Normandy in the summer of 1944, the rate of desertion and psychiatric collapse was such that senior commanders began to worry that their pre-war fears that the morale of their troops would be too fragile to sustain combat might be about to come true. They reacted by demanding the reintroduction of the death penalty in the hope that it would discourage the many from following the example of the few.[104] In fact, however, their concerns proved to be unjustified. The British army never experienced a widespread and paralysing refusal of its men to fight.

Desertion was the most common way in which men deliberately absented themselves from the battlefield, but it was not the only response. Others chose self-inflicted wounds, attempted suicide, neglected to take proper anti-malarial precautions, or courted a 'blighty' wound by holding their arms above their slit trenches when they were being bombarded.[105] Nervous collapse could be infectious. A private in

[100] Wingfield, *The Only Way Out*, 63; Holding, *Since I Bore Arms*, 80–2.
[101] PRO WO 71/700, Proceedings of the Field General Court Martial of Gnr. Z, RHA, Jan. 1941.
[102] PRO WO 71/1043, Proceedings of a General Court Martial of Bdr Y, 11 Sept. 1940.
[103] D. Houldsworth, *'One Day I'll Tell You'* (Marlborough, Wilts, 1994), 5.
[104] French, ' "Tommy is no soldier" ', *passim*; French, 'Discipline and the Death Penalty', *passim*.
[105] Dyson, *Tank Twins*, 65, 67; IWM Eric A. Codling MSS88/4/1, TS memoirs, 51–2;

7th Rifle Brigade in Normandy himself broke down in July 1944 because a man in a nearby slit trench 'was showing signs of panic, crying out and saying he could not stand it'.[106] The nature of the battlefield, with its requirement that men fight dispersed in small groups and often at night, made it comparatively easy for men to avoid combat if they wished.[107] In the opinion of one infantry officer in Normandy, 'People get lost all over the place in battle, some deliberately, most quite by accident.'[108] In September 1942 Douglas Tobler met a small group of men in the desert

who for their own reasons had deserted their units or perhaps made no effort to get back to their own lines after getting lost during an engagement with the enemy. Glad to be out of the fighting, they were content to live by their wits knowing it was unlikely anyone would check on their credentials.[109]

The treatment of men who left the battlefield without permission or who refused to fight varied between units. Some battalion officers accepted that all men had only a limited stock of courage and that while most men could endure a certain amount of exposure to the dangers of the battlefield, all of them would eventually break down if they were not first killed or wounded.[110] Others were convinced that the personnel selection system had failed in that too many men who were mentally unfit for front-line service had, none the less, been drafted into the infantry. They were, therefore, predisposed to treat men who refused to fight as medical casualties or to find them employment away from the front line.[111] Deserters who were well known to their officers, who had fought in several engagements, and who had a reputation for honestly trying, had more chance than men who were newcomers to a unit and who broke down in their first action, of escaping with a light punishment or of being treated as psychological casualties. An Irish Fusilier who was arraigned before his colonel on a charge of desertion in Italy in late 1943, escaped scot-free when he reminded him that they had been

Whitefield, *The Eyes and Ears of the Regiment*, 86–7; Whitehouse and Bennett, *Fear is the Foe*, 155.

[106] PRO WO 71/925, Proceedings of a Field General Court Martial of Rfn. C, 23 Oct. 1944.

[107] IWM R. Gladman MSS 92/1/1, TS memoirs, 15; Crimp, *The Diary of a Desert Rat*, 58–9.

[108] IWM Lieut. H. T. Bone MSS 87/31/1, Bone to his mother, 4 July 1944. See also PRO WO 231/16, 152nd Infantry Brigade, Discussion of Lessons learned during the year of fighting from Alamein to Messina, 6 Nov. 1943; PRO WO 231/14. Lieut.-Col. T. N. Grazebrook, Memorandum, 4 Jan. 1944.

[109] D. H. Tobler, *Intelligence in the Desert. The Recollections and Reflections of a Brigade Intelligence Officer* (Victoria, BC, 1978), 45.

[110] IWM Lieut.-Col. A. T. A. Browne MSS 86/4/1, 'Destiny. A Portrait of a Man in Two World Wars', TS memoirs; Jary, *Eighteen Platoon*, 110; Bowlby, *Recollections of Rifleman Bowlby*, 128.

[111] A. M. Cheetham, *Ubique* (London, 1987), 139.

with the battalion in a recent battle when it had been decimated and had promised himself, ' "Mac, if I ever gets out of this, I'm going on the piss. And, Sir, *I've been*!" '[112] Before 1939, army doctors had been instructed that, if the flow of physically wounded men was not too great, divisional medical officers might use one of their field ambulances to form a divisional rest station. Here, men suffering from minor and unspecified disabilities could be sent for a few days. 'They fulfil a useful purpose, as the soldier while freed from the strain and exposure of fighting remains under divisional control.'[113] The first formations to develop forward psychiatric services were 9th Australian division in Tobruk in 1941 and 2nd New Zealand division in North Africa in the summer of 1942. Treatment, which took place in front-line casualty clearing stations, consisted of administering sedatives to ensure that the patient received adequate sleep, followed by a brief discussion during which he was encouraged to talk about his fears with a doctor. Doctors claimed to be able to return between 30 to 40 per cent of patients to their units. This provided a model treatment regime for British formations, but they were much slower to adopt it.[114] It was not until August 1942 that 8th Army established its first centre where troops suffering from battle exhaustion could be sent for a short period to recuperate.[115] In April 1943, the War Office issued a circular to all medical officers identifying the problem and recommending treatment as far forward as possible at a rest station or casualty clearing station. They hoped that such measures would enable casualties to return to duty in a few days.[116] A comprehensive forward psychiatric service was established in 21 Army Group prior to D-Day and it functioned throughout the North West European campaign. However, its success in returning more than a handful of men to active service in the front line was debatable.[117]

But not every man who gave up trying to fight was treated leniently or classified as a psychiatric casualty. Some officers, angry that men who absented themselves had placed their comrades in greater danger, had little hesitation in charging them with an offence against the Army Act.[118] In September 1944, a company commander of 1st Black Watch was so disgusted by the behaviour of two deserters that when they were

---

[112] C. Gunner, *Front of the Line. Adventures with the Irish Brigade* (Antrim, 1991), 57.

[113] War Office, *Royal Army Medical Corps Training, 1925* (London, 1925), 111–12.

[114] T. Copp and B. McAndrew, *Battle Exhaustion. Soldiers and Psychiatrists in the Canadian Army, 1939 to 1945* (Montreal and Kingston, Ont., 1990), 48–9.

[115] PRO WO 177/324, Medical War Diary, DDMS 8 Army, Report on tour of 8 Army, 18–24 July, 1942, by Consultant in Psychological Medicine, Brig. G. W. B. James, 28 July 1942; Crew, *Army Medical Services*, ii, 472–3.

[116] AMD 2, *Army Medical Directorate Bulletin Suppl. no. 5, Early Recognition and Treatment of Psychiatric Battle Casualties*, Apr. 1943.

[117] French, ' "Tommy is No Soldier" ', 168–9.

[118] Lindsay, *So Few Got Through*, 99.

returned to his company he had them manacled and sent into no man's land at night with a patrol as an example to others.[119] In February 1945 the CO of a Guards battalion in Italy ordered his supporting artillery to fire on a deserter as he ran across no man's land towards the German line.[120] Between 1939 and 1945, 167 men were convicted for cowardice, 800 for mutiny, 3,854 for sleeping at, or deserting, their post, and 30,740 for desertion.[121] Soldiers accused of serious offences such as these were usually tried before a Field General Court Martial. A FGCM was convened by a senior officer (usually a brigadier or above), and consisted of a President, who had to be of field rank and two other officers, each of whom was required to have had only a year's commissioned service.[122] The system produced a conviction rate for men accused of deserting or going AWOL of over 90 per cent. In North West Europe in 1944–5, men found guilty of desertion were sentenced to up to ten years in prison, although reviewing officers habitually reduced such sentences to three years and the offender usually only served six months before being returned to the front line and given an opportunity to redeem himself.[123] Such penalties did not appear to have been much of a deterrent. Private Gladman of the 1st Hampshire regiment 'often saw the charges being read out with an officer sitting on a box, hats off, marched up etc. These things were recorded but no one was shot as in previous wars.'[124]

Habitual deserters who absented themselves during quiet periods because of boredom, but who had a reputation as effective fighting soldiers, were apt to receive more lenient treatment.[125] Most front-line soldiers 'knew the difference between cowardice, as with some of the "accidental on purpose" injuries, and those unfortunate instances where the psychological pressure became too much to bear'.[126] Men who cried and trembled under stress were not usually regarded as cowards by their comrades, provided they made an effort to overcome their fears and do their job.[127] The experience of witnessing several men tried in the Anzio bridgehead for desertion persuaded John Hillier that the officers running the court martial did not know 'what shock was'.[128]

The incidence of battle exhaustion was highest amongst the infantry, for they were the soldiers who faced the most severe physical and mental stresses. One brigade commander who served in Italy in 1943–5 esti-

[119] Whitehouse and Bennet, *Fear is the Foe*, 63.
[120] P. Brutton, *Ensign Italy. A Platoon Commander's Story* (London, 1992), 116.
[121] PRO WO 277/7 McPherson, *Discipline*, Appendix 1(a).
[122] Ibid. 49.
[123] Lindsay, *So Few Got Through*, 225, 258; PRO WO 277/7, McPherson, *Discipline*, 33–4.
[124] IWM R. Gladman MSS 92/1/1, TS memoirs, 15.
[125] IWM E. P. Danger MSS 82/37/1, 'Diary of a Guardsman', TS memoirs, ii.
[126] Dyson, *Tank Twins*, 67.
[127] C. R. Eke, *A Game of Soldiers* (Brighton, 1997), 99–100.
[128] Hillier, *The Long Road to Victory*, 142.

mated that it was common to have as many as twenty men per battalion who were what he called 'battle absentees'.[129] A study of 2,000 deserters in 21 Army Group in 1944–5 showed that no fewer than 1,200 (60 per cent) were infantrymen, a figure entirely out of proportion to the infantry's total strength in 21 Army Group. The next highest number, 47 (2.35 per cent), were gunners.[130] However, in North Africa in 1942–3 the Royal Armoured Corps also provided a disproportionately large share of psychiatric casualties, a reflection of the intensity of tank fighting in that theatre.[131]

The number of deserters tended to rise sharply during periods of positional warfare, such as troops experienced in the Anzio and Normandy beachheads in 1944. Soldiers confronted 'the interminable round of standing to, cleaning weapons, administration, feeding under difficulties, digging better defences and observing the Bosche all too near for our comfort', and a steady trickle of casualties caused by artillery and mortar fire.[132] Men who were continually cowering in slit trenches came to see themselves as the helpless victims of a distant enemy against whom they could not retaliate.[133] Junior officers and NCOs were rather less likely to become psychiatric casualties because their responsibilities for their subordinates gave them less time to brood about the dangers they confronted. Even men who did not break down in combat carried mental scars with them for the rest of their lives. Tom Barker, who was lightly wounded when he took part in a bayonet assault on the Italian position at Sidi Barrani in December 1940, recorded long afterwards: 'The blue scar [on my leg] I can put up with but memories at night are something else.'[134]

Another choice facing soldiers in the front line was to remain in place but take little or no part in the fighting or at least to determine for themselves how they would participate. Discipline rested upon the tacit consent of the vast majority of those upon whom it was applied. When that consent broke down, soldiers either went through the motions of obeying orders, or ignored them.[135] In July 1944, a company of the 2nd Rifle Brigade operating just north of Rome, was ordered to board some Sherman tanks and advance against Germans holding a nearby hill. A battalion of Guardsmen had tried the same tactic the previous day and suffered heavily. The Riflemen protested to their company commander, refused to board the tanks and 'stood around their vehicles like pickets

---

[129] LHCMA Maj.-Gen. J. Scott Elliot MSS, 'The Fifth Casualty', 1947.

[130] PRO WO 277/7. McPherson, *Discipline*, 50–1.

[131] Crew, *Army Medical Services*, ii, 492.

[132] IWM Lieut. H. T. Bone MSS 87/31/1, 23 July 1944.

[133] Trevelyan, *The Fortress*, 66.

[134] T. Barker, '2982252, 1st Battalion Argyll and Sutherland Highlanders', WWW, accessed 14 June 1998 at *stead@iinet.net.au*.

[135] R. Holmes, *Firing Line* (London, 1987), 332–4.

in a strike'. It was simply not practical to deal with a refusal to obey orders on such a scale by disciplinary means. The order was therefore cancelled, and the men were told that they would attack the hill the next day on foot, which they did.[136]

The final choice, which was the one taken by most soldiers most of the time, was to remain in danger and to participate in the fighting. Many factors sustained men in combat and encouraged them to stay on the battlefield, but ideological fervour was usually not one of them. Philip Fielden, an officer in an armoured car regiment in North Africa in July 1941, reminisced that when his squadron came out of the line 'he found it difficult to remember what was the background of the War at that time, and I don't think that any of us were very interested in it'.[137] Adequate supplies of food and drink were more important. They were essential not merely because they provided physical sustenance, but because their preparation and consumption bonded men together. 'The desert army', according to one veteran, 'was broken up into thousands and thousands of little groups whose very core was a fire tin and a brew can.'[138] Cigarettes were equally important because they 'soothes ones nerves'.[139] The quality of rations made a considerable difference to morale. Before late 1942, the basic battle ration consisted of bully beef, hard biscuits, tea, sugar, tinned milk, jam, and margarine. It was only intended for consumption for a week, but was often issued for much longer periods, although some effort was made to supplement it with limited quantities of tinned vegetables, tinned herrings, and rice.[140] Typically, breakfast consisted of fried bully or porridge made from crushed biscuits, lunch of biscuits and cheese, and dinner of bully stew and rice pudding. 'Compo rations', first introduced in late 1942, were widely considered to be an improvement because they contained a much greater variety of foods.[141] But official rations contained little if any fresh food, and troops took every opportunity to supplement their rations with fresh food, either bought, bartered, or stolen, from local inhabitants.[142]

Few men were driven to fight by the quest for medals, although most recipients of decorations did feel pride in their achievements. Medals were granted either to men who carried out special acts of bravery on the battlefield or 'for steady bravery and good work rather than specific

[136] Bowlby, *Recollections of Rifleman Bowlby*, 45–6.
[137] Fielden, *Swings and Roundabouts*, 31.
[138] Roach, *The 8.15 to War*, 49.
[139] IWM Tilly MSS PP/MCR/328, Maj. G. Tilly to his wife, 8 July 1944.
[140] PRO WO 106/2223, Notes from Theatres of War no. 4. Cyrenaica, Nov. 1941–Jan. 1942.
[141] IWM E. P. Danger MSS 82/37/1, 'Diary of a Guardsman', TS memoirs, i; LHCMA Paton-Walsh MSS 4/4/10, Operational Feeding, The Use of Field Rations.
[142] Dyson, *Tank Twins*, 43–6.

acts of gallantry'. However, the usual allotment for men who fell into the latter category was, in the opinion of many front-line soldiers, woefully inadequate.[143] The granting of gallantry awards was a cumbersome process. Recipients had to be recommended by their CO and the recommendation then had to be ratified by every step in the chain of command until it reached a committee at the War Office that made the final decision. It was not uncommon for the intended recipient to be wounded or killed in the meantime. Many men regarded the system with cynicism, convinced that it rewarded the wrong people and withheld rewards from the really deserving.[144] Sir Brian Horrocks thought that the US Army's system, which allowed divisional commanders to make gallantry awards to men coming straight out of the line was better because it had an immediate positive impact on morale 'and that, after all, is the object of awarding decorations in war'.[145] Some British units therefore began to bypass the official system by issuing their own unit citations in lieu of official medals.

Far more important in sustaining men was good news from home and the conviction that what they were enduring and achieving was appreciated by friends and family in Britain. Soldiers did not shed their responsibilities as sons, lovers, and fathers when they enlisted. They were perpetually anxious for reassuring news from their families and complaints about the slow arrival of mail, particularly in the Middle East, were commonplace.[146] Mail that brought good news raised morale, just as mail that brought bad news lowered it.[147] Marital infidelity was a growing source of worry for men on long overseas postings. By mid-1943, the Legal Advice Service in the Middle East was dealing with thirty divorce applications each day.[148] Troops overseas anxiously scanned newspapers and BBC broadcasts to discover if the media was reporting their own doings to friends and families at home. English and Scottish troops, for example, who had taken part in the Greek campaign in 1941 were annoyed at the way in which the British press wrote up the exploits of the Anzacs but overlooked their own.[149] Similarly, troops in Italy in early 1944 were aggrieved because the BBC carried more stories about the Red Army than it did about their own operations.[150]

[143] Lindsay, *So Few Got Through*, 118, 252.
[144] IWM E. P. Danger MSS 82/37/1, 'Diary of a Guardsman', TS memoirs, ii; Dyson, *Tank Twins*, 169.
[145] Horrocks, *Corps Commander*, 215.
[146] PRO WO 163/52/AC/G(43)17, WO Committee on Morale in the Army, Fifth Quarterly Report, 3 July 1943; PRO WO 214/62, Montgomery to Alexander, 23 Sept. 1943.
[147] Crimp, *The Diary of a Desert Rat*, 27.
[148] PRO WO 277/16, Sparrow, *Morale*, 9–10; PRO WO 163/52/AC/G(43)27, WO Committee on Morale in the Army, May–July 1943, 5 Oct. 1943.
[149] C. Seton-Watson, *Dunkirk–Alamein–Bologna. Letters and Diaries of an Artilleryman 1939–1945* (London, 1993), 84.
[150] PRO WO 163/53/AC/M(44)1, Minutes of the Army Council, 21 Jan 1944.

The regimental system did play a limited role in sustaining morale in combat. Once in action, for some soldiers their regiment came to mean something far more tangible and important than it had ever meant to them during training. John Hillier, who served with 2nd Wiltshires in Italy, recalled that 'The Battalion became a large family, and also a circle of friends. Discipline and good humour went hand in hand with cleanliness and smartness. Men would lay down their lives for their comrades in battle, so that their friends or pals could live for another day.'[151] Soldiers sometimes showed their identification with their regiment by creating regimental symbols where none had existed before. The men of the first three battalions of the Parachute regiment, for example, designed and wore their own distinctive coloured lanyards made from dyed parachute rigging lines.[152] Men who felt such loyalties were understandably resentful, therefore, if they were arbitrarily drafted into an unfamiliar unit. When, for example, in March 1944 the 6th battalion of the Grenadier Guards was disbanded in Italy and its men sent as reinforcements to the 5th battalion, considerable numbers of the new men quickly absented themselves.[153] The fact that the absentees were members of the same *regiment* indicated that the military authorities and ordinary soldiers constructed regimental loyalty in quite different ways. The former regarded it as loyalty to an abstract concept of 'the regiment'; the latter were only prepared to give their loyalty to a concrete human organization represented by their own battalion and composed of men they knew. Some commanders realized this. When 1st Bucks was disbanded in July 1944 and its men drafted to units of 51st Highland division, care was taken to post men in their existing platoons in order to maintain their morale.[154]

The problems associated with the cross-posting of men trained in one regiment to serve in a different regiment became increasingly common in the second half of the war. Until 1941 each infantry regiment retained its own Infantry Training Centre which supplied it with recruits. But in March 1941 the War Cabinet capped the size of the army and in August the Army Council reduced the number of ITCs to twenty-five. Henceforth, one ITC had to serve several different regiments. The differing incidence of casualties between regiments soon meant that large numbers of men were posted to units where they found themselves amongst strangers. As Adam admitted in March 1942, 'The drafting of infantry by Regiments had completely broken down'.[155] By 1943 regiments overseas were allocated a draft of twenty men per month from

---

[151] Hillier, *The Long Road to Victory*, 1.
[152] Sims, *Arnhem Spearhead*, 21.
[153] IWM E. P. Danger MSS 82/37/1, 'Diary of a Guardsman', TS memoirs, ii.
[154] Whitehouse and Bennett, *Fear is the Foe*, 47–8.
[155] PRO WO 205/1c, Minutes of the C-in-C's conference held at GHQ, 17 Mar. 1942.

their own regiment; any deficiency had to be made up with men from other regiments.[156]

The military authorities thus found it impossible to maintain the regimental system in the second half of the war. The troops were, therefore, increasingly thrown back upon their own more human loyalties. Some senior regular regimental officers were offended by this, but in July 1941 the Adjutant General believed that their wartime commissioned juniors 'did not worry unduly about regimental identities and traditions provided they belonged to a live and efficient unit'.[157] One of the first lessons front-line soldiers learnt was that they depended for their survival on the small group of men around them and, perhaps for the first time in their lives, they felt themselves to be totally bound up with another group of people who were not members of their own family.[158] During training Raleigh Trevelyan, who was commissioned into the Rifle Brigade, 'had it dinned into me day and night that I now belonged to a crack regiment'. But as soon as he arrived in Italy he was posted to a battalion of the Green Howards. After three weeks of sharing their hardships at Anzio, loyalty to and identification with his original regiment gave way to a new loyalty and sense of identification. He concluded that 'I'm not sure if my ties with the blokes in this platoon don't outweigh any nebulous loyalty I may have felt towards the traditions of the regiment'.[159] Infantrymen invariably dug two-man slit trenches and this bred what Norman Craig called 'the inseparability of mates. They would live, eat, work and sleep together and could not bear to be parted. If one of them was killed or wounded the other was quite lost.'[160] The importance of such bonding was underlined in North Africa in the summer of 1942. Doctors reported that one reason for a decline in morale was the hasty creation of composite units in which officers and men did not have the opportunity to get to know each other before they went into action.[161]

But it would be a mistake to believe that primary group loyalty always provided a sound bedrock for combat morale. There is plenty of evidence to suggest that some primary groups developed norms of behaviour that placed the survival of the group above the goals of the army and so actually encouraged their members to refuse to fight. Two incidents, which took place in Normandy in August 1944, illustrate this point. In one, a section of 2/6th Staffs collectively refused to obey an order by their

---

[156] PRO WO 163/92/ECAC/P(43)109, Adjutant-General, Infantry of the Line, Regimental System of drafting to units overseas, 4 Oct. 1943.
[157] PRO WO 163/50/ACM(41)9, Minutes of the Army Council, 18 July 1941.
[158] Bowlby, Recollections of Rifleman Bowlby, 4; Roach, The 8.15 to War, 49.
[159] Trevelyan, The Fortress, 48.
[160] Craig, Broken Plume, 81.
[161] PRO WO 177/324, DDMS 8 Army, Report by Brig. G. W. B. James, 28 July 1942.

company commander to advance.[162] A few days later a section of the 1st Gordon Highlanders deserted *en masse* after seeing their company continuously reduced by casualties since D-Day. 'They all marched back together under a corporal carrying their arms and kit . . .'[163]

Furthermore, at some stages of the war casualty rates amongst front-line units were so high that primary groups were quickly destroyed and hardly had time to reform before they were again dissolved. During the First World War the British army suffered 705,000 fatalities and 1,165,000 wounded. Compared to this its losses in the Second World War—144,000 dead and 425,500 wounded, missing, or taken prisoner—were comparatively light.[164] However, these figures conceal the fact that during some battles losses approached or exceeded the worst experiences of the First World War. The British army lost an average of 2,324 men each day over the 105 days of the Third Battle of Ypres. Allied losses in Normandy, at 2,354 men per day, were therefore actually higher.[165] These losses were concentrated disproportionately in the infantry. Seven British infantry divisions fought in Normandy.[166] Each division contained approximately 7,200 all-ranks in its nine rifle battalions. In the eighty-three days between 6 June and 28 August 1944, each division lost on average 341 infantry officers and 5,115 infantry other-ranks, or three-quarters of its infantrymen. (By contrast, the three British armoured divisions fighting in Normandy—7th, 11th, and Guards Armoured—suffered casualties at only half the rate of the infantry.)[167] Individual units could suffer seemingly light casualties but still have their fighting edge blunted. The 1943 pattern infantry battalion had a total of 36 officers and 809 other ranks. But only about 400 men performed the most dangerous function, wielding rifles and light machine-guns in combat. The rest serviced support weapons or served in administrative jobs.[168]

The effectiveness of primary group loyalty in persuading men to remain in the front line depended on the human stability of each primary group and on the fact that leaders and men knew each other intimately. Heavy losses sustained over a brief period made it difficult to sustain such relationships. Between 6 June and 18 July 1944, the signals

[162] PRO WO 71/902, Proceedings of a Field General Court Martial of L/Cpl. D. and Ptes., E, F, G, H, I, and J, 22–3 Aug. 1944.

[163] Lindsay, *So Few Got Through*, 64.

[164] PRO WO 277/12, Pigott, *Manpower Problems*, 80.

[165] T. J. Copp, 'Battle Exhaustion and the Canadian Soldier in Normandy', *British Army Review*, 85 (1987), 47.

[166] 3, 15, 43, 50, 51, 53, 59 divns.

[167] PRO WO 285/13, Casualties and Ammunition, 2 Army, 1944–5. The 3rd divn. suffered the heaviest losses—7,267 all-ranks, followed by 50th (6,630 all-ranks). Fewest losses (3,639 all-ranks) were suffered by 53rd divn.

[168] PRO WO 32/10400, An Infantry Bn. (Higher Establishment), Notified in ACI for 19 May 1943.

platoon of 2nd battalion the East Yorkshire Regiment, for example, lost twenty-two out of its original thirty-five members.[169] Maintaining primary group loyalty became even more problematic when units sustained heavy losses amongst their officers.[170] In North West Europe between August and November 1944, about one-third of rifle platoon and company commanders in the seven infantry divisions of the BLA became casualties each month.[171] That meant that by 2 September 1944, 2nd Argyll and Sutherland Highlanders, which had landed in Normandy with a complement of thirty-six combatant officers, had been reduced to only twenty-five officers, of whom only seven had been with the battalion on D-Day.[172] The 4th battalion of the Dorset Regiment had suffered similar losses. By 26 August it had been reduced to twenty-eight out of its original complement of thirty-six combatant officers and only nine of the survivors had been with the battalion when it landed in France.[173] Between D-Day and March 1945, the 1st Gordon Highlanders had an average of thirty officers serving with it at any one time, but 102 officers had served with the battalion at one time or another. The twelve rifle platoons were led by no fewer than fifty-five different officers and their average length of service with the battalion was only thirty-eight days.[174] Losses on this scale, when coupled with the inability of the regimental system to function effectively to replace them, meant that primary group loyalty was a decidedly uncertain foundation for morale. Pitched in amongst strange officers and NCOs, a man had 'No traditions, no influence, no one to look after his interests and no one to whom he could turn for advice.'[175]

Heavy losses amongst junior leaders were particularly dangerous, because effective leadership was probably the most important single factor that sustained men in combat. Leadership at unit and sub-unit level was crucial in persuading men to remain on the battlefield, and units which lacked sufficient numbers of effective leaders were always liable to fail.[176] There were many ways in which officers could earn the respect of their men. Some like Lieutenant Woods, the mortar platoon commander of 2nd Parachute battalion in September 1944, were effec-

---

[169] IWM Lieut. H. T. Bone MSS 87/31/1, Signals Platoon Roll.

[170] The ratio of officer to other rank casualties in the infantry was 1.48 : 1. Even in armoured formations officers suffered a higher proportion of casualties than other ranks. See PRO WO 106/1024. Military Operational Research Unit, Report no. 23, Battle Study, Operation Goodwood.

[171] PRO WO 291/1331, Operational Research in North West Europe, Report no. 19, Infantry Officer Casualties.

[172] PRO WO 171/1262, War Diary, 2 Argyll and Sutherland Highlanders, 2 Sept. 1944.

[173] PRO WO 171/1286, War Diary, 4th Bn. Dorset Regt., 26 Aug. 1944.

[174] Lindsay, *So Few Got Through*, 114, 267–8.

[175] IWM E. P. Danger MSS 82/37/1, 'Diary of a Guardsman', TS memoirs, ii.

[176] Lindsay, *So Few Got Through*, 132.

tive leaders because they had a reputation for being 'efficient and cool under fire'.[177] Officers and NCOs who were willing to treat their men with consideration, to lead by example and not to risk the lives of their men unnecessarily, also found it easier to gain that confidence.[178] '[I]t was your willingness', wrote one gunner to his former section commander in January 1945, 'to listen to our petty troubles, and your rational dealing with them that made us a happy section. We always regarded you as an officer, and a friend. Army discipline usually ensures respect for officers, while nobody ever let a friend down if he could possibly help it.'[179] Lieutenant Colonel K. C. Hooper, CO of 2nd Royal Sussex, was respected because of his ability to speak to his men with 'prosaic simplicity' on the eve of Alamein.[180] Good relations were often fostered by the simple fact of physical proximity, for, unlike the situation in barracks, platoon and troop commanders usually lived with and slept beside their men in combat. Lieutenant Sydney Jary, who led an infantry platoon throughout most of the North West European campaign, thought that successful leadership depended on two factors. Soldiers had to have faith in the professional ability of their officers and 'they must trust them as men'.[181] However, Stan Whitehouse's platoon commander had only a sketchy knowledge of infantry tactics: 'But for all that he was a gentleman through and through and we respected him.'[182] Physical courage was an essential element in the make-up of any leader. The CO of 2nd Wiltshires during the Sicilian campaign earned the respect of his men because of his refusal to take cover when the battalion was being shelled. In their opinion, 'He was a real leader of men.'[183]

Some forms of behaviour had the opposite effect. Officers who were too keen and seemed to be intent on seeking out action to further their own careers, and so threatened to lead their men into unnecessary danger, were bitterly resented.[184] Officers who railed against their men when they failed, or NCOs who were needlessly officious, only demoralized their men.[185] In May 1940, the CO of 7th Hussars provoked a mutiny in his regiment as a result of the resentment provoked by his continual fault-finding.[186] Similarly, a failure on the part of provost

---

[177] Sims, *Arnhem Spearhead*, 24.
[178] Jary, *Eighteen Platoon*, pp. xvi–xvii; Wingfield, *The Only Way Out*, 14.
[179] IWM L. W. Cannon MSS, Gnr. D. A. Mitchell to Mr Bowyer, 18 Jan. 1945.
[180] Craig, *Broken Plume*, 53.
[181] Jary, *Eighteen Platoon*, 8.
[182] Whitehouse and Bennett, *Fear is the Foe*, 94.
[183] Hillier, *The Long Road to Victory*, 99.
[184] Crimp, *The Diary of a Desert Rat*, 93–4.
[185] Bowlby, *Recollections of Rifleman Bowlby*, 86; Hamerton, *Achtung Minen*, 90.
[186] PRO WO 71/694, Proceedings of Field General Court Martial on Trooper X and 7 others, 1940.

and embarkation officers at Durban in January 1942 to fumigate a verminous troop ship, the *City of Canterbury*, precipitated a mutiny amongst troops ordered to embark on it.[187]

Senior officers could exercise a more remote but still powerful influence over their troops. When Tim Bishop glimpsed Auchinleck near Alamein in early July 1942, 'I thought he looked reassuringly unperturbed.'[188] At a lower level in the command structure in May 1940, Major-General G. Le Q. Martel, GOC 50th division, posted himself and other senior officers behind sections of his line which were being particularly heavily shelled, in an attempt to rally stragglers.[189] But it was not until Montgomery arrived in the desert in August 1942 that a senior officer began to make a deliberately populist appeal to his troops in an effort to sustain their morale. He set about creating 'a Montgomery fable' in order to wean his troops away from their admiration for Rommel.[190] The responses of other ranks varied. Sapper Richard Eke looked upon Montgomery as 'well loved' in part because of his unorthodox dress and because of his willingness to tolerate similar habits amongst his troops.[191] His apparent willingness to tell all ranks down to the private soldier what he was going to do, and why he was doing it, was particularly appreciated.[192] Others, whilst holding Montgomery's obvious professionalism in high regard, were less impressed by what they regarded as his vulgar publicity gimmicks.[193] Troops about to go into action for the first time usually found his pep talks reassuring. A trooper in 107th RAC who heard him just before D-Day spoke for all of his mates when he muttered, without any trace of irony, 'It's like the coming of the Messiah'.[194] However, experienced troops, especially if they felt that they had already done their share, were less likely to be impressed. When 5th Royal Sussex received one of Montgomery's orders of the day while they were resting after Alamein they regarded his intimation that they ought to be upset that they were not taking part in the pursuit with incredulity.[195] When he told the men of 78th division, which had fought throughout the Tunisian campaign as part of 1st Army, that they should feel proud to be joining 8th Army 'the temperature dropped below freezing in a second'.[196] Men of the 2nd Devons,

---

[187] PRO WO 71/734, Proceedings of a Field General Court Martial of Sgt. A, 7 Feb. 1942.
[188] Bishop, *One Young Soldier*, 92.
[189] Martel, *An Outspoken Solider*, 159–60.
[190] Lieut.-Gen. Sir B. Horrocks, *A Full Life* (London, 1960), 120.
[191] Eke, *A Game of Soldiers*. See also Lee Harvey, *D-Day Dodger*, 60.
[192] PRO WO 163/52/AC/G(43)27, WO Committee on Morale in the Army, May–July 1943, 5 Oct. 1943.
[193] Carrington, *Reflect on Things Past*, 35–6.
[194] Dyson, *Tank Twins*, 17.
[195] Craig, *Broken Plume*, 100.
[196] D. Healey, *The Time of My Life* (London, 1990), 55.

part of the highly experienced 50th division, booed him when he visited them shortly before D-Day.[197]

Most soldiers found the war was too impersonal and prolonged to allow them to hate their enemies for more than a brief period.[198] In many instances, the image of the enemy as an inhuman Hun faded after first contact with him, especially if he was a prisoner. Norman Craig thought that the Afrika Corps prisoners he saw at Alamein 'looked very different from the newspaper photographs of the victorious German army in France'.[199] Once their surrender had been accepted, most prisoners were treated in accordance with international law.[200] The one exception was that they were almost invariably relieved of their personal valuables. When formations failed to meet their proper legal obligations to their prisoners, it was usually the result of administrative shortcomings, rather than deliberate malice.[201] A feeling of grudging respect for the bravery and military skill of the average German soldier was the most common response of front-line troops to their adversaries.[202] The one major exception to this was the SS. The War Diarist of 11th Royal Scots Fusiliers noted laconically that, when two prisoners from 2nd SS division captured in July 1944 'Reported that they had not fed for five days—this report did not melt the heart of any Jock to the extent of sharing his rations'.[203]

British infantrymen rarely killed their enemies with much relish. Senior officers recognized this and tried constantly to reinforce the message that the war could only be won by killing. In September 1942 for example, when X Corps was training for Alamein, its commander, Lieutenant-General Herbert Lumsden, issued a training instruction which began with the uncompromising injunction: 'This war cannot end in our favour until we have killed sufficient Germans.'[204] When soldiers did use their personal weapons to kill their enemies, they often did so out of self-preservation or in revenge for friends who had been killed.[205] Because few soldiers actually fought in the teeth arms in the front line,

[197] Houldsworth, 'One Day I'll Tell You', 11.

[198] McCallum, Journey with a Pistol, 105–6; IWM Sgt. E. P. Danger MSS 82/37/1, 'Diary of a Guardsman', TS memoirs, i.

[199] Craig, Broken Plume, p. 59.

[200] S. P. Mackenzie, 'The Treatment of POWs in World War Two', Journal of Modern History, 66 (1994), 490; General Staff, War Office, Field Service Pocket Book. Pamphlet No. 3. Intelligence—Information and Security (London, 1939), 19–20; General Staff, ATM No. 44 (London, 1942); IWM Brig. J. N. Cheney MSS 80/3/1, DPM's lecture, 13 May 1944.

[201] LHCMA Brig. E. J. Paton-Walsh MSS 1/1/12, Brig. A/Q, 1 Army, to Paton-Walsh, 11 Apr. 1943; 1/1/4, DPM, V Corps, to Patton Walsh, 24 May 1943.

[202] Holding, Since I Bore Arms, 90.

[203] PRO WO 171/1365, War Diary, 11 Royal Scots Fusiliers, 1 July 1944.

[204] PRO WO 201/537, Xth Corps Training Instruction no. 1, 11 Sept. 1942.

[205] Crimp, Diary of a Desert Rat, 46; Whitehouse and Bennett, Fear is the Foe, 98; Jary, Eighteen Platoon, 60.

comparatively few men were actually required to kill an enemy face to face. Front-line infantrymen on both sides were trained to practice concealment and many small unit actions took place in the dark when men shot at shadows and sounds.[206] Ambushed at night in southern Holland in October 1944 by a German patrol he could hear but not see, Stan Whitehouse reacted in blind self-defence. 'I felt I was about to be killed and there was nothing I could do about it. To combat my "bomb-happiness" I stood up and hosed another magazine down the road, this time finding relief by shouting "Come on you bastards, come on".'[207] The reaction of those who did have the opportunity to fire at a visible enemy was varied. Sydney Jary 'had little stomach for sniping. More often than not, it was a cold and calculated way of killing which achieved no military advantage.'[208] Some regarded killing almost dispassionately. Phillip Brutton recorded of a German he shot at close range in Italy in 1944 that 'The .45mm soft-nosed Tommy gun bullet did not bounce off the German parachute helmets at close range. In any case, he was hit below the rim. His face disappeared before he fell.'[209] Others took a quiet professional pride in their skill.[210] Troops rarely crossed bayonets, perhaps because the mere threat of hand-to-hand combat sufficed to make one side or the other flee.[211] Most front-line soldiers regarded their enemies without sustained rancour, and were reluctant to kill them at close quarters unless circumstances forced them to do so, and sometimes regretted doing so after the event. In the autumn of 1944, a corporal in the 1st Black Watch shot an armed German soldier who was running directly at him. But when he examined the corpse and found a wallet of family photographs, he broke down and 'cursed at the system that had made him kill this family man'.[212] It was, therefore, as well that British doctrine prescribed that battles were won by generating overwhelming quantities of mechanized fire-power. Montgomery was right when he wrote shortly after Alamein that 'The trouble with our British lads is that they are not killers by nature'.[213]

Superficially, British and German recruits underwent a similar experience as each army tried to transform them from civilians into soldiers. Both were drilled and disciplined until obedience to orders

[206] For a vivid description of a brief night action, see Trevelyan, *The Fortress*, 24.
[207] Whitehouse and Bennett, *Fear is the Foe*, 98.
[208] Jary, *Eighteen Platoon*, 60.
[209] Brutton, *Ensign Italy*, 82.
[210] T. Barker, T., '2982252, 1st Battalion Argyll and Sutherland Highlanders', (World Wide Webb accessed 14 June 1998 at *stead@iinet.net.au*).
[211] PRO WO 201/527, Extracts from the report of a War Office observer in North Africa, May 1943.
[212] Whitehouse and Bennett, *Fear is the Foe*, 120.
[213] LHCMA Alanbrooke MSS 14/61/9, Montgomery to Alanbrooke, 27 Nov. 1942.

became instinctive. But there the similarities ended. German soldiers were taught from the outset that they had a duty to use their initiative in order to further their commander's intentions. British soldiers were taught that their first duty was to obey their superior's orders. The German army went to considerable lengths to inculcate into its troops the issues at stake in the war. Even before they had enlisted, they were indoctrinated into the principles of the National Socialist state and imbibed a combination of anti-Semitism, racism, and anti-Bolshevism. They saw the war, particularly in Russia, as an ideological struggle against an enemy that threatened the validity of the Nazi state. Most of them were deeply committed to that state because they believed that it had redeemed Germany's defeat in 1918 and had restored a sense of identity to the German nation.

However, ideological commitment was not the only reason why they endured so much. The German army did not suffer the same incidence of recorded psychiatric breakdown as the British because the German army did not recognize such diseases. Soldiers whose mental well-being snapped under the stress of battle were dealt with in one of two ways. They were either treated as medical casualties who were suffering from some form of organic disease. When a senior British doctor visited a number of sick POWs he concluded that soldiers who would have been classified as psychiatric casualties in the British army were 'masquerading under a diagnosis of organic disease such as "commotic cerebri", a heart disease, gastritis, etc'.[214] Furthermore, unlike the British army, the Germans retained the death penalty for a wide range of political and military offences. Between 13,000 and 15,000 German soldiers were executed by their own army during the Second World War.[215] German soldiers were so brutalized by the disciplinary system of their own army that they sought and found a vicarious release from a near-intolerable situation by brutalizing in turn those weaker than themselves. The result was that, on the one hand, many ordinary German soldiers continued fighting despite casualty rates that rapidly undermined any primary group loyalties. But they also showed a barbarous disregard for the inhabitants of the countries they fought over and the prisoners they captured.[216]

---

[214] PRO WO 177/316, Brig. E. Bulmer, Quarterly report of consulting physician 21 Army Group 1 July–30 Sept. 1944.

[215] M. Messerschmidt, 'German Military Law in the Second World War', in W. Deist (ed.), *The German Military in the Age of Total War* (Leamington Spa, 1985), 323–5.

[216] S. G. Fritz, *Frontsoldaten. The German Soldier in World War Two* (Lexington, Ky, 1995); idem., ' "We are Trying to Change the Face of the World"—Ideology and Motivation in the Wehrmacht on the Eastern Front: The View from Below', *Journal of Military History*, 60 (1996), 683–710; O. Bartov, *Hitler's Army: Soldiers, Nazis and War in the Third Reich* (Oxford, 1991); idem., 'Daily Life and Motivation in War: The Wehrmacht in the Soviet Union', *Journal of Strategic Studies*, 12 (1989), 200–14; E. Shils and M. Janowitz, 'Cohesion

By contrast, British attempts to indoctrinate their troops were half-hearted and often ineffectual. With the exception of SS soldiers, the British entertained a grudging respect for their enemies and treated their prisoners largely in accordance with international law. British doctrine prescribed that battles were won by mechanized fire-power, which was just as well as many British soldiers exhibited a marked reluctance to use their personal weapons to kill at close quarters. British soldiers were the products of a civic culture that deprecated public violence. They were largely apolitical. They identified more strongly with their families and their homes than with any public institution or ideology.[217] Unlike the Germans, they were not subject to a brutal disciplinary system and they, therefore, had less need to vent their own pent-up aggression on those weaker than themselves. Their objective was to defeat, not to exterminate, their enemies, and then to return home to their families as soon as possible. The army may have transformed them into soldiers. It did not transform them into warriors. It was perhaps that failure, more than the actual incidence of desertion or self-inflicted wounds, that encouraged senior officers to continue to harbour serious doubts about the fragile morale of their troops. As the DMT lamented in December 1943,

The army can achieve nothing if the young soldier has been brought up from the cradle, and during the most impressionable period of his adolescence, to look upon wars and battle as beyond human endurance and something not to be even contemplated. No wonder that men brought up in this way get "pinned down" or "mortared off" or "shelled out" by the first missile that arrives anywhere in the vicinity. And this is the way we did in fact bring up our present fighting men between the last war and the present one. Books, literature, cinemas, plays, education, and propaganda were all turned to this end.[218]

The morale of the British army during the Second World War was, therefore, not uniformly poor or fragile. Front-line soldiers were at least as ready as their fathers had been to suffer in their nation's cause. On the Western Front between 1914 and 1918 battalions suffered an average of 100 casualties each month. In North West Europe between 1944 and 1945 the figure was exactly the same. In Normandy allied troops endured higher daily losses than had Haig's army during the Third

and Disintegration in the Wehrmacht', *Public Opinion Quarterly*, 12 (1948), 280–315; J. Förster, 'Motivation and Indoctrination in the Wehrmacht', in P. Addison and A. Calder (eds.), *Time to Kill. The Soldiers' Experience of War in the West, 1939–45* (London, 1997), 263–73; T. J. Schulte, 'The German Soldier in Occupied Russia', in Addison and Calder (eds.), *Time to Kill*, 275–83; A. Steim, 'International Law and Soviet Prisoners of War', in B. Wegner (ed.), *From Peace to War. Germany, Soviet Russia and the World, 1939–41* (Providence, RI, 1997), 293–308.

[217] McKibbin, *Classes and Cultures, passim*.

[218] PRO WO 231/8, Director of Military Training, General lessons of the Italian campaign, 18 Dec. 1943.

Battle of Ypres in 1917. Senior officers were probably wrong to believe that folk memories of the First World War had left their men so traumatized that they would be unwilling to fight. They were less deferential towards authority than their fathers, but those memories actually helped to sustain their morale by persuading them that, bad as their own situation might be, it was not as bad as that which their fathers had endured.[219] Too much should not be made of the unwillingness of most soldiers to close with the enemy and to kill him at close quarters using their personal weapons. British doctrine placed a premium on long-range mechanized combat. Morale was a dynamic force. It changed over time and it changed between, and within, units. It was affected by a large number of factors. Just as unrelenting physical hardships, mounting casualties, and in particular the loss of trusted leaders, served to degrade a unit's morale, so effective leadership, the presence of trusted comrades, and adequate food and shelter sustained it. 'The marvellous thing', the DMT concluded, 'is not that young soldiers under fire for the first time get "pinned down", but that they later fight as magnificently and courageously as they have done.'[220]

[219] G. D. Sheffield, 'The Shadow of the Somme: The Influence of the First World War on British Soldiers' Perceptions and Behaviour in the Second World War' in P. Addison and A. Calder (eds.), *Time to Kill. The Soldier's Experience of War in the West 1939–45* (London, 1997), 35–6.
[220] PRO WO 231/8, Director of Military Training, General lessons of the Italian campaign, 18 Dec. 1943.

CHAPTER FIVE

The Pre-War Army and the British Expeditionary Force, 1940

In retrospect Sir Henry Pownall, the Chief of Staff of the BEF in 1940, thought that Britain's defeat at Dunkirk had the inevitability of 'a Greek tragedy'.[1] It did not. When the BEF was expelled from the Continent in June 1940, it left behind 68,111 casualties of whom only 3,500 were killed and 40,000 were prisoners, 88 per cent of its artillery, and 93 per cent of its motor vehicles.[2] The Germans did not win a bloodless victory in France. But nor did they outfight the BEF. Instead they outthought and outmanoeuvred it.

The British defeat in 1940 owed much to a poor allied plan of campaign. At the grand strategic level, as early as 1935 the General Staff had decided that a future war against Germany, in which Britain was allied to France, would fall into three phases. The experience of the First World War, they believed, had convinced the Germans that they could not win a long war. They would therefore employ masses of tanks and aircraft to try to gain a rapid victory either by attacking the Maginot Line or by outflanking it through Switzerland or the Low Countries. The war would, therefore, begin with a short period of mobile warfare, and it was essential that the BEF arrive in France in time to assist the French army in repulsing the initial German onslaught. Provided they were successful in doing so, in the second stage the fronts would be stabilized, both sides would mobilize their full resources, and the allies could employ their air and naval power to degrade the German economy. In the final stage, once the Germans had been suitably weakened, the allies would mount a decisive counter-offensive.[3] At the operational level, the small size of the BEF left the British with little choice but to fall in with French wishes and rush to the defence of the Low Countries when they were attacked. But this plan played directly into the Germans' hands. It enabled them to cut off the best-equipped and most mobile allied forces

---

[1] *Chief of Staff. The Diaries of Lieutenant General Sir Henry Pownall*, i, ed. Bond, 352.

[2] Maj. L. F. Ellis, *The War in France and Flanders in 1940* (London, 1953), 326–7; LHCMA Adam MSS, Adam 3/1, Notes for the Secretary of State's Estimates speech, 15 Feb. 1941.

[3] PRO WO 32/4612. Montgomery-Massingberd, Future re-organisation of the army, 9 Sept, 1935.

by advancing rapidly westwards to the Channel coast and severing their communications.[4]

The campaign in France and Flanders in 1940 showed that the British were unable to mount successfully either a static defence or a mobile counter-offensive. At one level this was because the British army lacked sufficient men and equipment to do so. In May 1940 Gort commanded a mere thirteen divisions. It was not until the spring of 1939 that the Chamberlain government finally reversed its policy of refusing to mount a continental commitment, introduced conscription, and decided to form a field force of thirty-two divisions.[5] These measures were meant to signal Britain's determination to resist aggression. All they did was to disrupt the organization of the Regular and Territorial Armies only a few months before the start of the war. The Treasury remained sceptical of their efficacy. It believed they would place an insupportable burden on the economy, that their training and the production of their equipment would take at least another eighteen months, and that they might actually provoke Hitler into acting.[6] Even so, on 8 September the War Cabinet's Land Forces Committee recommended that all planning should be based on the assumption that the war would last for at least three years. Britain should raise a field force of fifty-five fully equipped divisions (thirty-two British, fourteen Dominion, four Indian divisions, and equipment for five allied divisions). It believed that it would be possible to equip twenty divisions by September 1940, provided that steps to extend factory space were begun at once, that the Ministry of Supply was given first priority for labour and raw materials, and that the Schedule of Reserve Occupations, which protected skilled labour from the call-up, was rigorously enforced.[7]

This plan not only threatened the other service programmes, it also ran contrary to Chamberlain's insistence that the Polish campaign had

[4] M. S. Alexander, 'Maurice Gamelin and the Defeat of France, 1939–40', in B. Bond (ed.), *Fallen Stars. Eleven Studies of Twentieth Century Military Disasters* (London, 1991), 107–40; idem, *The Republic in Danger. General Maurice Gamelin and the Politics of French Defence, 1933–40* (Cambridge, 1992), *passim*; idem, ' "Fighting to the Last Frenchman"? Reflections on the BEF's Deployment in France and the Strains of the Franco-British Alliance, 1939–40', *Historical Reflections/Reflexions Historiques*, 22 (1996), 235–62; D. W. Alexander, 'Repercussions of the Breda Variant', *French Historical Studies*, 8 (1974), 459–88; B. Bond, *Britain, France and Belgium, 1939–40* (2nd edn., London, 1990), *passim*.

[5] Bond, *British Military Policy*, *passim*. The field force was to consist of 3 armoured divns., each of 2 armoured bdes. and a support group, plus 5 army tank bdes., or roughly the equivalent of another 2.5 armoured divns., 22 infantry divns. on a 3-bde. basis, and 6 motor divns., on a 2-bde. basis. The whole force was to be made ready in increments and the final division was to be fit to take the field eleven months after mobilization. PRO WO 277/8, Anon., 'Fighting, Support, and Transport Vehicles', 13.

[6] PRO PREM 1/296, Treasury to Chamberlain, 28 Mar. 1939; Peden, *British Rearmament and the Treasury*, 148–9.

[7] PRO CAB 92/111/LF(39), Minutes of 2 Meeting, 8 Sept. 1939; PRO CAB 92/111/LF(39)5, Hoare, Land Forces Committee, Report, 8 Sept. 1939.

demonstrated that Britain must have a powerful air force. But Hore-Belisha, Lord Halifax, the Foreign Secretary, and Churchill, who had just joined the government as First Lord of the Admiralty, coalesced behind the committee's recommendation. They believed that Britain was obliged to do everything it could to assist the French. On 22 September, the War Cabinet accepted the fifty-five-division programme as a basis for industrial planning.[8] However, the Treasury was right to be sceptical of the ability of the economy to equip such a force. The defence industrial base had shrunk to such an extent since 1919 that production of essential items such as field and anti-tank guns, tanks, and mortars accelerated only very slowly in the winter of 1939–40. By February 1940 the War Cabinet was compelled to accept that the fifty-five-division army should remain its ultimate target, but that henceforth it was to be attained 'at the earliest possible date rather than within the first two years of the war'. The War Office reluctantly accepted that the most that the Ministry of Supply could do was to equip thirty-six divisions by September 1941.[9]

However, the slowness with which the BEF received the men and equipment it needed was not merely a product of industrial bottlenecks. It was also a reflection of a deeper malaise within the British government. It had embarked upon the war with the utmost reluctance. By early 1940, with the 'Phoney War' at its height, some ministers were beginning to hope that it might be possible to end the war without significant land fighting. In February 1940, Oliver Stanley, the Secretary of State for War, informed Sir Alan Brooke, then commanding II Corps of the BEF, that he thought it unlikely that the Germans would attack in the West in 1940.[10] A month later Lord Chatfield, the Minister for the Co-ordination of Defence, told ministers 'It might be that eventually Germany would have to capitulate owing to her condition, without any great land fighting. Our great weapon, as he had remarked at previous meetings, was our sea power and blockade, and we were ever tightening the screw.'[11] Such complacency bred a dangerous lack of urgency in

---

[8] PRO CAB 65/1/WM9(39), Minutes of the War Cabinet, 9 Sept. 1939; W. S. Churchill, *The Second World War, i. The Gathering Storm* (London, 1948), 360; PRO CAB 65/3/WM(39)20, War Cabinet, Confidential Annex, 19 Sept. 1939; PRO CAB 92/111/LF(39), Minutes of 4 meeting, 19 Sept. 1939; PRO CAB 92/111/LF(39)14, Land Forces Committee, Second Report, 19 Sept. 1939.

[9] PRO CAB 65/5/WM40(40), Minutes of the War Cabinet, 13 Feb. 1940; PRO WO 277/8. Anon., 'Fighting, Support, and Transport Vehicles', 17–18; PRO WO 163/49/OS21, Memo by the Army Council as to the basis on which requirements up to Z plus 24 shall be calculated and communicated to the Ministry of Supply, 26 Feb. 1940.

[10] LHCMA Alanbrooke MSS 5/2/15, Alanbrooke, 'Notes from My Life, iii, BEF France-Flanders, 1939–40', 121.

[11] PRO CAB 65/56, A meeting of Ministers held at Richmond Terrace at 6 p.m. on Thurs., 7 Mar. 1940.

ministerial circles when it came to finding men and equipment for the army. Only the shock of defeat dispelled it.

Thus, in May 1940 Gort possessed only ten infantry divisions (five regular and five first line Territorial) and a single army tank brigade, with only two of its three battalions present. In April 1940, three further Territorial divisions had arrived in France, minus all of their heavy equipment, for labouring duties. Elements of 1st Armoured division did not begin to arrive until 14 May, and the whole division never assembled as a single formation. By contrast, on 10 May the Germans committed 135 divisions, including ten Panzer divisions, to their offensive in the West. Civilian politicians, therefore, bore a considerable share of the responsibility for the BEF's defeat in 1940.

However, it would be quite wrong to place the whole burden of responsibility for the BEF's defeat upon their shoulders. The campaign also revealed major weaknesses in the army's own preparations for war. These were most apparent in the areas of training and command, control, communications, and intelligence. A poor allied plan, shortages of equipment, and inadequate numbers of troops did not alone cause the defeat of Gort's army. The British were also defeated because they failed to foresee how German doctrine and organization would interact with their own on the battlefield. The Polish campaign had given the British ample opportunity to analyse German doctrine, but they failed to take full advantage of it. On 4 September 1939, the CIGS, Sir Edmund Ironside, told the War Cabinet that he did not think that the Germans would be able to crush Poland rapidly.[12] That they did so was an unpleasant surprise, but the British had little difficulty in gathering information to explain it away. The British military mission to Poland, led by Major-General Sir Carton de Wiart, escaped and furnished the War Office with a plethora of reports. These were supplemented by others supplied by escaped Polish officers. From the reports it was apparent that the German victory had rested on three factors. In the air the Luftwaffe had played a vital role in destroying the Polish air force, in disrupting the Polish army's command and control system, in providing CAS to the Panzer spearheads, and in preventing the movement of reserves to counter-attack the German penetrations. On the ground, the Germans had concentrated their tanks and thrust them boldly and rapidly forward. And the Polish army had been unable to match the tempo of German operations on the ground or in the air. According to de Wiart, it was broken up into a series of pockets by deep thrusts by German mechanized forces and '[Polish] GHQ was always 24 to 48 hours late in ordering retirements necessitated by German

---

[12] PRO CAB 65/1/WM2(39), War Cabinet, 4 Sept. 1939.

penetration and outflanking'.[13] When these reports were sent to GHQ in France, Gort's staff concluded that 'The German armoured forces and the German Air Force played a preponderating part in bringing about the rapid collapse of Polish resistance.'[14]

However, knowledge of how Poland was defeated was one thing. The willingness to translate that knowledge into appropriate counter-measures was another. That the Wehrmacht would be able to emulate its success in Poland against the Franco-British armies was beyond the imagination of many senior British officers. They found it easy to think of reasons why the Polish collapse could not be replicated in the West. For many years the Poles had planned for a war against Russia, not Germany.[15] The British and French were preparing for war against Germany. The Poles had been taken by surprise. The Germans attacked before parts of the Polish army had even mobilized. The British and French were fully mobilized and would not be surprised. In Poland the Germans had the great good fortune to strike when unexpectedly dry weather made it possible for their tanks to range widely across country and prevented the Poles from using rivers as natural anti-tank obstacles. The Germans had acted boldly because they knew that the Poles had no mobile forces with which to counter-attack. These, in the opinion of the British Military Intelligence, were conditions that 'will rarely present themselves in other theatres of war'.[16] The BEF's command and control system would not collapse. Even if bombing destroyed the civilian tele-phone and telegraph system, they could rely on wireless for, unlike the Poles, their ciphers would not be captured.[17] The Luftwaffe and the Panzers would not enjoy the same freedom to operate unchecked, because powerful allied air forces would oppose them.[18] Above all, the Russians would not attack the Anglo-French armies in the rear. After the Polish campaign, the War Office issued a series of pamphlets explaining the latest information about German operational techniques but many officers seem to have paid little attention to them. They had lulled them-selves into a false sense of security, with the result that the speed and violence of the German onslaught took them by surprise in May 1940.

[13] PRO WO 106/1747, British Military Mission to Poland, Despatch by Maj.-Gen. A. Carton de Wiart [c.Oct. 1939]; PRO WO 287/226, Tactical and Technical Notes on the German Army no. 2, 20 Sept. 1939; PRO WO CAB 65/1/WM26(39), War Cabinet, 25 Sept. 1939; PRO WO 287/226, Tactical and Technical Notes on the German Army no. 3, 27 Sept. 1939.

[14] PRO WO 197/66, Notes on German air operations in Poland, GHQ pamphlet no. 9, 4 Nov. 1939; T. Harrison-Place, 'British Perceptions of the German Army, 1938–40', Intelligence and National Security, 9 (1994), 495–519.

[15] PRO WO 287/226, Tactical and Technical Notes on the German Army no. 6, Oct. 1939.

[16] PRO WO 287/266, MI 3b, Tactical and Technical Notes on the German Army no. 7 [c.Oct. 1939].

[17] PRO WO 287/226, Tactical and Technical Notes on the German Army no. 5, Nov. 1939.

[18] PRO WO 167/203, War diary, G. branch, 2 divn., 9 Dec. 1939.

After the Dunkirk evacuation one divisional commander candidly admitted that the Germans had won not merely because of the greater weight of their material but because of 'surprise in the use of new tactical methods'.[19]

British command, control, and communications doctrine, with its commitment to an inflexible and autocratic management system, was ill suited to counter these 'new tactical methods'. If the British system was to work, an effective C3I system was essential. But its efficiency was degraded by no less than six factors: overreliance upon detailed written orders; poorly trained and organized staffs; a selection system which sometimes produced senior officers who were professionally or temperamentally ill prepared for battlefield command and gave them little opportunity to practise commanding large formations in manoeuvres; an overreliance on cable communications; and a lack of appreciation of the importance of intelligence.

Reliance upon detailed, written orders was not merely a product of the failure of many senior officers to anticipate the highly mobile operations they found themselves involved in after May 1940. They also reflected how peacetime training had been conducted and how the army was organized. In peacetime exercises they were convenient because they were often the only way in which umpires and members of the directing staff could discover what commanders and their staffs were attempting to do.[20] Commonly understood and well-practised drills might have obviated the need for such a cumbersome system of transmitting orders.[21] Reliance upon detailed written orders also reflected the army's hierarchical ethos and structure. A subordinate commander rarely had available the means to provide sufficient covering fire to operate independently. The result, as the Kirke Committee noted, was 'As soon as he has to appeal to higher authority for help, centralised control and complicated orders naturally ensue. The fire plan is the forcing house of the voluminous order.'[22] To achieve what the committee identified as 'The ideal [which] is that a commander should be able to carry on with his own resources on simple verbal orders or instructions containing the superior's object and general plan, until a change in the general situation requires the intervention of higher authority on broad lines', the entire organizational structure and hierarchical ethos of the army would have required radical modification. Every commander would have had to

---

[19] PRO WO 197/118, Maj.-Gen. H. O. Curtis, Report on the operations of Polforce, 20–5 May, and 46 Divn. 25 May–1 June 1940, 19 June 1940.

[20] PRO WO 279/65, Report on the Staff Conference, Comments by the DMT; PRO WO 33/1305, Notes on certain lessons of the Great War, 6 Apr. 1933.

[21] Brig. I. C. Mackay-Dick, 'The Desert War 1940–43: Are any of the Lessons Relevant to NATO's Central Front Today?' in Maj.-Gen. J. J. Mackenzie and B. Holden Reid (eds.), Central Region Versus Out-of-Area: Future Commitments (London, 1990), 230.

[22] PRO WO 33/1305, Notes on certain lessons.

command sufficient organic support weapons to enable him to operate without being forced to appeal to a higher authority for fire support. But the British were never willing to allow subordinates so much initiative or to devolve the control of support weapons to the same extent as the Germans. They, therefore, continued to rely perforce far more heavily upon detailed orders than did their enemies, with all the consequences that had for the tempo of their operations.

The army wanted senior officers who accepted responsibility, could earn the confidence of their superiors and subordinates, were calm under pressure, and had the intellect to be able to analyse problems and see solutions. Such an officer needed a strong personality, physical and moral courage, clear judgement, and a thorough knowledge of war based upon prolonged study. Above all, he needed the physical and mental stamina that would enable him to work successfully under enormous stress.

The system by which senior officers were appointed and promoted was only partly suited to produce such men. By reserving the senior ranks of the inter-war army to regular officers who were Staff College graduates, it ensured that only experienced officers, who had received the best training that the army could provide, got to the top. But the system also offered considerable scope for the operation of favouritism and 'buggins turn'.[23] The selection of officers for promotion to ranks ranging from Lieutenant-Colonel to Lieutenant-General was the task of the Selection Board. Its core members were the president, the CIGS, the Adjutant General and the GOC-in-Cs of the Aldershot, Eastern, and Southern Commands. The Military Secretary and his Deputy acted as its secretaries. Up to the rank of Major-General the Board acted upon the principle of seniority tempered by rejection of the unfit, rather than upon identifying particularly meritorious candidates and promoting them over the heads of competent, but less meritorious, colleagues.[24] His colleagues rarely gainsaid a CIGS with strong personal preferences. Above the rank of Major-General, the Board presented three names in order of seniority to the Secretary of State and he made the final decision.[25] Senior appointments by arm of service largely followed the proportion of each arm in the army. The line infantry, therefore, dominated the senior ranks of the army. (The one exception to this was that the Guards received a slightly disproportionate share of senior appointments, largely at the expense of the Royal Engineers and the Royal Tank

[23] The Private Papers of Leslie Hore-Belisha, ed. Minney, 66.
[24] PRO WO 32/3737, Report of the Committee on Promotion of Officers in the Army, 6 Jan. 1925; LHCMA Montgomery-Massingberd MSS 133/1, Chetwode to Montgomery-Massingberd, 4 Aug. 1921.
[25] PRO WO 32/3740, Précis for the Army Council no. 1242, Feb. 1926.

Corps.) Examples of nepotism abounded. The first batch of post-war divisional commanders was, for example, heavily weighted towards officers who had served on the Western Front. This was hardly surprising, as Haig was the chairman of the *ad hoc* board that had selected them. Officers who had served with Milne on the staff of 4th Division in 1914 or at Salonika between 1916–18 received their opportunity when he was CIGS. Subsequent CIGS followed suit in furthering the careers of their protégés.

The Kirke Committee, in accordance with its wish that the army establish a 'smaller and handier division, with much more "punch" behind it for mobile warfare', recommended that it also needed younger, fitter, and more aggressive commanders.[26] Its recommendation was timely, for by the mid-1930s the senior ranks of the army were in danger of becoming a self-perpetuating gerontocracy. In 1937 the senior ranks remained dominated by officers who had served in the Boer War. Divisional commanders were nearly four years older, Generals holding the major home commands were nearly six years older and the Military Members of the Army Council were five years older than their predecessors had been in 1914.[27] Hore-Belisha insisted that 'All promotions and appointments must be guided by the urgent sense that we are preparing for a war not only having the material but the men ready.'[28] He reduced the compulsory retirement age for all Generals, abolished the half-pay system, reduced the normal tenure of staff and command appointments from four to three years, and persuaded the Treasury to agree to a temporary increase in the establishment of Lieutenant-Generals and Major-Generals to ease the path upwards of younger officers.[29] The result was that younger men did now begin to reach the top of the army. But even so the average age of his divisional commanders (52.5 years) still compared unfavourably with the men commanding divisions at the Armistice in 1918, whose average age was only 46.7 years.[30]

Reliance upon Staff College graduates to fill the ranks of senior command positions in the army had two drawbacks. Camberley and Quetta between them graduated only about 50 British-service officers annually. This sufficed to produce enough staff officers and commanders

[26] PRO WO 33/1297, Report of the Committee on the Lessons of the Great War, 13 Oct. 1932.

[27] B. H. Liddell Hart, 'High Command in the Army', *The Times*, 16 Sept. 1937.

[28] CCC Hore-Belisha MSS HOBE 5/8, Hore-Belisha to Deverell, 27 Aug. 1937.

[29] PRO WO 163/608, Committee on the conditions of service of officers in the Royal Navy, the Army, and the Royal Air Force, July 1938; Bond, *British Military Policy*, 54; CCC Hore-Belisha MSS 5/8, Hore-Belisha to Gort, 1 Sept. 1937; PRO WO 32/4466, Minute by Military Secretary, 3 Feb. 1938.

[30] I am again grateful to Dr John Bourne for supplying me with information concerning the age of divisional commanders in Nov. 1918.

for the peacetime regular army. It did not suffice to provide the senior leaders of a greatly expanded wartime army. Secondly, the training aspiring senior officers received at the Colleges was not entirely appropriate for future commanders. It placed too much emphasis on training officers in the arts of grand strategy and too little on learning operational techniques. It was hardly surprising that Rommel concluded that 'the higher ranking British officers thought more in terms of strategy than tactics.'[31] In the mid-1920s two commandants at Camberley, Sir Edmund Ironside and Sir Charles Gwynn, suggested establishing a new war college to train officers in the operational techniques of commanding large formations. However, Milne insisted on retaining the existing system by which senior officers were supposedly trained by their own commanders.[32]

Senior commanders could not rely upon their staffs to make good their own deficiencies in training because the latter were inadequately manned and trained, and poorly organized. The staff's functions were to collect, collate, and disseminate information about their own and the enemy's forces, to submit plans for operations to their commander, and to issue orders translating their commander's wishes into action. Between the wars, too few staff officers were posted to field force formations. In 1936 the GOC 1st Division at Aldershot had only three staff officers permanently attached to his headquarters, although he could count himself better provided than commanders of Territorial Divisions, who had only two.[33] During manoeuvres or on mobilization, staffs had to be improvised around this inadequate nucleus. The system also placed an unnecessary burden on the commander because it left him responsible for co-ordinating the work of the different branches of his own staff.[34] This was in contrast to the German system that interposed a Chief of Staff between the commander and his staff and gave the CGS the power to issue orders in his commander's absence. The possibility of imitating the German system was rejected in 1919. Too many commanders were afraid that if the CGS became the sole conduit of information between the commander and his staff he would constitute a dangerous bottleneck in the flow of information and orders.[35] The

---

[31] *The Rommel Papers*, ed. Liddell Hart, 531.

[32] D. French, 'Colonel Blimp and the British Army: British Divisional Commanders in the War against Germany, 1939–1945', *English Historical Review*, 111 (1996), 1189–90.

[33] Brig. C. N. Barclay, *The History of the 53rd (Welsh) Division in the Second World War* (London, 1956), 9.

[34] General Staff, *FSR. Vol. 1. Organisation and Administration. 1930*, 23, 30–3.

[35] PRO WO 32/11357, Major-General, General Staff, GHQ, to DSD, War Office, 18 Dec. 1918, Appendix, Note on organization of General Staff in War, and remarks by Brig.-Gen. J. E. Edmonds; PRO WO 32/5153, Secretary, War Office, to Commanders-in-Chief France, Egypt, Mesopotamia, Salonika, India, Italy, and East Africa, 30 Dec. 1918, and Haig to Secretary of War Office, 24 Mar. 1919 and enc., Report of the committee on Staff Organization, 6 Mar.

British thus deprived themselves of the possibility of commanders commanding from the forward edge of the battle, confident that the work of their headquarters would not stop in their absence.

The inability or unwillingness of commanders to go right forward to command placed a special premium on effective communications. However, the rapid flow of information up and down the chain of command was impeded by shortcomings in the available technology and the way it was employed. Despite a great deal of wireless experimental work—in 1931 it was the British who first demonstrated the practicality of controlling the movement of an entire Tank Brigade using r/t—in 1939 the army's communications system was still fundamentally the same as that which they had employed in 1918. It possessed three means of communication, cable (line telegraphs and telephones), wireless (either by morse key or r/t), and despatch riders. Ideally, the most effective signals system employed all three means, because each possessed advantages denied to the other two.[36] Wireless was, in theory, regarded as the primary means of communication forward of divisional HQs.[37] In 1918–19 the government had established a W/T Board to co-ordinate the service's research into radio. However, development work was hampered by a general shortage of funds and by the fact that most British commercial manufacturers only had experience of making receivers, whereas the army also required transmitters.[38] Many of the sets developed between the wars suffered from serious practical limitations. It was not until 1937–8, with the issue of the No. 9 set which had a range using r/t of about 10 miles, that the army had a radio which could receive and transmit on the move over tactically useful distances.[39] Even so, radios were still far from being completely reliable and there was much reluctance outside the tanks and artillery to rely on them as the primary means of communication. More often than not, therefore, communications both in front and to the rear of divisional HQs relied largely on cable. Compared to the uncertainty of radio, cable offered known advantages. It could carry a much larger volume of traffic than wireless. It did not require elaborate codes to ensure the security of its messages, and it could meet the needs of a command system designed for slow-moving, attritional warfare.

In practice by 1939–40, the use of radios at the tactical level was

1919. Milne dissented from this opinion: see PRO WO 32/5153, Milne to Secretary, War Office, 23 Mar. 1919.

[36] FSR (1935), ii, 35–7.

[37] Ibid. 136.

[38] PRO WO 277/25, Gravely, Signals Communications, 167.

[39] IWM Dept. of Sound Recordings, Accession no. 000887/05: Col. R. N. Seddon, 62–3; IWM Dept. of Sound Recordings, Accession no. 000933/04: Col. K. E. Savill, 22; IWM Dept. of Sound Recordings, Accession no. 000991/03: Visc. Bridgeman, 18.

limited to armoured and artillery units. Infantry divisions had so few radios that, if they ever became dependent upon them for communications, each divisional HQ would have to try to command three brigades using a single set. Infantry battalions had only one set, for rear communications to brigade. Battalion commanders relied on runners to communicate with their forward companies. No radios had been allocated for administrative communications. The unevenness of the distribution of radios across the army had important repercussions for all-arms co-operation. Brigadier Hobart, who commanded the 1st Tank Brigade from 1934 to 1937, was one of the dominant influences in the development of armoured tactics in the late 1930s. He shunned all-arms co-operation in favour of self-sufficient all-tank formations, in part because the artillery and infantry lacked the same flexible communications system his tank regiments possessed. According to one of his brigade majors, G. W. Richards, who himself commanded an armoured brigade in 1942–3, the gunners could take up to twenty minutes to engage a target. 'Well, we wanted them to get on to a target in three minutes not twenty minutes. The result was that we probably wasted all that time instead of getting a move on. So until they had proper communications I don't think General Hobart had much use for them.'[40] The infantry were even more handicapped in Hobart's eyes. The outcome was that in North Africa in 1941–2, the British tried to use tanks without infantry or artillery support. That, in Richards's opinion, 'was a great pity because the only way you get success in an armoured brigade or anything like that was good co-operation between the Gunners, the Infantry and yourselves'.[41]

In view of their numerical inferiority, the army would have benefited enormously in the early stages of the war if they had possessed a sound understanding of the utility and requirements of both intelligence and security. The former might have provided a much-needed force-multiplier; the latter might have prevented the enemy from exploiting its manifold weaknesses. The British enjoyed neither advantage in 1939–40. The First World War had taught the British army about the need for signal security, but the need to practise it was almost forgotten after 1918.[42] It was not until 1935 that *FSR* included a section on security precautions and listed the means by which enemy intelligence organizations gathered information. They included not only overhearing careless conversations of troops on leave, but captured orders, diaries, and private letters, the interrogation of POWs, and the careless use of w/t

[40] IWM Dept. of Sound Recordings, Accession no. 000866/08: Maj.-Gen. G. W. Richards, 67–8.
[41] Ibid. 69.
[42] J. Ferris, (ed.), *The British Army and Signals Intelligence during the First World War* (London, 1992), *passim*.

and r/t ciphers.[43] It enjoined officers not to transmit orders using r/t in plain language unless they were of such immediate tactical importance that the enemy would not have sufficient time to act upon the information if he intercepted the message.[44] In 1922 Cavan looked forward to the day when the army would acquire mechanical cipher machines 'which will enable messages to be de- or enciphered at the rate of five or six words per minute in a battalion or brigade'.[45] However, the services were extremely tardy in producing a reliable mechanical cipher machine, and, although the 'Typex' machine they adopted was robust and secure, too few were available in the early stages of the war. The result was that between 1939 and 1942 the Germans often had little difficulty in reading British messages.[46] Equally little thought was given between the wars as to how the army might gather information by listening in to enemy radio transmissions or practising means of destroying his communications system. The signals officer of a tank battalion who 'intercepted' the plain text messages of an opposing force during exercises on Salisbury Plain in 1929 was roundly condemned by the GOC-in-C Southern Command. He told him that in real life the enemy would be communicating in a foreign language that he would not understand.[47]

The parochialism and inter-unit jealousy supposedly bred by the regimental system was not responsible for the fact that the army was so bad at practising combined arms tactics after 1939.[48] There was nothing in the regimental system *per se* that precluded effective combined arms co-operation. Looking back to the opening days of the Gazala fighting, Robin Dunn, a regular gunner officer whose battery was affiliated to the Bays, and formed part of the 2nd Armoured Brigade Group, believed that

Much of the success of 2nd Armoured Brigade was because all the regimental groups had lived and trained together for three months. All the officers knew one another intimately and could appreciate what the other ones were likely to do. Although we all wore different cap badges we were all intensely loyal to the Bays Group.[49]

The pre-war army hierarchy recognized the importance of such co-

---

[43] *FSR (1935)*, ii, 77–8.
[44] Ibid. 39.
[45] PRO WO 279/54, Report on the Staff Exercise.
[46] J. Ferris, 'The British "Enigma": Britain, Signals Security and Cipher Machines, 1906–1946', *Defence Analysis*, 3 (1987), 153–63.
[47] IWM Dept. of Sound Recordings, Accession no. 000954/07: Brig. W. R. Smijth-Windham, 15–16, 48.
[48] Cf. English, *The Canadian Army and the Normandy Campaign*, 25; Bond and Murray, 'British Military Effectiveness', 110–11.
[49] IWM Dunn MSS 94/41/1, R. Dunn, 'The Battle of Knightsbridge', 1942.

operation. Speaking after an exercise in 1927, Milne said that 'It is the co-operation of all necessary arms that wins battles and that is your basis for training for the future. I want that to be your principle in train-ing—combination and co-operation of arms.'[50] However, the experience of the first half of the Second World War demonstrated that it was a lesson that the army had been slow to put it into practice. There were many reasons for that, not least the helter-skelter expansion of the army between 1939 and 1941 that led to a dangerous dilution of its trained cadre. But what must not be overlooked was that the cadre itself had been inadequately trained to practise combined arms tactics between the wars.

This was only partly because of uncertainty over the army's mission. After 1918 its everyday function was to garrison the empire. It therefore confronted four different types of conflict: imperial policing, minor wars that it could fight on its peacetime establishment, major wars that might or might not require the government to mobilize the Territorial Army, and a major national war. Each kind of operation required different kinds of organization, equipment, and training.[51] However, it was only for a very brief period, between the signing of the Kellogg-Briand Pact and the collapse of the Geneva Disarmament Conference, that the army at home concentrated its training on imperial operations to the exclu-sion of preparing for war against a European enemy.[52] For the rest of the 1920s and much of the 1930s, whilst preparing to fight mobile opera-tions on the periphery of the empire, it never entirely lost sight of the need to fight a European enemy with modern equipment.[53] Hitler's accession to power and Germany's withdrawal from the League of Nations and the Disarmament Conference, persuaded the new CIGS, Sir Archibald Montgomery-Massingberd, that henceforth its main mission was to prepare for a continental land war.[54] In September 1934 the Director of Military Training ordered 'that the Army is to train for European Warfare next year (and [against] a best equipped enemy)'.[55]

---

[50] PRO WO 279/59, War Office Exercise no. 2, Winchester, 9–12 May 1927. See also PRO WO 32/2382, Memorandum on Army Training Collective Training period 1928, 26 Nov. 1928.

[51] General Staff, *Training Regulations 1934* (London, 1934), 1.

[52] Capt. J. R. Kennedy, 'Army Training', *Journal of the Royal United Services Institute*, 77 (1932), 714.

[53] LHCMA Kirke MSS 2/1/3, Kirke, 'The Experimental Brigade'; PRO WO 279/54, Report on Staff Exercise; PRO WO 279/55, Report on Staff Exercise; PRO WO 279/60, Report on the Staff Conference; PRO WO 32/3115, Milne, *Army Training Memorandum No. 4A. Guide for commanders of regular troops at home, 1932*, 29 Dec. 1931.

[54] PRO AIR 2/1664. Slessor to Peck, 18 June 1934; Larson, *The British Army and the Theory of Armoured Warfare*, 176; PRO WO 32/2847, Minute, Montgomery-Massingberd to Military Members of Army Council, 15 Oct. 1934.

[55] LHCMA Liddell Hart MSS 11/1934/48, Talk with Col. G. Le Q. Martel, 9 Sept. 1934; PRO WO 277/8, Anon., 'Fighting, Support, and Transport Vehicles', 2.

Despite its inability to persuade its political masters of the need to accept a continental commitment until February 1939, the General Staff remained wedded to this priority, and it guided training at home for the rest of the 1930s.[56]

The most fundamental reason why the army experienced such difficulty in practising combined arms operations after 1939 was that it had failed to train sufficiently thoroughly to do so before 1939. The training of the regular army was governed by an annual cycle. Individual training extended from October to February. It was followed by collective training in the spring and summer, culminating in the autumn formation manoeuvres.[57] Brigade and divisional manoeuvres, designed to train commanders and units of different arms to co-operate, were crammed into a five-week period at the end of the cycle. But between the wars the army held manoeuvres only twice in which corps-sized formations were pitted against each other. These took place in 1925 and 1935, but they lasted only for a few days. The principal causes of this lacuna were lack of funds, lack of sufficiently large manoeuvre areas, and lack of troops. In 1933 Eastern Command, centred on Colchester, did not have a training ground large enough to take more than a single brigade.[58] The situation abroad was frequently just as bad.[59] In 1937 Deverell inaugurated a new two-year cycle for higher training in Britain that was intended to enable corps level manoeuvres to be held biannually, beginning in September 1939.[60] But the outbreak of war precluded them from taking place.

None of the officers who commanded major formations in 1939–40, therefore, had any experience of doing so in peacetime manoeuvres. Senior officers had to make do with other forms of training—signals exercises, TEWTS, war games, and staff tours. They were easier to organize but often lacked realism. Officers taking part in a combined RAF–army signal exercise in May 1933, for example, kept office hours, beginning work at 10 a.m. and finishing by 3 p.m. each day.[61] Staff exercises were a poor substitute for the opportunity to practise with live soldiers across real ground, particularly in the light of the wholesale

[56] See e.g. LHCMA Liddell Hart MSS 11/1936/99, Talk with FM Sir C. Deverell, 12 Nov. 1936.

[57] General Staff, *Training Regulations 1934*, 8–10.

[58] LHCMA Aston MSS, *The Times*, 22 Apr. 1933.

[59] General Staff, *Training Regulations 1934*, 118–28; LHCMA Liddell Hart MSS 1/401, Ironside to Liddell Hart, 26 Jan. 1929.

[60] General Staff, *ATM No. 19 December 1937* (London, 1937); General Staff, *ATM No. 21. Individual Training Period 1938/39* (London, 1937); PRO WO 33/1635, Army Manoeuvres, 1939.

[61] LHCMA Liddell Hart MSS 15/3/114, General Staff, *Memorandum on Army Training. Collective Training Period for 1926* (London, 1926); Aston MSS 2/2, *The Times*, 26 May 1933; Lt. Gen. Sir F. Morgan, *Peace and War. A Soldier's Life* (London, 1961), 101.

mechanization which overtook the army in the late 1930s.[62] In April 1938 a staff officer attending a TEWT held in Southern Command was horrified to note the propensity of many of his seniors 'to carry out direct attacks on strong enemy positions'.[63]

At a lower level, training was often stymied by the personalities of senior officers. Some like Wavell, Hobart, and Burnett-Stuart, were enthusiastic trainers who imbued their subordinates with their own enthusiasm and tried to make training as realistic as possible. When Burnett-Stuart was C-in-C in Egypt in 1931, he insisted that schemes be continued night and day until a conclusion was reached and the troops be pushed to the limits of their physical endurance.[64] But the pitfall of a training system dominated by the personalities of senior officers was that promising innovations could quickly be stifled when they were posted or retired. Thus for example, Northern Command's experiments with realistic live-firing exercises in the aftermath of the Armistice were brought to an abrupt halt when the GOC, Sir Ivor Maxse, retired in 1924.[65] Other senior officers adopted a *laissez-faire* attitude towards training. When Sir Charles Bonham-Carter left the War Office to command 4th division in 1931, he was delighted with the more relaxed regime of his new job. He regularly visited the scattered stations of the division at Shorncliffe, Lydd, Colchester, Norwich, and Woolwich, 'but left the training of units and brigades to Commanding Officers and Brigade Commanders, controlling only by general directions and by advice during my visits'. When he was at the division's headquarters at Colchester, he spent a couple of hours each day in his office 'and then rode about the training area, watching work being carried out but not interfering, and that was my day's work'.[66] Other officers, like Sir Andrew Skeen, the CGS in India in 1924–8 were antediluvian, and in the absence of actual modern weapons like tanks and aeroplanes, forbade their subordinates even to consider their impact on the conduct of operations.[67] Some had so little imagination that they failed to recognize the need to explain to their subordinates the lessons which a particular exercise was intended to highlight.[68] Different arms of the service also

[62] Lieut.-Col. A. G. Cunningham, 'The Training of the Army', *Journal of the Royal United Services Institute*, 9 (1934), 725; LHCMA Lindsay's papers, Liddell Hart MSS 15/12/14, Wavell to Lindsay, 28 Mar. 1936.

[63] LHCMA Liddell Hart MSS 1/132/28, Macleod to Liddell Hart, 11 Apr. 1938.

[64] LHCMA Burnett-Stuart MSS 3, Burnett-Stuart, Training, 1931; Maj.-Gen. C. H. Miller, *History of the 13th/18th Royal Hussars (Queen Mary's Own) 1922–1947* (London, 1949),14; Taylor, *Infantry Colonel*, 16–17.

[65] LHCMA Liddell Hart MSS 1/344/1, Liddell Hart to Maj.-Gen. Hakewill-Smith, 3 Apr. 1951.

[66] CCC Bonham-Carter MSS BHCT 9/3, Bonham-Carter, 'Autobiography, 1921–39'.

[67] LHCMA Liddell Hart MSS 1/401, Ironside to Liddell Hart, 29 May 1929.

[68] LHCMA Liddell Hart MSS 11/1927/1b, Diary entry, 28 Mar. 1927; PRO WO 32/2382, Milne to Birdwood, 28 Nov. 1928.

had different attitudes towards training. A junior cavalry officer whose regiment trained alongside the RTC battalions at Tidworth in 1929–32 was convinced that the RTC had a much more professional attitude towards training than his own regiment.[69]

Even enthusiastic trainers had to battle against a host of practical obstacles. The army's commitment to imperial garrison duties impeded training, for it meant that battalions in Britain were regularly stripped of trained soldiers to provide drafts for their sister battalions abroad.[70] The need to avoid damaging civilian property meant that on exercises road-blocks, craters, and trenches had to be represented by white tapes, anti-tank mines by buried bricks, and fire by thunder-flashes, Very lights, signalling lamps, and blank ammunition. Lack of modern equipment meant that 15 cwt. trucks painted grey were used as substitutes for light tanks, trucks fitted with a conspicuous wooden 'T' represented infantry tanks, and anti-tank guns were wooden mock-ups or flags.[71] Indeed, coloured flags sometimes represented whole sub-units of infantry, tanks, and artillery.[72] Training also required realistic and imaginative umpiring, something that became harder to ensure as the inter-war period progressed and the number of officers with wartime experience declined and the introduction of new weapons and equipment made umpiring decisions more problematic.[73] It was not unknown for the judgements of umpires to be flouted by commanders who were senior to them.[74] Some umpires were suspected of favouring their own units. But their most important failing was their tendency to halt operations when the two sides approached within 200 yards of each other lest they become so intermingled that the resulting confusion could not be rectified. In doing so, they encouraged the infantry to assume that their supporting gunners would be able to suppress the defenders' fire by killing them before they arrived at their objective. The infantry, therefore, learnt that there was no need for them to practise their own minor tactics and fieldcraft. In reality, the best the gunners could usually do was to neutralize the defenders' fire until the moment came when they had to lift their

[69] IWM Dept. of Sound Records, Accession no. 000893/03: Col. G. W. Draffen, 24, 28.
[70] PRO WO 279/60, Report on the Staff Conference held at the Staff College Camberley, 16–19 Jan. 1928, Remarks by Maj.-Gen. W. H. Bartholomew, Director of Recruiting and Organization at the War Office; LHCMA Montgomery-Massingberd MSS 122/1, Chetwode to Montgomery, 30 Dec. 1920.
[71] LHCMA Liddell Hart MSS 15/3/114, Maj.-Gen. A. E. MacNamara, Instructions Regarding Training in the Manoeuvre Area for 1935 (London, 1935); 15/3/23, General Staff, ATM No. 20, April, 1938 (London, 1938).
[72] General Staff, Training Regulations 1934, 68.
[73] LHCMA Liddell Hart MSS 15/3/114, General Staff, ATM No. 20, April, 1938 (London, 1938); Montgomery-Massingberd MSS 133/1, Chetwode to Montgomery-Massingberd, 26 Jan. 1921; PRO WO 279/76, Report on Army Manoeuvres, 1935.
[74] LHCMA Liddell Hart MSS 1/269, Liddell Hart to Essame, 25 Jan. 1952.

supporting-fire although their own infantry were still some 200 yards from their objective.[75]

The training of the Territorial Army was impeded by even more severe handicaps. Progressive training, even of single sections, was difficult because of the rapid turnover in personnel and because only rarely did all the men of a section actually attend a drill meeting on the same evening.[76] Local training facilities varied greatly. Many units in rural areas were scattered across half a dozen stations and lacked adequate drill halls or parade-grounds. Company and platoon commanders had different levels of enthusiasm and knowledge, making it difficult for unit commanders to lead them as a single body.[77] It was, therefore, difficult to inculcate a common standard of efficiency and a common doctrine into the whole unit. London Territorial units received a good deal of assistance in training from nearby regular units, whereas Territorials in Western Command, which had few regular units, received much less help. In any case, by 1938–9 regular units were too busy learning how to use the new equipment they were receiving to spare much time to help the Territorials.[78] In theory, Territorial units and formations were supposed to undergo tactical training at one of the four weekend camps each unit attended and at their annual camp, which lasted for a fortnight. In reality, combined arms training rarely took place even at the annual camp. So rudimentary was the state of individual training that many Territorials confined their work at camp to unit and sub-unit training.[79] The only training most senior Territorial officers received in combined arms operations took the form of TEWTs, with the result that they rarely had 'the actual chance of seeing the co-operation of all arms'.[80] The result, according to one Territorial CRA, was that by 1939 the Territorials knew even less of combined arms practices than the regulars.[81]

As early as 1922, Cavan recognized that the intimate all-arms co-operation, which had characterized the operations of the army in the closing stages of the First World War, was already being lost.[82] The

[75] Col. L. G. S. Harvey, 'Military Umpiring', *Journal of the Royal United Services Institute*, 76 (1931), 560.

[76] LHCMA Liddell Hart MSS 1/519/2, Montgomery to Liddell Hart, 16 July 1924.

[77] Capt. P. A. Hall, 'The Training of Junior Leaders in a County Territorial Battalion', *Journal of the Royal United Services Institute*, 77 (1932), 586–8.

[78] LHCMA Liddell Hart MSS 15/3/23, General Staff, *ATM No. 20, April 1938* (London, 1938); PRO WO 279/65, Report on the Staff Conference, Comments by Col. R. N. Dick and Col. E. H. Kelly.

[79] PRO WO279/75, Report on the Staff Conference, Comments by Maj.-Gen. E. F. Marshall.

[80] PRO WO 279/70, Report on the Staff Conference, Comments by Maj. R. H. Lorrie.

[81] Brig. R. G. Cherry, 'Territorial Army Staffs and Training', *Journal of the Royal United Services Institute*, 84 (1939), 551.

[82] PRO WO 279/55, Report on the Staff Exercise held by CIGS, 9–13 Apr. 1922.

manifold obstacles in the way of realistic combined arms exercises meant that troops taking part became disheartened because of their lack of realism, and neither commanders nor regimental officers and their men were given sufficient opportunity to experience the fatigue and fog of war.[83] Even more significantly, the army's *laissez-faire* approach to training and the interpretation of doctrine meant that senior officers could evolve their own understanding of how doctrine should be implemented so that 'when you changed your commander you changed your doctrine; everything was chaotic'.[84] This was the single most important obstacle impeding combined arms co-operation in the British army. The lack of uniformity in the army's training could have been overcome only if the CIGS had had a stronger management system in place which could have imposed a common understanding of its doctrine. However, before 1939 no CIGS saw the need to impose his own interpretation of doctrine on the army and the inspection system was too weak to ensure that commanders were training their troops in accordance with a common interpretation of the official doctrine. It was not until July 1939, when two senior officers, Ironside and Kirke, assumed the duties of Inspectors General of Overseas and Home Forces respectively, that the inspectorate finally acquired the authority it required and then it was too late.[85] Ironside's jaundiced comment that 'The War Office have no idea of the importance of this [Higher Training]. They have simply played at it' was largely justified.[86]

Thus, the inter-war army possessed a paper doctrine that promised to secure victory through mechanized, combined arms operations. But it lacked a commonly understood interpretation of that doctrine, an appropriate command and control system, and a training regime, to exploit the advantages which mechanization and the co-operation of all arms might have conferred upon it. It found itself at a particular disadvantage in 1940–2 when confronted by an enemy committed to manoeuvre warfare, because success so often depended upon being able to outwit the enemy. British commanders had little practice at doing so because few of the peacetime exercises they had undergone had been genuinely two-sided. Britain went to war with an army whose senior officers and equipment were largely untested at the highest level of field operations. Many senior officers had only a limited practical knowledge of how recent developments would affect field operations and most regi-

[83] LHCMA Kirke MSS 10/21, Maj.-Gen. J. Kennedy, 'Lessons of the War on the Western Front, 1915–16' [c.Oct. 1932]; PRO WO 32/2984, Finlayson to GOC-in-C Southern Command, 15 Jan. 1936.

[84] IWM Maj.-Gen. R. Briggs MSS 66/76/1, Opening Address delivered by FM the Rt. Hon. Visc. Montgomery of Alamein, CIGS, on the occasion of Exercise 'Evolution', held at the Staff College Camberley, 14 Aug. 1946.

[85] *The Ironside Diaries*, ed. Macleod and Kelly, 76.

[86] Ibid. 87.

mental officers and men had probably never taken part in a realistic large-scale exercise. This was doubly unfortunate, because the tactical and higher training of the German army was far more realistic. The Germans trained their leaders to act speedily. During TEWTs, for example, German infantry officers were given only a few minutes to propose a solution to the tactical problems they were set. Their British counterparts were usually given a whole hour.[87] Moreover, unlike the British, the inter-war German army did not neglect multi-divisional manoeuvres. From 1926 onwards the Reichswehr had held corps manoeuvres on an annual cycle, and by the time it confronted the BEF in 1940, it had already fought in Poland and absorbed the lessons of that campaign.[88]

The British army was defeated in 1940 for a variety of reasons. Some, such as its paucity of troops, equipment, and air support, and a poor allied plan that thrust the BEF into Belgium and exposed its lines of communication to a devastating German riposte, were beyond its control. But other factors were not. The British were also defeated because they did not foresee how German doctrine and organization would interact with their own on the battlefield. They had failed to take advantage of the lull in operations in the winter of 1939–40 to train for the campaign they actually fought, and their C3I system could not cope with the tempo of operations that the Germans imposed upon it.

By 1939 the British had decided that the way to stop a German armoured attack was not to try to outmanoeuvre the Panzers. Instead, they wanted to create a deep defensive front that would absorb the shock of their attack and prevent them breaking out into open country.[89] The Poles believed that in-depth defences against the Panzers required two lines of defences, the second based on a series of natural obstacles and out of range of German artillery, and that they had to have the support of adequate anti-aircraft artillery, fighter cover, and mobile armoured formations available to counter-attack.[90] However, the BEF lacked the material to produce such a system, although some senior officers deluded themselves into believing that it could cope.[91] In October 1939, Pownall rejoiced that if the BEF advanced to the Escaut it would have no fewer than three anti-tank obstacles upon which it could base its defences and that it possessed a higher proportion of anti-tank guns than either the French or German armies.[92] In fact, 2nd division

---

[87] A. Farrar-Hockley, *Infantry Tactics 1939–1945* (London, 1976), 14–15.
[88] Corum, *The Roots of Blitzkrieg*, 183–6.
[89] PRO WO 287/226, Tactical and Technical Notes on the German Army no. 7, Oct. 1939.
[90] PRO WO 287/226, Tactical and Technical notes on the German Army no. 8, Nov. 1939.
[91] J. B. A. Bailey, *Field Artillery and Firepower* (Oxford, 1989), 168–9.
[92] *Chief of Staff*, ed. Bond, i, 243.

had only sixty-three anti-tank guns to cover a front of nearly 12,000 yards, giving a ratio of one gun for every 180 yards. German doctrine suggested the proper ratio was one gun for every 34 yards. The divisional commander blithely disregarded such calculations, confident that the Germans were wrong because their doctrine took no account of the plenitude of anti-tank rifles with which his troops were equipped.[93]

Throughout the campaign, the shortage of troops meant that the BEF was compelled to hold far longer stretches of front than was practicable, given its paucity of mobile reserves ready to seal off German penetrations. GHQ hoped that each division would only be required to hold between 5,000 and 6,000 metres of front, and even then conceded that it would only have sufficient reserves for local counter-attacks.[94] On the Dyle, Gort deployed his nine divisions in depth, but the three in the front line were each holding nearly 10,500 yards. On the Escaut, he deployed seven divisions to hold a front of nearly 53,000 yards, or 7,500 yards per division. Each battalion in the forward positions was required to hold about a mile of winding riverbank. On the south-western front, such a density of troops to front was regarded as a luxury. On 18 May, for example, 'MacForce', a single infantry brigade supported by two field regiments and a battery of anti-tank guns, was deployed on a front of over 26,000 yards between Raches and St Amand in an effort to deny the Scarpe crossings to the Germans. By the evening of 22 May, Gort had established a thinly held line stretching 45 miles from Gravelines on the coast along a series of canals to St Omer, Béthune, and La Bassée. Just how thinly this was held can be judged when it is noted that the line had no fewer than forty-four crossing-places and each battalion was required to hold an average of over 12,000 yards. The BEF's greatest extension came on 25 May, when seven divisions, with three in reserve, were trying to hold a front of over 150,000 yards.[95] The fact that the British habitually prepared their positions for all-round defence was of little help. The extended fronts between the localities often made it impossible for them to give each other mutual support.[96]

German tactics were well suited to exploiting these weaknesses. Their operations were characterized by speed and heavy fire-power at the point of maximum effort.[97] As soon as their reconnaissance units had

[93] PRO WO 167/203, War Diary, G. branch, 2 divn., 5 Nov. 1939.

[94] *Chief of Staff*, ed. Bond, i, 237; LHCMA Bridgeman MSS 2/1, Bridgeman, Notes on operations in Belgium and Flanders, 10 May–3 June, compiled by the General Staff of GHQ, BEF.   [95] Ellis, *France and Flanders*, 38, 64, 69, 117–18, 147.

[96] PRO WO 106/1775, Montgomery, Important lessons from the operations of the BEF in France and Belgium—May 1940, 14 June 1940; PRO WO 106/1775, Maj. R. B. B. Colvin to 'My dear Alex[ander]', 5 June 1940; PRO WO 277/5, Pemberton, *Artillery Tactics*, 37.

[97] PRO WO 106/1775, Maj. R. B. B. Colvin to 'My dear Alex[ander]', 5 June 1940; LHCMA Bridgeman MSS 2/1, Bridgeman, Notes on the operations in Belgium and Flanders 10 May–3 June 1940.

made contact with the BEF's forward positions, they mounted a series of probing attacks 'which taps along the front line until a weak spot or gap is found'. Once they found it, they crossed the obstacles covering the British front, established a bridgehead, widened it, and built a bridge so that they could bring tanks and other support troops across. If the reconnaissance unit failed to find a weak spot, their follow-up forces put down a concentration of gun and mortar fire, sometimes assisted by Stukas, and crossed the obstacle behind a curtain of fire. Once they had established a bridgehead, they infiltrated between the British-defended localities, with apparent disregard for their flanks, and pushed mobile troops well forward to further disrupt the defenders by seizing focal points such as towns and road junctions.[98]

The BEF's attempts to deny roads to the Panzers by holding and forti-fying villages was often rendered nugatory by the German practice of employing dive-bombers to drop incendiary bombs on them.[99] The Luftwaffe's ability to deliver close air support within as little as 45 minutes of the troops requesting it, impressed and demoralized the British.[100] By contrast, inadequate air support handicapped the BEF. The lessons of Spain and Poland had further reinforced the RAF's dislike of providing aircraft for CAS. The Germans had developed powerful light flak weapons that could exact an excessively heavy toll on aircraft flying such missions.[101] Throughout the winter of 1939–40, GHQ and the War Office fought a largely unsuccessful running battle to persuade the Air Ministry to place more aircraft at Gort's disposal in case of a German attack. The RAF's only concession was to accept that in some circum-stances the light bombers of the Advanced Air Striking Force in France might be required to act in direct support of the BEF. However, they continued to resist the idea that the whole of Bomber Command should be diverted to attacking German troops if they invaded the Low Countries.[102]

Without adequate fighter support, the light bombers of the AASF and of the BEF's air component were quickly decimated when they tried to attack German communications centres behind the lines. After the fall of Abbeville, the Air Component was evacuated to England and henceforth

---

[98] PRO WO 106/1775, Report of the Bartholomew Committee, 2 July 1940; LHCMA Bridgeman MSS 2/2, Bridgeman, Notes on the operations in Flanders and Belgium 10–31 May with particular reference to the present problem of home defence [c.July 1940]; PRO WO 106/1775, Montgomery, Important lessons.

[99] PRO WO 167/203, War diary, G branch, 2 divn. Intelligence summary No. 102, 30 June 1940.

[100] PRO WO 106/1775, Report of the Bartholomew Committee, 2 July 1940.

[101] PRO WO 277/34, Army Air Support and Photographic Interpretation, 1939–45, 12.

[102] Chief of Staff, ed. Bond, i, 237; PRO CAB 92/111/LF(39), Minutes of 4 meeting of the Land Forces Committee, 23 Oct. 1939; PRO CAB 65/2/WM75(39), War Cabinet, 8 Nov. 1939; PRO CAB 65/2/WM106(39), War Cabinet, 8 Dec. 1939.

the RAF flew missions in support of the BEF from the far side of the Channel. Bereft of adequate communications, this meant that little effective bomber support could be provided for Gort's troops before they reached Dunkirk and only intermittent fighter cover was supplied as they waited to embark.[103] In contrast, after achieving air superiority, the Luftwaffe played a major role in disrupting the BEF's C3I system, interdicting its supply lines, and undermining its morale.[104] German air attacks often caused little material damage. The commanding officer of the 1st Tank Brigade at Arras reported that although his formation had been heavily attacked by Stukas, they had knocked out only two tanks.[105] But the psychological impact of even a near miss could be devastating. An infantryman whose battalion was attacked by fifty Stukas in fifteen minutes thought that

An attack by Stukas in these numbers cannot be described, it is entirely beyond the comprehension of anyone who has not experienced it. The noise alone strikes such terror that the body becomes paralysed, the still active mind is convinced that each and every aircraft is coming for you personally, you feel that you have grown so large that they cannot possibly miss.[106]

The RAF did exact a heavy toll of German aircraft in its efforts to protect the allied armies during the evacuation.[107] However, most air battles took place away from Dunkirk and out of sight of the troops on the beaches. Confronted by an enemy against whom they could not retaliate, they arrived in England bitterly angry at the apparent inability of the RAF to protect them.[108]

Shortages of men, material, and air cover only partly explain the BEF's defeat in 1940. To these must be added another cause, the failure of the army's C3I system to cope with the high tempo of operations that the Germans forced upon it. The secret of the success of the German blitzkrieg in 1940 was not that it killed large numbers of enemy soldiers but that it destroyed the allied command, control, communications, and

[103] PRO WO 277/34. Army Air Support, 16; B. Collier, *The Defence of the United Kingdom* (London, 1957), 113–16; Ellis, *France and Flanders*, 53–4, 60; PRO WO 197/97, GSO2, HQ, BEF, The work of the Air Component during May 1940, c.4 June 1940.

[104] W. Murray, *Luftwaffe. Strategy for Defeat 1939–45* (London, 1988), 71–2; Corum, 'The Luftwaffe's Army support doctrine', 68–73; Bryant, *Turn of the Tide*, 105.

[105] B. Greenhous, 'Aircraft versus Armour: Cambrai to Yom Kippur', in T. Travers and C. Archer (eds.), *Men at War. Politics, Technology and Innovation in the Twentieth Century* (Chicago, 1982), 96, 98; J. S. Corum, 'From bi-planes to blitzkrieg', 97; PRO WO 277/5, Pemberton, *Artillery Tactics*, 39; PRO WO 231/1, DMT to C-in-C Home Forces, Notes on the tactical and administrative lessons of the campaign in Norway, 7 June 1940.

[106] Holding, *Since I Bore Arms*, 129.

[107] Murray, *Luftwaffe*, 75.

[108] Seton-Watson, *Dunkirk–Alamein–Bologna*, 29; PRO WO 197/97, GSO2, HQ, BEF, The work of the Air Component during May 1940, c.4 June 1940.

intelligence system. What that meant was, according to Brigadier Oliver Leese, who joined GHQ as DCGS on 10 May, that

Decisions had to be made so very quickly and so often could not be confirmed on the basis of the information coming in. Because of these armoured vehicles, the general moves the Germans made were so quick and where you may have a stable situation in the morning, by 7 o'clock or 8 o'clock in the evening, if you did not act and do something, the situation might be irretrievably lost.[109]

He believed 'we never really got a good working system going in the time with the speed with which the operations went'.[110] This was not just a problem for army headquarters. It affected headquarters at all levels. On 20 May 48th Division's intelligence summary admitted, for example, that 'Events have moved so swiftly since the period covered by this report that it is impossible to deduce a course of conduct based purely on the information given'.[111]

The efficient functioning of the British C3I system was impeded by a number of factors. Gort was handicapped by having to act not only as an army commander but also as the C-in-C of all British forces in France.[112] He did not make his own task any easier by the way he organized his staff. Fear of air attack persuaded him to disperse his HQ across fifty square miles around Arras, although its war establishment had been prepared on the assumption that it would be concentrated in a single town.[113] Communications between its various components were already difficult even before active operations began in May 1940. They then became infinitely worse when Gort formed a Command Post forward of GHQ. In particular, the collection and dissemination of intelligence material almost ceased, and the QMG found that he had too few staff officers to perform his duties adequately.[114]

With the exception of I Corps, all the BEF's higher staffs had to be improvised after the start of the war. Individual staffs took their tone and acquired their efficiency from their commander. Officers who came into contact with them habitually compared the efficiency of Lieutenant-General M. Barker's I Corps or Major-General H. C. Loyd's 2nd division unfavourably with that of Brooke's II Corps or Montgomery's

---

[109] LHCMA Bartholomew MSS 3/1, WO, DMT, Notes of a committee set up to consider the lessons learnt from the operations in Flanders [c.June 1940].

[110] Ibid.

[111] PRO WO 167/289, War dairy, G branch, 48th divn., Intelligence summary no. 12, 20 May 1940.

[112] Lieut.-Gen. Sir P. Neame, *Playing with Strife. The Autobiography of a Soldier* (London, 1947), 256.

[113] *Chief of Staff*, ed. Bond, i. 242.

[114] PRO WO 197/111, DQMG, BEF to CGS and QMG, BEF, 17 June 1940; J. R. Colville, *Man of Valour. Field-Marshal Lord Gort* (London, 1972), 190, 194–5; PRO WO 197/110, Lindell, 'Q' notes in connection with operations in France and Belgium 10–31 May 1940, 17 June 1940.

3rd division.[115] This was a product of their relative state of training. The BEF's commanders knew that their troops suffered from a training deficit. In September 1939, for example, the divisions and brigades in II Corps had done no brigade or divisional training.[116] The Territorials who joined the BEF in early 1940 were even worse prepared.[117] It was hardly surprising, therefore, that the CIGS told Gort that 'he [was] to train his army first when he [got] to France'.[118] But the obstacles in the way of doing so were formidable. They included not only the lack of modern equipment and manoeuvre-grounds, but also the fact that units spent too much time building fortifications along the Franco-Belgian frontier. GHQ was uncertain about the kind of operation for which the troops should train, in November 1939 issuing orders for them to pre-pare for both a defensive battle against German air, armoured, and mobile formations and for offensive operations against fortified posi-tions.[119] Finally, recognizing the need to train troops in the field was one thing; doing so was another. The pernicious effect of allowing com-manders wide latitude to train their own troops was soon visible, for some senior officers failed to translate the realization that their troops needed more training into action. In the winter of 1939–40, whereas 3rd Division (II Corps) held no fewer than four divisional exercises, each of which lasted for several days, 2nd division (I Corps) conducted only two short movement exercises. The upshot was that on the eve of the German onslaught Gort believed that his regular divisions were still not as well trained as their 1914-vintage counterparts and his Territorials were fit only for static operations.[120] Something of the flavour of this failure of imagination was made apparent by the report of two staff officers who visited seven of the divisions that had fought in France.

There was a general complaint that training up to the time of active opera-tions had been lacking in realism and that the written word of reports on German methods was insufficient to prepare troops for actual operations. The continuous appearance of enemy aircraft, the wide frontages of units, resulting in the frequent penetration of enemy troops, and the speed of development of the enemy attack, all surprised our troops and created a tendency to "keep look-ing over the shoulder to the rear."[121]

[115] Sir B. Bartlett, *My First War. An Army Officer's Journal for May 1940* (London, 1940), 85; Henniker, *Image of War*, 23.

[116] LHCMA Alanbrooke MSS 5/2/14, Alanbrooke, 'Notes from my Life, ii. The Inter-War Years, 1919–39', 94.

[117] D. Lindsay, *Forgotten General. A Life of Sir Andrew Thorne* (London, 1987), 137; PRO WO 197/129, Extracts from war diaries of the BEF reviewed by the General Staff [*c.*Jan. 1941].

[118] Maj.-Gen. Sir J. Kennedy, *Business of War* (London, 1957), 22.

[119] LHCMA Bridgeman MSS 3/1, Pownall to I and II Corps and GHQ troops, Training instructions for the BEF, 10 Nov. 1939.

[120] PRO WO 259/59, Gort to Stanley, 11 Apr. 1940.

[121] PRO WO 208/2050A, Lessons in organization and staff duties and minor tactics from BEF, May 1940.

The first symptom of the fact that the BEF could not cope with the pace of operations was the collapse of its communication system. Soon after the start of the German attack, the BEF discovered that its reliance upon cable communications was dangerously misplaced. The British and French believed that telephone communications would be safe because the main French trunk lines were carried by buried cables. However, many of them ran alongside main roads and were quickly cut by German bombing. The telephone system also restricted the movement of GHQ because it could move only to where it could tap into the international telephone system. Even when the cables had not been cut, French telephone operators were not always co-operative, and were liable to break the connection in mid-call or to close down the system entirely when their shift had finished.[122] Attempts to link corps and lower headquarters to the international telephone system failed because the distances involved were too great for the available cable and because lower headquarters moved too frequently.[123] The task of the signal staff was made even more difficult by the propensity of some Operations Staff officers to forget to warn them of impending moves.[124]

The BEF was, therefore, compelled to rely upon radio communications to a much greater extent than it had envisaged before 1939, only to discover that it had too few of the right kind of sets, too few trained operators, and that its security procedures placed an unacceptable delay on the speed of transmissions. After the campaign, the British blamed the French for causing their communications to collapse by insisting the BEF maintain radio silence during the 'Phoney War'.[125] But that was only one reason why the BEF's communications failed. By 1944, each infantry division had nearly 1,000 wireless sets. In 1940, they had only 75, and many of those could only transmit Morse, lacked sufficient range, and were too cumbersome for mobile operations. Crucial units within the division, like RE field companies, had no wireless transmitters.[126] Forward of corps headquarters, the transmission of wireless messages in cipher, rather than the employment of simple code words for places, names, and formations, placed an intolerable delay in trans-

---

[122] A. Wade, *A Life on the Line* (Tunbridge Wells, 1988), 96; PRO WO 197/103, Maj.-Gen. R. Chenevix-Trench, Operations from 10 May. Lessons of campaign, 17 June 1940; M. Reid, *Last on the List* (London, 1974), 26; R. Ryder, *Oliver Leese* (London, 1987), 75.

[123] PRO WO 197/103, Wade, Operations from 10 May 1940, Lessons of campaign, 31 May 1940.

[124] PRO WO 197/103, Maj.-Gen. R. Chenevix-Trench, Operations from 10 May; PRO WO 197/103, GSO2(Wireless) BEF, Recommendations for improvement of GHQ wireless communications as a result of the Flanders campaign, 8 June 1940.

[125] PRO WO 197/103, Maj.-Gen. R. Chenevix-Trench, Operations from 10 May; PRO WO 167/203, War diary, G branch, 2nd divn., GSO 2 to bgd. commanders, 11 Oct. 1939.

[126] Henniker, *Image of War*, 15; PRO WO 277/25, Gravely, *Signals Communications*, 6, 138; PRO WO 106/1775, Report of the Bartholomew Committee, 2 July 1940; PRO WO 277/5, Pemberton, *Artillery Tactics*, 37.

mitting information.[127] Wireless, therefore, proved to be no substitute for cable.

Like the rest of GHQ's staff, Gort's intelligence organization was improvised at the start of the war. The Germans achieved complete tactical surprise on 10 May and within a few days GHQ's intelligence staff had virtually ceased to function. The Germans had maintained wireless silence during the 'Phoney War' and so the British had no practice at breaking into the German army's radio traffic.[128] However, they could intercept the many plain text tactical messages that the Germans sent, and, beginning on 22 May, GC&CS began to decipher Luftwaffe Enigma messages. But the real potential of these sources was never utilized. The BEF's intercept service lacked sufficient linguists who were well versed in German military terms and the dissemination of intelligence between intercept stations, GHQ, and lower headquarters suffered from the same weaknesses as the rest of the BEF's communications system.[129]

Handicapped by the rapid collapse of their C3I system, senior commanders had to improvise ways of commanding. In the early part of the campaign, GHQ relied upon Number 3 Air Mission, which had been renamed 'Phantom' in February 1940, as a general news-gathering service independent of the normal chain of command.[130] As early as 16 May, Corps and Divisional commanders had stopped issuing detailed written orders. Instead they were going forward to subordinate headquarters to hold orders groups, issuing verbal orders, followed, only if time allowed, by brief written confirmation or map tracings showing objectives and boundaries between units.[131] They also employed motor contact officers, who not only delivered orders, but, if they were properly trained, could give their own commander a first-hand account of the position at the front. But there were too few of them, many were not trained, and refugees blocking the roads often delayed their progress.[132]

That the BEF escaped from Dunkirk owed much to the qualities of its

[127] PRO WO 106/1775, Report of the Bartholomew Committee, 2 July 1940.

[128] F. H. Hinsley et al., *British Intelligence in the Second World War* (London, 1979), i, 146.

[129] Colvile, *Man of Valour*, 199; Bond, *Britain, France and Belgium*, 104; Hinsley *et al.*, *British Intelligence*, i, 144–5; H. Skillen, *Spies of the Airwaves. A History of Y Sections during the Second World War* (Pinner, Middx., 1989), 56–7; PRO WO 106/1775, Report of the Bartholomew Committee, 2 July 1940.

[130] R. J. T. Hills, *Phantom Was There* (London, 1951), 18–31.

[131] PRO WO 208/2050A, Lessons in organization; Bryant, *Turn of the Tide*, 120, 142; PRO WO 167/203, War diary, G Branch, 2 divn., 16 May 1940. Between 26 and 29 May Montgomery held no fewer than three orders groups with his unit commanders; PRO WO 167/218: War Diary, G. Branch, 3rd divn., entries for 26, 27, 29 May 1940.

[132] PRO WO 106/1775, Report of the Bartholomew Committee, 2 July 1940; PRO WO 208/2050A, Lessons in organization; PRO WO 197/103, Maj.-Gen. R. Chenevix-Trench, Operations from 10 May.

commanders. Gort's 'mental toughness' was his greatest contribution to the conduct of operations.[133] Unlike many of his French colleagues, he preserved an equable temperament and inspired confidence in his subordinates. Despite the collapse of his C3I system, he maintained a bleakly realistic understanding of the predicament within which the BEF found itself, and issued the appropriate orders to extricate it from what would otherwise have been a complete débâcle. On 20 May he had the moral courage to oppose pressure from Ironside and the War Cabinet to retreat south-westwards towards Amiens to link with the main French forces. Such an operation would have exposed the whole of his force to a flank attack by the German Panzers. He also acted sufficiently swiftly to improvise scratch formations to protect his rear. On 25 May he had the good sense to withdraw the 5th and 50th divisions from a projected Anglo-French counter-offensive southwards and to use them to plug a dangerous gap between the BEF and the Belgians to the north. In doing so, he forestalled a German attack that would have broken through the BEF's left flank and surrounded it.[134] Given the odds stacked against him, it was inconceivable that he could have won a great victory. At least he avoided an even greater defeat.

Gort's divisional and corps commanders were amongst the beneficiaries of Hore-Belisha's determination to reduce the age of senior officers. Gort's divisional commanders on 10 May 1940 were on average just over fifty-three years old. After a brief visit to the BEF, Ironside told the War Cabinet on 21 May that 'On the whole our own High Command were standing up well to the situation, although one or two changes had been made among the corps and divisional commanders'.[135] In reality, what the campaign demonstrated was that Hore-Belisha's reforms had placed too much emphasis on relative youth as a qualification for high command. In early May, Brooke had decided to replace D. G. Johnson, GOC of 4th division, because he was fifty-six years old. However, active operations began before he could act, Johnson remained, and at the end of the campaign Brooke had no regrets that he had done so.[136] By contrast, as early as 16 May, H. C. Loyd, GOC 2nd division and, at forty-nine, one of the youngest divisional commanders, broke down under the strain.[137] Brooke, who was fifty-seven in 1940, existed on four or five hours sleep each night and still appeared imperturbable despite his own private doubts and fears.

[133] Horrocks, *A Full Life*, 80.
[134] Bond, *Britain, France and Belgium*, 108–112, 135; Sir J. Smyth, *The Only Enemy. An Autobiography* (London, 1959), 148–9; Ellis, *France and Flanders*, 148–9.
[135] PRO CAB 65/7/WM132(40), Minutes of the War Cabinet, 21 May 1940.
[136] LHCMA Alanbrooke MSS 5/2/15, Alanbrooke, 'Notes from My Life, *iii*. BEF. France-Flanders 1939–40', 102, 135.
[137] Henniker, *Image of War* (London, 1987), 18–19; LHCMA Liddell Hart MSS 1/460, *The Times*, 12 Nov. 1973.

By contrast Lieutenant-General Michael Barker, GOC of I Corps, who was a year younger, became 'very tired and', in Pownall's opinion, 'gave us all a lot of fuss later in the evening about when he could or could not start the retirement . . . He is much too excitable for a Corps Commander'.[138] The breakdowns of Loyd and Barker suggest that the real fault of the pre-war system of selecting senior officers was not that it promoted them when they were too old. Rather, it failed to test their ability to withstand the physical and mental strains of active service and to discard those found wanting.

For all its shortcomings, the BEF's C3I system operated just well enough to enable its commanders to extricate it from a disastrous situation. The retreat from the Dyle to the French frontier was carried out successfully and under GHQ's control in a series of bounds from one river line to the next. However, it was fortunate that Von Rundstedt issued his 'halt' order on 24 May, for that gave the British vital time to recover some of their balance. The claim later made by Major-General Viscount Bridgeman, who served as GSO1(Staff Duties) at GHQ that Gort 'never lost control at any stage of the battle' was an exaggeration. By 26 May, it was common for headquarters to be out of contact with both their superiors and their subordinates. Typical was the experience of Major-General E. A. Osborne, GOC 44th Division. From 26 May until the evacuation, he had no contact with his corps headquarters except for three messages, each of which arrived so late that it was out of date.[139]

The Dunkirk campaign, and the coterminous Norwegian campaign, therefore, revealed a long list of shortcomings in the training, equipment, and doctrine of the British army. On 30 May 1940, in the midst of evacuating his troops from Norway, Sir Claude Auchinleck still found time to write to Sir John Dill, the CIGS, hoping that

I may be able to help you make a new army. It will have [to be] a very different one from our last. War has changed. We are in the same position as were Napoleon's adversaries when he started in on them with his new organization and tactics. I feel we are much too slow and ponderous in every way.[140]

Auchinleck's thumbnail analysis of the problem was right. It remained to be seen how effectively the army could find an effective counter to this new Napoleon.

---

[138] *Chief of Staff*, ed. Bond, i., 320; Bryant, *Turn of the Tide*, 127.
[139] IWM Osborne MSS. Con Self, Diary entry, 27 May 1940.
[140] LHCMA Alanbrooke MSS 6/2/9, Auchinleck to Dill, 30 May 1940.

CHAPTER SIX

The Reformation of the Army, Home Forces, 1940–1943

Historians are divided over the extent to which the British army learnt the lessons of 1940. Some believe that, spurred on by Sir Alan Brooke, the training regime of Home Forces became tougher and more realistic. Others contend that the army failed to learn the lessons of 1940 because it did not train sufficiently hard, and because it lacked a single doctrinal centre able to disseminate the same lessons to the whole army. The result was that the army pursued a series of 'decentralised training programmes' which did not reflect a consistent battle doctrine.[1] There is a kernel of truth in both interpretations. Training, particularly at the tactical level, did become more realistic after Dunkirk. But, at the operational level, despite the shock of Dunkirk, little happened to alter the peacetime practice of allowing senior officers to interpret doctrine as they saw fit with the result that the army at home was slow to develop a consistent battle doctrine.

The fall of France undermined most of the major assumptions upon which the General Staff had based their strategic plans. Until June 1940, they expected to win the war by weakening the Axis powers through a combination of economic blockade, propaganda, and aerial bombardment. Only when they had sufficiently enfeebled their enemies did they intend to mount a final offensive, probably in 1942, to overthrow them.[2] The French collapse rendered that strategy obsolete. On 4 September 1940, the Chiefs of Staff presented 'An Appreciation on Future Strategy' to the Cabinet, the first full-scale review of British grand strategy since Dunkirk. The possibility of engaging in a climactic land offensive in western Europe was now a distant possibility and would not be possible unless German resistance had already been mortally weakened by blockade and air attacks. The immediate demands of home defence necessitated the production of warships and fighter planes before tanks and field guns. In the medium term, they determined to give priority to bombers because the only means Britain could employ to hurt Germany

---

[1] Fraser, *And We Shall Shock Them*, 87; Murray, 'British Military Effectiveness', 112.
[2] Gibbs, *Grand Strategy*, i, 668–80.

were blockade, bombing attacks, and support for indigenous resistance movements.[3] After Dunkirk, the army was, therefore, accorded a secondary role, for, as Churchill wrote in March 1941, the strategic situation, and in particular the size and strength of the German armed forces,

make it impossible for the Army, except in resisting invasion, to play a primary role in the defeat of the enemy. That task can only be done by the staying power of the Navy, and above all by the effect of Air predominance. Very valuable and important services may be rendered overseas by the Army in operations of a secondary order, and it is for these special operations that its organization and character should be adapted.[4]

Although a handful of formations were sent overseas in 1941–2, home defence remained the army's major mission until the end of 1942.[5] This had major repercussions on the pace and shape of the reformation of the army after Dunkirk.

Determined not to commit the same mistakes as the Asquith government of 1914–15, and allow the indiscriminate recruitment of soldiers before their equipment was ready, the Chamberlain government had decided to recruit no more than 60,000 conscripts per month. Young men in reserve occupations would be left in the factories while older men not doing essential war work were called up.[6] But in the summer of 1940 the Churchill government abandoned this rational policy of balancing the needs of industry and the army. Under pressure to do something to demonstrate its determination to continue fighting, it resorted to grand gestures. Between June and August 1940, 324,000 men were enlisted. The decision was taken against the advice of the Adjutant-General, who knew that the training system could not cope with such numbers. They were organized into 122 new infantry battalions, not because the army needed such a large increase in its infantry, but because the only weapons it had in stock were 300,000 First World War pattern rifles.[7]

---

[3] *Churchill War Papers, ii. Never Surrender, May–December 1940*, ed. M. Gilbert, ii, 492, 510, 762–3, 1,010–11; Butler, *Grand Strategy*, ii, 209–17, 251–2, 343–4.

[4] PRO PREM 3/55/1, Churchill, Directive by the Minister of Defence, 6 Mar. 1941.

[5] PRO WO 193/221, Directive for the guidance of the C-in-C, Home Forces for training of two Corps for operations overseas in 1941, 10 Oct. 1940; PRO WO 193/230, Extract from the minutes of the 307 & 310 meetings of COS committee, 2 & 3 Sept. 1941; PRO WO 193/230, FOPS, Continental operations on the lines foreshadowed in Section 9, Future Strategy Paper, Progress Report, 4 Sept. 1941; Collier, *Defence of the United Kingdom*, 100–6; PRO WO 193/786, DMO&I, Future army operations, 25 July 1940; PRO WO 193/101, Minute of the COS Committee, 7 Dec. 1942.

[6] PRO CAB 92/116/RF(40), War Cabinet Committee on Recruitment of the Armed Services, 26 Apr. 1940.

[7] PRO WO 163/48/ACM(AE)2, Minutes of the proceedings of the Army Council, 17 May 1940; PRO WO 163/48/ACM(AE)5, Minutes of the Army Council, 14 June 1940, and enc. Memorandum by the Adjutant-General on a proposal to increase home defence units, 14 June 1940; PRO WO 163/48/ACM(AE)7, Minutes of the Army Council, 17 June 1940; PRO WO

Much of the army's effort in the winter of 1941–2 and in 1942–3 was devoted to converting many of these battalions into armoured and artillery units when equipment for them became available. This accretion of strength meant that Churchill's government could reaffirm the fifty-five-division programme.[8] By March 1941, their target had risen to fifty-nine and one-third 'equivalent divisions', a figure that included a much higher proportion of armour—twelve armoured divisions and eight army tank brigades—than hitherto.[9] The final plan, FFC-36, prepared in May 1941, envisaged a field force by March 1942 of forty-seven infantry divisions, twelve armoured divisions, and eight independent tank brigades. Of this, the British were expected to find twenty-seven infantry divisions, ten armoured and seven independent tank brigades. The remainder was to be furnished by India, the Dominions, and the exiled allies.[10]

The army could not grow even larger because the necessary manpower was not available. In August 1940, Ernest Bevin, the Minister of Labour, inaugurated an inquiry into the manpower needed to fulfil the services' production programmes. It concluded that if the government met the army's demands for a million extra men by October 1941, the troops could not be equipped because industry would face a manpower famine.[11] Even the VCIGS admitted in November 1940 that 'you cannot at one and the same time have more men in the Army and greater production for the Army'.[12] Churchill's initial reaction was to create a leaner army. The 'divisional slice' of formations in the Middle East was 35,000 men and of field force divisions in the UK 24,000 men. The establishment of an infantry division was 15,500 men, yet only 6,750 of them were front line infantrymen. In Churchill's opinion there was too much 'fluff and flummery behind the fighting troops'. The Adjutant-General argued in vain that many of the units Churchill dismissed were 'not ineffectives' but fighting troops. The large number of line of com-

163/48/ACM(AE)12, Minutes of the proceedings of the Army Council, 27 July 1940; *Hansard* 362 HC Deb. 5s., cols. 11–12, 53, 18 June 1940; PRO WO 163/48/ACM(AE)10, Minutes of the Army Council, 28 June 1940.

[8] PRO WO 163/48/ACM(AE)4, Minutes of the Army Council, 7 June 1940; PRO WO 260/41, DSD to PUS, War Office, 12 June 1940; PRO WO 163/48/ACM(AE)3, Minutes of the Army Council, 3 June 1940; PRO WO 163/48/ACM(AE)30, Minutes of the Army Council, 16 Dec. 1940.

[9] F. W. Perry, *The Commonwealth Armies. Manpower and Organization in Two World Wars* (Manchester, 1988), 55; Butler, *Grand Strategy*, ii, 2, 256–7.

[10] PRO WO 277/8, Anon., 'Fighting, Support, and Transport Vehicles', 20–1; PRO WO 193/37, Field Force Committee, FFC 36, 6 May 1941; PRO WO 193/980, Lt.-Col. V. Dykes to DMO&P, 7 May 1941.

[11] Hancock and Gowing, *British War Economy*, 283–8; PRO WO 163/48/ACM(AE)28, Minutes of the Army Council, 14 Nov. 1940; (AE)69, Adjutant-General, Manpower, 12 Nov. 1940; (AE)70 Permanent Under Secretary, Manpower, 13 Nov. 1940.

[12] PRO WO 163/48/ACM(AE)29, Minutes of the Army Council, 26 Nov.1940.

munications units sent to the Middle East was essential because the Dominions provided only divisional formations and the British had to provide the rearward services they required.[13]

By March 1941, Churchill's manpower economy drive had failed to show sufficient results. The War Cabinet, therefore, promulgated the Army Scales Directive, setting the manpower 'ceiling' of troops raised in Britain at 2,195,000 men. This figure was arrived at after an assessment of the country's manpower resources, economic capacity, and the immediate strategic situation. Shipping shortages meant that no more than three or four divisions could be sent from Britain to the Middle East. The strength of the German army meant that the army need prepare no more than eight to ten divisions, with a high proportion of armour, as an amphibious striking force for operations elsewhere. Most troops would, therefore, remain committed to Home Forces and unless the army experienced heavier than expected casualties, its intake would be confined to annual cohorts of about 240,000 eighteen- and nineteen-year olds, just enough to replace 'normal' wastage.[14] Although some slight upward adjustments were allowed later in the war, the size of the army was now fixed.

In view of these constraints, the British government could only come close to achieving the targets in Field Force Conspectus-36 by resorting to a series of increasingly desperate expedients. At the outbreak of war in September 1939, the army could claim that it could field thirty-three divisions, two armoured, seven regular infantry divisions, twelve first-line territorial divisions and the same number of second-line Territorial divisions, and five independent tank brigades. However, all of them were short of equipment, and the dozen second-line Territorial divisions, the product of the Chamberlain government's hasty decision to double the size of the Territorial army, really only existed on paper. By the end of 1939 two more divisions, one armoured and one cavalry, were being raised, making a total of thirty-five divisions. In 1940 a further three armoured and two 'County' divisions were formed. Equipped on a much lower scale than field force divisions, the function of the latter was to delay a German landing on the beaches long enough to allow mobile field force divisions to mount a counter-attack.[15]

However, in February 1940 an infantry division was disbanded in Palestine and, following the Dunkirk evacuation a further four Territorial divisions were disbanded. The net strength of the army's Order of Battle had, therefore, remained the same. The following year

[13] PRO PREM 3/55/7, Churchill to Eden, 9 Dec. 1940; PRO PREM 3/55/7, Churchill to Margesson, 29 Jan. 1941; PRO PREM 3/55/7, Lindemann to Churchill, 24 Jan. 1941.
[14] PRO PREM 3/55/1, Churchill, Directive by the Minister of Defence, 6 Mar. 1941; PRO WO 193/979, DSD to General Staff Directors, 13 Mar. 1941.
[15] PRO WO 260/43, DSD to Brooke, 15 Feb. 1941.

witnessed what seemed at first sight to be a major expansion of the army, with the formation of no fewer than four more armoured divisions, one airborne division, two infantry divisions, and eight 'County' divisions. However, the latter were very short lived and by the end of the year all ten County divisions had been disbanded, the 2nd Armoured division had been destroyed in North Africa and not re-formed, and one of the new Armoured divisions had been formed by re-equipping the Cavalry division. By the end of 1941 the total number of British field force divisions stood at one airborne, nine armoured, and twenty-seven infantry, plus eleven independent tank brigades. In 1942 another armoured division (79th Armoured) was added, as were two further tank brigades and the 78th Infantry division. But in February the 18th Infantry division was captured at Singapore and never re-formed and two tank brigades were also disbanded.

However, the army's ability to increase very slightly the number of its field force divisions in 1942 hid a growing weakness. It was only able to maintain this number of divisions by resorting to two expedients. Between November 1941 and January 1942, lack of equipment, and in particular shortages of motor transport and artillery, forced the War Office to place no fewer than six infantry divisions on a new lower establishment. They had two rather than three field regiments, were without either a machine gun or a reconnaissance battalion, had fewer engineers and only a single RASC company compared to three in a higher establishment division.[16] Furthermore, the War Office was only able to find lines of communications troops and drafts for formations overseas by disbanding a growing number of airfield defence battalions, independent brigades and the 'County' divisions and by milking the lower establishment divisions.[17] By 1943, however, this expedient was exhausted, and the disbandment of first-line field force formations began. Although another airborne division was formed in May 1943 and a weak infantry division had been added to the order of battle in January, no fewer than two armoured and three infantry divisions were disbanded in the course of the year. Therefore, at the beginning of 1944 the army could field eight armoured, two airborne, and twenty-five infantry divisions. However, of the latter only seventeen were higher establishment divisions and fit to fight overseas. The remainder were on lower establishments or acting as holding and training formations in Britain and so could not be sent abroad. The commitment of troops to both Italy and North West Europe in the second half of 1944, and the army's inability to make good its losses, meant that the process of dis-

---

[16] PRO WO 260/43, DSD to Brooke, 11 Nov. 1941
[17] PRO WO 199/453, Paget to PUS, War Office, 2 June 1942; PRO WO 193/230, DSD to DCIGS, 18 July 1942.

banding whole divisions accelerated in 1944. A further three armoured divisions and four infantry divisions were disbanded, losses for which the formation of a single new infantry division was no real compensation. By the end of 1944 the army possessed only five armoured divisions, seven independent tank brigades, and twenty-one infantry divisions. This meant that, as the war continued and casualties rose as increasing numbers of divisions became engaged in active operations, commanders had constantly to be calculating the possible rewards of offensive operations against the growing likelihood that their losses could not be replaced.

The army lost no time in analysing the lessons of the Dunkirk campaign. Nevertheless, despite the magnitude of their defeat and the celerity with which the War Office acted, the recommendations that they gathered and implemented were not fundamentally radical. They remained committed to their belief that the army able to deploy the greater weight of material won wars and that fire-power generated by combined arms action was essential to facilitate mobility and win battles. They did recognize that one of the main reasons why the Germans had won was because the BEF's C3I system could not cope with the rapid tempo of operations the Germans forced upon them. But they believed that high morale, stricter discipline, greater organizational decentralization in the shape of brigade groups, and more weapons would suffice to overcome them.

By 12 June 1940, a committee under Lieutenant-General Sir William Bartholomew, GOC Northern Command, was taking evidence on the course of operations in France. Its other members consisted of the DMT at the War Office, Major-General C. C. Malden, and three officers with actual experience of the campaign, Major General N. M. S. Irwin, GOC 2nd Division, and the BGGS of I and III Corps, W. C. Holden and D. G. Watson. They were asked to consider the lessons of operations in France and Flanders and to suggest any necessary modifications to the army's organization and training in the light of the threatened German invasion. They took oral or written evidence from divisional, brigade, and artillery commanders, as well as a handful of battalion and regimental commanders. Their report was ready by 2 July.[18] The Royal

---

[18] PRO WO 106/1775, Report of the Bartholomew Committee, 2 July 1940; LHCMA Bridgeman MSS 2/1, Notes on the operations in Flanders and Belgium, 10–31 May 1940 [c.July 1940], and Notes on the operations in Belgium and Flanders, 10 May–3 June 1940 compiled by the General Staff of GHQ, BEF; PRO WO 197/111, DQMG, BEF to CGS and QMG BEF, 17 June 1940; PRO WO 197/110, Lindsell, Q notes in connection with operations in France and Belgium, 10 May–31 May 1940, 17 June 1940; PRO WO 197/103, Maj.-Gen. R. Chenevix-Trench, Operations from 10 May, Lessons of Campaign, 17 June 1940; PRO WO 208/205A, Lessons in organisation and staff duties and minor tactics from BEF, May 1940, Memo; PRO WO 32/9642, Martel to Dewing, 9 July 1940.

Artillery and the RAC formed their own committees, and a separate committee presided over by Lieutenant-General Sir G. W. Howard collected the lessons of operations which took place on the lines of communication south of the Somme after 10 June.[19]

These reports highlighted several major lessons and a long list of minor ones. Fostering high morale was essential, and troops had to possess 'The offensive spirit'. They also had to be much more physically fit and all units, particularly rear echelon ones, had to be more disciplined. Tactically, the campaign showed that river lines and obstacles not covered by fire would not stop the Germans. Gort's General Staff believed that the French had lost the campaign because 'The "Maginot line complex" had led them to forget defence in depth'.[20] Henceforth, all defended localities had to be organized for all-round defence. Troops had to stand fast when surrounded in the certain knowledge that reserves were on hand to mount an immediate counter-attack to relieve them. The Panzers were the cutting edge of the German army. To defeat them the British army not only needed more tanks and anti-tank guns, but troops had to lose their fear of enemy tanks. The latter could be stopped if they were divorced from their supporting infantry. Defending infantry, strongly supported by medium machine-guns, could deal with the latter, whilst anti-tank weapons, well-concealed and sited in great depth, could surprise the Panzers by hitting them in the flank. British tanks and infantry could complete the victory by counter-attacking.[21]

To achieve these goals, the army needed a more flexible organization, an improved reconnaissance capability, and heavier and more effective fire-support. As early as 27 May, faced with the possibility of a great number of German landings at different points, Ironside told the War Cabinet that 'We were working on the basis of small, mobile columns'.[22] The Bartholomew Committee concluded that in view of the extended fronts across which the army would probably have to fight in the event of an invasion, pre-war teaching about the primacy of the division as the basic tactical unit was misplaced. The committee's ideal was a flexible division, one which could be controlled centrally, but which could also be divided into three brigade groups. The army retained its basic

---

[19] PRO WO 32/2384, Report of a committee to enquire into the lessons to be learned from the evacuation from the area south of the River Somme after 10 June 1940, with special reference to the possibility of whether the evacuation of arms, equipment, vehicles and stores could reasonably have been increased under the existing circumstances, and to report, 4 Nov. 1940; PRO WO 106/1775, PA, IMT co-ordination papers, n.d.

[20] LHCMA Bridgeman MSS, Bridgeman, Notes on the operations in Belgium and Flanders, 10 May–3 June 1940 compiled by the General Staff of GHQ, BEF.

[21] LHCMA Bridgeman MSS 2/2, Bridgeman, Notes on operations in Flanders and Belgium, 10–31 May 1940 with particular reference to the present problem of home defence [c.July 1940].

[22] PRO CAB 65/7/WM141(40), /WM147(40), Minutes of the War Cabinet, 27, 30 May 1940.

divisional structure but, within days of Dunkirk, formations in Britain were being reorganized into brigade groups with the aim, according to Brooke, of ensuring that 'the various arms were in intimate co-operation for offensive action'.[23] Each brigade group was to consist of three infantry battalions, a battery of anti-tank guns, a field regiment, a machine-gun company, and an AA platoon of heavy machine-guns.[24] This organization did undoubtedly provide a more flexible formation, but it did so, as Montgomery recognized, at the expense of the Bartholomew's Committee's other goal, of providing heavier and more effective fire-support because the new organization impeded 'centralised artillery control'.[25] The Army Council therefore decided to retain the basic pre-war organization of divisions but insisted that 'The affiliation of artillery regiments and field companies [of the Royal Engineers] to infantry brigades must, however, be much closer than heretofore'. The adoption of the brigade group organization therefore antedated the desert campaign of 1941.

The provision of effective fire-support in France had also been impeded because, while artillery regiments were organized on a two-battery basis, infantry brigades were organized on a three-battalion basis. Bartholomew and the Royal Artillery's own enquiry agreed that each field regiment should be reorganized on a three-battery basis to foster closer co-operation.[26] But the infantry did not entirely trust the gunners to be constantly on tap. They had been so impressed by the weight of mortar fire directed against them that they wanted more of their own pocket artillery and insisted that the number of 3-in mortars per battalion should be tripled.[27]

Tactical reconnaissance had also been seriously deficient throughout the campaign. The armoured cavalry regiments which had formed part of the regular divisions (but not the Territorial divisions) of the BEF were to be replaced by reconnaissance regiments, which were to be part of the establishment of all infantry divisions. The commander of 1st Armoured division in France, Major-General Roger Evans, and his senior officers, believed that, like the infantry, their formation had lacked sufficient reconnaissance capability and wanted their own armoured car unit. They also decided that mixing cruiser and light tanks in the same brigade was a mistake, because of their different speeds and ranges. However, what they could not agree upon was the correct

[23] PRO WO 199/1647, Minutes of a meeting of C-inCs held on 2 June 1940; PRO WO 199/1649, Minutes of a conference held by GOC-in-C Southern Command, 7 Aug. 1940.

[24] PRO WO 193/221, GS(P) to DMO&P, 4 June 1940.

[25] PRO WO 106/1775, Montgomery, Important lessons from the operations of the BEF in France and Belgium, May 1940, 14 June 1940.

[26] PRO WO 106/1775, Report of the Bartholomew Committee, 2 July 1940, Minute by VCIGS, 23 Aug. 1940.

[27] Ibid.

proportion of tanks and infantry in the division. Evans thought that the division's two motor infantry battalions were insufficient, they ought to be replaced with a whole motor infantry brigade, and that the support group needed more field-, anti-tank, and light anti-aircraft artillery and engineers.[28] But his successor, Major General C. W. Norrie, deprecated adding more motor infantry to the division because 'the type of unit suggested is copied from the German organisation which was essentially based on fighting an opponent weak in armoured troops and against whom, therefore, such a unit could be used boldly in reconnaissance in front of the tank formation'. This was inappropriate, because the Germans were anything but weak in armour. Consequently, each armoured division retained two armoured brigades, although each of them had an organic motor battalion. Rather than the Support Group including a whole motor brigade, it had only now incorporated a single lorried infantry battalion.[29] The British thus retained their tank-heavy divisions and forfeited another opportunity to transform their armoured divisions into more balanced all-arms formations.

The War Office began to put Bartholomew's recommended organizational changes into effect in the autumn of 1940. However, the post-Dunkirk reports were equally significant for what they did not say. Dunkirk did not shake the faith of the great majority of senior officers in the army's fundamental doctrinal commitment to 'top-down' command and control. Bartholomew did not recommend that organizational decentralization should be accompanied by a similar devolution in command and control. Manuals and *ATMs* continued to play lip-service to the need for senior officers to allow their subordinates to exercise a proper degree of initiative.[30] But that was more than counterbalanced by their continued insistence on the overriding need for senior officers to make plans and issue orders and for their subordinates to obey not only their spirit but also their letter.[31] Only one witness before the Bartholomew Committee believed that, to be effective, organizational decentralization had to be accompanied by a corresponding devolution in authority. The BEF's QMG, Lieutenant-General Sir W. G. Lindsell, suggested that one of the BEF's basic faults was that its command and control system was too rigid. It had stifled the initiative of junior commanders by placing too much authority in the hands of senior officers. The only member of the committee to support him was Major-General Irwin, who, significantly, was also the only member who had

[28] PRO WO 199/3186, HQ 1 Armoured divn. to Morgan, Crocker, and McCreery, 26 June 1940; Maj.-Gen. R. Evans to GOC VII Corps, 15 July 1940.

[29] PRO WO 199/3186, Norrie to Pope [c.1 Sept. 1940]; PRO WO 199/3186, Minutes of a meeting presided over by the DAFV, held in the War Office, 11.15 a.m., 3 Sept. 1940.

[30] See e.g. *ATM No. 36* (London, 2 Oct. 1940); *ATM No. 38* (London, 11 Feb. 1941).

[31] PRO WO 106/1775, Report of the Bartholomew Committee, 2 July 1940.

actually commanded a division during the campaign. Irwin was an out-spoken character. In 1942, he was dismissed from a Corps command in England because he told his commander to his face that he had no confidence in him. During the committee's deliberations he argued that 'We must train commanders to act on their own much more. I would like this to be put in as a major lesson and one which is going to be more applicable than ever, now we are dealing in Brigade Groups etc.' But Irwin's suggestion was too revolutionary for the other members of the committee. They insisted that Lindsell was the only witness to raise the point and had done so in conjunction with administrative and not operational arrangements. They believed that the real fault was not that subordinates were allowed too little initiative but that their seniors had committed the cardinal sin of issuing too many vaguely worded verbal orders.[32] More prescription, not less, was their recipe for the future. Underlying their reluctance to give their subordinates more latitude was a new factor, a developing fear that if the latter made mistakes, it was they who would bear the blame. 'The shadow of the bowler hat often stultifies initiative' noted an *ATM* in May 1942.[33] The rapid turnover of divisional commanders in wartime, and the short period of their tenure in command (eleven months on average), gave substance to their concerns. But the cost was high, for 'this attitude of mind on the part of senior commanders is likely to be reflected in their subordinates, and fear of making mistakes leads to fear of action'.[34]

Dunkirk thus did little to change the mind-set of senior regular officers, who continued to place a premium on instant compliance before all else. Many returned from Dunkirk convinced that their troops needed more, not less, training in formal drill and obedience to orders.[35] They were supported in the highest quarters. On 3 June Churchill insisted that, as soon as units had reassembled after Dunkirk, 'the first days after re-assembly should be spent in good steady parade drill. There has not been enough of this since the war began.'[36] A month later, the CIGS issued orders reminding all unit commanders that close-order drill was the basis of good discipline, and in June 1941 Montgomery told some of his subordinate commanders that

I am a tremendous believer in the value of close order drill as an aid to opera-tional and collective discipline, and to mental alertness. I have not been impressed by the standard of operational discipline that I have seen recently in

[32] LHCMA Bartholomew MSS 3/3, Criticisms of draft report by members of the committee [*c.*late June 1940].
[33] *ATM No.* 42 (London, 23 May 1942).
[34] Ibid.
[35] PRO WO 208/2050A, Lessons in organisation and staff duties and minor tactics from BEF, May 1940.
[36] PRO CAB 120/234, Churchill to Ismay, 3 June 1940; Haining to Ismay, 4 June 1940.

12 Corps. Any drill done must be good drill; bad drill is worse than useless—it is definitely harmful.[37]

At the tactical and operational levels, this meant that the exploitation of success continued to be limited by the need for superior officers to retain control of their subordinates. If advancing troops escaped beyond their commander's control, they would be easily become the victims of a swift German riposte. In July 1941, for example, the General Staff's latest pronouncement on *The Infantry Division in the Attack* laid down that 'Modern warfare demands considerable decentralisation, and every subordinate must be encouraged to make his own decisions on no more than very general instructions'. But on the same page it then added that, once a breakthrough had been achieved, 'the rapid co-ordination of all arms will depend upon the timely arrival of the divisional commander, with the minimum of staff necessary to collect reports and issue orders, at a position from which he can make decisions that may affect the whole future course of the operations'.[38] This was a recipe for military arthritis.

There were numerous reasons why the army did not undertake a more radical reappraisal of its fundamental doctrine. In the first instance, it did not have the luxury of digesting the lessons of defeat at its leisure. In the summer of 1940, it was facing the imminent threat of invasion.[39] It was, therefore, 'impractical at this stage to contemplate any radical alteration to the organization, armament and training of the basic formations and units of the Army.' The most that could be done was to adapt existing organization and doctrine to meet the immediate problem of how to counter an invading army that was likely to be better equipped and capable of operating at a much faster tempo than the British.[40] But such considerations cannot explain why, after the immediate threat of invasion had passed in the autumn and winter of 1940–1, the army did not embark upon a more fundamental overhaul of its doctrine to make it better suited to exploit the possibilities offered by tanks, motor transport, aircraft, and radio communications.

Senior officers anxious to cling to what they understood did not have to look far for reasons for doing so. There was an element of genuine confusion over what were the appropriate lessons to draw from the

---

[37] LHCMA Allfrey MSS 1/4, Corps Commanders personal memorandum for commanders, 1 June 1941; Bridgeman MSS 3/8, *ATM No. 33* (London, 1940).

[38] General Staff, *MTP No. 23. Operations. Part IX. The Infantry division in the Attack* (London, 1941), 4.

[39] On the importance of the time factor as an impediment to wartime innovation, see S. P. Rosen, *Winning the Next War. Innovation and the Modern Military* (Ithaca, NY, 1994), *passim*.

[40] LHCMA Bridgeman MSS 2/1, Bridgeman, Notes on the operations in Belgium and Flanders, 10 May–3 June 1940.

defeats of 1940. In December 1940, the DSD referred to the Dunkirk campaign as 'a special set of circumstances which are unlikely to arise again'.[41] Fundamental faults in the army's doctrine could be glossed over by placing the blame for defeat on the French or Belgians. The Bartholomew Committee insisted that, despite the Germans' material and numerical superiority on the ground and in the air, British formations, including those that were improvised to hold the south-western front, were never forced to relinquish their posts because of a successful German frontal assault. This, the committee concluded was proof that, 'given a reasonable fighting chance the British Army may fight with confidence of success'. With a defeated army on home soil and in imminent expectation of an invasion, the committee may have felt it essential to find every possible crumb of comfort they could discover. But, while noting the fact a few lines later that it was standard German doctrine to avoid heavy frontal assaults in favour of infiltrating between and around the flanks of defended localities, they ignored its implications.

Defeat could also, plausibly, be blamed upon shortages of essential equipment, another factor entirely beyond the control of the army.[42] They could fall back on the notion that 'the Briton was man for man the better' and that the BEF had only been defeated because 'the campaign was not really one of man against man but a campaign of equipment. In aircraft, in anti-aircraft weapons, in offensive engineer equipment and most of all in armoured vehicles, the enemy was immeasurably the stronger.' It was an explanation that was entirely consonant with the insistence of British pre-war doctrine that battles were won by the side with the heavier guns.[43] But even this analysis was flawed. British intelligence greatly exaggerated German numerical superiority in key items such as tanks. In May they believed the Germans possessed between 7,000 and 7,500 armoured fighting vehicles, compared to the 2,574 tanks that they actually deployed in the West.[44] It also failed to take account of the fact that the allies as a whole enjoyed rough parity in terms of the numbers and quality of the weapons they deployed. Where the allies failed was in the absence of a coherent coalition strategy and in the ways in which they organized their resources. By emphasizing the importance of material over doctrine, the British analysis provided a superficial and, at best, a partial answer to the question of what the army had to do to beat the Germans.

Finally, there was an undoubted reluctance amongst senior officers to

[41] PRO WO 193/69, DSD to DMO&P, 24 Dec. 1940.

[42] PRO WO 106/1775, Report of the Bartholomew Committee, 2 July 1940; LHCMA Bridgeman MSS 2/6, Bridgeman, Notes of a lecture [c.late 1940].

[43] LHCMA Bridgeman MSS 2/6, Bridgeman, Notes of a lecture [c.late 1940].

[44] PRO WO 167/203, War diary, G branch, 2 divn. Intelligence summary no. 102, 30 June 1940; Cooper, *German Army*, 209.

admit that they had taken decisions before 1939 that had contributed to the débâcle of 1940. Laurence Carr, the ACIGS, exemplified this tendency in 1940. As the DSD in 1938–9, Carr bore considerable responsibility for formulating pre-war doctrine. In July 1940, contemplating a list of reforms advocated by the Bartholomew Committee, he wrote that

there is an element of risk in circulating these controversial points too widely as they may cause dissatisfaction at a critical stage. They may create a feeling that the organisation of the army and some of its methods are faulty. I do not dispute that the organisation is not susceptible to improvement, but it is on the whole sound, and it might cause more harm than good if we tried any considerable scale of reorganisation at this stage.[45]

Carr ignored the obvious fact that the Dunkirk débâcle had already undermined confidence in the army's methods and organization.

In 1941–2 Home Forces contained the majority of British field force formations. They trained to fight a campaign to eject a German army, well equipped with Panzers and supported by aircraft and airborne troops that had landed in southern or eastern England. But merely because the army was on the strategic defensive did not mean that it prepared to fight defensively. Attempts to hold linear defence lines along water obstacles had failed in France. On becoming C-in-C Home Forces in July 1940, Brooke immediately told his subordinates that the basis of defensive operations must be mobile, offensive action. 'The idea of linear defence must be stamped out', he insisted in August 1940. '[W]hat is required to meet the dual threat of sea-borne and airborne attack is all round defence in depth with the maximum number of troops trained and disposed for a rapid counter-offensive.'[46] The only major fixed defences would be along the beaches and around ports. Their defenders would impose a sufficient check on the German advance to enable Home Forces' mobile reserves to deliver a crushing counter-attack.[47] Commanders and troops, therefore, had to learn how to interpret doctrine to perform this task.

Despite organizational changes, the manuals and training memoranda issued between 1940 and 1942 emphasized the same basic doctrine that was contained in their pre-war predecessors. There was a continued insistence that combined arms action and the generation of overwhelming fire-power facilitated mobility and won battles. 'Fire dominates the battlefield', asserted a General Staff pamphlet in 1942.[48] Senior officers

[45] PRO WO 106/1775, ACIGS to VCIGS, 11 July 1940.
[46] PRO WO 199/1647, Minutes of a meeting of C-in-Cs held on 6 Aug. 1940.
[47] PRO WO 199/314, Brooke to War Office, 14 Dec. 1940.
[48] General Staff, *Military Training Pamphlet no. 23. Operations. Part I. General Principles. Fighting Troops and their Characteristics* (London, 1942), 5.

were still expected to exercise the closest possible control over their subordinates through the medium of their plans. 'There must be clear direction and firm control by army and corps commanders. Divisions and
armoured divisions will each be given definite tasks which will con-
tribute directly to the success of the army or corps plan', insisted GHQ
Home Forces in October 1942 in one of its own manuals. The greater
the degree of enemy resistance, the more carefully they had to make their
preparations and the more elaborate had to be their fire-plan. Their
object was to destroy as many of the enemy's defensive weapons as
possible before the assault and to neutralize the remainder while it took
place. The infantry, advancing close behind the barrage, could then
arrive at their objectives with the fewest possible losses. These were the
basic lessons that were taught by senior commanders in innumerable
exercises.[49]

There were, however, some changes of emphasis. *Army Training
Instruction Number 1*, published in January 1941, placed more stress
than previous doctrinal publication on how to employ brigade groups,
rather than divisions, as the army's basic tactical formation.[50] Most
wartime manuals placed more importance than *FSR (1935)* had done on
the vital need to secure surprise, in both attack and defence. There was a
more explicit insistence on the need to ensure that troops going into
battle enjoyed the highest possible morale. That, in turn, was thought to
depend upon a combination of the troops' confidence in their equipment
and their leaders, on their own mental and physical fitness, on the provision of adequate food and rest, and on firm discipline.

There was also a clearer appreciation of the need to secure closer and
more effective ground–air co-operation. The army now thought it was
essential to ensure that ground forces enjoyed at least a modicum of air
superiority. After Dunkirk, army–airforce relations were poor on almost
all levels. The army hankered after an air support system comparable to
what it thought the German army enjoyed. They wanted to be able to

---

[49] See e.g. General Staff, MTP No. 23. *Operations. Part IX. The Infantry Division in the
Attack* (London, 1941), *passim*; , MTP No. 23. *Operations. Part IX. The Infantry Division in
the Advance* (London, 1941), *passim*; General Staff, *Field Service Pocket Book. Pamphlet
Number 2 (Reprinted with amendments, 1941.) Orders and Intercommunication* (London,
1941); General Staff, MTP No. 23. *Operations. Part I. General Principles. Fighting Troops
and their Characteristics* (London, 1942), *passim*; General Staff, MTP No. 23. *Operations.
Part II. The Infantry Division in the Defence* (London, 1942), *passim*; PRO WO 232/41,
*Doctrine for the Tactical Handling of the Division and the Armoured Division. Issued by the
C-in-C Home Forces* (London, 1942). Senior commanders like Montgomery emphasized this
doctrine in their training exercises. See e.g. LHCMA Allfrey MSS 1/9, S. E. Army Exercise
TIGER, Final conference—4 June 1942, Remarks of army commander; PRO WO 199/2623,
Army Commanders' Personal Memorandum no. 3, 22 June 1942.

[50] PRO WO 193/223, General Staff, *Army Training Instruction No. 1. Notes on Tactics as
Affected by the Reorganisation of the Infantry Division. Prepared under the Direction of the
CIGS* (London, 1941).

summon powerful forces of dive-bombers at short notice and thought that the only way they could do so was by having an air force under their own command. This was a mistake, because it overlooked the fact that the RAF's first priority had to be to establish air superiority over the battlefield. Without it, the Germans would be able to bomb the army, and RAF air interdiction and CAS missions in support of British troops would be difficult if not impossible.[51] Senior RAF officers were equally mistaken, for they remained convinced that effective army co-operation only required a willingness to work together and a more efficient inter-service signals system. In August 1940, two middle-ranking RAF and army officers devised the basis of a workable scheme. At its heart was a mobile operations room, known as an Air Support Signals Unit. It was commanded by an army officer, but was located at a combined Army–RAF headquarters. It sent forward tentacles—officers in cars equipped with radios who sent back the latest information about the progress of the battle and calls for air support. The mobile headquarters sifted these requests and then passed then back to nearby airfields, where an RAF Group Commander ordered his squadrons into the air. After being tested in Britain, the first ASSU went into action in autumn 1941 with 8th Army in North Africa.[52]

The British believed that the Germans had been able to sustain a much more rapid tempo of operations than they could because of more efficient staff practices. Staff officers and commanders were henceforth expected to rely on verbal, rather than written, orders. They were encouraged to transmit these either at face-to-face meetings or by wireless or radio-telephone. Pre-war fears that w/t or r/t transmissions might provide the enemy with an inestimable source of intelligence waned. The British now realized that, in many cases, if they acted sufficiently fast, by the time the enemy had gathered the information, it would be too late for them to act.[53] But this was only half the answer. It overlooked the fact that the Germans also allowed subordinate leaders at every level far more scope to use their own initiative, and that this enabled them to respond to changing circumstances more rapidly than the British could. Two orders issued by senior officers in Home Forces in 1941–2 illustrate both the confusion into which the army had fallen and the General Staff's continued commitment to allowing senior officers to interpret doctrine as they saw fit. In November 1941 Montgomery, then GOC

[51] Muller, 'Close Air Support, 183–4; PRO WO 199/1647, Minutes of a meeting of C-inCs held on 6 Aug. 1940.

[52] Lieut.-Col. C. E. Carrington, 'Army-Air Co-Operation, 1939–43', *Journal of the Royal United Services Institute*, 115 (1970), 37–41; PRO WO 277/34, Army Air support and Photographic Interpretation, 1939–45, 18–19; LHCMA Liddell Hart MSS 15/8/149, *Army Training Instruction No. 6. Air Forces in Support of the Army* (London, 1941).

[53] General Staff, War Office, *Field Service Pocket Book. Pamphlet No. 2. (Reprinted with amendments, 1941). Orders and Intercommunication* (London, 1941).

South Eastern Army, told his subordinates that when troops met organized resistance all supporting arms, but particularly artillery, had to be controlled by the highest-ranking commander possible so as to maximize their hitting-power. Only when that resistance had been overcome should self-contained groups of all arms under their own commanders be allowed to operate on their own initiative in order to exploit any gains.[54] But two months later, Alexander issued a circular to Southern Command stating that 'Over centralisation is probably most marked in the sphere of tactics. To develop initiative and self-confidence subordinate commanders must be allowed latitude of action. The guide should be "Tell him what you want done and let him do it in his own way".'[55]

The military authorities were in no doubt that, compared to the Germans, Home Forces had a serious training deficit to make up. However, many of the same obstacles that had impeded the training of the pre-war army persisted. Equipment, accommodation, ammunition, and land for training were in chronically short supply, as priority was given to field force units, rather than to the training organization.[56] It was not until March 1942, with the opening of a battle-training area on the South Downs, that Home Forces had sufficient land for a whole brigade to exercise with live ammunition and air support. 'This', according to Sir Bernard Paget, who succeeded Brooke as C-in-C Home Forces in December 1941, 'enabled a proper battle to be staged, living dangerously and abolishing all unnecessary safety-first precautions.'[57] Other obstacles were the creation of wartime conditions. Skilled instructors, well versed in modern war, were in short supply. Many instructors had little aptitude for teaching and it was not until December 1942 that the War Office instituted a system of formal training for them.[58] Company and platoon commanders had themselves received only very sketchy tactical training.[59] Many units were dispersed in billets, which made collective training difficult to organize. The wholesale conversion of units from one arm of service to another that took place in the winters

[54] PRO WO 199/2623, Army Commander's personal memorandum to commanders, 28 Nov. 1941; LHCMA Allfrey MSS 1/7, Montgomery, XII Corps Study Week for Commanders, 15–20 Dec. 1941, Note by Corps Commander, 11 Nov. 1941.

[55] LHCMA Lt.-Col. Maturin-Baird MSS, Alexander to Maturin-Baird, 29 Jan. 1942.

[56] See e.g. PRO WO 163/49/OS11, Lt.-Gen. Sir R. Adam to War Office, 21 Jan. 1940, for the difficulties encountered by III Corps prior to its embarkation for France in early 1940; PRO WO 199/1647, Minutes of a meeting of C-in-C held on 20 Apr. 1940; PRO WO 260/41, DSD, War Office to General Staff, Staff Duties, Home Forces, 24 Aug. 1940; PRO WO 216/87A, Col. Digby to Inspector General Training, 10 Aug. 1942, and minutes by DAG(B) to VCIGS, 16 Aug. 1942, and Adam to VCIGS, 14 Sept. 1942.

[57] PRO WO 205/1c, Minutes of the C-in-C's conference held at GHQ, 17 Mar. 1942.

[58] PRO WO 277/36, Gibb, Training, 23.

[59] LHCMA Allfrey MSS 1/6, Montgomery to GOCs-in-C 43rd, 44th, and 56th Divns., 27 Aug. 1941.

of 1941–2 and 1942–3 disrupted training. It meant that troops who had just mastered one set of skills had to begin to acquire another set from scratch.[60] The need to prepare defences consumed time that might have been spent in field training.[61]

Much tactical training lacked realism and a sense of urgency.[62] The standards of umpiring varied, and badly trained or biased umpires could ruin exercises. The infantry continued to devote too little time to practising minor tactics and fieldcraft.[63] TEWTS remained a favourite method of teaching, but, as one junior officer who participated in many of them noted, 'Since there was no actual troops and—more important still—no live enemy, one always chose a dynamic solution to show the required spirit of well-bred aggression.'[64] It remained difficult to replicate the sounds and confusion of a real battlefield.[65] A training pamphlet issued in 1940 still recommended representing an artillery barrage by a row of men carrying flags.[66] The overriding need for realistic field training to prepare troops for the first time they encountered the demoralizing noise, confusion, danger, and physical exhaustion of battle was underlined by the fighting in France and Flanders in May and June 1940. Even so, as late as February 1943, the Guards Armoured division gloried that, at the end of an exercise, 'The division ended with a good tank gallop through some of the best of the hunting country near Towcester, which gave it great satisfaction even if it did not please the umpires'.[67]

Training regimes also continued to exhibit a lack of uniformity. By November 1940, the task of producing training manuals and memoranda had been centralized in the Directorate of Military Training and the latter developed an elaborate bureaucracy for overseeing the training of the various arms of service.[68] However, this did not mean that the army now followed a uniform training programme, because, like the pre-war army, a single interpretation of doctrine was not enforced at either the tactical or the operational level. Responsibility for training remained divided. After Dunkirk, GHQ Home Forces become a major operational headquarters, and each of the Home Commands was transformed into an Army Command. Together they were responsible

[60] PRO WO 205/1c, Lt.-Col. Jones to CGS, Home Forces, 22 Apr. 1942.
[61] PRO WO 199/2623, Army Commander's Personal Memorandum no. 2, 21 Mar. 1942.
[62] PRO WO 199/1650, Army Commander's Conference—points raised, 4 Feb. 1941.
[63] PRO WO 199/1650, Army Commanders' Conference, Southern Command, 26 Oct. 1940; T. Harrison Place, 'Tactical Doctrine and Training in the Infantry and Armoured Arms of the British Home Army, 1940–44', Ph.D. thesis, (Leeds, 1997), chs. 2–4 passim.
[64] Craig, Broken Plume, 32.
[65] General Staff, ATM No. 36 (London, 1940).
[66] General Staff, Training in Fieldcraft and Elementary Tactics. Military Training Pamphlet No. 33 (London, 1940).
[67] Capt. the Earl of Rosse and Col. E. R. Hill, The Story of the Guards Armoured division (London, 1956), 25.
[68] PRO WO 277/36, Gibb, Training, 15, 17.

for training all field force units and formations in Britain. However, the War Office retained direct control both of training units responsible for recruit training and of the training of formations earmarked for despatch overseas.[69] New inspectors were appointed to oversee the training of the infantry, RAC, and signals on the outbreak of war, but they had no powers to impose uniform practices on field force formations.[70] After Dunkirk, Gort was appointed as the Inspector General of Training, but the post carried so little real power that Gort's biographer recorded that he 'had nothing constructive to do' and he was soon replaced by a more junior officer.[71] The post was abolished in December 1942, and the various inspectors of the arms of service henceforth reported directly to the DMT. However, their remit was confined to the work of army schools and training establishments and they were forbidden to inspect the training done by field force units and formations.[72]

Training pamphlets and memoranda issued in the early years of the war continued the pre-war practice of prescribing general principles but allowing individual commanders to decide how to interpret them.[73] In June 1940, for example, the General Staff issued a pamphlet instructing unit commanders how to train their battalions. It began by asserting that 'It is not intended that the application of the instructions should be followed slavishly or that the initiative of officers responsible for training should be in any way cramped. Variation and originality in method of instruction should be encouraged provided that they produce good results.'[74]

The very plethora of instructions issued by the War Office defeated their own purpose. In October 1941, Lieutenant-General K. A. N. Anderson, then commanding VIII Corps, complained that they 'are (despite all orders) largely unread or merely skimmed through'.[75] By May 1942 even the General Staff admitted that all the average officer knew was that

there exists an assortment of manuals in red covers, manuals in blue covers, pamphlets in binders, pamphlets with manila covers, and pamphlets with no covers at all. He may not know what they are, what should be done with them,

[69] PRO WO 277/25, Gravely, *Signals Communications*, 22–3; PRO WO 199/1649, Agenda for meeting of GOC-in-Cs of Commands with CIGS and C-in-C Home Forces, at 3 p.m., Tues. 6 Aug.

[70] PRO WO 277/36, Gibb, *Training*, 12.

[71] Colville, *Man of Valour*, 236.

[72] PRO WO 193/981, DMT to C-in-C Home Forces, 12 Dec. 1942.

[73] PRO WO 32/9834, DMT to VCIGS, 6 Nov. 1940.

[74] General Staff, *The Training of an Infantry Battalion. Military Training Pamphlet no. 37 (1940)* (London, 1940), 1.

[75] PRO WO 199/1654, Anderson to Alexander and Director General of Training, Home Forces, 20 Oct. 1941.

or where to look for any information he requires on points not connected with his own customary duties.[76]

The plethora of training schools for company officers and NCOs that sprang up in the aftermath of Dunkirk did nothing to reduce this confusion.[77] Variations in methods of instruction soon lead to variations in what was taught. Much of the difficulty that units experienced in co-operating with each other on the battlefield during the Second World War was a consequence of the General Staff's continued *laissez-faire* attitude towards how doctrine was interpreted and how training was conducted.

Such a regime could only have produced a common understanding of how to interpret doctrine if two conditions had been met. Senior commanders themselves had to learn a common approach to operational and tactical problems, and they had to remain in their posts sufficiently long to impose their understanding on their subordinates. The second condition was never fulfilled; the first was only fulfilled, as subsequent chapters will show, from late 1942 onwards. Brooke was ruthless in sacking senior officers who he thought were inadequate.[78] When Laurence Carr, promoted to be GOC Eastern Command, mishandled his armoured formations during a major exercise in the autumn of 1941, Brooke immediately decided to relieve him.[79] Two other senior officers, Lieutenant General E. A. Osborne (II Corps) and Lieutenant-General H. R. S. Massy (XI Corps) were also relieved shortly afterwards.[80] Brooke would have liked to be even more merciless with divisional and corps commanders whom he thought not up to their job, but he did not think he could find better men to replace them.[81] His ruthlessness had an obvious advantage in that it did rid the army of potentially inadequate commanders. However, it had a corresponding disadvantage. Senior officers enjoyed a leasehold, not a freehold, on their commands, and they acted accordingly. Officers like G. I. Thomas, who took command of 43rd division in March 1942 and remained in command until the end of the war, were exceptional. His long tenure of command meant that he had sufficient time to impose his personality and his preferred manner of conducting operations onto his entire division before it landed in Normandy in June 1944.[82] But the average divisional commander had too little time to impose their own ideas on

[76] General Staff, *ATM No. 42* (London, 23 May 1942).
[77] PRO WO 199/1647, Minutes of a meeting of C-in-Cs held on 6 Aug. 1940.
[78] LHCMA Alanbrooke MSS 5/2/17, Alanbrooke, 'Notes from My Life, iv, Home Forces', 239.
[79] Ibid. 295.
[80] LHCMA Liddell Hart MSS 11/1941/68, Talk with T. P[ile], 5 Oct. 1941.
[81] LHCMA Alanbrooke MSS 5/1/4, Diary entry, 8 Oct. 1941.
[82] Maj.-Gen. H. Essame, *The 43rd Wessex Division at War 1944–45* (London, 1952), 4, 8–9.

his command before he was either dismissed or promoted and a new commander, with new ideas, was imposed on the formation.[83]

However, in 1941 and 1942 there were four significant improvements in the army's training regime. Exercises did become more realistic. At the tactical level battle drills were introduced to enable units to operate at a faster tempo. Battle inoculation was introduced to prepare troops for the sights and sounds of a real battle. And, finally, at the operational level senior officers were given the opportunity to practise the art of commanding corps and armies in large-scale manoeuvres.

Despite the manifold obstacles outlined above, tactical training for units and formations did become more realistic after Dunkirk. Brooke supplied the initial impetus behind this. As C-in-C Home Forces, he insisted that exercises should take place in both summer and winter, last for several days, and that troops should march thirty miles or more and still be able to fight.[84] His successors followed suit, and exercises came to reflect some of the confusion of the battlefield. Len Waller remembered them as being

highly disorganised affairs, and we couldn't help thinking that if real war was going to be anything like this it was God help us. Whenever we were supposed to meet up with somebody or other you could bet they wouldn't be there; the cook house got lost and there'd be no hot meal for us; we stumbled for miles across fields in the wrong direction; at nightfall we were told that 'the enemy' had captured our blankets. But the worried expressions on the faces of the senior officers confirmed our suspicions that the enemy were in our midst. Some of these exercises were more physically arduous than anything we were to experience in true combat.[85]

Guardsman Waller's experiences were not unique. Eric Codling was a private in 8th Middlesex Regiment (43rd division). He recorded, that after taking part in numerous exercises, some lasting for several days, in the winter of 1943–4 in Kent 'We had become used to being hungry and uncomfortable'.[86]

Pre-war training manuals laid down a series of generalized rules, but gave individual commanders a good deal of latitude in interpreting them. Many of them rationalized their distaste for drills by insisting that the actual conditions of battle would rarely conform exactly to a text-book. Drills would inhibit leaders from using their knowledge, intelligence, and initiative to adapt the principles to the particular situation they faced.[87] But, in 1941, some senior officers reluctantly accepted that

[83] French, 'Colonel Blimp and the British Army', 1,182–1,201.
[84] LHCMA Alanbrooke MSS 6/2/6, Brooke to Wavell, 5 July 1942.
[85] IWM Waller MSS 87/42/1, 'How ever did we win?'
[86] IWM Codling MSS 88/4/1, TS memoirs, untitled.
[87] General Staff, ATM No. 41 (London, 1941).

the wholesale dilution of the army's pre-war trained cadre by hundreds of thousands of conscripts and wartime volunteers meant that these qualities, particularly knowledge, were in short supply. The army needed a training regime more attuned to the rapid mass production of tactical leaders. Senior officers like Alexander, Montgomery, and Dill began to accept the best way to do this was through teaching tactical drills. By ensuring that every man knew his precise role, drills could ensure that orders were much briefer and the tempo of operations thereby hastened.

Alexander's experiences during the Dunkirk campaign showed him that the army's propensity to shun tactical drills was mistaken, because, under the stress of battle, most soldiers were too beset by fear and doubt to exercise their initiative; while they remained paralysed, the Germans practised their infiltration drills, penetrated between their positions, and forced them to retire. In October 1940, he issued a set of 'Tactical Notes' to I Corps commanders in which he insisted that it was

Better to know instinctively some orthodox line of conduct than to be paralysed by the uncertainty of what to do.

Let us, therefore, study and draw up lines of conduct for the simple soldier—so that we may ensure that our soldiers when faced with problems on the battlefield will have an answer to them.[88]

In January 1941, Alexander sent a copy to Dill, who quickly had it reprinted with only minor changes and issued throughout the army.[89] By October 1942, the General Staff had accepted Alexander's argument and issued a training memorandum stressing that simple and widely understood battle drills were applicable not only to infantry sub-units but also to other arms of the service. 'To some extent it may be regarded as the teaching of tactics by numbers, in order to secure a common doctrine and a common approach to a problem.'[90] As casualties mounted and the process of dilution gathered pace in the final years of the war, the need to teach drills became even more urgent.[91] By May 1944, the General Staff admitted that training and tactics had to be altered to suit the limitations of the soldiers employed in the front line.

After more than four years of war, though the army has greatly expanded, it has also lost many of its most resolute and efficient soldiers. For this reason, it is inevitable that the ratio of experienced to inexperienced men should have steadily fallen, and must continue to fall. Unless they are given sound, basic

[88] LHCMA Alanbrooke MSS 6/2/1, Alexander to Dill, 4 Jan. 1941, and enc. Tactical notes, I Corps, Oct. 1940.

[89] LHCMA Liddell Hart MSS 15/8/146, General Staff, *Infantry Training 1937. Supplement. Tactical Notes for Platoon Commanders (1941)* (London: War Office, 1941).

[90] General Staff, *ATM No. 44* (London, 1942).

[91] PRO WO 231/10, Memorandum, 1 Divn., Lessons of the Tunisian campaign, 30 May 1943.

training in simple, well understood drills for all normal types of fighting, the bulk of these less experienced men cannot be expected to adapt quickly to new and unexpected situations.[92]

Infantry battalions and armoured and artillery regiments were all expected to practise standard drills in order to carry out the more common types of manoeuvres. In 1943 the School of Artillery was, for example, teaching regiments how to prepare standard barrage-plans that could be applied in all but the most unusual fire-support tasks. In doing so, they halved the time it took to lay on a barrage.[93] The School also held exercises to give commanders and staffs practice in how to lay on divisional and corps fire-plans.[94] By 1943–4 drills were being devised to fit new tactical situations and changes in the nature of the army itself. In May 1943, troops in Britain were ordered to practise night battle drills, as night fighting was now common practice at the front.[95] The establishment of the School of Infantry in July 1942 meant that, for the first time, the infantry, like the other combat arms, had an establishment 'for ensuring common doctrine and keeping abreast of modern developments'.[96] Montgomery pioneered the adoption of drills at the divisional level.[97] In May 1942 he told senior officers in South Eastern Army that only by developing and applying a proper drill would they achieve 'the successful handling of the new model armoured division [which] depends on the intimate co-operation of all arms'.[98] The enhanced ability of the army to practise combined arms operations in the second half of the war owed much to these developments.

Training in minor tactics also became much more realistic after late 1941. The first divisional battle school was established in Britain by 47th Division in July 1941 and was placed under the command of Captain Lionel Wigram.[99] Its purpose was to offer soldiers some experience of the noise and chaos of battle by giving them the opportunity to train under live-firing conditions.[100] By December 1941, thanks to Paget's enthusiastic support, GHQ was in the process of establishing its own GHQ's Battle School at Barnard Castle to provide instructors

---

[92] General Staff, *ATM No. 48* (London, 1944).

[93] PRO WO 277/5, Pemberton, *Artillery Tactics*, 99.

[94] PRO WO 277/36, Gibb, *Training*, 59–60.

[95] General Staff, *ATM No. 45* (London, 1943).

[96] PRO WO 216/82, Report of a joint committee on instruction of officers and schools, 17 May 1942.

[97] PRO WO 199/2623, Army commander's personal memorandum to commanders, 28 Nov. 1941.

[98] LHCMA Allfrey MSS 1/9, S. E. Army, Exercise TIGER, Final Conference—4 June 1942, Remarks by Army commander.

[99] T. Harrison Place, 'Tactical Doctrine and Training in the Infantry and Armoured Arms of the British Home Army, 1940–44', Ph.D. thesis (Leeds, 1997), ch. 4, *passim*.

[100] LHCMA Liddell Hart MSS 15/8/168, General Staff, *The Instructor's Handbook on Fieldcraft and Battle Drill* (London, 1942), *passim*.

for the schools he had ordered every division to form.[101] The schools trained unit instructors in battle drill, and helped to counter the often exaggerated fears of green troops by providing soldiers with a course of 'battle inoculation' through the gradual introduction to the sights and sounds of the battlefield.[102]

Some senior officers had recognized shortly after Dunkirk that it was essential to give their men some instruction in how to manage their fear. In a series of exercises, troops were now placed in slit trenches and over-run by tanks, advanced to the edge of artillery bombardments, heard shell fragments whistle over their heads, and were fired over by small arms. In February 1942, Home Forces lifted some of the safety pre-cautions that had hitherto restricted live-firing exercises. Occasional accidents made it plain to all concerned just how realistic was the new training regime. Commanders knew that boredom with a repetitive training regime was one of the great enemies of high morale and troops at home generally enjoyed strenuous and realistic training. Most, there-fore, welcomed battle drill and field-firing exercises.[103]

Senior officers who supported battle drills did so because they hoped that they would increase the tempo at which the British army could operate and enable it to compete on more equal terms with the Germans. But Wigram wanted to go much further. He hoped that the combination of battle drill and realistic battle inoculation would so raise the morale of British infantrymen that they could win without

heavy and accurate covering fire of all descriptions. To-day, against exceedingly quick and bold opponents who rely for success on surprise in the form of rapid infiltration, we shall find ourselves at a grave disadvantage if we cannot be as fit, as quick, as bold and as enterprising as they are.

The modern German army has never yet met an opponent who can play them at their own game—and we may be sure that if we develop the technique of speed in offensive operations they in turn will be surprised and will fall an easier prey than we imagine.[104]

His experience of taking part in infantry operations in Sicily showed Wigram that few infantry units actually employed battle drill in action

---

[101] PRO WO 205/1c, Gen. Sir B. Paget's conference as C-in-C Home Forces, 16 Jan. 1942.
[102] Ibid.; Rees, *Shaping of Psychiatry*, 80–1; PRO WO 199/799. Major Main, Object of battle inoculation [*c.*April 1942].
[103] PRO WO 163/51/AC/G(42)20, Adjutant-General, Morale Committee, Report, Feb.–May 1942, 12 June 1942; PRO WO 163/51/AC/G(42)32. WO Committee on Morale in the Army, Second Quarterly Report, May–July 1942; PRO WO 163/52/AC/G(43)10, WO Committee on Morale in the Army. Fourth Quarterly Report, Nov. 1942–Jan. 1943, 7 Apr. 1943; Morgan, *Peace and War. A Soldier's Life*, 145–6; PRO WO 199/799, CGS Home Forces to GHQ Battle School, Safety rules for use of live ammunition for training purposes, 3 June 1942; PRO WO 199/2623, Army Commanders' Personal Memorandum no. 2, 21 Mar. 1942.
[104] LHCMA Liddell Hart MSS 15/8/168, General Staff, *The Instructor's Handbook on Fieldcraft and Battle Drill* (1942), 50.

in the way he envisaged it because most platoons contained few men willing to close with the enemy. When enemy machine-guns opened fire, it was common for most of the platoon to seek cover. Only the platoon commander and a handful of men continued to advance, usually without any covering fire. 'The positions are taken', Wigram concluded, 'by what I call "Guts and Movement".'[105] His solution was to devise a simpler drill 'based on acceptance of the fact that there are only from four to six men in the platoon who can be absolutely relied on to do as they are told under enemy fire'.[106] Montgomery instantly dismissed his suggestion.[107] He had no intention of discarding the most basic tenets of British doctrine, especially as Wigram's assumption that the best way to beat the Germans was to ape their own doctrine was in any case flawed. Rather than downgrade reliance on mechanized fire-power in favour of better-trained infantry, senior officers married the two together whilst continuing to give precedence to fighting their battles using machinery rather than manpower.

They were right to do so. Sub-unit for sub-unit, German platoons and companies were larger and armed with more and better automatic weapons than their British counterparts. By 1942, for example, a German rifle company mustered three light mortars, fifteen machine pistols, twelve light machine-guns, and eighty-four rifles. This compared to a British company that had the same number of light mortars, but only nine tommy-guns, nine Brens, and fifty-four rifles.[108] At the unit level the only factor which worked to mitigate the German battalion's superior fire-power lay in the fact that British battalions had four rifle companies compared to the three in a German battalion. It was only when British unit commanders summoned support from their gunners that they could hope to deploy sufficient fire-power to neutralize their opponents' fire long enough to close with them. Battle drill, therefore, continued to be taught in such a way as to emphasize that the infantry was part of a combined arms team. 'No solo parts were written into the score, nor was there scope for small groups of performers in this mammoth ballet of machines', wrote one platoon commander who fought in North West Europe in 1944–5.[109]

Progress was more limited at the operational level, as was shown by the three largest exercises ever held in Britain. Exercise BUMPER (27 September to 3 October 1941) involved a quarter of a million troops

[105] PRO WO 231/14, Current Reports from Overseas no. 15, Section 1, Infantry Tactics in Sicily, 16 Aug. 1943.
[106] Ibid.
[107] D. Forman, *To Reason Why* (London, 1991), 72–5.
[108] LHCMA Liddell Hart MSS 15/8/168, General Staff, *The Instructor's Handbook on Fieldcraft and Battle Drill*, 182.
[109] Jary, *Eighteen Platoon*, 19.

organized into a dozen divisions, including three armoured divisions. It was designed to give senior commanders practice in handling motorized and mechanized formations, to investigate the proper composition of an expeditionary force, and to test Britain's defences against invasion.[110] It showed that although Home Forces had made significant advances since Dunkirk, serious problems persisted, particularly in the realm of command and control. Commanding officers sited their headquarters too far to the rear, and remained reluctant to accept that in fast, mobile, operations they had to rely upon verbal orders otherwise the Germans would run rings around them. Wireless discipline was poor, headquarters failed to pass information forwards, backwards, and laterally with sufficient speed, and corps headquarters could not communicate by radio when they were moving. Air–ground co-operation was unsatisfactory because army commanders delegated the call-up of air support to their corps commanders before they had seen how operations would develop.

Brooke recognized that at the operational level his senior officers had not yet learned how to use their armour. Carr, in particular, dispersed his two armoured divisions. Instead of using them to outflank Alexander's forces, he dashed one of them to pieces in a wide frontal attack in a manner that suggested that neither he nor the divisional commander concerned (Major-General M. B. Burrows, 9th Armoured) understood the need for tanks to operate in close co-operation with other arms. Some infantry division commanders also dispersed their strength by attacking on fronts that were too wide. This pointed to the fact that the primacy given to the Brigade Group after Dunkirk had been mistaken. Divisional commanders had forgotten the power of concentrated artillery. They employed brigade groups in cases where they would have been more successful had they committed a portion of their infantry but given them the assistance of all of their division's artillery.[111]

Four months later, Exercise VICTOR 2 (15–19 February 1942), another large-scale home defence exercise, showed that some of the command and control problems that had been revealed by BUMPER persisted. Major headquarters lacked adequate wireless communication. Some headquarters issued orders that were too vague, others that were too detailed and therefore took too long to transmit and failed to take proper account of local circumstances. Commanders and their staffs at all levels were still bad at passing vital information to flanking forma-

[110] PRO WO 277/36, Gibb, *Training*, 191; PRO WO 199/2469, GHQ Exercise BUMPER, 27 Sept.–3 Oct. 1941, Comments by C-in-C Home Forces.

[111] PRO WO 277/36, Gibb, *Training*, 191–2, 199; LHCMA Alanbrooke MSS 5/2/17, Alanbrooke, 'Notes from my Life, iv. Home Forces', 295; PRO WO 199/2469, GHQ Exercise BUMPER, 27 Sept.–3 Oct. 1941, Comments by C-in-C Home Forces.

tions, and there was generally insufficient liaison between field force formations.[112]

Finally, Exercise SPARTAN (4–12 March 1943), involving no fewer than five separate corps, was designed to analyse the problems that would arise after a force had landed on a hostile shore and was advancing from a bridgehead. It was the largest exercise ever held in Britain. It demonstrated that, although Home Forces had made considerable strides forward since BUMPER, the most serious weaknesses sapping the army's combat capability lay at the top. Senior officers had still not yet mastered all of the problems of command and control in mobile operations. Neither of the army commanders, Andrew McNaughton and J. H. Gammel, displayed sufficient forethought in making their plans, and both gave their Corps commanders too little notice of future operations. McNaughton allowed some of his orders groups to degenerate into debates. Command, control, and communications systems had improved markedly but shortcomings persisted. Armoured divisions were usually more adept than infantry divisions in using radio as their main means of communication. The pace of movement was hindered by traffic control problems.[113] Army–air co-operation was satisfactory in as much as the joint headquarters of the two services worked well together. Commanders largely used verbal orders, although they did not always make their meaning perfectly clear. However, essential information from subordinate headquarters frequently failed to get through, and staffs continued to fail to convey vital information to units on their flanks. Wireless security was poor throughout the exercise.[114]

The handling of large armoured formations still left a great deal to be desired. Several armoured division commanders mounted attacks without proper reconnaissance. One Corps Commanders had learnt so little from reports about German anti-tank tactics in North Africa that he 'destroyed' a complete armoured brigade by attacking across a minefield on a narrow front without infantry support against an infantry brigade covered by ample anti-tank guns.[115] But the lingering impact of the Bartholomew Committee's support for Brigade Groups had faded. Divisional commanders had now learnt how to centralize the control of their artillery. However, some divisional commanders, such as Major-

---

[112] PRO WO 199/860, Exercise VICTOR 2, 15–19 Feb. 1942, Report by Army Section, Central Control Staff on military problems during VICTOR 2.

[113] PRO WO 199/818, Exercise SPARTAN, Reports on movement control in Second British army, 20 Mar. 1943.

[114] PRO WO 199/817, GHQ Home Forces to War Office, 22 Mar. 1943; PRO WO 277/36, Gibb, *Training*, 194–5; PRO WO 199/232, Exercise SPARTAN, Comments by C-in-C Home Forces, Mar. 1943.

[115] PRO WO 199/232, Exercise SPARTAN, Comments by C-in-C Home Forces, Mar. 1943.

General Aizlewood of 42nd Armoured division, failed to make the best use of the artillery of neighbouring formations which might have supported them. Other formations had little idea of how to create a radio network that would link their infantry and artillery. On the defensive, formations tended to disperse their units too widely and failed to mount vigorous counter-attacks when the enemy penetrated between their positions.[116]

Paget, the director of the exercise, was particularly critical of McNaughton's plan, because the latter showed too little sense of urgency and failed to recognize how swiftly the Germans would react to any attack.[117] McNaughton's lethargy was symptomatic of a more fundamental weakness shared by commanders on both sides of the exercise, their inability to cope with the demands of mobile operations and their preference for limited, attritional battles.

I noticed that commanders generally appeared more confident when they had come to close grips with the enemy than when there was scope for manoeuvre and surprise. This was probably due to lack of practice in command and at some periods to lack of reliable intelligence. Modern battles will generally include certain periods of mobile operations in which bold decisions confidently and quickly executed may result in forcing the enemy into a disadvantageous position for the main battle.

This lack of confidence resulted in missed opportunities, delayed decisions, frequent changes of orders and frequent and conflicting short moves of units and formations.[118]

Paget was right to highlight lack of practice in large-scale exercises as one reason why commanders lacked confidence in mounting mobile operations. However, he missed the more fundamental reason. Dunkirk changed the strategic role of the British army. But the experience of defeat did not persuade the army to change its basic doctrine of command. To have done so would have been to admit too many past errors and, in the midst of a great national emergency, might have simply piled confusion upon confusion and further sapped the troops' faith in their leaders. Organizational changes were easier and quicker to implement, and created at least the appearance that the high command was reacting positively. The army, therefore, retained a hierarchical command system that allowed subordinate commanders too little initiative to enable them to grasp fleeting opportunities on the battlefield as they arose. Brooke did eventually succeed in energizing the way the army trained at home; what he failed to do was to centralize it. Until the

[116] Ibid.
[117] Ibid. Liddell Hart shared his opinion: LHCMA Liddell Hart MSS 1/613, Liddell Hart to Rowland, 18 Mar. 1943.
[118] PRO WO 199/232, Exercise SPARTAN, Comments by C-in-C Home Forces, Mar. 1943.

second half of the war, commanders were still allowed a free hand to interpret doctrine as they saw fit. The full drawbacks of this system, or lack of it, were revealed in North Africa in 1941–2.

CHAPTER SEVEN

The Desert War, 1940–1942

The army's fortunes in the field reached their nadir in June 1942 when Tobruk fell to Rommel's army. The press blamed the senior commanders on the spot. In the *Daily Express* Alan Moorehead opined that the Germans were better trained than their opponents, used their tanks *en masse* in co-operation with other arms rather than in small packets without infantry or artillery support, and that what the British needed was 'Quick decision men, that's what we lack most of all'. Alexander Clifford in the *Daily Mail* pointed to 8th Army's inability to react with sufficient speed to Rommel's actions. And Richard Macmillan in the *Daily Mirror* said that front line units complained 'of the absence of control. That was the keynote of criticism one heard.'[1]

There was a kernel of truth in each of their assessments. British training was deficient in many respects. British formations were not as skilful as the DAK at mounting combined arms operations. The British army's C3I system was not able to react to changing situations as rapidly as Rommel's system could do so. But what their criticisms overlooked was the fact that the British had made considerable, albeit imperfect and incomplete, efforts to remedy each of these shortcomings.

If the Dunkirk campaign demonstrated the weaknesses of British doctrine, higher training, and equipment, Lieutenant-General Sir Richard O'Connor's defeat of the Italian 10th Army revealed some of the strengths of the inter-war regular army. The offensive, Operation COMPASS, began on 9 December 1940. By its end, on 7 February 1941, O'Connor had advanced 500 miles. The Italians had lost 5,000 dead, 8,000 wounded, and over 100,000 prisoners, as well as 180 medium tanks and 1,000 guns.[2] The cost to the British was only 2,000 casualties, including 500 dead. O'Connor did not win because he outnumbered his opponent. His force, a mere two divisions, totalling approximately 36,000 men, was heavily outnumbered by Marshal Graziani's army of over 100,000 men. He won because his army was better prepared than its opponents to confront the peculiar conditions of the desert. The

---

[1] These cuttings, each dated 23 June 1942, can be found in LHCMA Hobart's papers, Liddell Hart MSS 15/11/12.

[2] J. J. Sadkovich, 'Understanding Defeat: Reappraising Italy's Role in World War II', *Journal of Contemporary History*, 24 (1989), 41.

wide-open spaces of the desert placed a premium on mobility, and the British were much better equipped, both materially and conceptually, to take advantage of those conditions. O'Connor's force was entirely motorized and he possessed more and better tanks than the Italians. The Italians, by contrast, lacked much of the modern equipment necessary to fight effectively in the desert. Their army was composed almost entirely of unmotorized infantry and they had fewer than 4,000 lorries in Cyrenaica. Their tanks were mostly light and mechanically unreliable and their field artillery was out-ranged by the British. With only about half the artillery of a British division, and with only two infantry regiments, Italian divisions lacked fire-power, manoeuvrability, or the capability to defend in depth.[3]

Graziani's troops were poorly trained and suffered from low morale. In contrast, O'Connor took the utmost care to rehearse his troops before their opening attacks against the Italian's forward posts. He insisted that 'all troops taking part must be trained to such a pitch that their action is almost automatic.'[4] The initial order for the operation was issued a month before it was mounted. It was thus possible for him to organize a full-scale dress rehearsal some days before the actual operation. It paid handsome dividends.[5]

Italian doctrine stressed fire at the expense of movement and their defensive tactics place little emphasis on the need to counter-attack. This produced a very fragile defence that was particularly vulnerable if ammunition ran low. The Italians' lack of motor transport placed them at a fatal disadvantage. It meant that they could neither mount swift counter-attacks to support their isolated forward positions nor withdraw rapidly out of reach of the British offensive.[6] They therefore dug in, and the British were able to deal with them piecemeal in a series of set-piece operations for which their doctrine and training had suitably prepared them.[7]

The British C3I was also better adapted to the demands of mobile warfare than was the Italian system. A German General Staff officer described Italian methods as being 'pedantic and slow. The absence of sufficient communications equipment renders the links to the sub-

[3] B. R. Sullivan, 'The Italian Soldier in Combat, June 1940 to September 1943: Myths, Realities and Explanations', in P. Addison and A. Calder (eds.), *Time to Kill. The Soldiers' Experience of War in the West 1939–1945* (London, 1997), 178–86, 197.

[4] PRO WO 201/3526, O'Connor to 4 Indian and 7 Armoured divns., 29 Nov. 1940.

[5] PRO WO 201/352, Report on capture by 4 Indian divn. of enemy position at Nibeiwa, the Tumars, etc. south of Sidi Barrani, culminating in the capture of Sidi Barrani itself, 9, 10, 11 Dec. 1940.

[6] Sadkovich, 'Understanding defeat',39–41; Sullivan, 'The Italian soldier', 188.

[7] Maj.-Gen. I. S. O. Playfair, *The Mediterranean and Middle East, i. The Early Successes against Italy (to May 1941)* (London, 1954), 267–361; PRO WO 201/2586, Middle East Training Pamphlet no. 10, Lessons of Cyrenaica campaign, Dec. 1940–Feb. 1941.

ordinate units precarious. The consequence is that the leadership is poorly informed about the friendly situation and has no capacity to re-deploy swiftly.'[8] Before the operation, O'Connor compensated for his own weaknesses by explaining his intentions to his subordinates in a series of conferences. Once the attack had begun, he allowed them a good deal of initiative within his plan, and maintained contact through liaison officers and by continuing to visit them himself.[9] He commanded by issuing brief verbal orders and retained control of his own forces by ignoring *FSR*, and dividing his HQ into three echelons. The first consisted of his own commander's group—himself, two staff officers, and a wireless that was fully mobile. This enabled him to go forward and yet to remain in contact with his staff. The second was an Advanced HQ commanded by his BGS and including the heads of each of his services. The third was a rear HQ consisting of the administrative staff.[10] Some of his subordinates followed his example. Brigadier Horace Birks, in temporary command of 4th Armoured Brigade, led his command from a tactical HQ that consisted of only two tanks and travelled just behind the leading unit.[11]

The British also made use of surprise as a force-multiplier. As early as October 1940, they had begun an active deception campaign to deceive the Italians. Through a combination of physical security measures—moving troops by night—and active deception—employing dummy tanks, aircraft, and guns and spreading false information through neutral diplomatic channels and bogus w/t traffic—they misled the Italians about their strength and intentions at the outset of the campaign.[12] They also possessed a technological surprise, in the shape of the single battalion of Matilda I tanks that were used to spearhead the opening phase of the offensive. They proved to be virtually impervious to Italian anti-tank fire, although they were vulnerable to mechanical breakdowns and mines.[13]

Intelligence, provided by a combination of intercepted signal traffic, aerial reconnaissance, and armoured car patrols, proved to be a second force-multiplier of considerable magnitude. It not only provided

[8] M. Knox, 'The Italian Armed Forces, 1940–43', in A. R. Millett and W. Murray (eds.), *Military Effectiveness, iii. The Second World War* (London, 1988), 152.

[9] LHCMA O'Moore Creagh MSS, Creagh to Barnett, 8 Feb. 1959.

[10] PRO WO 201/2586, Middle East Training Pamphlet no. 10, Lessons of Cyrenaica campaign, Dec. 1940–Feb. 1941; PRO WO 201/352, General Staff, XIII Corps, Operations Western Desert, Dec. 40, Lessons from, 18 Jan. 1941.

[11] Roberts, *From the Desert to the Baltic*, 29.

[12] PRO WO 201/2588, Middle East Training Memorandum no. 1, 5 Oct. 1940; PRO WO 201/2586, Middle East Training Pamphlet no. 10, Lessons of Cyrenaica campaign, Dec. 1940–Feb. 1941; M. Howard, *British Intelligence in the Second World War, v. Strategic Deception* (London, 1990), 32–3; H. O. Dovey, 'The Eighth Assignment, 1941–42', *Intelligence and National Security*, 11 (1996), 672–3.

[13] PRO WO 201/2505, Wavell to CIGS, 2 Jan. 1941.

O'Connor with an accurate picture of the Italians' order of battle but it also gave him crucial information about their intentions. His surprise advance across the cord of Cyrenaica that enabled him to cut off the remnants of the 10th Army at Beda Fomm, was made possible because intercepted Italian radio traffic provided by his Y service showed that the Italians were incapable of mounting any serious opposition to his advance.[14]

However, the campaign also produced some unfortunate legacies. Seventh Armoured division's success in rounding up the remnants of the Italian forces at Beda Fomm, an operation its commander likened to a fox-hunt, reinforced the conviction of many RTR officers that they could win battles by manoeuvre alone, 'as one normally only had to place oneself behind them for a decision to be reached'.[15] The one tank versus tank engagement of the campaign, at Mechili on 24 January 1941, did at least convince the senior RTR officers present that armoured divisions needed more artillery. But it was to be over a year before they learnt how to combine tanks and artillery successfully within an armoured division.[16] Nor did the campaign do anything to persuade the British that infantry had to co-operate more closely with tanks within the armoured division or that anti-tank guns should be employed offensively against enemy tanks.[17]

It also seemed to suggest that dispersal could bring major tactical benefits. The wide-open spaces of the desert made concealment from the air almost impossible. O'Connor's forces, therefore, operated in widely dispersed formations as a way of minimizing the impact of air attack.[18] This was essential until the British enjoyed air superiority. But it held its own dangers, because it made tactical concentrations, and the concentration of fire-power at the decisive point, extremely difficult.[19] Finally, O'Connor fought the campaign on a logistic shoestring. To conserve his equipment in periods between major operations, he deployed small 'Jock columns'—so named after Lieutenant Colonel 'Jock' Campbell of 4th RHA—who pioneered them. Consisting of a company of motorized infantry, a battery of field guns, and a handful of armoured cars, the columns' task was to harass the Italians and to persuade them that they

[14] PRO WO 201/2586, Middle East Training Pamphlet no. 10, Lessons of Cyrenaica campaign, Dec. 1940–Feb. 1941; R. Bennett, *Behind the Battle. Intelligence in the War with Germany 1939–45* (London, 1994), 71; Hinsley et al., *British Intelligence*, i, 375–9.

[15] LHCMA Liddell Hart MSS 1/153, Carver to Liddell Hart, n.d.

[16] PRO WO 193/25, Notes on lessons learnt from the recent employment of an armoured division and an Army Tank battalion in the Western Desert, 8 Jan. 1941; PRO WO 201/2586, Middle East Training Pamphlet no. 10, Lessons of Cyrenaica campaign, Dec. 1940–Feb. 1941.

[17] PRO WO 201/352, Report on lessons of the operations in the Western Desert, Dec. 1940, 31 Dec. 1940.

[18] Ibid.

[19] PRO WO 201/2586, Middle East Training Pamphlet no. 10.

were faced by a much larger force than was the case. Their very success led the British to exaggerate their power when confronted by a more resolute enemy.[20] They were formed again in late November 1941 to counter Rommel's 'dash to the wire' during CRUSADER, and were reputed to have done 'excellent work and inflicted considerable damage and casualties to Enemy formations and Transport'.[21] It was not until mid-1942 that opinion definitely turned against them. Major-General Frank Messervy, who, as the temporary commander of 1st Armoured division, had employed them to harass Rommel as the British withdrew from El Agheila to Gazala in February 1942, deprecated them. 'We are very liable to send out columns hither and thither; they achieve little and use up a large proportion of our guns, which are not then available, or at any rate are not fit and fresh for the main battle.'[22] But it was not until after the fall of Tobruk that 8th Army issued an order banning them except in exceptional circumstances.[23]

The final lesson that 7th Armoured division learnt from its campaign against the Italians was that 'This defensive attitude [of the Italians] has given us the opportunity of taking very great risks, risks which would be quite unjustifiable against German troops'.[24] Just how unjustifiable was demonstrated later in 1941 when Axis forces inflicted three consecutive defeats on the British. In March and April they expelled the British from Cyrenaica, invested Tobruk, and established themselves on the Egyptian frontier; in May and June they defeated two British counter-attacks, operations BREVITY and BATTLEAXE. In November and December 1941 the British mounted a third offensive, on a much larger scale than their previous two efforts, Operation CRUSADER. It was a British victory in that the Axis lost more heavily than the British and the offensive achieved its objective of relieving Tobruk.[25] But, for several reasons it left a taste of bitter disappointment in the mouths of many of those involved on the British side. Victory owed a great deal to superior British logistics, and Rommel's handling of his own forces was inept and head-

---

[20] LHCMA O'Moore Creagh MSS, Interview, 13 July 1945, with Maj.-Gen. Sir O'Moore Creagh, who commanded 7 Armoured divn. in 1940–1; M. Carver, *Dilemmas of the Desert War. A New Look at the Libyan Campaign 1940–42* (London, 1986), 15–16; PRO WO 106/2223, Notes from Theatres of War no. 1, Cyrenaica, Nov. 1941.

[21] PRO WO 106/2255, Lessons from operations in Cyrenaica no. 4, 12 Dec. 1941.

[22] PRO WO 106/220, Report on operations in the Libyan desert by commander (temporary) 1 Armoured divn., 21 Jan.–4 Feb. 1942.

[23] PRO WO 106/2223, Notes from Theatres of War no. 6, Cyrenaica, Nov. 1941–Jan. 1942, July 1942.

[24] LHCMA O'Moore Creagh MSS, Advanced HQ, 7 Armoured divn. to Col. G. E. Younghusband, 2 Armoured divn., 9 Jan. 1941.

[25] PRO CAB 146/10, Enemy Documents Section, Appreciation no. 9, Appendix 9; Playfair, *The Mediterranean and Middle East, iii,* 97.

strong.[26] Furthermore, the Axis forces escaped utter annihilation, and in January 1942 were able to mount a counter-offensive that drove 8th Army back to the Gazala line.

For most of 1941–2 there were never more than three German divisions in North Africa. By November 1941 the DAK consisted of three divisions, 15th and 21st Panzer and 90th Light division. Although they lost several divisional commanders, Rommel, either as commander of the DAK or, after August 1941, commander of the larger Panzer Gruppe Afrika, consisting of the DAK and two Italian Corps, remained in supreme command throughout.[27] This was an advantage, for it gave the Germans much greater continuity of command and the opportunity to amass far more institutional experience than the British. The Western Desert Force (or the 8th Army as it became in September 1941) had no fewer than six commanders in sixteen months, and some twenty different divisions or their equivalents went into action under its control in 1941–2. Only four of them (1st and 7th Armoured divisions, 4th Indian, and 1st South African divisions) fought in more than two battles. The upshot was that the British 'seemed incapable of profiting by our experience. No one seemed able to analyse our weaknesses, and those of the enemy; there was no development of a dynamic tactical policy'.[28] The danger of committing inexperienced formations to war in the desert was demonstrated with painful clarity on at least two occasions. In March and April 1941 Rommel totally destroyed the inexperienced, undertrained, and under-strength 2nd Armoured division in a matter of days. Nine months later he routed the almost equally inexperienced 1st Armoured division south-east of Agedabia.[29]

The greater institutional experience of the Axis forces showed itself at the tactical level in their superior combined arms tactics. Unlike the British, they believed that the best antidote to the tank was not another tank, but an anti-tank gun. In BREVITY, BATTLEAXE, and CRUSADER, DAK employed anti-tank guns aggressively in close co-operation with their own tanks to blunt the advance of the British armour. Their 50mm. and 88mm. anti-tank guns gave them a distinct advantage, especially as they were distributed in greater proportion to all arms than were British anti-tank guns. When taking the offensive, Panzer divisions moved in compact, all-arms battle groups so organized that tanks, motorized artillery, anti-tank guns, and infantry could quickly give each other

[26] Gen. S. Westphal, 'Notes on the campaign in North Africa, 1941–43', Journal of the Royal United Services Institute, 105 (1960), 75.

[27] P. Griffiths, 'British Armoured Warfare in the Western Desert, 1940–43', in J. P. Harris and F. N. Toase (eds.), Armoured Warfare (London, 1990), 83–4; R. Lewin, The Life and Death of the Afrika Korps (London, 1977), passim.

[28] LHCMA Liddell Hart MSS 1/56/20, Maj.-Gen. D. Belchem to Liddell Hart, 31 Jan. 1954.

[29] PRO WO 106/2149, Report on the action of the 2 Armoured divn. during the withdrawal from Cyrenaica, Mar.–Apr. 1941, June 1941; Carver, Dilemmas of the Desert War, 54–5.

mutual support.[30] Each Panzer division advanced in a tight 'box' formation, tanks moving ahead accompanied by some field guns. When the box encountered the enemy, it halted and the division took up position for all-round defence. Tanks deployed on a wide front and then withdrew slowly to positions on either side of the box. When the British armour pressed home their attack, the German tanks withdrew further, so that the advancing British could be engaged from the flank by antitank guns and frontally by tanks. Meanwhile, German tanks from the disengaged side of the box could swing around and attack the British in the rear.[31]

Rommel's senior commanders could lead from the front because they had special command tanks stripped of their guns and equipped as mobile command posts.[32] To enable divisional commanders to issue orders rapidly, each of them travelled in a vehicle equipped with an ultra-short wave radio. They could thus monitor their own tanks' radios and so did not have to wait for 'sitreps' to reach them through the normal chain of command. Another vehicle in radio contact with reconnaissance units and Corps HQ always followed closely behind the divisional commander. Between their arrival in North Africa and CRUSADER, 15th Panzer division, and then the whole DAK, developed a series of battle drills to enable formations to operate on the briefest of verbal orders. This ensured close co-operation between all arms and allowed units to move at maximum speed, with the minimum of orders.[33] When the British captured a copy of a German divisional order at the end of 1941, they realized that 'Here, obviously, is the basis on which all arms can work out combined action, "in the way the higher commanders would have ordered", that is, it brings into prominence the thoroughness and uniformity of German training'.[34] This meant that when both sides' C3I systems collapsed in the chaos of battle, DAK was generally able to adapt to the confusion better than could the British. The Germans' commitment to 'mission command' meant that subordinate commanders were much better able to act on their own initiative than could their British counterparts.

However, it would be a mistake to explain away the setbacks the

[30] PRO CAB 146/10, Enemy Documents Section, Axis Operations in North Africa, Part I, The new battle tactics developed by the Panzer formations, Nov. 1941.

[31] PRO WO 277/5, Pemberton, *Artillery Tactics*, 109–10; LHCMA General Sir H. Pyman MSS, 3/1, Maj.-Gen. W. H. E. Gott, 7 Armoured divn., An account of the operations in Libya, 18 Nov.–27th Dec. 1941, 31 Jan. 1942; PRO WO 106/2223, Notes from theatres of war no. 6, Cyrenaica, Jan.–June 1942, Oct. 1942.

[32] PRO WO 32/10135, Minutes of meeting of Middle East Research Committee, 4, 24 Dec. 1941.

[33] PRO CAB 146/10, Enemy Documents Section. Axis Operations in North Africa, Part 1.

[34] PRO WO 106/2223, Notes from Theatres of War no. 2, Cyrenaica, Nov.–Dec. 1941, 7 Mar. 1942.

British suffered solely by reference to superior German tactics and organization. Italian formations also played an important role in Rommel's successes in 1941–2, contributing more men than the Germans and roughly equal numbers of tanks. After Beda Fomm the Italian forces in North Africa underwent a renaissance. By September 1941 two motorized divisions (the Trento and Trieste) and an armoured division (the Ariete) had arrived, together with a trickle of modern equipment. Italian anti-tank guns took a significant toll of British tanks during both BREVITY and BATTLEAXE. It was the Ariete that blunted the advance of 2nd Armoured Brigade at El Gubi on 19 November 1941 at the start of CRUSADER and it continued to take a major toll of British armour in the opening phase of the battle. During the Gazala fighting in May and June 1942, the motorized and armoured formations of the Italian army made a substantial contribution to the fall of Tobruk. Had it not been for the efforts of Ariete and Trieste in overrunning British positions and linking up with the DAK on 28–9 May, and the work of the Italian X Corps in opening a path through the British minefield, DAK might have been destroyed in the 'Cauldron'.[35]

The British experienced so many reverses because they committed errors both at the tactical and operational level in 1941–2. At the operational level, the most egregious was their failure to focus their forces at the decisive point. Sir Alan Cunningham had more tanks than Rommel at the beginning of CRUSADER, but he lost that advantage by failing to concentrate them. Although his three armoured brigades were all under the command of 7th Armoured, they operated in close conjunction only on the first day of the offensive.[36] Rommel, who kept 15th and 21st Panzer divisions concentrated in the DAK, was able to dispose of them piecemeal. At the end of May 1942, when Rommel attacked them on the Gazala line, the British once again enjoyed numerical superiority in tanks, but again they forfeited any advantage by failing to mass their forces. Lieutenant-General Neil Ritchie, who was preparing for a major offensive to expel the Axis from Libya, had established his infantry in seven defended 'boxes' along a fifty-mile line west of Tobruk stretching from Gazala in the north to Bir Hacheim in the south. Each box was prepared for all-round defence, manned by a brigade group and contained food and supplies for a week. The man who 'invented' them, Frank Messervy, had persuaded Auchinleck, who held a high opinion of the former's skills as an infantry and armoured commander, that it would matter little if the boxes were so far apart that they could not be

---

[35] Sadkovich, 'Understanding Defeat', 35, 44; J. J. Sadkovich, 'Of Myths and Men: Rommel and the Italians in North Africa, 1940–42', *International History Review*, 13 (1991), 288–91, 296–304; Sullivan, 'The Italian Soldier', 190–4, 198, 200.

[36] Carver, *Dilemmas of the Desert War*, 33; Playfair, *The Mediterranean and Middle East*, iii, 38–41.

mutually supporting. Their front and the gaps between them could be covered by minefields. A mobile striking force of armour, held centrally until the direction of the enemy's main thrust had been discerned, could 'attack him in flank and rear'.[37] The day before Rommel struck, Auchinleck told his commanders that, as an attacker could always mass sufficient force at the decisive point to penetrate fixed defences, 8th Army would therefore hold its front line with 'the minimum [force] which will preserve the semblance of occupation'. Enemy forces that broke through would be defeated by a powerful counter-attack, 'The object being to defeat the enemy by mobile action on that part of the battlefield in which we can organise superiority rather than attempt to defeat his attack in an area where he can inevitably develop crushing superiority of fire'.[38]

This was not necessarily an unsound way to dispose of his forces. It was not practical for Ritchie to do what O'Connor had done in late 1940, and hold his main force up to 60 miles back from the enemy, with only mobile covering forces in front of them. Rommel, unlike Graziani, could not be relied upon to remain passive, and Auchinleck had to hold the port of Tobruk if he was to prepare for his forthcoming offensive.[39] The crucial weakness of his plan was that it depended upon concentrating 8th Army's mobile troops so that they could crush Rommel's penetration. This they failed to do. Ritchie and most of his senior subordinates were convinced that, although Rommel might make a feint around their southern flank, his main thrust would come through the centre of their position.[40] They were wrong. Ritchie's mobile armoured formations were too far to the north and too slow to respond when Rommel's attack in the south began on the night of 26–7 May. In the absence of effective mobile troops, the 'boxes' proved to be predictably vulnerable to Axis attack.[41]

The British failure to concentrate their forces meant that at the tactical level, all too often single British brigades were confronted by whole Axis divisions. On 27 May 1942, the 3rd Indian Motor Brigade was overwhelmed by 21st Panzer and Ariete divisions, the 7th Motor Brigade was attacked by the whole of the 90th Light Division, the 4th Armoured Brigade by the whole of the 15th Panzer division, and the 22nd Armoured brigade by 15th and 21st Panzer divisions. On 29 May

[37] PRO WO 106/220, Auchinleck to Brooke, 24 Feb. 1942, and enc. Report on operations in the Libyan desert by commander (temporary) 1 Armoured divn., 21 Jan.–4 Feb. 1942.
[38] PRO WO 201/538, Lieut.-Gen. Corbett to 8, 9, and 10 Armies, 26 May 1942.
[39] Carver, Dilemmas of the Desert War, 62; Cf. Barnett, The Desert Generals, 140–1.
[40] LHCMA Liddell Hart MSS 1/507, Lieut.-Gen. Sir F. Messervy to Liddell Hart, 26 May 1954.
[41] PRO WO 204/7975, C-in-C 8 Army to XIII, XXX Corps, 50 divn., 10 Indian divn., 19 July 1942; PRO WO 106/2223, Notes from theatres of war no. 6, Cyrenaica, Jan.–June 1942, Oct. 1942.

the British were only able to commit a single armoured brigade (2nd Armoured) in an attack on the combined 15th and 21st Panzer divisions.[42]

Even when the British did manage to concentrate their tanks, their failure to use them in co-operation with other arms only served to multiply the scale of their defeat. The British armour suffered its biggest defeat of the desert war on 12–13 June 1942, when, in a series of confused actions, the tanks of 2nd, 4th, and 22nd Armoured brigades, fighting under the control of 1st Armoured division, once again impaled themselves on Rommel's anti-tank gun screen.[43] By the summer of 1942 losing large numbers of tanks to anti-tank guns was not a new experience for the British armour. BATTLEAXE (June 1941) was the first occasion a British armoured division engaged one of its German counterparts. It revealed a recurrent shortcoming—the inability of the British to practice combined arms tactics—which was to mar their operations in the desert for months to come. British tanks repeatedly charged, unsupported by infantry or artillery, against German and Italian anti-tank guns, and time and again they sustained disproportionate losses. On 19 November 1941, for example, 22nd Armoured brigade suffered heavy losses, when, unsupported by friendly infantry, it attacked an Italian anti-tank screen at El Gubi. The tanks passed through the Italian positions but were unable to take prisoner the many Italians who wanted to surrender because they were not accompanied by any infantry. They then encountered a large body of hostile tanks, who forced them back through the Italian positions, where they discovered that the anti-tank gun crews they had overran had still not been mopped up and had manned their guns and opened fire on them again.[44]

British tank regiments did not behave in this way because, in their earlier incarnation as cavalry, they had been taught to charge home with sword and lance and thought they could do the same when they had exchanged their horses for tanks. The First World War had disabused the cavalry of any idea that *armée blanche* tactics remained practical in the face of modern fire-power. As one of their officers remarked, by the mid-1920s 'nobody in their senses could think that the Cavalry would ever be used again in shock action since the machine gun had proved deadly in the last war'.[45] The cavalry's main roles between the wars were 'reconnaissance and protection.' Indeed, official doctrine deprecated their employment without the co-operation of other arms. Horsed

---

[42] Playfair, *The Mediterranean and Middle East*, iii, 223–4, 226.

[43] Ibid. 241–45; Barnett, *The Desert Generals*, 156.

[44] Maj. S. Pittman, *Second Royal Gloucester Hussars. Libya–Egypt 1941–42* (London, 1950), 11–15.

[45] IWM Dept. of Sound Records, Accession no. 000905/06: Col. Sir Andrew Horsborough-Porter (12th Lancers), 2.

cavalry regiments had been trained to move mounted, but usually expected to fight dismounted with rifles and light machine-guns.[46] The propensity of armoured regiments, both of the RTR and of the cavalry to charge hostile anti-tank guns owed far more to the deficiencies of the inter-war training regime and tank doctrine. The former had given them too little opportunity to practise combined arms operations, and the latter was suffused with the idea that tanks could operate successfully without the intimate co-operation of artillery and infantry.[47]

In an effort to improve combined arms co-operation, from CRUSADER onwards each armoured brigade was given its own affiliated artillery regiment. But the destruction or even neutralization of a series of point targets, such as anti-tank guns, required far more shells than a single field regiment could fire. When 2nd RHA, attached to the 2nd Armoured brigade, engaged German anti-tank guns on 23 January 1942, the Brigade commander complained: 'Enemy very distant and hard to identify. Ronald continues to engage. Artillery fire (own) disappointing (No real volume? FOO's poor).'[48] Rather than spend time in careful reconnaissance to pinpoint and then to engage hostile anti-tank guns with high explosive shells, the British armour preferred to use their own artillery and close-support tanks to create smokescreens and to rely on the speed of their cruisers, coming in preferably from a flank, to engage the enemy's armour.[49] Tactical co-operation became worse as battles proceeded. Heavy casualties amongst men who had trained together forced commanders to replace losses with worn-out tanks, replacement crews that did not know each other, and even to amalgamate whole regiments into composite units.[50]

More success might have been achieved if armoured divisions had employed their motor infantry, with their comparatively lavish scale of anti-tank guns, in close co-operation with armoured brigade groups. But they were wasted, either employed in a static role, holding 'boxes' or, like 7th Motor Brigade during the Gazala fighting, divided into columns to harass the Axis line of communication around Bir Hacheim.[51] Thus,

[46] *FSR* (1929), 12–14; *FSR* (1935), ii, 6; IWM Dept. of Sound Records, Accession nos. 000893/03: Col. G. W. Draffen (Queen's Bays), 10; 000905/06: Col. Sir Andrew Horsborough-Porter (12th Lancers); 2; 000892/06: Col. G. J. Kidston-Montgomerie of Southannan, 4; 000933/04: Col. K. E. Savill, 3.

[47] Griffith, 'British Armoured Warfare', 72; Playfair, *The Mediterranean and Middle East*, ii, 159–61, 167–74. An officer in the 3rd Hussars training in Egypt in the late 1920s remembered carrying out exercises with the RHA, 'but practically nothing with the infantry'. See IWM Dept. of Sound Records, Accession no. 000968/02: Col. Sir Douglas Scott, 6.

[48] IWM Briggs MSS 66/76/1, Notebook no. 1, Entry dated 23 Jan. 1942.

[49] PRO WO 106/2223. Notes from Theatres of War no. 1, Cyrenaica, Nov. 1941.

[50] LHCMA Liddell Hart MSS 1/507, Lieut.-Gen. Sir F. Messervy to Liddell Hart, 26 May 1954; PRO WO 106/2235, Report of a Court of Enquiry, vol. 2, Statement by Maj.-Gen. Lumsden—Comdr. 1 Armoured divn., n.d.

[51] PRO WO 106/2235, Report of a Court of Enquiry, vol. 2, Statement by Maj.-Gen.

when 2nd and 22nd Armoured Brigade Groups attacked Rommel in the 'Cauldron' on 30 May 1942, they were quickly brought to a halt. They had no infantry to move forward and overcome Rommel's anti-tank screen, and their supporting artillery, unable to spot such small targets as anti-tank guns, was reduced to laying down smoke ineffectively.[52]

In the middle of the fighting around the 'Cauldron' in June 1942, Herbert Lumsden, GOC 1st Armoured division, concluded that the only way to overcome Rommel's anti-tank defences was to mount a night attack using infantry. Its failure revealed the depths to which the British had sunk in carrying out combined arms operations. On the night of 4–5 June, 10th Indian brigade tried to punch a hole through the anti-tank screen so that 22nd Armoured Brigade could exploit it in daylight. The infantry thought that they had been successful, and blamed the tanks for a lack of 'push' and an unwillingness to co-operate when they failed to advance. One of the battalion commanders involved commented that 'The action was quite useless and to my mind quite hopeless. I must say I really lost faith in the RAC that day.'[53] These aspersions were unwarranted. Poor reconnaissance by the infantry had failed to discover the position of the main German anti-tank gun screen. The crews of 22nd Armoured Brigade were by now sufficiently experienced to recognize, in the words of the second-in-command of one squadron, that 'a frontal attack by armour on a defended position, and an attack of this kind by cavalry tanks, though even then considered part of their role, is one of the surest methods of suicide that exists'.[54] Moreover, lack of co-ordination cut both ways. When the infantry were counter-attacked later in the day, the tanks did not go to their assistance because the commander of 22nd Armoured Brigade had been told by his divisional commander that he had no responsibility for protecting the infantry.[55]

This sad story of failed combined arms co-operation was symptomatic of what was amiss with 8th Army in 1941–2. Despite suffering so many early defeats at Rommel's hands, most British commanders took a long time to recognize that their combined arms tactics were at fault. They believed that when they encountered German armoured formations

Messervy commanding 7 Armoured divn., 27 Feb.–19 June 1942; PRO WO 106/2223, Notes from theatres of war no. 6, Cyrenaica, Jan.–June 1942, Oct. 1942.

[52] PRO WO 106/2235, Report of a Court of Enquiry, vol. 2, Statement by Maj.-Gen. Lumsden–Comdr. 1 Armoured divn., n.d.; IWM Sir Robin Dunn MSS 94/41/1, 'The Battle of Knightsbridge', 1942.

[53] PRO WO 106/2235, Statement by Lieut.-Col. D. G. Thorburn, commanding 2 HLI from 18 May 1941.

[54] Pittman, Second Royal Gloucester Hussars, 67.

[55] Playfair, The Mediterranean and Middle East, iii, 228, 231–3; Barnett, The Desert Generals, 151; M. Carver, Tobruk (London, 1964), 197–9; PRO WO 106/2234, Report of a Court of Enquiry assembled by order of the C-in-C, Vol. 1, Report.

they had been bested in tank-versus-tank actions. In reality, they had dashed themselves to pieces by attacking the German anti-tank screen without proper infantry and artillery support.[56] They put the responsibility for their failures on a series of prosaic causes: the inexperience of commanders, a lack of training, a lack of equipment, the poor mechanical reliability of much of the equipment that was available, a lack of air superiority, the fact that they could not manoeuvre as they wished because they were tied to the infantry's apron-strings, and the supposedly poor quality of British as compared to German tanks.[57]

It was only in the aftermath of CRUSADER that 8th Army appreciated that it had to improve its combined arms tactics. On 7 January 1942, 8th Army HQ issued an edict that henceforth 'tanks must never move, once contact has been made, unless adequately covered by artillery'.[58] The main function of armoured divisions remained to seek and destroy enemy armoured formations, but, as an after-action digest of the battle explained, 'tanks alone cannot win battles . . . In the armoured division, tanks must act in the closest co-operation with infantry and artillery in order to defeat the German armoured forces.' In the infantry division, Infantry tanks were essential, but they could not overcome enemy anti-tank defences without the close support of infantry and artillery. 'Modern anti-tank defences have not rendered the heavily armoured tank obsolete but they have destroyed the legend of its invulnerability.'[59]

This recognition promised a major step towards improving the army's battlefield performance. However, three factors impeded real progress. The first was inherent in the new tactics. Henceforth, the task of the British armour was to seize ground vital to the enemy and lure him to destruction on the British anti-tank screen. But doing so would require a far greater degree of co-operation between tanks, field artillery—8th Army's best 'tank-killer' in the absence of a better anti-tank gun than the 2-pdr.—and anti-tank guns than had hitherto been achieved.[60] But employing field artillery in an anti-tank role threatened to rob the infantry of the concentrated artillery support they required, for field guns dispersed as anti-tank weapons could not also provide con-

[56] Roberts, *From the Desert to the Baltic* , 51.

[57] W. S. Churchill, *The Second World War*, iii, 192, 304; Carver, *Dilemmas of the Desert War*, 23–4; PRO WO 32/9765, Committee to examine questions relating to defence against enemy tanks, 8 June 1941; LHCMA Liddell Hart MSS 1/705, DMT's tour, Note C, Brig. Tuker, 18 Aug. 1941; PRO WO 201/2588, Middle East Training Memorandum no. 16, 30 June 1941; LHCMA Hobart's papers, Liddell Hart MSS 15/11/10, DAFV to ACIGS, 24 Aug. 1941; See e.g. LHCMA Gen. Sir H. Pyman MSS 3/1, Maj.-Gen. W. H. E. Gott, 7 Armoured divn., An account of the operations in Libya, 18 Nov.–27 Dec. 1941, 31 Jan. 1942.

[58] PRO WO 201/527, BGGS, 8 Army, to XIII and XXX Corps, 7 Jan. 1942.

[59] PRO WO 106/2223, Notes from Theatres of War no. 4, Cyrenaica, Nov. 1941–Jan. 1942, May 1942.

[60] PRO WO 106/2223, Notes from Theatres of War no. 2, Cyrenaica, Nov.–Dec. 1941, 7 Mar. 1942; PRO WO 201/527, BGGS, 8 Army, to XIII and XXX Corps, 7 Jan. 1942.

centrated indirect fire support.[61] The absence of any significant quantity of medium artillery made the provision of concentrated artillery support doubly difficult. Eighth Army began the Gazala fighting with an 8 : 5 superiority in artillery. It failed to reap the benefits, because it abandoned any possibility of maximizing its fire-power by centralizing command of its artillery. Even when guns were employed to give indirect fire-support, their weight of fire was wasted because commanders failed to carry out a proper reconnaissance before preparing their fire-plan, or went into action without any fire-plan at all.[62]

Secondly, this dispersal of fire-power was institutionalized in early 1942 when Auchinleck decided that

Everything we have learned from our operations in Libya goes to show that the association between armoured units, infantry and artillery must be far closer than it has ever been before, and that any attempt at segregation is wrong and most dangerous. I have definitely come to the conclusion, and so has everyone in a position of responsibility here, that the Armoured Brigade Group as a permanent organization is a necessity and I am not prepared to put armoured troops into battle in any other form. We are working hard at this now and will send you our considered opinion as soon a possible. I feel also that our divisional headquarters must not be classified as 'armoured' or 'infantry', but must be prepared to control a collection of brigades of varying composition as the occasion demands.[63]

Like Home Forces after Dunkirk, Auchinleck believed that the path to better combined arms co-operation and tactical flexibility lay through organizational decentralization. Existing divisions should be replaced by a series of divisional headquarters, each of which was to be capable of commanding a varying number of armoured, motorized, or lorried infantry brigade groups. Each brigade was to be organized so that they could, if necessary, operate entirely independently of any divisional organization.[64] This organization, he hoped, would overcome the major operational weakness that CRUSADER had disclosed, the inability of the British to co-ordinate the operations of their three teeth arms on the battlefield.[65]

The third and final factor that continued to impede significant improvements in 8th Army's combat capability even after CRUSADER was the result of defects in its C3I system and its training regime. Shortcomings in communications technology were beyond the control

[61] PRO WO 106/2223, Notes from Theatres of War no. 2, Cyrenaica, Nov.–Dec. 1941, 7 Mar. 1942.

[62] PRO WO 201/452, Notes on main lessons of recent operations in the Western Desert, 13 July 1942.

[63] PRO WO 216/70, Auchinleck to Brooke, 28 Dec. 1941.

[64] PRO WO 193/224, Auchinleck to Brooke, 12 Jan. 1942.

[65] LHCMA Alanbrooke MSS 6/2/12, Auchinleck to Churchill, 12 Jan. 1942; 6/D/4d/j, Auchinleck to Brooke, 21 Jan. 1942.

of field commanders. Radios remained in short supply.[66] When he took command in Cyrenaica on the eve of Rommel's counter-offensive in March 1941, Sir Philip Neame discovered that he depended on the Italian telephone system, and Italian operators, for much of his communications. The radios of 2nd Armoured divisions quickly failed in April 1941 because units went into action without the proper apparatus to charge their batteries.[67] In early 1942, armoured units were short of wireless sets.[68] As late as November 1942, radio communications in 1st Armoured division almost failed because of a shortage of battery-charging units.[69] But armoured divisions were well supplied compared to the infantry. They were short of wireless equipment throughout 1941 and many of the sets they did possess were too bulky to be manhandled easily in forward positions.[70]

The sets that were available suffered from serious technical shortcomings.[71] Reception was sensitive to geography—during Rommel's counter-attack in January 1942, 4th Indian division's wireless communications was subject to 'fading' in the 'dead pocket'[72] around Benghazi. Atmospheric conditions, particularly at night, often interrupted radio communications.[73] 'It meant', according to one officer, 'having to shout at the top of one's voice coded stuff such as: "Monument nuts playbox peddler" etc through a wild mixture of what sounded like an Egyptian funeral, dance music and the foreign tongues of announcers.'[74] In 1941, Corps Commanders discovered that the ranges of their sets were inadequate and asked for better ones. 'Without it', Beresford-Pierse wrote after BATTLEAXE, 'control is bound to be lost at one stage or another.'[75]

The system could only be made to work by skilled personnel, and they, too, were in short supply. The goal the army strove for was not simply to train signallers so that they were sufficiently skilled to

[66] PRO WO 216/69, Auchinleck to War Office, 7 Jan. 1942.

[67] Neame, *Playing with Strife*, 269–70, 272; PRO WO 106/2149, Report on the action of the 2 Armoured division during the withdrawal from Cyrenaica, Mar.–Apr. 1941, June 1941.

[68] PRO WO 216/69, Auchinleck to War Office, 7 Jan. 1942.

[69] IWM Dept. of Sound Records, Accession no. 000954/07: Brig. W. R. Smijth-Windham, 50.

[70] PRO WO 201/357, Lessons of the campaign in the Western Desert, Battle of Capuzzo, Report by Commander 4 Indian divn. on operations in Western Desert, 15–18 June 1941, 6 Aug. 1941.

[71] IWM Dept. of Sound Records, Accession no. 000954/07: Brig. W. R. Smijth-Windham.

[72] Tuker, *Approach to Battle*, 55, 64.

[73] PRO WO201/357, Lessons of the campaigns in the Western Desert, Battle of Capuzzo, 14–17 June 1941, 6 Aug. 1941; PRO WO 106/2223, Notes from Theatres of War no. 1, Cyrenaica, Nov. 1941, 19 Feb. 1942; IWM Dept. of Sound Records, Accession no. 000991/03: Visc. Bridgeman, 31–2.

[74] Bishop, *One Young Soldier*, 95.

[75] PRO WO201/357, Lessons of the campaigns in the Western Desert, Battle of Capuzzo, 14–17 June 1941, 6 Aug. 1941.

communicate with each other, but 'to get the headphones on the commander's head' so that they could use r/t to speak directly to their subordinates. In 1939 only a few artillery, RTR, and mechanized cavalry units had reached that stage of proficiency. In early 1942 some units in 1st Armoured division still had not done so.[76]

British communications, therefore, remained highly vulnerable even to small breakdowns. When the 4th Armoured Brigade lost four radios on 22 November 1941, command and control throughout the brigade vanished for a whole day. The virtual collapse of the army's signals system in the first week of CRUSADER was one reason why armoured formations became so widely scattered that they often fought in isolation. Even when the system was functioning at maximum efficiency, situation reports were usually twelve hours out of date by the time they reached Army HQ. It was not unusual for Corps and Army HQ, often twenty-four to thirty-six hours behind the times in their understanding of the battle, to be incapable of co-ordinating the operations of subordinate formations.[77] The German intercept service was often quicker at intercepting and passing on British messages to their own commanders.[78]

Commanding by means of brief verbal orders worked only if all staffs and troops involved had already learnt a set of common operating procedures. After COMPASS, 7th Armoured division attributed much of its success to the fact that most of its units had been training together in the desert since 1938. They had thus been able to develop a series of standing orders defining drills to meet common situations.[79] Unfortunately, other formations did not have their good fortune in being able to train together in the desert for such long periods before going into action. Between 1940 and 1942 British forces in North Africa, like the rest of the British army, were the victim of the army's expansion. The surviving senior officers of the 2nd Armoured division ascribed its destruction in March and April 1941 partly to the fact that 'This division had not, in fact, had opportunity for adequate training as a team. It was a collection of Units, three of which had only joined shortly before the action, rather than a trained formation. The breakdown in control and administration was largely due to this fact.'[80] Staffs of higher formations were often

[76] IWM Dept. of Sound Records, Accession no. 000954/07: Brig. W. R. Smijth-Windham, 27–8.
[77] PRO WO 277/25, Gravely, *Signals Communications*, 383; Belchem, *All in the Day's March*, 102–3.
[78] PRO WO 106/2223, Notes from Theatres of War no. 6, Cyrenaica, Nov. 1941–Jan. 1942, July 1942.
[79] PRO WO 201/352, General Staff, XIII Corps, Operations Western Desert, Dec. 40, Lessons from, 18 Jan. 1941.
[80] PRO WO 106/2149, Report on the action of the 2 Armoured divn. during the withdrawal from Cyrenaica, Mar.–Apr. 1941, June 1941.

hastily thrown together only shortly before the onset of major operations. On the eve of CRUSADER, for example, the staff of 8th Army had been in existence for only eight weeks, that of XXX Corps for only six weeks, and neither had sufficient time to train together.[81]

However, the British command and control system also suffered from defects that field commanders themselves could have done something to rectify, even if they probably could not have overcome them completely. A few commanders did follow O'Connor's example and led from the forward edge of the battle. During CRUSADER, Lieutenant-General C. Willoughby Norrie commanded XXX Corps from a mobile tactical HQ consisting of four vehicles carrying a couple of staff officers, a wireless on the corps forward net, and another wireless tuned to intercept messages from Rommel's Panzer divisions.[82] Similarly, Major-General W. H. E. Gott commanded 7th Armoured division from a tank up to 20 miles ahead of his Advanced HQ.[83] But many senior commanders reverted to the more remote approach to C3 embodied in *FSR* and were reluctant either to delegate command to their subordinates or to go forward themselves.

They failed to do so for what must have seemed to be compelling reasons. Generals who went to the front line risked becoming casualties, as O'Connor's own fate demonstrated when he was captured in April 1941. Indeed, within days of his capture, GHQ Middle East issued an order that, although it did not forbid senior commanders and staff officers from going up to the front, did enjoin them to take care that they did not become unnecessary casualties.[84] Major-General Messervy, GOC 7th Armoured division, was also captured in May 1942 when his Advanced HQ was overrun, but, luckier than O'Connor, he was able to escape after a few hours. Even so, for nearly two days his division was without an effective commander. Far more important were the difficulties of communication experienced by commanders who tried to lead from the front. Lacking suitable command vehicles, they knew that if they went forward themselves they risked losing contact with their own HQs.[85] But, if they remained at their main HQ, where they could remain in contact with GHQ in Cairo and their supporting air units, they risked

[81] PRO WO 106/2223, Notes from Theatres of War no. 1, Cyrenaica, Nov. 1941, 19 Feb. 1942; Notes from Theatres of War no. 4, Cyrenaica, Nov. 1941–Jan. 1942, May 1942; Carver, *Out of Step*, 77–9.

[82] Carver, *Out of Step*, 84–6, 89.

[83] LHCMA Pyman MSS 3/1, 7 Armoured divn., An Account of the operations in Libya, 18 Nov.–27 Dec. 1941, 31 Jan. 1942.

[84] PRO WO 201/2588, Middle East Training Memorandum no. 9, Avoidance of excessive officer casualties, 14 Apr. 1941.

[85] PRO WO201/357, Lessons of the campaigns in the Western Desert, Battle of Capuzzo, 14–17 June 1941, 6 Aug. 1941; PRO WO 106/2255, Lessons of the operations in Cyrenaica no. 3, 18 Nov.–3 Dec. 1941; LHCMA Liddell Hart MSS 1/154/30b, Caunter to Liddell Hart [*c*.May 1943].

losing contact with their own forward units. This was the problem that confronted Beresford-Pierse during BATTLEAXE and Cunningham and Ritchie during CRUSADER.[86] It was why one of Cunningham's senior staff officers believed after the war that 'By modern standards control was not properly exercised by the Commander. The battle was largely decentralised to the Corps. The decentralisation resulted in an untidy development of operations, and failure to exploit opportunities.'[87]

Command also depended upon the human qualities of the men making up the team. Some generals, like O'Connor, had the gift of inspiring their subordinates by radiating confidence, integrity, and calmness.[88] He was also assisted by an outstanding BGS, whom he had chosen himself, John Harding.[89] Similarly, Lieutenant-General A. R. Godwin-Austen, GOC XIII Corps during CRUSADER, impressed his subordinates as a robust, shrewd, and energetic leader.[90] It was, therefore, doubly unfortunate that both men were lost to the army. O'Connor was captured and Godwin-Austen asked to be relieved after the fall of Benghazi in January 1942 because his army commander, Ritchie, had persistently ignored his advice.[91] In the opinion of one of Godwin-Austen's subordinates, 'His going was the latest of many misjudgements which had started to shake the confidence in the leadership'.[92] Until Montgomery's arrival in August 1942, too many of the commanders in post did not radiate the necessary inspiration, confidence, and calmness. Cunningham, for example, was 'remote, showing no warmth of personality; he made no attempt to exude confidence, nor to encourage us, and he was unnecessarily sharp-tempered'.[93] Auchinleck dismissed him in the middle of CRUSADER because he 'had lost his nerve'.[94]

Relations between commanders were sometimes marred by 'personal quarrels and ruthless "breaking or rocketing up" of friends and foes up and down'.[95] In mid-1942, senior officers, particularly his two corps commanders Norrie and Gott, who were close personal friends, thought that Ritchie was too much under the influence of Auchinleck. They

[86] Roberts, *From the Desert to the Baltic*, 48–9; PRO WO 106/2223, Notes from Theatres of War no. 1, Cyrenaica, Nov. 1941, 19 Feb. 1942.

[87] LHCMA Liddell Hart MSS 1/56/20, Maj.-Gen. D. Belchem to Liddell Hart, 31 Jan. 1954.

[88] LHCMA Liddell Hart MSS 1/553, Copy of notes from Ronald Lewin, 29 Aug. 1968, Notes on a discussion with Gen. Sir Richard O'Connor, 11 July 1968; LHCMA O'Moore Creagh MSS, Creagh to Barnett, 8 Feb. 1959.

[89] LHCMA O'Connor MSS 8, 'Some notes and opinions on the selection of Officers for senior appointments, with some remarks about Generalship', A paper by Maj. J. K. Nairne, Feb. 1971; Hunt, *A Don at War*, 69.

[90] Hunt, *A Don at War*, 68–9.

[91] PRO WO 259/73, Auchinleck to War Office and encs., 20 Feb. 1942.

[92] Tuker, *Approach to Battle*, 81; Carver, *Dilemmas of the Desert War*, 56–8.

[93] Belchem, *All in the Day's March*, 98.

[94] LHCMA Liddell Hart MSS 1/444, Lewin to Liddell Hart, 18 Mar. 1967 (recounting a conversation with Auchinleck).

[95] CCC R. Lewin MSS RLEW 2/1, Notes for History, Brig. A. G. Kenchington, n.d.

believed that many of his orders had come directly from Cairo and he had not modified them sufficiently to meet local conditions.[96] Both before and during the Gazala fighting the situation was not helped by Ritchie's preference for holding lengthy and inconclusive conferences rather than issuing precise orders.[97] The repercussions of this seeped downwards and reached its nadir at the beginning of June during the planning and execution of the offensive to eliminate the 'Cauldron'. The task of doing so was assigned to 5th Indian and 7th Armoured divisions. The divisions were from two different Corps, but neither of 8th Army's Corps commanders was anxious to assume responsibility for the offensive. To complicate matters further, Ritchie failed to assign the responsibility to either of them.[98] The result was such a lack of urgency in preparing and staging the attack that Rommel was able to recover his balance and repulse the blow when it came.

Similar problems existed at a lower level. In June 1940 the commander and second in command of 4th Armoured Bridge were on such bad terms that the divisional commander was compelled to replace the latter with his own GSO1.[99] Co-operation between 1st and 7th Armoured divisions during the opening phase of the Gazala fighting was impeded because their commanders, Lumsden and Messervy, did not get on. Lumsden also had little time for his Corps commander, Norrie.[100] Gott, as GOC XIII Corps, had to expend a good deal of time refereeing arguments between two of his divisional commanders, Pienaar (1st South African Division) and Ramsden (50th Northumberland division) because they 'could never see eye to eye over any subject'.[101]

However, the problem of command went beyond the personal. Often, through no fault of their own, many senior officers lacked experience of armoured warfare. At the start of CRUSADER, neither the army commander nor his two corps commanders had any experience of desert fighting or of armoured warfare.[102] Critics of the performance of the army in North Africa have ascribed many of its problems to the fact that its senior ranks were dominated by cavalrymen who knew little about armoured warfare.[103] Such strictures are exaggerated. Of the nine

[96] LHCMA Liddell Hart MSS 1/339/2c, Notes for History, The Libyan campaign, May–Aug. 1942, Talk with Dorman-Smith, 2 Nov. 1942; Carver, *Dilemmas of the Desert War*, 252; PRO WO 236/1, Erskine to Latham, 23 Sept. 1949.
[97] Barnett, *The Desert Generals*, 150–1.
[98] PRO WO 106/2235, Report of a Court of Enquiry, vol. 2, Statement by Maj.-Gen. Messervy, commanding 7 Armoured divn. 27 Feb.–19 June 1942; PRO WO 106/2234, Report of a Court of Enquiry assembled by order of the C-in-C, vol. 1.
[99] LHCMA Liddell Hart MSS 1/154/28, Brig. J. A. Caunter to Liddell Hart, 16 May 1943; 11/1942/80, Notes for History, Talk with Brig. R. L. Scoones (DDMT) and Lieut.-Col. H. C. J. Yeo, 24 Sept. 1942.   [100] Carver, *Out of Step*, 100–1, 105, 128–9.
[101] PRO WO 236/1, Erskine to Latham, 23 Sept. 1949.
[102] Belchem, *All in the Day's March*, 100–1.
[103] Ibid. 19.

officers who commanded the three armoured divisions which served in North Africa between December 1940 and August 1942, only three were cavalrymen, and one, Major-General Herbert Lumsden, was a member of a regiment (12th Lancers) that had been mechanized as long ago as 1928. The others included two light infantrymen, a gunner, and three officers from the RTC. The latter were not all military paragons. The rapid collapse of 2nd Armoured division in March 1941 was partly caused by the ineptitude of its undertrained staff and because its commander, Major-General Michael Gambier-Parry was, in the opinion of one of his seniors, 'a conventional and slow minded soldier who couldn't cope with the unexpected'.[104] But Gambier-Parry was not a cavalryman. He had transferred from an infantry regiment to the RTC in 1924.

That some senior officers of mediocre calibre were appointed to posts in North Africa in 1941–2 may have been because Auchinleck, the C-in-C from July 1941 to August 1942, was himself an Indian Army officer in a theatre dominated by senior British officers. This placed him at a disadvantage, because he knew few of his senior subordinates personally and had to lean heavily upon his military secretary for advice. The outcome was a number of mistaken appointments, the most egregious of which was the appointment of Ritchie, who had never commanded anything bigger than a division, to command of 8th Army after Cunningham's dismissal.[105]

After Rommel's arrival in the desert, the British also lost some of the advantage of being able to rely upon their superior intelligence and security organizations as force-multipliers that they had enjoyed when O'Connor confronted the Italians. In June 1941, British intelligence seriously underestimated the number of tanks that the Axis forces could commit against them.[106] In January 1942, they exaggerated Rommel's tank losses during CRUSADER and failed to note the supplies that he had received from Italy since then.[107] And, in mid-May 1942, they discounted evidence derived from prisoner interrogations and signals intercepts provided by their Y service that Rommel's main thrust at Gazala would come in the south and wrongly insisted it would come through the centre of their positions.[108] Shortages of such intelligence-gathering assets as armoured cars and reconnaissance aircraft only partly

[104] LHCMA Liddell Hart MSS 1/553, Copy of notes from Ronald Lewin, 29 Aug. 1968, Notes on a discussion with Gen. Sir Richard O'Connor, 11 July 1968.
[105] LHCMA Alanbrooke MSS 11/7, Notes by Mrs M. Long, Confidential Interviews, 1941–6.
[106] LHCMA O'Moore Creagh MSS, Creagh to ?, 30 July 1941.
[107] Carver, *Dilemmas of the Desert War*, 54.
[108] Ibid. 75–6; PRO WO 106/2235, Report of a Court of Enquiry, vol. 2, Statement by Maj.-Gen. Messervy commanding 7 Armoured divn., 27 Feb.–19 June 1942; Hinsley et al., *British Intelligence*, ii, 722–7.

explained these failures.[109] More important was the fact that, although the British had little difficulty in reading high-grade Italian ciphers, for a long time high-grade German Enigma ciphers eluded them. In April 1941 they did break into the Enigma key used for army–air co-operation in North Africa, and this proved to be a very fruitful source of intelligence. But until August 1941 its utility was limited because it was not sent beyond GHQ in Cairo.[110] It was not until September 1941, and then only with great effort and often with some weeks' delay, that GC&CS managed to crack German army Enigma.[111] Y intercepts became a major source of information during periods of active operations, but they were less useful during quiet periods because the enemy made less use of w/t. Even when sigint did provide information, the British communications system could not always get it on time to the commanders who needed it.[112] Furthermore, until January 1942 any advantage the British did gain from reading German traffic was largely cancelled out because the Germans were reading British messages.[113] Rommel's signals intercept company eagerly fed off British signallers' lack of security. Before CRUSADER, the British did attempt to improve their signals security and their combination of wireless silence and active deception measures allowed them to take Rommel by surprise on 18 November.[114] However, the advantage was short-lived. By the eve of Rommel's offensive at Gazala, the British knew that the Germans were still receiving much valuable intelligence because of poor British wireless security, although 'We also have been receiving information from the enemy'.[115] Intelligence, therefore, did not confer a decisive advantage on either side.

Underlying all of these problems was the fact that 8th Army was insufficiently trained to practise successful combined arms operations. That some improvement had to be made was apparent as early as June 1941. Following BATTLEAXE, GHQ Middle East issued an edict stating that 'A war of movement such as this one requires troops to be trained

---

[109] PRO WO 193/25, Notes on lessons learnt from the recent employment of an armoured divn. and an Army Tank Bn. in the Western Desert, 8 Jan. 1941; PRO WO 201/2588, Middle East Training Memorandum no. 5, Notes on air co-operation Western Desert, Dec. 1940, 14 Jan. 1941.

[110] Hinsley et al., *British Intelligence*, i, 393–4.

[111] Ibid. ii, 280, 295–6.

[112] Ibid. ii, 308.

[113] J. Ferris, 'The British Army, Signals and Security in the Desert Campaign, 1940–42', in M. Handel (ed.), *Intelligence and Military Operations* (London, 1990), 269–74; PRO CAB 146/10, Enemy Documents Section, Axis Operations in North Africa, Part 1.

[114] General Staff, *ATM No. 44*, Appendix B. 'As the Germans see us' (London, 1942); PRO CAB 146/10. Enemy Documents Section. Axis Operations in North Africa. Part 2. Appendix 9: Appreciation of the fighting between 11 November 1941 and 6 Feb. 1942, Trans. from Panzergruppe Afrika's battle report.

[115] PRO WO 201/2591, Notes on the training conference held at GHQ Middle East on 10 May 1942.

to a considerably higher degree than was necessary in the last war'.[116] Auchinleck deliberately postponed his next offensive because, as he informed Churchill, 'BATTLEAXE showed that present standard of training is not (repeat not) enough, and we must secure that team spirit which is essential for efficiency'.[117] But CRUSADER indicated that much remained to be done.[118] In January 1942, BGS 8th Army issued orders that

Every opportunity will be taken to carry out training in the tactical methods described above so as to develop an established technique for this type of operation, and to ensure that different units can carry it out in combination even if they have not had an opportunity of training together beforehand.[119]

In early 1942, Auchinleck's recently appointed DMT, Major-General John Harding, planned to co-ordinate all training efforts by holding monthly meetings with staffs of all armies in the Middle East, by creating training establishments and schools, by establishing a higher commanders' course for selected senior officers, and by allocating collective training areas, each large enough to exercise a complete division. Training was to be conducted on clearly defined lines. 'There is too great a tendency to disperse our forces, and too great an inclination to play for safety. Risk must be taken and weakness in certain areas accepted in order to achieve concentration of effort in the right place and at the right time', he insisted.[120] Night training, training in deception, and battle inoculation were all to be practised. Auchinleck thought that he was doing an excellent job. None the less, the Court of Enquiry that investigated the reasons for the fall of Tobruk highlighted many of the same faults in achieving combined arms co-operation that had become apparent in the previous year.[121]

Harding's failure resulted from the fact that he had not had sufficient time to dispel the very real and often intractable problems that had impeded realistic training since the end of COMPASS. At the level of the individual soldier, training units in Britain were under pressure to produce 'trained' men for field force units. As a result they had to abbreviate their training syllabus and there was seldom enough time to give each man proper training. In September 1942, the GOC of 50th division complained that out of a draft of 860 reinforcements, very few had fired

[116] PRO WO 201/2588, Middle East Training Memorandum no. 16, 30 June 1941.

[117] LHCMA Alanbrooke MSS 6/2/11, Auchinleck to Churchill, 15 July 1941.

[118] PRO WO 106/2223, Notes from Theatres of War no. 4, Cyrenaica, Nov. 1941–Jan. 1942, May 1942.

[119] PRO 201/527, Harding to 1 Armoured and 4 Indian divn., 4 Jan. 1942.

[120] PRO WO 201/2591, Notes on the Training Conference held at GHQ Middle East on 10 May 1942.

[121] LHCMA Alanbrooke MSS 6/2/13, Auchinleck to Brooke, 3 May 1942; PRO WO 106/2234, Report of a Court of Enquiry assembled by order of the C-in-C, vol. 1, July 1942.

an anti-tank rifle or a 2-in. mortar and only a quarter had done any field training.[122] At unit and formation level, Britain's temperate climate made it impossible to simulate desert conditions. The most the War Office could do was 'to suggest [that] the formations be supplied with the latest tactical lessons and general information from the Middle East and Burma to enable them to make a special study of the fighting in such areas.'[123]

Consequently, formations always required a period of intensive local training before they were ready for combat, although they did not always realize that fact. When 1st Armoured division, which had been training in Britain since Dunkirk, arrived in the Western Desert in January 1942, to the experienced eyes of an 8th Army staff officer it was apparent that

they had done a great deal of training in that starry-eyed, dedicated way in which training was carried out in Britain, especially in the first two years of the war. They had a most admirable self-confidence, but they tended as a result to think that there was not much for them to learn.[124]

Rommel soon taught them otherwise. Frank Messervy, who commanded no fewer than three different divisions in North Africa, estimated that 'it is necessary to give troops 3 months training after arrival from Europe or any other non-desert country before they can be confidently thrown into battle in the desert'.[125] British formations rarely enjoyed such a luxury. By late 1941, British formations were beginning to develop drills, but initially they applied them to cross-country movements rather than tactical deployments. During CRUSADER, for example, some divisions and brigades evolved drills for both day and night movement so that divisions could move up to 30 miles in one night without becoming disorganized.[126] Messervy himself had grasped by early 1942 that part of DAK's success lay in its highly developed battle drills and wanted the British armour to follow their example. In February 1942, he suggested the adoption of 'Battle array and drill for armoured division', because he explained, 'it is necessary to have some framework I am certain, otherwise there will be nothing but confusion of thought and consequently confused action.'[127] But he was replaced before he could do anything, and when the division next went into action in May 1942 it

[122] PRO WO 201/2590, Maj.-Gen. J. S. Nichols to GHQ 8 Army, 21 Sept. 1942.
[123] PRO WO 260/16, DSD to C-in-C Home Forces, 9 Mar. 1942.
[124] Hunt, *A Don at War*, 93; LHCMA Liddell Hart MSS 1/56/20, Belchem to Liddell Hart, 31 Jan. 1954.
[125] PRO WO 106/220, Report by Maj.-Gen. Messervy on operations of 1 Armoured divn. in Western Cyrenaica, 24 Feb. 1942.
[126] PRO WO 106/2223, Notes from Theatres of War no. 2, Cyrenaica, Nov.–Dec. 1941, 7 Mar. 1942.
[127] PRO WO 106/220, Report by Maj.-Gen. Messervy on operations by 1 Armoured divn. in Western Cyrenaica, 24 Feb. 1942.

did so piecemeal. The advice old hands gave to troops new to the desert was not always particularly enlightening. Just before CRUSADER, an officer of 7th Hussars told the 2nd Royal Gloucester Hussars that battle 'always looks a muddle, it often is . . . but the actual business of fighting is easy enough. You go in, you come out, you go in again, and you keep on doing it till they break or you are dead.'[128]

The polyglot nature of the Commonwealth forces in North Africa further complicated the problem. In February 1941, Wavell complained that 'it is not always easy to persuade Dominion troops of the need of long training and they appear to want preferential treatment in matters of equipment.'[129] Auchinleck shared his opinion that Australian, South African, and to a lesser extent New Zealand units, 'are apt to think that once they have been in battle, they have little to learn and are on the whole deeply suspicious of any attempt by us to teach them'.[130] This attitude was not confined to Dominion formations. A senior Indian Army officer who visited 7th Armoured division before BATTLEAXE noted that 'there seemed to by [sic] no intensive training going on to remedy this or their obvious lack of proper tactical training.'[131]

Other factors were beyond the control of field commanders. O'Connor's success left him convinced of the necessity of continuing to train troops on active service.[132] But operations were sometimes mounted at such short notice that there was little or no time to rehearse them. In exculpation of 7th Armoured division, it was given only two weeks to prepare for BATTLEAXE.[133] Training in North Africa, particularly amongst units stationed 'up the blue' (in other words in the front line) was hampered by logistical problems. As late as July 1942, Auchinleck was still so short of transport that he found it impossible to give formations in training more than a small proportion of their full establishment of transport.[134] Some infantry units were issued with the new 6-pdr. anti-tank gun only days before the Gazala fighting began, and did not have time to train with it.[135] Petrol was often in short supply and commanders were anxious not to wear out their vehicles before they went into action.[136] The too-frequent transfer of

---

[128] Pittman, *Second Royal Gloucester Hussars*, 5.
[129] LHCMA Alanbrooke MSS 6/2/4, Wavell to CIGS, 11 Feb. 1941.
[130] LHCMA Alanbrooke MSS 6/2/14, Auchinleck to Brooke, 25 July 1942.
[131] LHCMA Liddell Hart MSS 1/705, DMT's tour, Note C. Brig. Tuker, 18 Aug. 1941.
[132] PRO WO 201/352, General Staff, XIII Corps, Operations Western Desert, Dec. 40—Lessons from, 18 Jan. 1940.
[133] LHCMA O'Moore Creagh MSS, Battleaxe, n.d.
[134] LHCMA Alanbrooke MSS 6/2/1, Auchinleck to Brooke, 25 July 1942.
[135] PRO WO 106/2234, Report of a Court of Enquiry assembled by order of the C-in-C, vol. 1, July 1942.
[136] Playfair, *The Mediterranean and Middle East*, iii, 5, 12; PRO WO 106/2255, Lessons of operations in Cyrenaica no. 3, 18 Nov.–4 Dec. 1941), 10 Dec. 1941; PRO WO 106/220,

units between formations interrupted formation training and hampered team building.

However, by mid-1942 there was one area in which British combined arms practice was at least as good as that of the Germans, if not better. It was in North Africa that the army and RAF developed the techniques of air support that became one of the distinguishing features of British operations in the second half of the war. However, for many months the effectiveness of the air support the army received was degraded by some of the same factors that affected the combat capability of the army on the ground. The most obvious was lack of equipment. At the start of COMPASS, the British could field 116 bombers but only 65 fighters compared to the 200 fighters of the Italian air force. In mid-December 1940, the Italians were therefore able to subject O'Connor's forces to heavy bombing attacks and to prevent his tactical reconnaissance aircraft from penetrating far behind their lines.[137] At the outset of Rommel's initial counter-offensive in March and April 1941, he enjoyed almost complete air superiority, using about 200 German and the same number of Italian aircraft. The British had to confine their own movements to the hours of darkness because most of their own AA artillery and aircraft had been sent to Greece. Similarly, at the start of BATTLEAXE the British had fewer serviceable aircraft than had the Axis forces, although they were not outnumbered to the same extent as they had been six months earlier.[138] The RAF's lack of numbers was often made worse by poor serviceability rates, a product of the intensity of air operations, and the harshness of the climate.[139] Furthermore, aircraft that might have served in the desert were diverted to other theatres, principally Greece in early 1941 and the Far East following the Japanese declaration of war in December 1941.

Poor communications and intelligence also reduced the effectiveness of air support. During COMPASS, O'Connor's air support was divided between a small air component consisting of two army co-operation squadrons and Number 202 Group RAF. Each army co-operation squadron had a specially trained air liaison officer who was able to brief pilots about the ground situation and interrogate them once they had landed. However, liaison with the squadrons of Number 202 Group was more haphazard. Its fighters were employed on ground strafing during COMPASS, but unless they happened to operate from an army co-operation squadron's airfield, there was no air liaison officer on hand

Report by Maj.-Gen. Messervy on operations of 1 Armoured divn. in Western Cyrenaica, 24 Feb. 1942.

[137] PRO WO 201/2588, Middle East Training Memorandum no. 5, Notes on air co-operation in the Western Desert, Dec. 1940, 14 Jan 1940; Playfair, *The Mediterranean and Middle East*, i, 262.

[138] Playfair, *The Mediterranean and Middle East*, ii, 166.

[139] Ibid. i, 253, 281.

to brief them.[140] Until CRUSADER, air–ground co-operation was also hamstrung by poor communications between forward troops and the aircraft supposed to assist them.[141] After BATTLEAXE, Western Desert Force's commander, Beresford-Pierse complained bitterly that air–ground co-operation had been handicapped from the outset because, while his own battle HQ was forward at Sidi Barani, the HQ of his supporting air group remained at Bagush, a hundred miles to the east. The lack of communications between the two made close air support and quick-response calls for fighters impossible.[142]

CRUSADER represented a significant turning point in air-ground co-operation. In July 1941 the AOC-in-C, Middle East, Air Chief Marshal Sir Arthur Tedder, created the RAF's first tactical airforce. He reorganized Number 204 Group into a new Air Headquarters, Western Desert, soon to be renamed the Desert Air Force.[143] He also began to take steps to improve the mobility of its ground organization so that it could keep pace with the rapid advances and withdrawals that characterized desert fighting. This helped to ensure that CRUSADER marked the first time that the RAF fielded more serviceable aircraft than did the Axis.[144] It was also the first occasion when the British operated a new system of air-ground control. Earlier in 1941, it had often taken three hours for air support to appear over their target, compared to the response time of the Germans, who could arrive within thirty minutes during BATTLEAXE.[145] Under the new system, the AOC of the Desert Air Force retained ultimate control of all air assets, but the army and RAF established a joint Air Support Control at each Corps and armoured division HQ. They were jointly staffed by the two services and linked by wireless 'tentacles' to Forward Air Support Links, with teams of RAF personnel attached to each brigade. These also had an r/t set enabling them to communicate directly to aircraft flying above them. A brigade could thus pass its request for air support back to the ASC, which, if they approved it, could summon help, again by radio, from nearby airfields. Once the aircraft were airborne, they could be directed onto their target by the RAF team at the brigade HQ.[146] The system also hastened the dissemination of RAF tactical reconnaissance reports. Pilots broadcast them while they were airborne and, in practice, tac/r

[140] PRO WO 201/2588, Middle East Training Memorandum no. 5, Notes on air co-operation in the Western Desert, Dec. 1940, 14 Jan 1940.

[141] PRO WO 201/2586, Middle East Training Pamphlet no. 10, Lessons of Cyrenaica campaign, Dec. 1940–Feb. 1941.

[142] PRO WO 201/357, Lessons of the campaign in the Western Desert, June–Nov. 1941.

[143] I. Gooderson, *Air Power at the Battlefront. Allied Close Air Support in Europe 1943–45* (London, 1998), 25–6.

[144] Playfair, *The Mediterranean and Middle East*, iii, 15.

[145] PRO WO 201/357, Lessons of the campaign in the Western Desert, June–Nov. 1941.

[146] PRO WO 277/34, Army Air Support and Photographic Interpretation, 1939–45, 44.

aircraft provided more targets for air attack than did the tentacles. With some modifications to hasten response times, this system remained in operation until the end of the war.

During CRUSADER the RAF achieved air superiority and prevented the Axis air forces from seriously intervening in the ground fighting. The RAF also inflicted considerable damage on enemy ground forces. However, RAF pilots reported that German armoured columns put up such heavy flak that low-level or dive-bombing attacks were impossible, and escaped British POWs reported that the enemy usually recovered from his confusion within an hour of the attack. The ASC system did hasten the arrival of air support. Nevertheless, because of the need to provide bombers with fighter protection, it still took two hours between the initiation of a request from brigade and the arrival of aircraft over their target. The army was understandably anxious to reduce this and did eventually succeed.[147] During the fighting around Gazala in June 1942, the time between the summoning of close air support and its arrival was on one occasion reduced to only thirty-five minutes.[148]

However, no foolproof solution had been found to the difficulty pilots experienced in distinguishing friend from foe in the swirling chaos of the ground war. Until ground forces discovered some reliable and rapid means of communicating their position to friendly aircraft, it was not safe for the latter to engage targets within 500 yards from their own troops.[149] It was for this reason that aircraft were more often employed on interdiction missions behind the enemy front line, where they was no chance of mistaking friend for foe, than in CAS missions, where they were more likely to attack friendly troops. One reason why the effectiveness of air support increased in the second half of 1942 was that from July onwards 8th Army occupied reasonably clearly defined positions on the Alamein line, thus making it easier for the RAF to distinguish friend from foe.[150]

By the time Tobruk fell, the German army recognized that the RAF had developed into a dangerous opponent. Improvements in intelligence gathering and communications enabled the British to direct their air assets more rapidly and more precisely onto their targets than ever before.[151] Seemingly continuous air attacks succeeded in degrading the effectiveness of German artillery. The Germans found RAF fighter–bomber attacks, first employed on a regular basis from May 1942,

---

[147] PRO WO 106/2223, Notes from theatres of war, Cyrenaica no 1, Nov. 1941, 19 Feb. 1942; no. 6, Nov. 1941–Jan. 1942, July 1942.

[148] PRO WO 277/34, Army Air Support and Photographic Interpretation, 1939–45, 47.

[149] PRO WO 277/5, Pemberton, *Artillery Tactics*, 103, 129–30; PRO WO 106/2223, Notes from theatres of war, Cyrenaica no. 1, Nov. 1941, 19 Feb. 1942.

[150] Carver, *Out of Step*, 124.

[151] B. Gladman, 'Air Power and Intelligence in the Western Desert Campaign, 1940–43', *Intelligence and National Security*, 13 (1998), 144–62.

particularly unpleasant because it was so difficult to predict when and where they would occur.[152] The 8th Army, by contrast, was almost immune to air attack during its long withdrawal to Alamein. This was not only because the Luftwaffe could not keep pace with the speed of Rommel's advance. It was also a testament to the fact that the Desert Air Force was sufficiently mobile to be able to leapfrog backwards and yet still maintain air superiority over friendly ground forces.[153] Whatever the reasons for the débâcle of the summer of 1942, lack of air support was not one of them.

After CRUSADER, Colonel Fritz Bayerlein, the DAK's chief of staff, concluded that the fundamental shortcoming of 8th Army was that its C3 system was an 'unwieldy and rigidly methodical technique of command, their over-systematic issuing of orders down to the last detail, leaving little latitude to the junior commander'.[154] The British agreed. Auchinleck was painfully aware of the dislocation that occurred when a major HQ was overrun, or even had to move. He correctly attributed it to 'our cumbrous and static system of control and command'.[155] In February 1942 he insisted that 'The old system of issuing orders and of control in general is not suitable for the swift moving warfare on very wide fronts which is likely to obtain all over this theatre'.[156] But the weaknesses of 8th Army went beyond that. During the desert war, both sides made mistakes. Rommel's tended to be at the operational level. His 'dash to the wire' in November 1941 and the way in which he allowed himself to become trapped in the 'Cauldron' at the end of May 1942 were two outstanding examples. But the DAK's battle drills and C3I system frequently sufficed to retrieve the situation. The British, thanks largely to inadequacies in their training, made mistakes at both the operational *and* tactical level, and paid the price accordingly.

[152] PRO CAB 146/15, Enemy Documents Section, Appreciation no. 9, Part IV, Appendix 9. DAK's report on fighting, May–July 1942, 10 Aug. 1942.

[153] D. Richards and H. St. G. Saunders, *Royal Air Force 1939–45, ii. The Fight Avails* (London, 1953), 210–16.

[154] *The Rommel Papers*, ed. Liddell Hart (London, 1953), 184.

[155] LHCMA Liddell Hart MSS 1/30/63, Auchinleck to Liddell Hart, 24 Oct. 1958.

[156] PRO WO 201/538, Auchinleck to Rear HQ, 8 Army and XII and XXX Corps, 8 Feb. 1942.

CHAPTER EIGHT

Monty's Army: Alam Halfa to the Rhine

It is easy to dismiss Montgomery as a Second World War general who applied the doctrines and methods of 1918 to win his victories.[1] Montgomery's insistence that his battles be fought according to a 'master plan', his employment of concentrated artillery and his insistence on not moving until he had adequate logistical support, combined to give his battles the outward appearance of the great offensives that Haig mounted in France between 1916 and 1918. He won because he enjoyed superiority in material, and was able to compel his opponents to fight a series of set-piece battles, not dissimilar to those of 1918, which minimized the British army's shortcomings.[2] Closer inspection reveals a different picture. Montgomery did enjoy a quantitative material superiority over his enemies. But so had Cunningham and Ritchie. Both had deployed more tanks than Rommel before CRUSADER and Gazala, and it had availed them nothing. Furthermore, as Chapter 3 has demonstrated, the British army's quantitative superiority was partially offset by the qualitative superiority of so many German weapons. Montgomery did not employ the same operational doctrine and techniques as Haig had done in 1918. His battles were a product of the doctrines that the army had developed between the wars, the lessons of its defeats in 1940–2, and his own personality.

Montgomery won his victories against an enemy who, from Alamein, through Tunisia, Italy, and Normandy, practised a highly effective defensive doctrine. The German army's defences increasingly relied upon deep, fortified positions, and deep minefields. They no longer deployed their tanks *en masse* but used them as mobile pill boxes.[3] The backbone of their defences consisted of small parties of infantry, lavishly equipped with machine-guns and mortars and supported by one or two

---

[1] Bidwell, and Graham, *Fire-Power*, 245, assert that 'He [Montgomery] turned back to the methods of 1918, not because he was a reactionary, but because he was a realist . . . When he chose what to many appeared to be the tactics of attrition he saw to it that the attrition was efficient. Where Gott hoped to avoid casualties by manoeuvre Montgomery used fire-power to batter down his opponent and reduce his ability to inflict injury on his troops.'

[2] Murray, 'British Military Effectiveness' 119; Fraser, *And We Shall Shock Them*, 233.

[3] Bailey, *Field Artillery and Firepower*, 190–2.

tanks or self-propelled guns. In Italy, they usually built their main defensive positions along natural lines, either rivers or mountains, or along a series of small towns commanding main roads.[4] In the bocage country of Normandy, visibility was so poor that they preferred to hold as strong points road junctions and villages rather than high ground.[5] A thinly held outpost line, usually on a forward slope, gave them warning of an attack. Their main defensive positions, covered by minefields, machine-guns, and anti-tank guns sited in enfilading positions, were on the reverse slope where they were concealed from British artillery observers. The Germans ranged their mortars and artillery onto ground where the British were likely to form up for an attack.[6] They held their positions in great depth, and, when attacked, usually mounted a swift counter-attack before the British were able to consolidate their gains.[7]

The Germans sometimes held their positions with properly constituted divisions. But the British frequently marvelled at their ability rapidly to form improvised battle groups from the remnants of formations and thought it one of the strengths of the German army. The Germans themselves were not so sanguine. A Corps commander who fought in Italy always preferred to fight with properly constituted divisions, saying of *ad hoc* groupings that 'In a major battle they melted away like butter in the sun'.[8] One reason for this was that such *ad hoc* groups often lacked proper artillery support. The Germans tried to use mortars to compensate for this weakness, and in Normandy British medical officers estimated that they caused as many as 70 per cent of infantry casualties.[9] When forced to withdraw, the Germans employed small, mobile rearguards equipped with handfuls of tanks, self-propelled guns, and anti-tank guns, mines, booby-traps, and snipers to slow the pace of the British pursuit.[10] They usually remained in position just long enough to enable their own engineers to carry out essential demolition work and began to withdraw when it was clear that the British advance guard was about to outflank them.[11] In the opinion of Major-General

[4] PRO WO 204/7976, Notes on fighting in Italy, 12 Mar. 1944.

[5] PRO CAB 106/963, Reports on the fighting in Normandy, 1944, Immediate Report no. 3, 12 June 1944; PRO WO 232/21, Notes from theatres of War, Report by Capt. L. C. Coleman, 3 Oct. 1944.

[6] PRO WO 232/14, Lieut.-Gen. K. Anderson to AFHQ, 16 June 1943; PRO WO 201/527, Extracts from the report of a War Office observer in North Africa, May 1943; PRO WO 232/17, DMT, CMF to DDMT, War Office, 25 Mar. 1944.

[7] PRO WO 291/1318, No. 1 Operational Research Section, Report no. 1/24/A, Effect of artillery fire in attacks in mountainous country [c.Nov. 1944]; PRO WO 232/21, Notes from theatres of War, Report by Capt. L. C. Coleman, 3 Oct. 1944.

[8] von Senger und Etterlin, *Neither Fear Nor Hope*, 223.

[9] PRO WO 291/1331, Operational Research in North West Europe no. 2 ORS, Report no. 11, The Location of enemy mortars, n.d.

[10] PRO CAB 106/1060, Report from Normandy, 6 June–6 July 1944, by Brig. J. Hargest.

[11] PRO WO 201/527, Part I, Seaborne Operations and Beach Organisation [c.Oct. 1943].

W. E. Clutterbuck, GOC 1st Division in Tunisia, the result for the British was that 'the A.Tank mine and the H[eav]y A.Tank gun has "seen off" the t[an]k to a great extent and while the tank is still most useful to inf[antry], its real helper is becoming massed Art[iller]y'.[12]

In finding ways of overcoming their opponents, from late 1942 onwards, British field commanders were compelled to operate within two constraints. The first was their long-held fear that the morale of their troops was dangerously fragile. The second was their knowledge that the army was fast running out of men. Together they meant that they had no option but to employ operational techniques that put a premium on minimizing casualties.

Even before the war senior commanders had harboured doubts about the fragile morale of their troops. By mid-1942 the string of defeats that they had suffered convinced them their worst fears were justified. In May 1942 Wavell decided that

we are nothing like as tough as we were in the last war and that British and Australian troops will not at present stand up to the same punishment and casualties as they did in the last war. It is softness in education and living and bad training, and can be overcome but it will take a big effort.[13]

A month later, worried about the apparently poor morale of units in 8th Army, Auchinleck asked the War Cabinet to reintroduce the death penalty as a deterrent to stem the rising tide of deserters. Two years later, again because of a growing incidence of desertion from front line units, Alexander followed suit.[14]

In all three cases there was a suspicion of commanders seeking easy solutions to complex, systemic problems. In making these requests, they were harking back to the same solutions that Haig and his contemporaries had espoused. They, too, had seriously doubted the willingness of the town-bred masses who filled the ranks of the army during the First World War to withstand the rigours of war with their morale intact. They, too, had believed that only an outward conformity to the tenets of military life and strict discipline would serve to maintain the army's cohesion.[15] Montgomery shared his contemporaries' concerns about the morale of their troops, but he never asked for the reintroduction of the death penalty. Instead, he adopted a holistic approach to conserving morale. Firm discipline was an essential factor in maintaining the willingness of troops to fight, but discipline alone was not enough. Troops also needed good leadership, realistic training, physical

---

[12] PRO WO 231/10, GOC, 1 Divn., Lessons of the North African campaign, 29 May 1943.
[13] LHCMA Alanbrooke MSS 6/2/6, Wavell to Alanbrooke, 31 May 1942.
[14] French, 'Discipline and the Death Penalty', 531–45.
[15] Travers, *The Killing Ground*, 51–2.

fitness, and professional man-management. But the single most important factor in sustaining morale was success in battle. 'I have *no failures*
in my Army and the troops know it', he told an audience of senior
officers in February 1943. However, the need to ensure that each operation was successful itself limited the scope of what he could ask his
troops to do. 'I limit the *scope of operations to what is possible*, and I
use the force necessary to ensure success.'[16] This meant, for example,
that at the operational level in early October 1942 he substituted a new
plan for the Alamein offensive because he believed that his troops were
insufficiently trained to carry out his original plan.[17] In Normandy, the
early stages of the campaign convinced him that some of the divisions he
had brought back from the Mediterranean were battle-weary.[18] For the
rest of the campaign he preferred to spearhead his operations with
formations like 15th and 43rd Infantry divisions and the 11th and
Guards Armoured divisions. Fresh from Britain, where they had been
training for four years, their morale was less fragile.

Haig had begun and ended the First World War believing that if two
sides were equally matched, the one with the stronger will to win would
be victorious. At the tactical level, Montgomery and his colleagues
shunned such simplicities. They put into practice the army's inter-war
doctrine that battles should be fought with the maximum quantity of
material and the minimum quantity of manpower. Concerned about the
morale of 6th Armoured division in January 1943, Lieutenant-General
C. W. Allfrey, GOC V Corps, insisted on the 'maximum use of Artillery
and minimum use of bodies'.[19] At the end of 1943, the DMT in Italy
concluded that a plentiful supply of armour was essential because the
infantry now expected its support as a right.[20] Lieutenant-General Sir
Sidney Kirkman, GOC of XIII Corps, echoed his opinion in November
1944.

We may at times be lavish with artillery expenditure, but the British soldier has
come to expect a certain measure of support and if at this stage support appears
inadequate, I consider that attacks will be launched in so half-hearted a manner
that we shall incur heavy casualties without success.[21]

But even if they had not been concerned about morale, senior officers
would have been impelled to rely more upon material. In late 1942, just

[16] *Montgomery and the Eighth Army,* ed. Brooks, 144–5.
[17] LHCMA Alanbrooke MSS 6/2/21, Montgomery, Review of the situation in Eighth Army,
12 Aug.–23 Oct. 1942 by Lieut.-Gen. B. L. Montgomery, 23 Oct. 1942; *Montgomery and the
Eighth Army,* ed. Brooks, 65–6.
[18] PRO WO 216/101, Grigg to Churchill, 3 Nov. 1944, and DCIGS to CIGS, 2 Nov. 1944.
[19] LHCMA Allfrey MSS 3/1, Diary entries, 13, 17 Jan. 1943.
[20] PRO WO 231/8, Directorate of Military Training, Lessons from the Italian Campaign, 18
Dec. 1943.
[21] LHCMA Kirkman MSS, Kirkman to Harding, 25 Nov. 1944.

as supplies and equipment began be delivered in quantities sufficient to enable the army to fight battles of material, manpower began to run dry. Recruits were so scarce by late 1942 that the army had to begin to disband formations. In December 1942, Alexander cannibalized 8th Armoured and 44th Infantry divisions to find drafts to maintain his remaining British formations.[22] In mid-1943 the equivalent of four divisions were disbanded in the UK. In the autumn of 1943, the War Cabinet, wrongly assuming that the war in Europe would end by the autumn of 1944, allocated the army an intake of only 150,000 recruits.[23] The only way the War Office could find sufficient men for 21 Army Group was by reducing the six Lower Establishment divisions in the UK to cadres. When that did not suffice, men were transferred to the infantry from the RAF Regiment and the Royal Artillery and, once those sources ran dry, Montgomery had no option but to disband two complete divisions in late 1944.[24]

The shrinking size of the army from late 1942 had political, operational, and tactical consequences. Churchill realized that it threatened Britain's political influence within the Anglo-American alliance. In November 1943 he insisted that the War Office find three more divisions to commit to the cross-Channel invasion so as to give the British parity with the Americans at least in the opening weeks of the campaign.[25] But the process of shrinkage was inexorable, and by December 1944 he could only lament that 'I greatly fear the dwindling of the British army as a factor in France as it will affect our right to impress our opinion upon strategic and other matters'.[26]

At the operational and tactical levels, Montgomery recognized, as early as December 1942, that 'In all my operations now I have to be very careful about losses, as there are not the officers and men in the depots in Egypt to replace them'.[27] Henceforth British field commanders could afford to be prodigal with munitions and equipment, but not with men. Faced with a possible shortage of artillery ammunition in March 1944, Alexander insisted that 'artillery has proved a battle winning factor in this war—and now it appears that we must give it up and sacrifice men's lives (which we haven't got) to do this job. I think it's dreadful.'[28]

[22] PRO WO 193/224, Alexander to Brooke, 3 Dec. 1942; PRO CAB 120/232, Brooke to PM, 4, 14 Dec. 1942.

[23] PRO CAB 78/184/Gen.26, Record of a conference of ministers held at No. 10 Downing Street on Friday 5 Nov. 1943.

[24] PRO PREM 3/55/6, Grigg to Churchill, 20 Oct. 1943; PRO CAB 106/313, DCIGS to CIGS, 15 and 21 Mar. 1944; PRO PREM 3/55/6, Grigg to Churchill, 25 Mar. 1944; IWM Montgomery MSS BLM 121/7, Montgomery to Adam, 2 Sept. 1944; PRO WO 216/101, Note on reduction of 50 divn. in 21 Army Group, 8 Dec. 1944.

[25] PRO WO 259/77, Churchill to Grigg, 6 Nov. 1943.

[26] IWM Visc. Montgomery MSS BLM 121, Churchill to Montgomery, 12 Dec. 1944.

[27] Montgomery and the Eighth Army, ed. Brooks, 96.

[28] LHCMA Alanbrooke MSS 6/2/19, Alexander to Brooke, 22 Mar. 1944.

Shortly before the Normandy landing, the Adjutant-General told Lieutenant-General Gerald Bucknall, GOC XXX Corps, whose troops were about to assault the beaches that the 'manpower & Reinforcement situ[atio]n [is] very touchy'.[29] The shortage of replacements severely constrained commanders' freedom of action. It reduced their willingness to seize fleeting opportunities, for fear that they might lead to heavy and unsustainable losses.[30] In March 1944, Montgomery concluded that 'We have got to try and do this business with the smallest possible casualties'.[31] Initially he pushed 2nd Army hard to take the area south-east of Caen in order to secure the airfields that his air support required. He told his army commanders that they must penetrate inland rapidly. 'We *must crack* about and force the battle to swing our way.'[32] But, by 10 July, faced by mounting casualties, he told Dempsey that, whilst he must enlarge the bridgehead, he had to avoid excessive losses. Second Army had plenty of tanks; what it lacked was a sufficiency of infantry.[33] Dempsey therefore persuaded Montgomery to allow him to mount an all-armoured attack, Operation GOODWOOD, on 18 July. In September 1944, confronted by an equally serious shortage of drafts in Italy, Alexander admitted that 'Commanders are forced to act cannily with serious adverse effects all the way down the tree'.[34] The need to keep casualties to a minimum in 1944–5 placed a premium on careful preparations and planning and the avoidance of all unnecessary risks. In June 1944 Leese ordered that, in a set-piece attack, infantry brigade commanders should issue their orders forty-eight hours before H-hour and that six hours of daylight should be left to enable platoon commanders and tank troop commanders to make their plans.[35] Two months later, Dempsey believed that if a battalion were ordered to attack an organized defensive position, it had a fifty per cent chance of success if it had two hours to make its preparations. It had a guarantee of success if it had twice as long.[36] Dwindling manpower and the perceived deficiencies of the morale of their troops meant that from late 1942 onwards the British could not afford to operate with the same

[29] IWM Lieut.-Gen. G. C. Bucknall MSS 80/33/1/folder 8, Diary entry, 1 June 1944.

[30] S. A. Hart, 'Field Marshal Montgomery, 21st Army Group, and North-West Europe, 1944–45', Ph.D. thesis (London, 1995), 95–6; PRO WO 204/1895, School of Infantry Training Conference, April 1944, Points raised by delegates, 23 April 1944.

[31] PRO CAB 106/313, Montgomery to DCIGS, 19 Mar. 1944.

[32] IWM Montgomery MSS BLM 107/2, Montgomery to Bradley and Dempsey, 20 Mar. 1944; CCC Sir P. J. Grigg MSS PJGG 9/8/5, Montgomery to Grigg and enc., 21 May 1944.

[33] LHCMA Liddell Hart MSS 1/230/22A, Liddell Hart, Operation GOODWOOD, 18 July 1944, Dempsey's expansion (18 Mar. 1952) of the notes he wrote down in brief form, 21 Feb. 1952.

[34] PRO WO 193/26, Alexander to War Office, 10 Sept. 1944.

[35] PRO WO 204/7957, Maj.-Gen. C. P. Walsh to V, X, XIII Corps, 28 June 1944.

[36] Taylor, *Infantry Colonel*, 86.

haste or develop the same disregard for casualties that characterized both the Russian and German armies.

The doctrine that Montgomery and his acolytes practised from Alamein onwards was not original, but neither was it the same as Haig had practised in 1918, although there were some superficial similarities. Indeed, recent research on the battles of 1918 has suggested that Haig in fact failed to practise any operational doctrine, and that he failed in a real sense to command the BEF.[37] Haig believed that it was his task as the C-in-C of the BEF to establish a 'master-plan' and then leave it to his subordinates to carry it out. If he interfered in the actual conduct of operations beyond deploying his own general reserve, he would paralyse their initiative. These ideas synergised with Haig's own personality. He was highly self-disciplined, he held himself aloof and found it difficult to form friendships with his equals. He liked order, disliked changing his mind or hearing his ideas opposed by subordinates. He picked weak and acquiescent men to fill staff posts at GHQ and dismissed officers who had crossed him. It was not surprising, therefore, that senior officers found it difficult to raise awkward questions with him. The result was that GHQ was isolated from the rest of the army, and from the realities of the battlefield. In 1918 Armies, Corps, and Divisions were left largely to their own devices to find solutions to the tactical problems that they confronted in the period of semi-mobile warfare that followed the collapse of the German spring offensive.

Montgomery's operational doctrine was an amalgam of inter-war doctrine, the lessons that the high command drew from operations in the field and in exercises at home since 1939, and his own ruthless personality that drove him to always seek to impose his will on those around him. The experience of defeat in France, Greece, and North Africa taught the British to avoid operational manoeuvres in favour of set-piece attrition battles based on the possession of superior quantities of material.[38] Montgomery agreed with Haig that battles should be conducted according to a 'master-plan', designed by the commander and intended to minimize the risk of confusion and error. To that end the plan had to be simple, for complex plans were inherently more likely to fail. He also agreed that subordinate commanders had to conduct their own part in the battle in accordance with the plan and their commander's wishes.

But as an army and army group commander, Montgomery did not believe that his job stopped there. He prepared the master-plan and

[37] The following paragraphs are heavily informed by T. Travers, 'A Particular Style of Command: Haig and GHQ, 1916–1918', *Journal of Strategic Studies*, 10 (1987), 363–76; idem, *How the War Was Won*

[38] The best analysis of Montgomery's doctrine is Hart, 'Field Marshall Montgomery', 26–7, 113–67. What follows is heavily informed by Hart's analysis.

allocated resources to his army and corps commanders, but he also co-ordinated their movements once the battle had begun and liased closely with the RAF to ensure proper air support for the ground forces.[39] Co-ordination was facilitated by the fact that Corps were deliberately organized flexibly so that their composition could be changed quickly to suit any particular operation.[40] But this high degree of flexibility was bought at some cost. In July 1944, when 15th (Scottish) division, was switched from VIII Corps to XXX Corps, its commander complained that 'their staffs are almost complete strangers to my staff and of course have different ways of working which require a certain time before we can say that we are in complete sympathy with them'.[41] It was the task of corps and divisional commanders to prepare their own plans to fight the tactical battle in accordance with the Army commander's plan.[42] Senior officers exercised control over their subordinates by setting them a well-defined centre line for their advance and ordering them to move along it in a series of 'bounds'.[43]

In order to enable him to exercise command without imposing unnecessary delays on the tempo of operations, Montgomery discarded written operational orders in favour of verbal orders, issued either in face-to-face meetings or, during mobile operations, using r/t. He expected his subordinates to do likewise. The issue to subordinate commanders of marked-up maps showing start lines and objectives usually supplemented verbal orders.[44] 'There is', according to one visitor in July 1943, 'a strong anti-paper complex everywhere in 8th Army HQ . . .'[45] Far from remaining aloof from the rest of the army, Montgomery went out of his way to maintain contact with them. To ensure that all ranks understood their part in the 'master-plan', Montgomery tried to address all officers down to the rank of Lieutenant-Colonel himself and again expected them to do the same to their subordinates.[46]

Nor did Montgomery employ a staff of yes-men. One of the first innovations that he introduced when he took command of 8th Army was to appoint Auchinleck's BGS, Freddie de Guingand, as his Chief of Staff.

---

[39] Gen. Sir C. Richardson, *Flashback. A Soldier's Story* (London, 1985), 130–3; Belchem, *All in the Day's March*, 167, 212; Montgomery, *Memoirs*, 81–2.

[40] LHCMA O'Connor MSS, 5/4/40, Montgomery to O'Connor, 4 Sept. 1944.

[41] LHCMA O'Connor MSS, Maj.-Gen. G. H. A. MacMillan to O'Connor, 22 July 1944.

[42] Horrocks, *Corps Commander*, 31–2.

[43] See e.g. PRO WO 232/17, Maj.-Gen. G. W. E. Erskine, 7 Armoured divn., Report on Operations, 20 Nov. 1943.

[44] General Staff, *MTP No. 41. The Tactical Handling of the Armoured division and its Components. The Armoured Regiment* (London, 1943); General Staff, *MTP Part 1. The Infantry Battalion (1944)* (London, 1944).

[45] PRO WO 205/39, Notes on visit to Mediterranean, July 1943; R. Ryder, *Oliver Leese* (London, 1987), 152; PRO CAB 106/1037, Notes of a Staff Conference, 13 Jan. 1944.

[46] LHCMA Liddell Hart MSS 6/2/23, Montgomery to Brooke, 3 July 1943; *Montgomery and the Eighth Army*, ed. Brooks, 25–8, 62–3.

The latter's role was not only to co-ordinate all staff functions, thus freeing the army commander to ponder how to fight the next battle. He also had the power to take decisions in Montgomery's name when the C-in-C was away from his main headquarters. This enabled Montgomery to go forward and command from near the forward edge of the battle.[47] Before D-Day, Montgomery urged all commanders down to Corps level to follow his example.[48] The Court of Enquiry that investigated the reasons for the collapse of the Gazala line and the fall of Tobruk in June 1942 concluded unequivocally that commanders had to command from the front.[49] By Alamein it had finally became common practice for formation commanders in 8th Army to exercise command in battle from a small tactical HQ.[50] However, until 1944, 8th Army's practice was not shared by formations training in Britain. Their commanders, preparing for D-Day, were told that forming a tactical HQ should be the exception, rather than the rule.[51] On taking command of 21st Army Group, Montgomery overturned this recommendation. He expected his subordinates down to the level of division to follow his example and fight the battle from a tactical HQ, and most did so.[52] Some paid the price by becoming casualties, but their readiness to command from the forward edge of the battle meant that Corps Commanders like Sir Brian Horrocks, who used a tank or a light aircraft to go forward to his division's HQs, could, in the eyes of their subordinates, develop 'a marvellous facility for turning up at the right moment'.[53] However, merely because commanders were on the spot did not necessarily mean that they invariably took the correct decisions. On the opening day of GOODWOOD, 'Pip' Roberts, then commanding 11th Armoured Division, was following closely behind his armoured brigade commander and ordered the latter to mask rather than capture the village of Cagny. It was only after the war that he discovered that in doing so he enabled the Germans to reinforce their defences and block the further advance of his division.[54]

[47] Guingand, *Operation Victory*, 157; Richardson, *Flashback*, 132; *Montgomery and the Eighth Army*, ed. Brooks, 27.

[48] PRO CAB 106/1037, Notes of a Staff Conference, 13 Jan. 1944.

[49] PRO WO 106/2234, Report of a Court of Enquiry assembled by order of the C-in-C, vol. 1.

[50] PRO WO 106/2223, Notes from theatres of War no. 6. Cyrenaica, Jan.–June 1942, Oct. 1942; Guingand, *Operation Victory*, 158–9; Richardson, *Flashback*, 120.

[51] General Staff, *ATM No. 45* (London, 1943).

[52] PRO WO 232/17, Maj. Gen. G. W. E. Erskine, 7 Armoured divn., Report on Operations, 20 Nov. 1943; PRO WO 232/21, Notes from Theatres of War, Report by Capt. L. C. Coleman AIF, 3 Oct. 1944; Roberts, *From the Desert to the Baltic*, 158–9, 172–3; *A Guard's General*, ed. Lindsay, 146.

[53] LHCMA Liddell Hart MSS 1/444, Lewin to Liddell Hart and enc., Notes of talk with Col. David Rooke, chairman of assault committee, 43–4, 10 July 1968; Horrocks, *Corps Commander*, 31, 68–9.

[54] Roberts, *From the Desert to the Baltic*, 173.

When he took command of 8th Army on 25 June 1942, Auchinleck realized that it was essential that commanders 'dispense with constant discussion with or reference to his subordinates' and actually command them.[55] Some of his senior staff officers thought that he was incapable of doing so.[56] Auchinleck's critics also thought he too-readily assumed that once an order had been given it would automatically be carried out. Montgomery did not make the same mistakes. Unlike Haig, he believed that it was an essential task of an army commander to monitor the execution of his orders to ensure that his subordinates were acting at all times in accordance with his master-plan. Just as he planned his battles two levels below himself, so he monitored the work of commanders two levels down. It was Montgomery's refusal to allow his senior subordinates the latitude customary in the British army to develop their own interpretation of orders that more than anything set him apart from his contemporaries. Determined to impose his will on the enemy, he knew that he first had to impose it on his own subordinates. What he called maintaining a 'firm grip' was 'essential in order that the master plan will not be undermined by the independent ideas of individual subordinate commanders at particular moments in the battle'.[57]

Montgomery established his 'firm grip' through a variety of means. He imposed a rigorous training regime at all levels of his army, and he insisted that units and formations devised and practised drills to ensure that they could carry out common tasks rapidly and efficiently. Most of the shortcomings in 8th Army's training had already been recognized by Wavell, Auchinleck, and their senior staff officers before Montgomery arrived. What Montgomery did do was to insist for the first time that all commanders took the training of their troops seriously. Only if they did so would 'the doctrine laid down permeate throughout the formation.'[58] Realism, including the lavish use of live ammunition was essential. 'We must', he told a Staff College audience in September 1942, 'adopt common-sense safety precautions and accept the risk of a few casualties in order to get the Army fit for battle.'[59] Whenever possible, he tried to rehearse operations before mounting them.[60] Before Second Alamein, X Corps practised how to effect a passage through deep minefields, putting special reference on preparing rapid artillery fire-plans to overcome enemy anti-tank screens.[61] Units earmarked for the landing in Sicily

[55] PRO WO 201/452, CGS, GHQ, Middle East, Notes on recent operations in the Western Desert, 13 July 1942.

[56] Richardson, *Flashback*, 102–3.

[57] Montgomery, *Memoirs*, 81–2.

[58] IWM Briggs MSS 66/76/1, 8 Army Training Memorandum no. 1, The approach to training, 30 Aug. 1942.

[59] *Montgomery and the Eighth Army*, ed. Brooks, 59.

[60] Ibid. 41–2.

[61] PRO WO 201/537, X Corps Training Instruction no. 1, 11 Sept. 1942.

practised assault landing techniques at the northern end of the Red Sea.[62] The 7th Armoured division spent three months in North Africa undergoing individual and unit training and combined operations training before landing in Italy in September 1943.[63] Training was also conducted when formations were at rest. By December 1942, 1st Armoured, 4th Indian, and 50th divisions had all been left behind by the speed of 8th Army's advance, but their Corps Commander, Horrocks, was busy chivvying them to ensure that they spent time in training. 'I am going off the day after tomorrow', he informed Montgomery, 'to spend two days each with 50 and 4 Ind[ian] Divisions, just to see that the training is not all on paper . . .'[64]

Much time was devoted to inculcating battle drills in the expectation that they would speed the tempo of operations. A week before Montgomery arrived in the desert, Auchinleck's newly appointed BGS, Brigadier de Guingand, asked Corps commanders to develop a battle drill for breaking through deep enemy positions protected by minefields. 'In the German Army this type of operation is carried out stage by stage in accordance with a standard procedure which may be modified for particular conditions. This has proved successful in recent operations.'[65] Montgomery had already enthusiastically embraced battle drills in Britain and lost no time in insisting that all arms develop them.[66] They 'will enable deployment to be speeded-up' as well as ensuring the proper co-ordination between all arms.[67] He appeared to have succeeded. At Alamein the Germans captured British orders that seemed to them to be clearer and briefer than anything they had seen before.[68] Almost simultaneously the General Staff formerly endorsed the practice in an *ATM*.[69]

Montgomery did not remain isolated from his generals. On the contrary he went out of his way to train them. 'I do concentrate', he wrote in, September 1943, 'on teaching my Generals, and I am certain one has got to do so.'[70] He spread his ideas through a series of short booklets distilling his experiences as a field commander and by

[62] Eke, *A Game of Soldiers.*

[63] PRO WO 232/17, Maj.-Gen. G. W. E. J. Erskine, 7 Armoured divn., Report on Operations, 20 Nov. 1943.

[64] PRO WO 201/537, Horrocks to Montgomery, c.Dec,. 1942.

[65] PRO WO 201/2590, De Guingand to XIII and XXX Corps, 5 Aug. 1942.

[66] PRO WO 199/2623, Army commander's personal memorandum to commanders, 28 Nov. 1941; IWM Briggs MSS 66/76/1, 8 Army Training Memorandum no. 1, The Approach to Training, 30 Aug. 1942.

[67] *Montgomery and the Eighth Army*, ed. Brooks, 54.

[68] PRO WO 201/2156, 8 Army Intelligence summary no. 462, 23 Mar. 1943, Appendix A, Report issued by HQ XC Army Corps (Intelligence), 11 Nov. 1942.

[69] General Staff, *Army Training Memorandum No. 44* (London, 1942); General Staff, *Military Training Pamphlet No. 41 The Tactical Handling of the Armoured division and its Components. The Armoured Regiment* (London, 1943).

[70] LHCMA Alanbrooke MSS 14/24, Montgomery to Nye, 11 Sept. 1943.

organizing lectures and study periods at which he presided. Before D-Day, he continued the process. On 13 January 1944, for example, he spoke to all Army, Corps, and Divisional commanders in 21st Army Group, explaining to them how he intended to stage-manage his battles and issued each of them with another pamphlet, *Notes on High Command in War*.[71]

Like Haig, Montgomery preferred to be surrounded by his own men, but the criteria he employed in selecting them was professional competence, not whether he found them personally congenial. He was ruthless in placing men who he had trained in his methods and who had demonstrated their ability as commanders in the field in command of units and formations under his command. Before Alamein, for example, he obtained not only two new Corps Commanders, Leese and Horrocks, but also a new CRA, Sidney Kirkman.[72] On returning from Italy to take command of 21st Army Group, he quickly installed a number of senior staff officers who had worked closely with him in 8th Army in key staff posts and throughout his tenure in command kept close control over appointments.[73] These measures went a long way to ensure that formations that had fought in the Mediterranean and formations that had been training in Britain since 1940 practised a common operational doctrine by 1944.[74]

However, Montgomery did not always get his own way over appointments. He did not think that Crerar was fit to command an army in action, only two of his original corps commanders in Normandy, Guy Simmonds and Gerald Bucknell, were his protégés and his attempt to dismiss the commander of the Guards Armoured division, Alan Adair, was blocked.[75] Officers excluded from his favoured circle were resentful, but he was hardly unique amongst Second World War generals in placing men he knew and trusted in key positions under him.[76] General Sir Richard McCreery, for example, began the war as a Lieutenant-

---

[71] PRO CAB 106/1037, Notes of a Staff Conference, 13 Jan. 1944.

[72] LHCMA Alanbrooke MSS 6/2/37, Montgomery, Review of the situation in 8 Army from 12 Aug. 1942 to 23 Oct. 1942.

[73] Richardson, *Flashback*, 170; Guingand, *Operation Victory*, 158.

[74] LHCMA Alanbrooke MSS 6/2/21, Montgomery to Brooke, 27 Nov. 1942; 6/2/23, Montgomery to Brooke, 14 Aug. 1943. In 1943 e.g. the General Staff issued a training pamphlet to all commanders in the UK embodying Montgomery's lessons. LHCMA Liddell Hart MSS 15/8/176, General Staff, *MTP No. 2. The Offensive* (London, 1943); Alanbrooke MSS 6/2/34, Montgomery to Nye, 31 Oct. 1944, Nye to Montgomery, 15 Nov, 1944, Montgomery to Nye, 26 Nov. 1944.

[75] LHCMA Liddell Hart MSS 11/1944/36, Notes for History, Talk with Evetts, 15 June 1944; Alanbrooke MSS 6/2/23, Montgomery to Brooke, 28 Dec. 1943; 14/27/6, Montgomery to Brooke, 7 July 1944; IWM Montgomery MSS BLM 119/29, Montgomery to Brooke, 2 Nov. 1944; LHCMA O'Connor MSS 5/4/4, Dempsey to O'Connor, 19 Feb. 1944; *A Guard's General*, ed. Lindsay, 136.

[76] Francis Tuker was a case in point. See LHCMA Liddell Hart MSS 1/705, Tuker to Liddell Hart, 2 Oct. 1954.

Colonel and GSO1 to Alexander, then commander of 1st division. When Alexander became C-in-C Middle East in 1942, McCreery became his CGS and ended the war, still under Alexander, as GOC 8th Army.

The extent to which other senior commanders followed Montgomery's example and reduced the latitude of their subordinates to interpret orders varied. Neither Alexander, when he commanded Army Groups in Tunisia and Italy, or Leese, when he commanded 8th Army in Italy, tried to do so to the same extent as Montgomery. The fact that their forces contained large allied contingents made it politically necessary for them to adopt a more relaxed policy towards those of their subordinates who were also allied or Dominion commanders responsible to their own governments.[77]

The reaction of subordinates confronted by this new regime varied. Some positively welcomed it. 'Pip' Roberts, who commanded an armoured brigade in the desert in 1942, contrasted Montgomery's precise orders before Alam Halfa favourably with Ritchie's indecisiveness before Gazala. 'There was one firm plan', he later wrote, 'and one position to occupy and we all felt better.'[78] When he commanded VIII Corps in Normandy, O'Connor found that 'what Montgomery gave to his commanders was a sense of assurance. A sense of confirmation having examined the plan.'[79] Others did not like his methods but they seldom lasted long. Montgomery did share another attribute with Haig, namely his willingness to dismiss senior officers who he believed had failed in action through showing insufficient determination and drive to carry out his orders. Since Ritchie's appointment to command 8th Army, senior officers had grown increasingly prone to question his orders.[80] But Montgomery would not tolerate this habit he called 'belly-aching'.[81] He dismissed Herbert Lumsden from command of X Corps and Alec Gatehouse from command of 10th Armoured division after Alamein because he had no time for officers he believed had shown signs of '"wilting under the strain"'.[82] Shortly after arriving in London, Lumsden was reputed to have entered his London club wearing a bowler hat and his uniform and said, 'I've just been sacked because there isn't enough room in the desert for two cads like Montgomery and me.'[83]

[77] Ryder, *Oliver Leese*, 174; W. F. Jackson, *Alexander of Tunis as Military Commander* (London, 1971), 144, 146; B. Holden Reid, 'Alexander', in J. Keegan (ed.), *Churchill's Generals* (London, 1991), 116–17

[78] Roberts, *From the Desert to the Baltic*, 94.

[79] LHCMA Liddell Hart MSS 1/553, Lewin to Liddell Hart and enc., 29 Aug. 1968.

[80] Belchem, *All in the Day's March*, 111.

[81] *Montgomery and the Eighth Army*, ed.Brooks, 27–8; Montgomery, *Memoirs*, 107.

[82] Playfair, *The Mediterranean and Middle East*, iii, 44–6; LHCMA Alanbrooke MSS 14/63, Alexander to Brooke, 10 Dec. 1942; 14/61/14 Montgomery to Brooke, 13 Dec. 1942.

[83] LHCMA Sir R. O'Connor MSS 11/14, Obituary of Gen. Sir R. McCreery.

Others whose careers suffered because they were insufficiently ruthless in driving their troops forward included D. C. Bullen-Smith (dismissed from command of 51st Highland division in July 1944), Bucknell, and 'Bobby' Erskine (dismissed from command of XXX Corps and 7th Armoured division in August 1944).

Again in contrast to Haig, Montgomery developed human and technological systems to monitor the work of his subordinate commanders. As an Army Group commander he could keep in close personal contact with his army and corps commanders. But he could not hope personally to visit each of his divisional commanders regularly, and so he employed a team of specially trained liaison officers to monitor their work. They visited divisional HQs in the afternoon when the commander was making his plans for the next day. They interviewed him, and he briefed them about his intentions. When Montgomery debriefed them in the evening, the liaison officers could tell him about not only each divisional commander's plans, but also his state of mind. If Montgomery was disturbed by anything they told him, he quickly contacted the relevant army or corps commander.[84] On top of this Montgomery also eavesdropped on his own subordinates. During CRUSADER some British commanders began unofficially to copy the Germans, and to monitor the operational traffic on their own units' wireless nets. By this method messages picked up from forward nets could be in the hands of Army HQ within ten to fifteen minutes, whereas normal 'sitreps' took up to twelve hours to filter through.[85] At Alam Halfa this process was systematized in the shape of the 'J' service, which was developed largely by the GSO1 (Operations) at 8th Army's HQ, Lieutenant-Colonel Hugh Mainwaring. It brought to light a worrying series of lapses in the command and control system. After Alamein the J system was established on a permanent basis.[86] Parallel developments took place in Britain. The result was that in North West Europe a 'Phantom' patrol was attached to each divisional HQ to intercept traffic on the divisional and brigade nets and pass it back immediately to army HQ.[87]

Montgomery and his colleagues were only able to command from near the forward edge of the battlefield because by late 1942 the army finally had the communications system that it required. They could now

[84] LHCMA Verney MSS IV/2, Montgomery, *Some notes on the Conduct of War and the Infantry Division in Battle*, 1 Nov. 1944; IV/3, Montgomery, *The Armoured division in Battle*, Dec. 1944; R. Dunn, *Sword and Pen. Memoirs of a Lord Justice* (London, 1993), 91.

[85] PRO WO 277/25, Gravely, *Signals*, 382–83; Carver, *Out of Step*, 94.

[86] PRO WO 204/7975, De Guingand to X, XII, and XXX Corps, 21 Sept. 1942; PRO WO 201/2596, Middle East Training Memorandum no. 8, Lessons from Operations, Oct.–Nov. 1942; Guingand, *Operation Victory*, 119; *Montgomery and the Eighth Army*, ed. Brooks, 303.

[87] PRO WO 232/21, Notes from Theatres of War, Report by Capt. L. C. Coleman AIF, 3 Oct. 1944.

rely on receiving a steady flow of up-to-date information about their own and the enemy's troops, and they could issue realistic orders in time for their subordinates to act upon them.[88] The army's mature system of C3I rested upon a greatly expanded signal establishment, and the manufacture of more and better equipment. In the course of the war the establishment of an infantry division's signals regiment increased from 491 to 743 all-ranks, and an armoured division's regiment from 629 to 753.[89] The army was also issued with more radios. Between 1939 and 1945, the Ministry of Supply produced over 550,000 wireless sets for the army.[90] It might have been better equipped sooner but for the fact that it received a lower priority than did the other two services for radio equipment.[91] The quality of radio equipment also improved, so that by 1943 armoured units, for example, had sets that enabled commanders to control their whole regiment on a single frequency.[92] However, the system did not depend solely on more and better radios. Cable retained its technical advantages over wireless in that it could carry a larger volume of traffic more securely.[93] At Alamein, in Tunisia, and for much of the fighting in Sicily, Italy, and North West Europe, the distances and speed with which operations were conducted diminished compared to the war in the desert, and mountains degraded the performance of radios. It therefore became possible and necessary for signallers to create elaborate systems of line communication.[94] This trend was most discernible in infantry formations, but it also occurred, although to a lesser extent, in armoured divisions. It was one reason why the British Army could employ large artillery concentrations in the second half of the war.[95] The outcome of these developments was a more flexible communications system, with inbuilt redundancies that both reduced the likelihood of communications collapsing and facilitated the rapid transmission of information and orders.[96] From 1942 onwards, commanders were far less likely to lose battles because their communications failed.

[88] PRO WO 201/452, CGS, GHQ, Middle East, Notes on recent operations in the Western Desert, 13 July 1942.

[89] PRO WO 277/25, Gravely, *Signals*, 270, 307.

[90] PRO WO 277/25, Gravely, *Signals*, 138.

[91] Postan, *British War Production*, 359.

[92] PRO CAB 106/963, Lieut.-Col. J. R. Bowring, Immediate Report no. 20, 19 June 1944.

[93] PRO WO 277/26. Gravely, *Signals*, 312–13; General Staff, *Field Service Pocket Book. Pamphlet No. 2 (Reprinted with Amendments (Numbers 1 and 2) and ATMs (Numbers 39, and 42, 1941) Orders and Intercommunication)* (London, 1941).

[94] PRO WO 260/50, Report on DMT's visit to the Mediterranean Theatre, Nov. 1943; PRO WO 204/7976, Report on No. 2 DMT Liaison Training Team: the defence battle of the Anzio bridgehead force, 9 Mar. 1944.

[95] PRO WO 201/2596, Middle East Training Memorandum no. 8, Lessons from Operations Oct.–Nov. 1942.

[96] IWM Dept. of Sound Records, Accession no. 000954/07: Brig. W. R. Smijth-Windham, 30–1; LHCMA Maj.-Gen. P. C. Hobart MSS 15/11/15, Hobart to Liddell Hart, 16 Jan. 1943.

The purpose of the 'master plan' was to produce the maximum concentration of force at the decisive point and time. One of the first things that Montgomery did when he arrived in the desert in August 1942 was to end Auchinleck's experiments with new forms of organization. Henceforth

Divisions must fight as divisions and under their own commanders, with clear-cut tasks and definite objectives; only in this way will full value be got from the great fighting power of a Division, and only in this way will concentration of effort and co-operation of all arms be really effective.[97]

This greatly assisted team-building, for it meant that divisions were more likely to reap the full benefits of their training. Raymond Briggs believed that one reason why his own 1st Armoured division performed more effectively than the other two armoured divisions in X Corps at Alamein was that, unlike them, all of its component units had been able to spend a month training together before the battle.[98]

The most obvious expression of Montgomery's pursuit of the principle of concentration, and the one which gave his battles the same outward appearance as those of the First World War, was the army's employment of concentrated artillery. But appearances were deceptive. It was only in Normandy that Montgomery was able to employ the same high concentrations of artillery that Haig had employed on the Western Front. On the opening day of the Somme, the latter had massed 92 guns per kilometre of front; at Vimy Ridge he had 161 guns per kilometre; at Pilckem Ridge 172 guns per kilometre, and at the Ghelveult Plateau 324 guns per kilometre. The latter represented the heaviest concentration of artillery employed by the BEF throughout the First World War. Comparable figures for Alam Halfa were 9 guns per kilometre, for Alamein 31 per kilometre, and for Cassino 127 per kilometre. Haig's concentrations dropped in the final year of the war. He employed only 125 guns per kilometre at the opening of Cambrai, 110 at Amiens, and 160 on the opening day of the assault on the Hindenburg Line. The only one of Montgomery's offensives in Normandy that exceeded these figures was GOODWOOD, when he employed 259 guns per kilometre. However, other offensives had the support of thinner concentrations of artillery. The opening day of EPSOM was supported by only 64 guns per kilometre, the Canadian attack towards Falaise on 8 August 1944 (TOTALIZE) by 98 guns per kilometre, and the opening of the Anglo-Canadian offensive in the Reichswald on 8 February 1945 (VERITABLE) by 105 guns per kilometre. To some extent Montgomery used air power to compensate for his relative paucity of artillery, but he could not

---

[97] IWM Briggs MSS 66/76/1, 8 Army Training Memorandum no. 1, The approach to training, 30 Aug. 1942.
[98] IWM Briggs MSS 66/76/1, Briggs to Tuker, 6 Feb. 1961.

always do so. GOODWOOD, TOTALIZE and VERITABLE were supported by large numbers of bombers, but bad weather ruled out the heavy air support planned for EPSOM.[99]

Furthermore, although some of the techniques that Montgomery and his colleagues employed were the same as those used by Haig between 1916–18, others were not. Montgomery was not the first Second World War field commander to recognize that massed artillery was a battle-winning factor of major importance. Auchinleck had employed it in July 1942 to inflict a series of hammer blows against the advancing Axis forces on the Alamein line. He was able to do so not only because the comparatively short line his troops held made the physical concentration of his guns possible, but also because sufficient 6-pdr. anti-tank guns had now been issued to relieve his field artillery of their anti-tank role.[100] It was this artillery, plus Rommel's own logistical problems, that were decisive in stemming the final German advance.[101] After being bombarded for seven hours, a German infantryman lamented that the barrage was 'such as I have never before experienced. Tommy has brought our attack to a standstill.'[102]

Montgomery discovered how to use massed artillery successfully on the offensive. By late 1942, confronted by deep German defensive positions, the British had learnt that no attack could succeed without overwhelming fire-support provided by artillery and air support. 'Fire dominated the battlefield. Fire is the chief antagonist of mobility',[103] and Montgomery did re-employ some of the same techniques that Haig's army had perfected twenty years before. The artillery battle, for example, began with a counter-battery programme to destroy, or at least neutralize, the enemy's guns. In Normandy each hostile battery that was located was deluged with an average of 20 tons of shells.[104] In principle, after 1942 covering fire for infantry and tanks could be called down by a FOO at the request of the unit his guns were supporting. In practice, the army usually employed techniques first devised in 1916. Because the precise position of enemy defences was rarely known with sufficient accuracy, concentrations on known targets were employed less frequently than timed creeping barrages.[105]

[99] These figures are gleaned from Prior and Wilson, *Command on the Western Front*, 314–15, 368–75; Bailey, *Field Artillery and Firepower*, Appendix A; Ellis, *Victory in the West*, i, 275, 412; Ellis and Warhurst, *Victory in the West*, ii, 257.

[100] Barnett, *Desert Generals*, 198; Tuker, *Approach to Battle*, 138; LMCMA Alanbrooke MSS 6/D/4f, Auchinleck to Brooke, 25 July 1942.

[101] Bidwell and Graham, *Fire-Power*, 239.

[102] PRO WO 201/2172, Extracts from the diary of a L/Cpl. of 104 PGR (21st Panzer Division), 24 Apr. 1943.

[103] LHCMA Liddell Hart MSS 15/8/157, Operations. MTP No. 23. *Operations, Part 1. General Principles, Fighting Troops and their Characteristics* (London, 1942), 5.

[104] PRO WO 277/5, Pemberton, *Artillery Tactics*, 223.

[105] PRO WO 201/431, RA Notes on the offensive by 8 Army from 23 Oct.–4 Nov., El

However, to dismiss the way in which the British employed their artillery as an outstanding example of the use of 'brute force' is to overlook the myriad ways in which forces in the field introduced innovations to enhance their combat effectiveness between 1942 and 1945. Some were relatively minor, like the use of 17-pdr. anti-tank guns to destroy concrete pillboxes that had proved resistant to field gun shells.[106] Far more important were the drills that the gunners devised to augment the speed and effectiveness of their fire. Standard concentrations ('stonks') were first employed by 8th Army at Alamein in October 1942 and later used by 1st Army in early 1943. By the eve of the Normandy landing they had been perfected. They were standard drills in which the fire of individual batteries and regiments were superimposed upon a single map reference and then moved about as necessary. They could be employed both to support attacks or to lay down defensive fire to break up enemy counter-attacks.[107] Air Observation Posts made their mark in the mountains of Tunisia, the first campaign when the army had a reasonable supply of medium and heavy guns. Flown by Royal Artillery officers, not RAF pilots, AOP pilots were soon entrusted with firing regimental and even divisional concentrations.[108] In 1942 a new type of formation entered the army's order of battle, Army Groups Royal Artillery (AGRA). Normally allocated on a basis of one per corps, AGRAs usually consisted of a mixture of field, medium, and heavy regiments. They provided a new element of flexibility in the provision of fire-support by enabling army commanders to mass their guns against a particular part of the enemy's defences.[109]

Developments such as these, when coupled with improved communications, produced an extremely flexible system of fire-support. Commanders could centralize control of their artillery at divisional, corps, or even army level, or decentralize it down to individual units. Hundreds of guns could be brought down quickly on a single target for a set-piece attack.[110] At Alamein, 1st Armoured division's gunners could produce a divisional concentration in five to ten minutes.[111] By July 1943 gunners in Sicily had cut the time to only two minutes, and, even in the

Alamein position, 14 Dec. 1942; LHCMA Lieut.-Gen. C. W. Allfrey MSS 2/5, Address by Allfrey [c.July 1944].

[106] PRO WO 277/5, Pemberton, *Artillery Tactics*, 199.

[107] PRO WO 201/431, RA Notes on the offensive by 8 Army from 23 Oct.–4 Nov., El Alamein position, 14 Dec. 1942; PRO WO 277/5, Pemberton, *Artillery Tactics*, 140–1, 143–4, 169, 208; PRO WO 232/14. Lieut.-Gen. K. Anderson to AFHQ, 16 June 1943.

[108] WO 277/5, Pemberton, *Artillery Tactics*, 158–9, 197.

[109] LHCMA Liddell Hart MSS 15/8/185, *ATM No.* 46 (London, 1943); IWM Visc. Montgomery MSS BLM 117/10, Address by C-in-C 21 Army Group to senior officers of the Royal Artillery, Larkhill, 30 Apr. 1944.

[110] PRO WO 204/7955, BRA, 8 Army, Memorandum no. 1, 12 June 1944.

[111] PRO WO 201/453, 1 Armoured divn., Lessons from Battle of Egypt, 31 Dec. 1942.

more difficult terrain of Italy, company commanders could summon a divisional concentration and expect to receive it in ten minutes.[112] Moreover, in more mobile operations, by mid-1943 improved command and communications systems made it possible (although each battalion could have its own affiliated battery and each brigade its own affiliated field regiment) for the divisional CRA to exercise almost instantaneous control over all the guns in his division when necessary. This produced a real camaraderie between the infantry and their supporting gunners. The Russian army also employed massed artillery in support of its ground operations. But by 1944–5, in the opinion of at least one senior German gunner, the British artillery outshone it both in tactical flexibility and the speed with which it could lay down effective fire.[113] Rommel himself was impressed, not just by the weight of fire that British gunners could deliver but by their 'great mobility and tremendous speed of reaction to the needs of the assault troops'.[114]

Montgomery's interpretation of the principle of concentration also meant attacking on much narrower fronts than the BEF had employed in the First World War.[115] Rawlinson's 4th Army attacked on a front of 15,000 yards at Amiens on 8 August 1918; a month later it broke the Hindenburg Line on a front of 11,000 yards.[116] By contrast Operation LIGHTFOOT, the opening stage of the Alamein offensive, was mounted on a front of about 7,000 yards.[117] On 26 March 1943, the 8th Armoured Brigade led the assault on the Tebaga Gap to outflank the Mareth Line on a front of less than 1,000 yards.[118] On 6 May 1943, Anderson mounted his final thrust in Tunisia on a front of only 3,000 yards.[119] The opening phase of Operation GOODWOOD was mounted on a front of only 2,000 yards.[120] From 1942 onwards, the British also mounted their offensives in considerable depth in order to sustain the momentum of the advance. Anderson employed two armoured divisions to exploit the gap he expected his infantry to make. For GOODWOOD, Dempsey's spearhead, 11th Armoured division, was followed by no less than two other armoured divisions.

[112] PRO CAB 106/531, Military Training Instructional Circular no. 13, 28 Apr. 1943; PRO WO 231/14, Maj. R. Long, Sicily, Reports on Operations, 1 Nov. 1943; PRO WO 260/50, Report on DMT's visit to Mediterranean Theatre, Nov. 1943.

[113] PRO WO 232/10A, Directorate of Tactical Investigation, German POW statements: General Jahn, n.d.

[114] The Rommel Papers, ed. Liddell Hart, 330.

[115] Belchem, All in the Day's March, 166.

[116] Prior and Wilson, Command on the Western Front, 318, 375.

[117] I. S. O. Playfair, The Mediterranean and Middle East, iv. The Destruction of the Axis Forces in Africa (London, 1960), 37; PRO WO 201/431, RA Notes on the offensive by 8 Army 23 Oct.–4 Nov., El Alamein position, 14 Dec. 1942.

[118] G. Blaxland, The Plain Cook and the Great Showman. The First and Eighth Armies in North Africa (London, 1977), 206.   [119] Blaxland, Plain Cook, 248–54.

[120] PRO WO 277/5, Pemberton, Artillery Tactics, 225.

Air superiority was an essential pre-requisite because attacks on the narrow fronts that Montgomery favoured required a very high density of troops to space. They were only possible from late 1942 onwards because allied air superiority denied the Germans the possibility of disrupting British forces before they attacked. Montgomery recognized that it could only be secured if ground and air force commanders worked in the closest co-operation. He strove to secure that by preparing his plans from the outset in co-operation with his air commander.[121] Air superiority prevented the Luftwaffe from interfering with his own operations. It supplied reconnaissance reports, and, either in the form of tactical air support or, less frequently, support provided by medium and heavy bombers, it supplemented the fire-power of his artillery. The latter could produce fire-support in all weathers and at any time of the day or night. But its range and the destructive power of its projectiles were limited. Air power could not operate at night or in bad weather. But when it was available, it enabled Montgomery to fight the kind of 'deep battle' that had been denied to Haig. It could hit the enemy far behind his front line, isolating the battlefield by destroying the enemy's supply lines, and delaying the arrival of his reserves. It also played a major role in reducing the tempo of German operations relative to that of the British by disrupting German communications.[122] Closer to the front line, when appropriate command and control techniques were in place, air power could deliver a demoralizing weight of high explosive onto enemy front line troops. In Normandy, the 2nd Tactical Air Force, sometimes assisted by the heavy bombers of Bomber Command and the US 8th Air Force, inflicted heavy losses on the Germans and denied them a large measure of tactical and operational mobility by forcing them to abandon movement in daylight.[123] But air attacks not only inflicted heavy material losses on the Germans. By investing their ground forces with a sense of their own inability to hit back, their morale was also undermined.[124] By Normandy, adding direct air support to the land operations, making a single integrated plan, had become a fundamental part of 21st Army Group's operational technique. Captured German officers frequently remarked that 'our overwhelming

---

[121] IWM Briggs MSS 66/76/1, Montgomery, Eighth Army Training Memorandum no. 1, The approach to training, 30 Aug. 1942; Montgomery MSS BLM 107/6, Montgomery to army and air commanders, May 1944.

[122] PRO WO 232/25, Special tactical studies no. 29, German views of allied combat efficiency, 17 Nov. 1944.

[123] PRO WO 205/1022, Interrogation reports of German Generals: Special Interrogation Report of Gen. Hans Eberbach, 9 Dec. 1946.

[124] LHCMA Liddell Hart MSS 15/8/203, ATM No. 50 (London, 1944); Greenhouse, 'Aircraft versus armour', 104–5; Gooderson, Air Power at the Battlefront, 57–248; LHCMA Dempsey MSS, 2 Army Intelligence summary no. 79, 22 Aug. 1944, Appendix C, Effect of allied air attacks, Prepared by 83 Group, RAF.

air superiority was one of the most, if not the most, important factor of our success'.[125]

Haig has been much criticized for the ways in which he employed intelligence material. With the exception of a handful of occasions, such as the opening of his offensives at Cambrai and Amiens, surprise and deception had rarely formed a central plank of his operations. In the second half of the Second World War, accurate intelligence, and the willingness to act upon it, and the use of security and surprise as a force-multiplier were vital components of British operational doctrine. On 29 October 1942, for example, Montgomery decided to shift the thrust line of Operation SUPERCHARGE further south when his intelligence discovered that Rommel had brought up the 90th Light Division to hold the line where he had originally intended to attack.[126] In February 1944, 'sigint' gave allied commanders in the Anzio beachhead ample warning of the timing and direction of a major German counter-offensive intended to drive them back into the sea and enabled them to mass sufficient forces to repulse it.[127] In Normandy the combination of signals intelligence and aerial reconnaissance enabled the British successfully to practise C3I warfare. They killed or captured some twenty German army, corps, or divisional commanders.[128] At the divisional level, the British improvised an intelligence organization to locate the numerous German mortars that caused them such heavy casualties.[129] At the unit level, they patrolled energetically to ascertain the position of the enemy's defences.[130] General von Obstfelder, GOC of LXXXVI Corps, warned his troops in July 1944 that the enemy employed 'tricks and is very cunning. During his attack he stages feints to provoke our anti-tank guns to open fire. If an anti-tank position is discovered it is as good as lost before it has a chance to fire.'[131]

Montgomery believed that surprise was second only to high morale as a factor making for success.[132] In January 1944 he told his senior officers that achieving surprise was an essential element in the stage management of battle.[133] The British multiplied the effectiveness of their own forces by combining surprise, achieved by security, and active decep-

---

[125] PRO WO 205/1021, Interrogation reports of German Generals: Vol. 1, Interrogation of Brigadeführer Wisch, 25 Aug. 1945.

[126] Hinsley et al., British Intelligence, ii, 444–45.

[127] Molony, The Mediterranean and Middle East, vi, 745–50; Hinsley et al., British Intelligence, iii, pt 1, 190–3.

[128] Belchem, All in the Day's March, 220.

[129] PRO WO 291/1331, Operational Research in North West Europe no. 2 ORS, Report no. 11, The Location of Enemy Mortars.

[130] PRO WO 232/17, DMT, CMF to DDMT, War Office, 25 Mar. 1944.

[131] LHCMA Dempsey MSS, 2 Army Intelligence summary no. 61. 4 Aug. 1944.

[132] Montgomery and the Eighth Army, ed. Brooks, 148.

[133] PRO CAB 106/1037, Notes of a Staff Conference, 13 Jan. 1944.

tion.[134] By 1943–4 the British had effectively blinded most German intelligence sources. Allied air superiority meant that the Luftwaffe was able to provide few reconnaissance reports. Although the Germans continued to capture POWs, most knew little about anything other than their own sub-unit's activities. The result was that the British could practice a successful deception policy and were repeatedly able to achieve tactical, operational, and sometimes even strategic surprise. The deception techniques that 8th Army successfully employed before Alamein to hide the direction, weight, and timing of the initial assault were not in themselves new. What was new was the thoroughness with which camouflage schemes were co-ordinated by the General Staff and incorporated into the main plan for the battle from the very beginning.[135] Before D-Day, not only had the allies persuaded the Germans that they had far more divisions in Britain than was actually the case, but they had also convinced them that the main allied landing would take place in the Pas de Calais. The result was that prisoners captured from 716th Infantry Division on D-Day complained bitterly that they had been utterly surprised by the allied landing.[136]

The British army that landed in Normandy in 1944 was not the sole creation of Montgomery. It was an amalgamation of formations that had fought under his command in the Mediterranean and the formations that had trained in Britain since Dunkirk. However, just as it would be wrong to attribute the causes of its successes and failures to one man, it would be equally wrong to ignore the fact that Montgomery made a major contribution to enhancing its combat effectiveness. He did not create the army's operational doctrine, but he did insist that formations under his command practised a common interpretation of it. The outcome was that by the second half of the war, the British possessed what was in some respects a military machine capable of considerable flexibility on the battlefield. Auchinleck had employed a series of thrusts along alternative axes to destabilize Rommel's army during the first battle of Alamein. But he had failed to break through in July partly because he lacked sufficient reserves and partly because, although he had concentrated his artillery, he continued to employ his infantry in brigade groups rather than divisions.[137] Montgomery also attacked along a series of different thrust lines, but, unlike Auchinleck, took care to ensure that he had the reserves necessary to exploit success. The first thrust

[134] LHCMA Liddell Hart MSS 15/8/157, *Operations. MTP No. 23. Operations, Part 1. General Principles, Fighting Troops and their Characteristics* (London, 1942), 6; 15/8/176, *MTP No. 2. The Offensive* (London, 1943), 1, 12–13.

[135] PRO WO 201/2596, Middle East Training Memorandum no. 8. Lessons from operations Oct.–Nov. 1942; Richardson, *Flashback*, 113, 115, 117.

[136] LHCMA Dempsey MSS, 2 Army Intelligence summary no. 7, 10 June 1944, Appendix A.

[137] Barnett, *The Desert Generals*, 212–15; LHCMA Alanbrooke MSS 6/D/4f, Auchinleck to Brooke, 25 July 1942.

compelled the enemy to begin to commit his reserves, the second, coming from an unexpected direction, left him unbalanced, and the third was a decisive break-through operation on yet another part of the line. Montgomery employed this technique at Alamein in October–November 1942, at Mareth in March 1943, and again around Caen during his attempts to encircle the town between June and August 1944.[138] His obsession with remaining 'balanced' throughout his operations was a product of his need constantly to create new reserves so that he had troops on hand to mount the next thrust.[139] The essence of Montgomery's generalship was to defeat his enemy by unbalancing him. This was an appropriate operational technique, because the combination of deception and security that the British practised plus allied air superiority meant that Montgomery could switch his main thrust lines far more speedily than could the Germans. Supplied with a sufficiency of equipment and an insufficiency of men, Montgomery's operational techniques were chosen to exploit the strengths and weaknesses of the army he commanded.

The ability of the British army to overcome the Germans in the second half of the war continued to depend, as it had done before Alamein, on its ability to mount successful combined arms operations. 'It cannot be emphasised too strongly', Montgomery insisted in August 1942, 'that successful battle operations depend on the intimate co-operation of all arms, whether in armoured or unarmoured formations. Tanks alone are never the answer; no one arm, alone and unaided can do any good in battle.'[140] Montgomery and his acolytes continued to reiterate this until the end of the war. The level of operational and tactical co-operation of British formations was undoubtedly better after 1942 than it had been earlier in the war. However, there is ample evidence that also points to continued serious shortcomings.

At the operational level, several factors degraded the effectiveness and reduced the tempo of British combined arms operations. Because attacks were usually mounted on narrow fronts, troops had little room for manoeuvre. They had to assault frontally, and consequently the Germans had only to move reinforcements to seal off a relatively narrow penetration. In one extreme case at the start of Operation BLUECOAT in Normandy on 30 July 1944, XXX Corps's axis of advance was a single

[138] Playfair, *Mediterranean and Middle East*, iv, 34–72; LHCMA Liddell Hart MSS 1/230/22A, Liddell Hart, Operation GOODWOOD, 18 July 1944, Dempsey's expansion (18 Mar. 1952) of the notes he wrote down in brief form, 21 Feb. 1952; PRO WO 201/2596, Middle East Training Memorandum no. 8, Lessons from Operations, Oct.–Nov. 1942.

[139] IWM Montgomery MSS BLM 122/4, Conference, General Officers of Second Army, 22 June 1944.

[140] IWM Briggs MSS 66/76/1, Montgomery, 8 Army Training Memorandum no. 1, The approach to training, 30 Aug. 1942.

track that was unsuitable for its tanks, and a single road that it shared with VIII Corps. It was, therefore, hardly surprising that the two German divisions holding the threatened sector quickly stalled the British advance.[141] Secondly, unless there were overwhelming operational needs, commanders never mounted a major operation without first ensuring that their maintenance was adequate to sustain the operation. Montgomery believed that the limits of what was operationally possible were set by the limits of what was logistically possible.[142] The German experience suggests that he was right. They concentrated on the tactical aspects of operations to the neglect of logistics, and in North Africa and Normandy they eventually paid a heavy price for doing so. In both theatres the final collapse of the German position owed a great deal to the prior collapse of their logistical support.[143] Thirdly, Montgomery was reluctant to let fluid operations develop. They did not permit the careful planning and control that characterized his approach to battle management. After Alamein, he therefore 'gave precise instructions to Lumsden about the development of operations for the pursuit to Agheila, and kept a firm hand on the battle to ensure the master plan was not "mucked about" by subordinate commanders having ideas inconsistent with it'.[144] One of his divisional commanders believed that the cause of his lackadaisical pursuit of Rommel after Alamein was his unwillingness to risk a failure.[145] But before Montgomery is dismissed as being hopelessly cautious, it is as well to examine his conduct of the pursuit from the Seine to Brussels. In twelve days, his armoured regiments travelled an average of 26 miles each day.[146] In 1940, by contrast, the German Panzers only managed an average of 21 miles per day between crossing the Meuse and reaching the Channel coast.[147] Moreover, Montgomery's caution ensured that the Germans were never able to mount the kind of riposte against his troops that Rommel had inflicted so successfully on the British in North Africa in 1941–2.

Despite the undoubted improvements made in British C3I since Dunkirk, in February 1944 Alexander still believed that British (and American) battle procedures were too slow compared to those of the German army.[148] There were several reasons for this. The command and

---

[141] IWM 80/33/1/folder 12, Bucknall to Dempsey, 3 Aug. 1944.

[142] PRO CAB 106/1037, Notes of a Staff Conference, 13 Jan. 1944.

[143] Van Creveld, *Supplying War*, 181–201; R. A. Hart 'Feeding Mars: The Role of Logistics in the German defeat in Normandy, 1944', *War in History*, 3 (1996), 418–35.

[144] Montgomery, *Memoirs*, 141–2.

[145] LHCMA Liddell Hart MSS 1/519/406, Notes on a conversation with Maj.-Gen. R. Briggs, 23 Sept. 1968.

[146] PRO WO 291/1331, Operational Research in North West Europe, Report no. 18, Tank casualties during the exploitation phase after crossing the Seine.

[147] G. L. Weinberg, *A World At Arms. A Global History of World War Two* (Cambridge, 1994), 127.

[148] LHCMA O'Connor MSS 5/2/19, Harding to O'Connor and enc., 26 Feb., 12 Mar. 1944.

control procedures of formations that had spent most of the war in the UK often lagged behind those that had honed them on the battlefield. As late as February 1944, the staff of VIII Corps still issued lengthy written orders for an attack when what was really necessary was for the CCRA to issue map tracings to his gunners and the Corps commander to visit his divisional commanders to explain his orders in person.[149] Even in Normandy, the wireless link between the Corps's HQ and its divisions operated too slowly because it was usually manned only by a signaller, rather than by a staff officer.[150] Despite improvements in signal security, intercepted wireless messages remained one of the German army's most valuable sources of intelligence.[151] Major-General von Broich, GOC 10th Panzer Division in Tunisia, for example, received ample warning about British air attacks by listening in to conversations between ground controllers and aircraft.[152]

The army also suffered because its pre-war training system had not prepared enough middle-ranking officers to jump several ranks in rapid succession to become formation commanders. Pre-war staff trained officers were spread very thinly in the army by 1944. In 7th Armoured division in September 1944, for example, there were only nine pre-war pscs in the entire division—the divisional commander, his infantry brigade and armoured brigade commanders, his signals officer, four regimental or battalion commanders, and a squadron commander.[153] Some commanders had not really understood that their job was to issue clearly defined orders. Major-General R. K. Ross, GOC of 53rd (Welsh) division, ran orders groups in 1944 that resembled 'councils of war, rather than occasions when clear and definite orders reflected the grip of the commander on the situation'.[154] As Harding admitted in September 1944, 'Many Division and Corps Commanders have failed, and involved casualties because [they were] not trained for such commands.'[155]

Senior officers themselves also continued to pay the penalty for leading from the front. In January 1943 Harding, then commanding 7th Armoured division, was so seriously wounded that he had to be evacuated, although he recovered sufficiently to resume his active career. Others were not so fortunate. In May 1943 Major-General E. G. Miles,

[149] LHCMA O'Connor MSS 5/2/10, Berney-Ficklin to O'Connor, 26 Feb. 1944.
[150] LHCMA O'Connor MSS 5/4/13, Erskine to O'Connor, 21 July 1944.
[151] PRO WO 231/8, DMT, Lessons from the Italian campaign, 18 Dec. 1943; General Staff, ATM No. 48 (London, 1944); PRO WO 205/1201, Interrogation Reports of German Generals, vol. 2: Brigadeführer Wisch, 25 Aug. 1945; Maj.-Gen. Kurt Meyer; PRO WO 277/25, Gravely, Signals, 322, 403–4, 406; Ritgen, The Western Front, 76; PRO WO 232/10A, Precis of report on interrogation of General Manteufel, 21 May 1945.
[152] IWM Briggs MSS 66/76/1/file 1, Notes on conversation with General von Broich, GOC10 Panzer, captured near Grombalia 12 May 1943.
[153] LHCMA Verney MSS II/5, Staff List–7 Armoured Divn., 30 Sept. 1944.
[154] Carver, Out of Step, 193.
[155] PRO WO 193/981, DMT's tour of the Mediterranean theatre, Aug.–Sept. 1944.

GOC 56th division, was so seriously wounded while reconnoitring that he had to be replaced.[156] Three days after landing in southern Italy, G. F. Hopkinson, GOC 1st Airborne division, was killed by a German machine-gunner. In 1944 two divisional commanders in Italy, W. R. Penny (GOC of 1st Division) and G. W. R. Templer (GOC 6th Armoured division) were both wounded by mines. In North West Europe, divisional commanders continued to be at risk. In June 1944 Major-General T. G. Rennie (GOC 3rd division) was wounded in Normandy. He returned to command of 51st Highland division, only to be killed crossing the Rhine in March 1945.

But it was at the tactical level that British combined arms operations were found most wanting, and where the army's shortcomings did most to reduce the tempo of its operations. Alamein had shown that infantry unsupported by tanks could take their objectives, provided they attacked at night and had plenty of artillery support. Thereafter, units typically only ever attacked behind heavy artillery support. By 1943, infantry were taught to advance close behind the barrage so they arrived on top of the German positions within two minutes of the barrage lifting, and before the neutralizing impact of the artillery had dissipated and the Germans were ready to fight back.[157]

There were plenty of occasions when successful co-operation was achieved between all three arms. In ideal circumstances, infantry operated with tanks and artillery with which they had trained. The attack was methodically planned, all arms had a chance to rehearse their part in it, and then had time to 'marry up' with their supporting arms.[158] Units that worked together on a regular basis could develop a close camaraderie. The 1st Gordon Highlanders of 51st Highland division, and a squadron of the Northants Yeomanry of 33rd Armoured Brigade, co-operated so frequently between Normandy and the Rhine crossing that the latter 'look on themselves as being almost Gordon Highlanders'.[159] On 16 June 1944, 49th division carried out an almost textbook combined arms attack. Operating in conjunction with a squadron of Shermans and with the support of seven field and four medium regiments, one of its battalions captured the village of Crisot, held by 12 SS Panzer Division at a cost of only three killed and twenty-four wounded.[160] In the bocage, where visibility was often limited by high banks and

---

[156] LHCMA Alanbrooke MSS 6/2/23, Montgomery to Brooke, 6 May 1943.
[157] LHCMA 15/8/176, MTP No. 2. *The Offensive* (London, 1943).
[158] LHCMA Liddell Hart MSS 15/8/180, *Army Training Instruction No. 2. The Co-operation of Infantry and Tanks, 1943* (London, 1943); PRO WO 231/10, 78 divn., Lessons from the Tunisian campaign with particular reference to . . . 22 Apr.–8 May 1943.
[159] Lindsay, *So Few Got Through*, 176.
[160] PRO CAB 106/963, Reports on the fighting in Normandy, 1944. Immediate Report no. 6, 16 June 1944.

hedges to only 150 yards, by August 1944 tanks and infantry developed a drill to reduce their losses that impressed even the Germans.[161] One or two squadrons of tanks supported the leading battalion. It advanced with two companies forward, using a road as its centre line. Each company had a single platoon as its spearhead, and it was supported by a troop of four tanks. The two leading tanks covered the infantry as they advanced to the next hedge, and were themselves covered by the rest of the troop. The infantry reconnoitred one field ahead of the tanks and one field outward to their flank. In this fashion infantry and tanks moved slowly forward by bounds from one hedgerow to the next.[162]

But the army's reliance upon heavy fire-support undoubtedly decreased the tempo of its operations. Faced by an enemy in a prepared position, battalion commanders were told that 'time is then required to "soften" the defences, to make preparations for the attack, and to apply a heavy methodical programme of bombardment to blast a path that their troops can take with the least loss to themselves'.[163] Fire-support could so crater the terrain that ground forces often found their way forward blocked.[164] The availability of heavy artillery support encouraged junior leaders to rely increasingly on the gunners to blast a way through for them. By the Sicilian campaign, infantry units had slipped into the habit, when they encountered resistance, of halting and calling down artillery support, rather than trying to outflank the enemy or fight their way forward with their own weapons. Infantry battalions in North West Europe, faced by stiff German opposition, advanced on average between 380–525 yards per hour in daylight and 305–420 yards at night.[165] The mountainous terrain meant that distances covered were even less in Italy. Such a slow rate of advance allowed the Germans to move up reserves to block the advance or to slip away unmolested.[166] The British also sometimes failed to reap the full benefits of carpet bombing by heavy bombers because fear of 'shorts' caused them to pull back their foremost troops before the bombing occurred. The result was that the infantry were slow to follow up the bombers and the Germans

[161] PRO WO 219/1908, SHAEF, G-2. Records: SHAEF Operational Intelligence Section, Intelligence Notes no. 23, 17 Aug. 1944.
[162] PRO WO 232/21, Notes from theatres of War, Report by Capt. L. C. Coleman, 3 Oct. 1944.
[163] LHCMA Liddell Hart MSS 15/8/206, *Infantry Training. Part 1. The Infantry Battalion (1944)* (London, 1944), 24.
[164] LHCMA Alanbrooke MSS 6/2/19, Alexander to Brooke, 22 Mar. 1944.
[165] PRO WO 291/1169, Army Operational Research Group, Report no. 17/52, An analysis of infantry rates of advance in battle, Nov. 1952.
[166] PRO WO 231/14, Lieut.-Col. W. I. Watson, 6 Durham Light Infantry, Notes on recent operations [Sicily], 24 Aug. 1943; PRO WO 231/14, Notes on the use of equipment and training of battle patrols [c.9 Dec. 1943]; PRO WO 231/14, Lieut.-Col. L. Wigram, Current Reports from Overseas no. 15, Section 1, Infantry tactics in Sicily, 16 Aug. 1943.

were given sufficient time to recover their composure and man their defences.[167]

The willingness of the infantry to move forward rapidly was essential, for the gunners could not win battles on their own. Against troops who were well dug-in, even massive concentrations of artillery killed or wounded remarkably few enemy soldiers. Men under cover were almost immune from anything other than a direct hit and calculations in Italy showed that only 3 per cent of field artillery shells actually fell into a trench.[168] In September 1944, a field and a medium regiment fired nearly 500 shells over a thirty-minute period at a small German strong point near San Martino in Gattara. The strong point consisted of four weapons pits containing machine-guns and three other slit trenches, all sited within a 50-yard radius of each other. When the infantry advanced, they approached within 40 yards of their objective before the Germans opened fire and stopped them. The (literally) fatal mistake the infantry had committed was to wait fifteen minutes between the end of the bombardment and arriving on their objective.[169]

The main effect of artillery was not to kill the enemy, but to degrade their morale. German soldiers defending the beaches in Normandy on 6 June 1944 reported that the 'drum fire inspired in the defenders a feeling of utter helplessness, which in the case of inexperienced recruits caused fainting or indeed complete paralysis. Their instinct of self-preservation drove their duty as soldiers, to fight and destroy the enemy, completely out of their minds.'[170] Later in the month Gefreiter J. Seibt wrote in his diary

I am writing my war adventures in a dug-out approximately 50 metres away from Tommy. It is a dark, foggy and cold day, and the clothes from yesterday are not dry yet. The frame of mind of all of us is miserable and the only thought is always: "How will this all end?" Everyone is absolutely fed up. Yes, that is due to the enemy artillery, which fired yesterday without a break. Today one hears the fire in intervals of minutes, but it was not so calm, particularly the drum fire. I don't know how long this will last. I also don't know whether today is the 24th, 25th or 26th or 27th of June. My watch was already knocked out of action during the first hour of the operation. Time, however, is not money here.

[167] LHCMA Dempsey MSS, 2 Army Intelligence summary no. 72, 15 Aug. 1944.

[168] PRO WO 201/2596, Middle East Training Memorandum no. 8, Lessons from Operations, Oct.–Nov. 1942; PRO WO 231/16, 152 Infantry Bde., Discussion of Lessons Learned during the year of fighting from El Alamein to Messina, 6 Nov. 1943; PRO WO 291/1318, No. 1 Operational Research Section, Report no. 1/24/A, Effect of artillery fire in attacks in mountainous country [c.Nov. 1944].

[169] PRO WO 291/1317, No. 1 Operational Research Section, Report no. 1/24, Report on effect of artillery fire, Italy, 1944.

[170] PRO WO 232/25, Special Tactical Study no. 30, German views of the Normandy landing, 28 Nov. 1944; LHCMA Dempsey MSS, 2 Army Intelligence summary no. 7, 10 June 1944, Appendix A.

One dare not stick one's head out of the dug-out, as otherwise one stops a bullet immediately. The only salvation is death.[171]

Experiments conducted in Britain, information gathered from battles from Alamein onwards and POW interrogation reports suggested that soldiers under continuous shellfire reached the limits of their psychological endurance after between two and four hours of shelling.[172] The crucial factor in undermining the enemy's morale was not the weight of individual shells but their number, and for that task field guns were better suited than medium or heavy artillery. Some formations, notably 43rd division, recognized the implications of this, and from Normandy onwards began to employ 'pepper-pot' tactics. At the start of an attack every weapon under the division's command, including not only its field guns and mortars, but also its light anti-aircraft guns, anti-tank guns, and medium machine-guns bombarded the enemy's positions in an effort to demoralize the defenders. By early 1945 such tactics were being employed on a grand scale. During the opening stages of Operation VERITABLE, the fire-power of XXX Corps 1050 artillery pieces was supplemented by 114 Bofors light anti-aircraft guns, 80 medium mortars, 60 Sherman tanks, 24 17-pdr. anti-tank guns, and 188 medium machine-guns.[173]

British commanders were slow to adjust their fire-plans to take account of the ways in which the Germans deployed their defending forces. The most common reason why attacks stalled was because they encountered unlocated German defences echeloned in depth beyond the range of their own artillery support.[174] In Normandy the bocage made it extremely difficult for the gunners to locate their targets. 21 Army Group's fire-plans tended to devastate the foremost German-defended positions, but to leave the main line of resistance relatively unscathed.[175] GOODWOOD failed because, although the initial British bombardment devastated the first German gun line and enabled VIII Corps's tanks to advance 4,000 yards, a second line some 3,000 yards behind it remained intact.[176] The first formation to recognize and try to overcome this problem was II Canadian Corps, in operation TOTALIZE in August 1944. The Canadians devised a fire-plan to co-ordinate the work of artillery,

---

[171] LHCMA Dempsey MSS, 2 Army Intelligence summary no. 25, 29 June 1944.

[172] LHCMA Alanbrooke MSS 6/2/48, Brooke to Wilson, 6 Mar. 1944.

[173] PRO WO 231/1331, ORS N-W Europe no. 2 ORS, Report no. 26, Fire support in Operation Veritable—effect on forward defensive positions, 8 Feb. 1945.

[174] PRO WO 232/17, Notes of an interview with Brig. G. P. Harding, commanding 138th Infantry Brigade, 29 Mar. 1944.

[175] LHCMA Liddell Hart MSS 1/153/20, Carver to Liddell Hart, 8 May 1952; PRO WO 232/21, Notes from theatres of War, Report by Capt. L. C. Coleman, 3 Oct. 1944.

[176] PRO WO 277/5, Pemberton, *Artillery Tactics*, 226; PRO CAB 106/959, Lieut.-Gen. Sir R. O'Connor, Corps Commander's Notes on 'Goodwood' meeting, 9 Sept. 1944; Roberts, *From the Desert to the Baltic*, 183–4.

heavy-bombers, and fighter-bombers to neutralize both the German defence lines blocking their advance.[177]

It was not until the middle of the Normandy campaign that the army finally abandoned the last remnants of its pre-war conviction that tanks and infantry within armoured divisions could and should operate separately. By Alamein the British accepted that each armoured division needed a whole lorried infantry brigade, but until Normandy they remained committed to the idea that armoured and infantry brigades should fight separate, albeit co-ordinated actions. The tanks' role was to forge ahead when the terrain was suitable, destroying the enemy's armoured and unarmoured forces and dislocating his lines of communication by deep penetrations or flank attacks. The infantry's function was to cover the advance of the tanks in close country, to mop up and hold ground taken by the tanks, and to form a secure pivot around which they could manoeuvre. In the close country of Tunisia and Italy, the two brigades usually tried to work closely together, one advancing close behind the other. But combined attacks by both the armoured and lorried infantry brigades were deprecated because they required exceptional co-ordination and left the divisional commander without any reserves.[178]   The role of the divisional artillery was to neutralize or destroy hostile anti-tank guns to enable the tanks to advance unhindered. To help them do so, by late 1942 most armoured divisions had a regiment of self-propelled guns attached to its armoured brigade. Von Thoma attributed Rommel's defeat at Alamein to the fact that the British gunners destroyed half of his anti-tank guns.[179] It was an indication of how dependent armour had become on artillery that during the North West European campaign 11th Armoured Division expended only 50,764 rounds of tank gun ammunition but 508,720 rounds of 25-pdr. ammunition.[180]

It took the defeat of 22nd Armoured Brigade at Villers Bocage and the abortive advance of the armoured divisions of VIII Corps during GOODWOOD before armoured commanders recognized that tanks and infantry had to operate on a far more intimate basis if they were to overcome the dense anti-tank defences that the Germans prepared in North West Europe.[181] After GOODWOOD, on O'Connor's initiative, 11th and

[177] Ellis, *Victory in the West*, i, 419–25.

[178] LHCMA 15/8/176, Military Training Pamphlet no. 2. The Offensive (London, 1943); PRO WO 232/41, *The Tactical Handling of the Armoured Division and its Components. Military Training Pamphlet No. 41* (London, 1943); PRO WO 204/7592, Brig. L. G. Whistler, The lorried infantry brigade: Its functions and difficulties, 20 Aug. 1943; PRO WO 232/14, Lieut.-Gen. K. Anderson to AFHQ, 16 June 1943; Carver, *Out of Step*, 165.

[179] PRO WO 201/431, RA Notes on the offensive by 8 Army, 23 Oct.–4 Nov., El Alamein position, 14 Dec. 1942.

[180] Anon., *Taurus Pursuant*, 119.

[181] LHCMA O'Connor MSS 1/5, O'Connor to Nairne [*c*.1970–2]; Liddell Hart MSS

Guards Armoured divisions did reorganize themselves more flexibly.[182] In close country, they operated in four regimental groups. One armoured regiment married up with a lorried infantry battalion, while the division's armoured reconnaissance regiment operated with the armoured brigade's motor battalion. Henceforth, infantry actually rode on the backs of the tanks so that they could give instant support to the armour.[183]

But there were also many occasions when co-operation broke down, sometimes with costly results. There were several common causes of failure. Sometimes the attacking troops failed to carry out a proper reconnaissance of enemy defences. On 23 April 1943, 2nd Infantry Brigade (1st division), supported by two squadrons of Churchills from 142nd RAC, failed to hold the gains it had made on Gueriat ridge in Tunisia because a line of unlocated anti-tank guns knocked out several of its supporting tanks and the Germans were able to mount a rapid counter-attack.[184] Sometimes fire-plans were inadequate. At Salerno a battalion attack failed because the artillery fire-plan had failed to provide for a reserve of guns to deal quickly with flanking machine-gun fire.[185] Sometimes units were thrown into an attack without sufficient time to 'marry up'. In July 1944 in Normandy, two companies of 4th Welch (53rd Welch Division) suffered sixty-seven casualties when they raided the village of Esquay in part because their supporting Churchill tanks arrived late at their rendezvous. The infantry commander had blithely assumed that they would be able 'to appear from out of the blue after the inf[antry] had advanced 900 yds and join smoothly in the attack'.[186]

Perhaps the most common cause of failures in combined arms operations was communications breakdown. The Royal Corps of Signals was responsible for providing communications down to unit level. But communications within each unit were provided by the unit itself. This was one reason why the weakest link in the army's communication system remained the infantry battalion. At the end of the Tunisian campaign, Anderson decided that 'The question of forward infantry communica-

15/4/85, Brig. W. R. N. Hinde, 22 Arm[oured] B[riga]de op[eration]s, 6–15 June 1944; PRO CAB 106/963, Reports on the fighting in Normandy 1944, Immediate Report no. 4, 11 June 1944.

[182] PRO CAB 106/959, O'Connor to Divisional Commanders, Notes by Commander VIII Corps on the employment of armour in battle, 26 July 1944.

[183] PRO WO 232/21, Capt. L. C. Coleman, Notes from Theatres of War, 3 Oct. 1944; Roberts, *From the Desert to the Baltic*, 159; G. S. C. Bishop, *The Battle. A Tank Officer Remembers* (Brighton, [c. 1969]), 59–60, 60, 62; *A Guard's General*, ed. Lindsay, 147, 152.

[184] PRO WO 231/14, 2 Infantry Bde., Lessons of the Tunisian Campaign, n.d.

[185] PRO WO 201/527, Part I, Seaborne Operations and Beach Organisation [c.Oct. 1943].

[186] PRO WO 205/401, Immediate Report no. 53, 25 July 1944, and Lieut.-Col.? for Maj.-Gen. RAC, 21 Army Group, 11 Aug. 1944.

tions required special study. Practically no progress has been made since the last war.'[187] Even during training, commanders of artillery and armoured regiments realized that their success depended on the efficiency of their signallers. But infantry commanders could carry on without any form of electrical communications by relying on well-trained runners. The result, according to one staff officer, was that 'The biggest clot in a battalion was made the Signal Officer'.[188] The infantry were also handicapped because they had to wait longer than other arms of service for sufficient radio equipment, and the sets they did receive were too heavy and operated on frequencies that were particularly susceptible to interference.[189] Their problems were made even worse by difficulties in providing sufficient batteries and replacement signallers.[190]

The result, according to the commander of an infantry training centre in the Middle East in 1943, was that 'The standard of r/t procedure is appallingly low'.[191] Communications between infantry and their supporting tanks remained an unresolved problem from Alamein to the end of the war.[192] When infantry and armoured units had the opportunity to train together before a battle, their communications were usually satisfactory. When they did not, they invariably broke down. This placed serious constraints on the infantry's tactical flexibility. They went into battle expecting that their communications would collapse and 'The result is that the plan had to be too rigid, and once troops are committed it is impossible for them to adjust themselves to the enemy's reactions'.[193]

Infantry that were closely supported by tanks and artillery usually found it comparatively easy to arrive on their objective, albeit often very slowly. But they also had to be able to hold it. Units that had studied German tactics knew they had to prepare to meet a swift counter-attack. Shortly after landing in Normandy, for example, a company of 10th

---

[187] PRO WO 232/14, Directorate of Tactical Investigation, Operational Report, North Africa, Lessons from Tunisian Campaign, 16 June 1943.

[188] CCC Ronald Lewin MSS RLEW 2/13, Belchem to Lewin, 21 Aug. 1980.

[189] PRO WO 232/14, Directorate of Tactical Investigation, Operational Report, North Africa, Lessons from Tunisian Campaign, 16 June 1943; PRO WO 231/14, Directorate of Military Training, 2 Infantry Bde., Lessons of Tunisian campaign, n.d; PRO WO 201/527, Role of Armoured Formations. Tactical Handling of Armoured Forces [c.June 1943]; PRO WO 232/77, Lieut.-Col. C. T. Honeybourne to DMT, Director of Infantry, 3 Dec. 1944; PRO WO 277/26, Gravely, *Signals*, 141.

[190] PRO WO 231/8, DMT, Lessons from the Italian campaign, 18 Dec. 1943; PRO WO 204/1895, Minutes of Infantry Conference held at CMTC on 2 Apr. 1944; PRO WO 231/14, DMT to 21 Army Group, Staff College, Director of Infantry, 9 Dec. 1943.

[191] PRO WO 201/2592, GHQ, MEF to 8 and 9 Armies, 23 May 1943; PRO WO 277/25, Gravely, *Signals*, 121.

[192] For comments on Alamein, see PRO WO 201/2592, GHQ, MEF to 8 and 9 Armies, PAIFORCE, c.May 1943.

[193] PRO WO 232/77,'Lieut.-Col. C. T. Honeybourne to DMT, Director of Infantry, 3 Dec. 1944.

Parachute battalion repulsed a German counter-attack by directing the fire of two field regiments onto the German troops as they formed up. They then allowed the survivors to approach their positions before opening rapid fire at short range with their own small arms and mortars.[194] On 8 July 1944, Lieutenant Ranzinger of 21st Panzer division, recorded that the previous day a counter-attack east of Caen by infantry and tanks of his division was quickly stopped by a combination of 'Murderous art[iller]y and mortar fire' and infantry small arms fire.[195] But British units that had not prepared to meet a swift German counter-attack and had not practised a drill to consolidate their gains rapidly and bring forward anti-tank guns and other heavy support weapons, were frequently driven off their gains.[196] On 18 June 1944, despite the support of several medium and seven field regiments, an attack mounted by 231st Infantry brigade was driven out of the village of Hottot in Normandy when German infantry infiltrated between its two leading battalions and German tanks attacked them from the front.[197]

Failures such as these suggest that even commanders as determined and energetic as Montgomery and Horrocks could not overcome that combination of weariness and sheer human inertia that overtook many units and formations coming out of battle and force them to begin training for the next one. After the occupation of Sicily, 50th division congratulated itself that, despite its inability to get behind and cut off the German rearguards that had opposed it, the division did not require any special training in operating in close country.[198] Time devoted to training was not always spent appropriately. In anticipation of a swift advance inland from the beaches, before D-Day 7th Armoured division trained almost exclusively for rapid, mobile exploitation operations, whereas they would have done better to work on effecting better infantry–tank co-operation.[199] A few weeks after the landing a tank troop commander in 24th Lancers noted in his diary 'In the afternoon all Officers are summoned to a lecture in a nearby field, given by Major Bourne, 2IC of the 3rd R.T.R., who has apparently had quite a lot of experience of fighting in this class of country. It is a warm day,

---

[194] PRO CAB 106/963, Reports on the fighting in Normandy, 1944, Immediate Report no. 23, 25 July 1944; Lieut.-Gen. Sir R. N. Gale, *With the Sixth Airborne Division in Normandy* (London, 1948), 57.

[195] LHCMA Dempsey MSS, 2 Army Intelligence summary, Trans. of extracts from diary of Lieut. Ranzinger of 21 Panzer Division, 8 July 1944.

[196] PRO WO 231/16, 152 Infantry Bde., Discussion of Lessons Learned during the year of fighting from El Alamein to Messina, 6 Nov. 1943; PRO WO 232/14, Lieut.-Gen. K. Anderson to AFHQ, 16 June 1943.

[197] PRO CAB 106/1060, Reports from Normandy, 1944. 6 June–10 July 1944, by Brig. James Hargest.

[198] PRO WO 201/527, Notes on operations—Sicily, Extract from reports on the operations of a Division in Sicily, 17 Aug. 1943.

[199] LHCMA Liddell Hart MSS 1/153/6, Carver to Liddell Hart, 22 Mar. 1950.

and a lot of drowsy Officers pay scant attention to this important advice . . .'.[200]

In December 1943 the DMT at 15 Army Group in Italy circulated, with Alexander's endorsement, a report on recent operations that concluded

Our tactical methods are thorough and methodical but slow and cumbersome. In consequence our troops fight well in defence and our set-piece attacks are usually successful, but it is not unfair to say that through lack of enterprise in exploitation we seldom reap the full benefit of them. We are too flank-conscious, we over-insure administratively, we are by nature too apprehensive of failure and our training makes us more so.[201]

It was, in fact, a remarkably candid and generally accurate assessment of the operational and tactical capability of the army. It omitted only one salient fact. This system served the British army's needs remarkably well. It delivered victory at an acceptable cost in human terms and without breaking the morale of front line units. The British army did not win its battles from Alam Halfa to the Rhine by the simple application of 'brute force' and a reversion to the methods of 1918. From the autumn of 1942 onwards, division for division, the British did enjoy a quantitative superiority in weapons and munitions. This was the product of three factors: their own factories were finally coming on full-stream; supplies were being delivered in growing quantities from the USA; and the bulk of the German army was being bled white in Russia. However, commanders in North Africa before Alamein had also enjoyed this superiority and had shown that they did not know how to exploit it. Furthermore, their quantitative superiority was to some extent offset by the qualitative inferiority of many of their weapons. Within a doctrine that continued to constrain the initiative of subordinate commanders, they developed more efficient C3I systems and new operational and tactical methods. The key to the British army's success from Alam Halfa onwards was that they had discovered how to employ the weapons they possessed in such a way as to exploit their opponent's weaknesses.

[200] Bishop, *The Battle*, 60.
[201] PRO WO 231/8, Directorate of Military Training, Lessons from the Italian Campaign, 18 Dec. 1943.

Conclusion

Critics of the British army have been too quick to echo the refrain that British intelligence analysts found in letters written by captured German soldiers in Normandy that, '"despite his heavy equipment, "Tommy is no soldier"'.[1] But the Germans overlooked the fact that the British had never believed that they could win their battles by pitting man against man, and indeed they never believed that they should even try to do so. In 1945, Britain was on the winning side, and Germany was one of the losers, because Britain was a member of a more powerful alliance. The British, Russians, and Americans were able to produce more guns, aircraft, ships, and all of the other paraphernalia required by armed forces in the industrial age than could Germany and its allies. They could place more soldiers, sailors, and airmen in the field than could the Axis powers, and they could maintain them there until they had done their job.

The British army played only a minor part in defeating Hitler's Germany. This was largely a factor of its small size. At its peak, in July 1944, Montgomery's force in Normandy had only fourteen British, three Canadian, and one Polish division in contact with the enemy. The US army had already landed twenty-three divisions, and by the end of the war, when Montgomery's armies were shrinking, American ground forces had grown to sixty divisions. But even this combined Anglo-American force could not, on its own, have matched the Wehrmacht. In mid-1944 the German army numbered 237 divisions. The fighting power of the Wehrmacht was worn down by a combination of the allied blockade, Anglo-American air attacks, and, crucially, the Red Army. From June 1941 onwards, the Germans never deployed less than two-thirds of their ground forces on the Eastern Front. By the beginning of 1944 the Red Army numbered 480 divisions, and it was in Russia that the bulk of the German army was eviscerated in an attritional struggle that dwarfed in terms of its sheer magnitude anything undertaken by the Anglo-American forces.[2]

Such disparities in size make any meaningful comparisons between the combat capabilities of the British and German armies at best problematic and at worst meaningless. The size of the British and

---

[1] PRO WO 219/1908, SHAEF, G-2, Records: SHAEF Operational Intelligence Section, Intelligence Notes no. 21, 3 Aug. 1944.
[2] R. Overy, *Why the Allies Won* (London, 1995).

German armies was a reflection of the place afforded to each of them in their respective national strategies. German national strategy, designed to afford Nazi Germany continental hegemony, placed a premium on the army at the expense of the navy and air force. The British army never enjoyed such favourable treatment because it was never accorded the leading role in British national strategy. Between the wars, whilst the British General Staff may have thought about how to fight a continental war, the British army actually spent most of its time garrisoning the empire, and, latterly, providing for the anti-aircraft defence of the United Kingdom. It was equipped accordingly. In 1939 the few actual preparations it had made to fight a continental land war were wrecked by a government intent on doing something spectacular in a vain effort to deter Hitler by a belated show of determination. Between the outbreak of war and Dunkirk, the main pillars of British strategy were the navy, the RAF, and the French army. The British army embarked on a slow build-up of its strength that, even when its plans were completed, supposedly in late 1941, would still have left it at about half the size of the French army. It was intended merely to assist the French army to deliver the *coup de grâce* against Germany after the latter had been suitably weakened by the naval blockade and air bombardment. The fall of France did not cause the army to be promoted as Britain's strategic mainstay. On the contrary, the demands of national survival caused Churchill's government to place even more emphasis on the navy and RAF. It continued to have to struggle with them for adequate resources. Churchill's army, therefore, never performed the role undertaken by Haig's troops in 1918. It never engaged and defeated the bulk of the enemy's land forces in a climactic offensive.

The combat capability of the British army was, therefore, constrained at the strategic level by decisions taken by politicians over whom it had little control. But this study has suggested that many of the other, frequently cited explanations for the British army's comparatively poor combat capability in the first half of the war, and for its improved performance after late 1942, are at best inadequate or are at worst positively misleading. Before 1914 the British army did not have a combined arms doctrine. All the other arms were regarded as being subservient to the infantry. However, that notion was abandoned in the midst of the First World War. By the end of the war, the army recognized that victory could only be secured by the proper combination of all arms. After 1918 the British army therefore developed a combined arms doctrine predicated on two assumptions. First, never again would society allow the army to be as prodigal with the lives of its men as it had been during the First World War. Secondly, it was unlikely that the troops themselves would be willing to make sacrifices on the same scale as their fathers had done. Henceforth, therefore, the army would have to engage the enemy with the minimum of manpower in the front line and employ the maximum of machinery to generate the overwhelming firepower required to suppress enemy fire and so make possible movement across the battlefield. Post-war doctrine abandoned a search for a 'human solution' to the conundrum of how to combine firepower, manoeuvrability, and surprise and enthusiastically embraced a technological solution. 'We must not forget', asserted the Adjutant-General, Sir Robert Whigham in 1927, 'that the object is to replace muscle power by some mechanical power and so reduce the wastage in war of human lives.'[3]

Far from seeing the army as some kind of refuge from the modern world, the General Staff regarded war against a first-class power as an industrial undertaking. They were, therefore, being entirely consistent when they tried to guide the development of the army along the same path towards a more capital-intensive future as did the managers of British industry. In the same way that managers of industry believed that capital-intensive technologies would increase the productivity of each worker, so senior officers believed that technology would increase the productivity of each soldier by enabling fewer soldiers to kill more of the enemy and at less cost to their own side. The essence of this system was explained in a paper prepared by the General Staff for Hore-Belisha in February 1939.

By reducing the size of the divisions a larger number of more compact formations can be organised, suitable for quick despatch and for effective action in any part of the world. The same number of guns, grouped in larger units for better development of their firepower, will give a proportionately increased support to smaller infantry units. The smaller divisions being more highly mechanized and more economically manned will not only enhance our tactical advantages in war but will enable the money devoted to the Army to be spent more usefully and with more effective results.[4]

At one level, this was a perfectly rational solution to the problem of how to win battles at minimum cost in human lives. However, throughout the inter-war period, the British army, like the German army before 1933, was largely bereft of the modern equipment to give it substance. However, confronted by a similar reality, the two armies adopted radically different doctrines. German doctrine, with its overriding emphasis on the need for each individual soldier to use his initiative within the broad confines of his commander's plans, promised to maximize the German army's main asset, high-quality manpower. The British did not

---

[3] PRO WO 279/57, Report on the Staff Conference.
[4] PRO WO 33/1502, Hore-Belisha, 'The organisation of the army for its role in war', CP26(1938), 10 Feb. 1938; *Chief of Staff*, ed. Bond, i, 129–33.

follow the same path. They opted instead for a doctrine that required weapons they did not have and which were unlikely to be available for a long time to come. They chose this path for several reasons. First, the British army lacked the high prestige of its German counterpart. It could not attract the same high-quality manpower that was so eager to enlist in Germany; furthermore, British commanders did not believe their soldiers would act appropriately if they were left without close and constant supervision. Secondly, before 1914, they had adopted a 'human-centred' solution to the problem of crossing the fire-swept zone, and it had brought them disaster in 1914–15. Thirdly, one reason they had done so was because the alternative required large quantities of expensive equipment that the pre-war Liberal government was reluctant to provide.[5] After 1919, they found it inconceivable that, if their political masters ever again required them to engage in a major continental war, that they would allow them to do so without proper equipment. When they did just that, their sense of betrayal was palpable and prolonged. After the war, Montgomery recalled that

Knowing the precise situation regarding the British Field Army in France in general, and in particular in my division, I was amazed to read in a newspaper one day in France in October 1939 the speech of the Secretary of State for War (Hore-Belisha) in Parliament when he was announcing the arrival of the B.E.F. He gave Parliament and the British people to understand that the Army we had just sent to France was equipped 'in the finest possible manner which could not be excelled'.[6]

Reliant, therefore, as it was on adequate quantities of high-quality equipment, the army's combat capability could only begin to improve significantly when that equipment at last became available in late 1942.

However, the notion that the British army won its battles by the employment of 'brute force' and a reversion to the tactics and operational art of 1918, and was wrong to do so, overlooks four factors. First, at the same time as sufficient quantities of weapons and munitions were at last coming off the production line, the size of the army began to shrink as British manpower reserves were exhausted. From 1942 until the end of the war British commanders, therefore, had an ever-more-pressing need to maximize the use of machinery and to minimize the possibility of heavy casualties. Secondly, it overlooks the fact that thanks to its commitment to colonial soldiering between the wars, many of the weapons the army adopted sacrificed fire-power to mobility. During the Second World War, British troops possessed small arms that were in some respects inferior to those issued to the German army. The

---

[5] K. Neilson, ' "That Dangerous and Difficult Enterprise": British Military Thinking and the Russo-Japanese War', *War and Society*, 9 (1991), 30.
[6] Montgomery, *Memoirs*, 50.

infantry, therefore, had to be able to summon support from the gunners because their own weapons were not good enough. The development of British tanks and anti-tank guns was the victim of political decisions taken about the strategic role of the army between the wars, and of the fact that proper development work had to be cut short after Dunkirk because of the overwhelming need to get any weapons into the hands of the troops quickly. The quantitative superiority that the British usually enjoyed from 1942 was, therefore, to some extent counterbalanced by the qualitative inferiority of too many of their weapons.

Thirdly, the 'brute force' thesis overlooks the plain fact that logistics mattered. In the short term, the tempo of British operations was retarded by the prominence British generals gave to supply and transportation in their calculations. For over 200 years the British army had fought overseas and far from its home bases. It had learnt the penalties of neglecting its logistical preparations the hard way. The Germans gave far less prominence to logistics because they were habituated to fighting continental wars across short distances and supported by good communications. Montgomery has frequently been castigated for waiting until his logistical preparations were complete down to the last gaiter button. Rommel, conversely, has been praised for his readiness to take risks with his logistics. This division of praise and blame is illogical. The German system worked across the short distances involved in fighting in France and Poland, and it worked against enemies with a rigid operational doctrine, without proper air support and handicapped by serious strategic errors. However, in Russia and North Africa, the Germans failed, in part because their ambitions outran their logistical infrastructure. In Normandy, distance was less of a problem, but German logistics could not cope with the twin handicaps imposed on them by allied air interdiction combined with the fact that many of the troops that might have defeated the invasion were otherwise engaged in Russia or Italy. In North Africa, Rommel repeatedly achieved tactical successes, but lack of transport meant that he could not transform them into operational victories. Montgomery's operations went forward at a more modest pace, and there were times, even in 1944–5, when his logistics system could not meet all the demands imposed on it simultaneously. However, from CRUSADER until the end of the war, no major British operation failed because the troops engaged did not receive adequate supplies.

Finally, the 'brute force' hypothesis overlooks the fact that by 1942, the British army was at last beginning to understand how to employ its weapons to reap maximum advantage from them. By 1918, the British Army had attained a high level of tactical and operational excellence. The reasons why it did not regain that level until late 1942 were manifold. Some were outside the army's control, and were the result of the political decisions about the role of the army already noted. But other causes of the army's shortcomings were the responsibility of the military authorities themselves. The problem was not at the level of failing to heed the experiences of 1914–18. The army did not wait for the Kirke Report of 1932 to try to learn the lessons of the First World War. It did develop a combined arms doctrine in the 1920s and 1930s and it did adopt new forms of organization designed to enhance its mobility. Rather, the failure was at the administrative level. The General Staff failed to impose a common understanding of doctrine on all units and formations. Nor did it ensure that all units and formations trained realistically, or prepare the 'middle piece' of the regular officer corps properly so that after 1939 its members could step up in rank and command the battalions and divisions of the greatly expanded wartime army.

Many of the difficulties that units experienced in co-operating with each other on the battlefield during the Second World War were a consequence of the General Staff's excessively *laissez-faire* attitude both before and during the war towards how training was conducted and how the principles enumerated in its doctrinal manuals should be interpreted in practice. In the late 1930s, the army adopted a smaller, mechanized divisional organization in the expectation that it would allow them to combine fire-power and mobility and thus permit an increase in the tempo of their operations. Beset by defeat after defeat in the first half of the war, at the hands of an enemy who could seemingly run rings around them, their immediate reaction was to conclude that organizational changes had not gone far enough. In the Home Forces after Dunkirk, the Brigade Group became the army's basic combined arms formation. It was only abandoned when experience in exercises indicated that, although it might enhance mobility, it was incapable of generating sufficient fire-power to cover its own movements. Ironically, just as Home Forces was reverting to divisional organization following the experience of its autumn 1941 exercises, 8th Army was moving in the opposite direction.[7]

This highlighted one of the army's most basic problems, the lack of a universal interpretation of the practical meaning of its doctrine. At the operational level, British doctrine promulgated the idea that it would be possible to bring order to the chaos of battle by practising an autocratic and highly centralized command and control system. This fundamental belief permeated the entire fabric of the army. Recruits were taught from the very beginning of their basic training that obedience to the letter and spirit of orders was the supreme military virtue. But paradoxically,

[7] LHCMA Alanbrooke MSS 6/2/12, Brooke to Auchinleck, 6 Feb. 1942.

senior officers shunned the most effective route to securing uniformity of behaviour on the battlefield, and refused to adopt tactical and operational drills until the second half of the war. In doing so they were reflecting a peculiarly British view of the proper relationship between authority and the individual. They were relying on the fact that senior officers had 'character', that apparently quintessentially British combination of perseverance, courage, and a sense of duty that was supposed to make them peculiarly well suited to reacting quickly and appropriately to whatever challenges arose on the battlefield.

The British army did actively seek to analyse and disseminate the lessons of its operations. One of the tasks of the Staff Duties branches at formations headquarters was to investigate tactical and operational level problems and find solutions to them.[8] At the War Office, the DSD's branch examined war diaries with a view to 'extracting in a systematic way—during the period of the war and not after its conclusion as was the case of the 1914–18 [war]—any information which could be turned to our advantage during the present war'.[9] Defeat encouraged the army to do even more. In August 1942, the Chief of Staff at GHQ in Cairo ordered all units and formations to produce brief preliminary reports highlighting any lessons so that these could be disseminated to others with the minimum of delay.[10] Simultaneously, the DSD at the War Office concluded that what was missing was 'a body which could study the lessons of the war and lay down a clear tactical doctrine for the various types of operation our troops would have to undertake. If such a doctrine could be established, its application would be comparatively simple and other requirements would automatically fall into place.'[11] The result was the establishment of the Directorate of Tactical Investigation which, from 1943 onwards, produced a series of lengthy reports on the lessons of major operations.

However, what the army still lacked was a single guiding executive able to impose a uniform understanding of that doctrine on all commanders. Even in wartime it continued with the pernicious peacetime practice of allowing senior commanders to interpret doctrine as they saw fit. 'As you know,' Sir Archibald Nye, the VCIGS, told Brooke in December 1943, 'each Army Group commander or indeed Army Commander can issue what training or tactical instructions he likes, provided they are not at variant with the doctrine and general policy laid down by the C.I.G.S. in M.T.Ps, A.T.I.s or A.T.M',[12] reservations which

[8] General Staff, *FSR, Volume 1. Organisation and Administration 1930*, 41–2.
[9] PRO WO 260/41, DSD to Auchinleck, 2 April 1940.
[10] PRO WO 201/538, McCreery to 8, 9, and 10 Armies, 20 Aug. 1942.
[11] PRO WO 163/183, Minutes of 8 meeting of the organisation and weapons policy committee, 28 Aug. 1942.
[12] LHCMA Alanbrooke MSS 6/2/23, Nye to Brooke, 21 Dec. 1943.

left local commanders ample scope for imposing their own ideas on their subordinates. It was not until Montgomery took command of 8th Army that it had a commander who was willing, sufficiently ruthless, and sufficiently confident in his own judgement to impose a single interpretation of doctrine on his subordinates. In the eyes of generals like Herbert Lumsden, Montgomery was a 'cad' because he had the very un-British habit of insisting on his own way. Cad he may have been, but Montgomery's genius lay in the fact that he realized that the British system could only be made to work at peak efficiency if it had an autocrat in charge.

Added to problems involving the interpretation of doctrine were the myriad of practical obstacles that hindered realistic training both before and during the war. They were made much worse because too much responsibility for training was left in the hands of individual commanders. Some were energetic and committed trainers who tried to make training realistic and interesting for their troops. But many others did not share their enthusiasm or commitment and the preparation of their troops for battle suffered accordingly. Senior British officers did not lack professional ambition. Those who rose to command formations after 1939 had worked hard to pass the necessary examinations to enter the Staff College, for possession of a coveted psc certificate became almost the *sine qua non* of high command. But, what they did all too often lack was adequate training at the tactical and operational level of war. Although most divisional commanders and their seniors had received the best professional training that the army had to offer by passing through the Staff College, the training they received there was defective. The Staff College devoted too much time to preparing officers to be strategists, rather than to training them to be divisional and corps commanders. At a lower level, the battalion and brigade commanders of the expanded wartime army were supposed to be provided from the ranks of the 'middle piece officers' of the pre-war regular army. That some of them did not function successfully was not the result of the fact that they were without professional ambition, or because they looked upon soldiering as a pleasant pastime, or because they saw the army as a refuge from the modern world. They failed because the inter-war army had not created a system to ensure that they received the appropriate training for their new role. Critics of the regimental system have exaggerated the ways in which it inhibited combined arms co-operation in the same way that its supporters have exaggerated the extent to which it sustained morale in the wartime army. It was the lack of opportunity given to the different arms to train together, not inter-arm or inter-regimental jealousy, which inhibited combined arms co-operation. When units did have the chance to train together, co-operation was usually good. When combined arms co-operation failed, the regimental system served as a convenient excuse to hide more intractable problems.

The British army's combat capability improved in proportion to the extent to which these myriad of shortcomings was overcome. British training did improve as the war continued. In the middle of the Normandy campaign, Paget received letters from junior officers who had been trained in Britain noting that 'what surprised and then reassured them most was how quickly they became accustomed to the real thing. This is the best test of training and we must never forget it.'[13] By 1943–5, the British had become highly competent in many aspects of waging war at the tactical and operational level. Montgomery did not simply revert to the tactical and operational methods that Haig had employed in 1918. Unlike Haig he kept a tight grip on the battle, attacked on narrower fronts but in greater depth, and developed the machinery of intelligence and deception in such a way as to be able regularly to employ surprise as an effective force-multiplier. British ground–air co-operation and artillery support techniques were far in advance of German practice. The British had also developed techniques to cross both man-made and natural obstacles in the shape of rivers and minefields. And they had become increasingly skilful at mounting large-scale offensives under cover of darkness. The ultimate proof of British competence was shown by the fact that they successfully conducted a series of the most difficult of all military operations, opposed amphibious landings. Even the Germans were impressed. In October 1942, Rommel noted approvingly the skilful way that the British combined their tanks, artillery, infantry, and sappers at Alamein to breach his defences and particularly the fact that they were able to do so at night.[14] Two years later, German reports from Normandy emphasized the very thorough training that the troops fighting them had received.[15]

By 1944, the British army's command and control system operated more rapidly than in the past not only because it had more and better technology, but because commanders used it differently. The army had shed its dependence upon cumbersome written orders in favour of verbal orders. Despite continued weaknesses particularly in infantry battalions, its systems were far faster, flexible, and robust than they had been in 1940. Commanders were now willing and able to lead from the front, although that did not always mean that in the heat of battle they issued the correct orders. They had accepted that battle drills were essential if units and formations were to act effectively on briefer orders. Senior commanders were now in place who accepted that orders were

[13] CCC Sir P. J. Grigg MSS PJGG 9/7/17, Paget to Grigg, 17 July 1944.
[14] *The Rommel Papers*, ed. Liddell Hart, 309, 330.
[15] PRO WO 232/25, Special Tactical Study no. 30, German views of the Normandy landing, 28 Nov. 1944.

not something to be argued over, but were to be obeyed within a framework provided by a common understanding of the meaning of doctrine. The hypothesis, therefore, that the British won their battles from Alam Halfa to the Rhine simply because they employed 'brute force' is an utterly inadequate explanation of its success.

The British had, therefore, discovered how to make their own system work. But what they had not done was to attempt to fight the Germans using German doctrine. The British did not have a doctrine that decentralized decision-making to subordinate commanders. The British army retained its commitment to autocratic, top-down managerial control. This did severely constrain the initiative of subordinates and it did confer a major advantage on the Germans. Despite all the improvements the British had introduced, the German C3 system continued to be better suited than the British system to cope with the inherent chaos of the battlefield. If a German commander's signals failed he usually acted on his own initiative in accordance with his understanding of his commander's intentions. A British officer was more likely to wait for them to be repaired before acting. Indeed, the very success of the British army in creating a flexible communications system may have served to curb the initiative of junior commanders. In the opinion of Montgomery's Operation's officer 'The development of modern radio communications may conceivably tend to curb dash and initiative. If the most junior leaders are in constant radio contact with their superiors, they may hesitate to proceed without instructions. If the radio networks breakdown, therefore, they may tend to feel lost.'[16]

The second factor that degraded the British army's combat capability has already been touched upon, the reluctance of British commanders to take risks. This was partly the product of the rapid turnover in divisional commanders. It left the incumbents reluctant to gamble for fear that if they did so and failed, they would be dismissed. It was also partly the product of their concerns for the supposedly fragile morale of their own troops. Too much was probably made of this both at the time and subsequently. Most of the conscripts enlisted after 1939 had little love of fighting. Few were driven into battle by a burning zeal to exterminate their enemies. But just because they lacked overt enthusiasm did not mean that they also suffered from poor morale. Front line units experienced casualty rates similar to those endured by their fathers' generation. Most soldiers regarded the war as an unpleasant but necessary duty that they had to undertake so that they could then return to their normal lives as soon as possible. The stresses of battle did some-

[16] LHCMA Liddell Hart MSS 1/56/6, Brig. D. Belchem to Liddell Hart, 7 Aug. 1952. Some German commanders noted the same problem with their own subordinates: see von Senger und Etterlin, *Neither Fear Nor Hope*, 220.

times produce an incidence of psychiatric casualties and desertions that worried senior commanders. But they never reached such a scale as seriously to endanger the combat capability of the army. That was in part because British doctrine was deliberately intended to minimize that possibility, and also because British commanders tailored their operations so as not to place an excessive burden upon their front line troops.

The reluctance of British commanders to take risks was also a product of their determination to conserve their rapidly dwindling manpower reserves. The more thoughtful German commanders themselves recognized this. 'The English' in the opinion of von Rundstedt, 'on the whole, were more cautious than the Americans. He understood that this was due to the imperative need of preserving as much life as possible due to the relatively small number of men available for the English land forces.'[17] American, German, and Russian commanders could afford to press forward more rapidly than the British because they could afford to accept higher casualties. The British knew they could not.

Whether they would have been right even to try is itself debatable. In April 1943 the Secretary of State for War, Sir P. J. Grigg, reiterated the army's standard doctrine that

The infantry cannot perform their task without firepower, and it is just as easy to fail to provide sufficient firepower as to fail to provide sufficient infantry. It is indeed more economical in infantry lives to have them well supported by firepower (our greatest life-saving element) than it is to have a larger number of men and inadequate support.[18]

In the Second World War the British army did not discover the answer to the question, 'how are you to succeed without causing losses?' But its total casualties, 385,000 killed and wounded, were only a fraction of the 2,370,000 casualties that it suffered during the First World War. This was partly the result of a strategic policy that relied upon economic blockade, the Anglo-American air-offensive, and, crucially, the Red Army, to wear-down the fighting power of the Wehrmacht. In absolute terms the British reduced their casualties simply by abstaining for long periods of the war from fighting the kinds of intensive land battles in which they were bound to incur heavy losses. In the strategic context, the British army, therefore, played only a comparatively small part in overthrowing Nazi Germany. But, the comparatively low casualties that the army suffered were also a consequence of its commitment to using mechanized fire-power to fight its battles, and the tactical and operational techniques that it developed after 1919 and that it employed and modified between 1939 and 1945. Together, these factors meant that

[17] PRO WO 205/1020, Interrogation Reports of German Generals, vol. 1, von Rundstedt, 1 Feb. 1946.
[18] PRO CAB 120/232, Grigg to Churchill, 12 Apr. 1943.

not only were the British army's losses far less in absolute terms than they had been during the First World War, but they also meant that its rate of losses was lower. Between 1914 and 1918, the army lost approximately 5.8 men per 1,000 per month killed on the battlefield. During the Second World War the figure fell to 3.6 men per 1,000 per month. Similarly, the proportion of men wounded was only 13.8 men per 1,000 per month during the Second World War, compared to 28.1 men per 1,000 per month between 1914 and 1918.[19] The British army's reliance on overwhelming fire-power did have the disadvantage that it led to a slow rate of advance. But it had the great advantage that it enabled troops to reach their objectives without intolerable losses and with their morale more-or-less intact. And even the Germans had to admit that less reliance on machinery, and more reliance upon audacity, would not necessarily have yielded better results. Asked by one of his interrogators 'Whether in the long run bold tactics would have saved more lives he [General Schwalbe] was not prepared to say.'[20]

[19] LHCMA De Guingand MSS IV/3/3, Anon., 'The Administrative History of the Operations of 21 Army Group', Appendix M.
[20] PRO WO 205/1020, Interrogation Reports, German Generals, vol. 1: Schwalbe, n.d.

Bibliography

UNPUBLISHED PRIMARY SOURCES

Public Record Office, Kew

Departmental Papers
Air Ministry:
  AIR 2, 5
Cabinet:
  CAB 4, 16, 53, 65, 78, 92, 98, 104, 106, 120, 146.
Prime Minister's Office:
  PREM 1, 3, 4.
War Office:
  WO 32, 33, 71, 106, 123, 163, 166, 167, 171, 177, 193, 197, 199, 201, 204, 205, 208, 214, 216, 219, 222, 231, 232, 258, 259, 260, 277, 279, 287, 291, 293, 365.

  Field Marshal Viscount Alexander (WO 216)
  Field Marshall Sir J. Dill (WO 282)
  General Sir M. Dempsey (WO 285)
  Field Marshal Lord Cavan (WO 79)

Churchill College, Cambridge

  Sir P. J. Grigg MSS
  Leslie Hore-Belisha MSS
  Ronald Lewin MSS

Imperial War Museum, Department of Documents

  G. H. C. Abrams MSS
  General Sir Evelyn Barker MSS
  Brigadier J. C. A. Birch MSS
  Major W. G. Blaxland MSS
  Lieutenant H. T. Bone MSS
  Brigadier R. A. Boxshall MSS
  Major-General R. Briggs MSS
  Brigadier R. H. Bright MSS
  Lieutenant-General G. C. Bucknall
  Major W. B. E. L. Burton MSS
  Signaller L. W. Cannon MSS
  Brigadier J. N. Cheney MSS
  Sir Robin Dunn MSS

Major J. H. Finch MSS
Captain H. T. Flanagan MSS
Private A. R. Gaskin MSS
Trooper W. Hewison MSS
Field Marshal Viscount Montgomery of Alamein MSS
Lieutenant-General E. A. Osborne MSS
F. Southall MSS

Imperial War Museum, Department of Sound Records

Major A. H. Austin, Accession no. 000944/03.
Major-General H. L. Birks, Accession no. 000870/09.
Viscount Bridgeman, Accession no. 000991/03.
Field Marshal Lord Carver, Accession no. 000877/03
Colonel G. W. Draffen, Accession no. 000893/03.
Major-General F. W. Gordon Hall, Accession no. 000858/05.
Brigadier R. N. Harding-Newman, Accession no. 000834/08.
Major-General P. R. C. Hobart, Accession no. 000857/02.
Colonel Sir Andrew Horsborough-Porter, Accession no. 000905/06.
Colonel G. J. Kidston-Montgomerie of Southannan, Accession no. 000892/
06.
Major-General H. M. Liardet, Accession no. 000862/05.
Colonel E. F. Offord, Accession no. 000867/06.
Major-General G. W. Richards, Accession no. 000866/08.
Colonel K. E. Savill, Accession no. 000933/04.
Colonel Sir Douglas Scott, Accession no. 000968/02.
Colonel R. N. Seddon, Accession no. 000887/05
Brigadier W. R. Smijth-Windham, Accession no. 000954/07.
Lieutenant-Colonel P. M. Wiggin, Accession no. 000918/04.

Liddell Hart Centre for Military Archives, King's College London

General Sir R. Adam MSS
Field Marshal Lord Alanbrooke MSS
Lieutenant-General C. W. Allfrey MSS
General Sir W. H. Bartholomew MSS
Major-General Viscount Bridgeman MSS
General Sir J. Burnett-Stuart MSS
Major-General Sir F. de Guingand MSS
General Sir Miles Dempsey MSS
Field Marshall Sir John Dill MSS
Brigadier Sir James Edmonds MSS
Major-General J. Scott Elliot MSS
Major-General P. C. Hobart MSS
Captain L. C. King-Wilkinson MSS
General Sir W. M. St. G. Kirke MSS
Lieutenant-General Sir Sidney Kirkman MSS

Sir Basil Liddell Hart MSS
Major-General George Lindsay MSS
Major-General Sir F. Maurice MSS
Field Marshal Lord Milne MSS
Field Marshal Sir A. A. Montgomery-Massingberd MSS
General Sir R. O'Connor MSS
Major-General Sir Michael O'Moore Creagh MSS
Brigadier E. J. Paton-Walsh MSS
Major-General W. R. C. Penny MSS
General Sir Harold Pyman MSS
Major-General G. L. Verney MSS

Staff College Camberley

Captain H. H. Dempsey MSS
Field Marshal Sir A. Montgomery-Massingberd MSS

World Wide Web

Barker, T., '2982252, 1st Battalion Argyll and Sutherland Highlanders', accessed 14 June 1998 at *stead@iinet.net.au*
Cheall, William, 'The War of a Green Howard', accessed 14 June 1998 at paul@paston.co.uk.
Martindale, S., 'Sid's War', accessed 14 June 1998 at *www.geocities.com. Heartland/Pointe/8180*
Tee, R. A., 'A British Soldier Remembers', accessed 14 June 1998 at *britvet@lks.net*

PUBLISHED PRIMARY SOURCES

Official Publications

Anon., *Standing Orders of the King's Royal Rifle Corps 1930* (Aldershot, 1930).
Boraston, Lieutenant-Colonel J. H. (ed.), *Sir Douglas Haig's Despatches (December 1915 to April 1918)* (London, 1919).
General Staff, *Field Service Pocket Book 1914* (London, 1914).
——*Field Service Pocket Book (1939). Pamphlets 1–11* (London, 1939).
——*Field Service Regulations, Pt 1. Operations (1909)* (London, 1909).
——*Field Service Regulations, ii. Operations (1920)* (London, 1920).
——*Field Service Regulations, ii. Operations (1924)* (London,1924).
——*Field Service Regulations, ii. Operations (1929)* (London, 1929).
——*Field Service Regulations, i. Organisation and Administration. 1930. Reprinted with Amendments (Numbers 1–11) 1939* (London, 1939).
——*Field Service Regulations, ii. Operations General (1935)* (London, 1935).
——*Infantry Training, i. Training* (London, 1932).
——*Infantry Training, ii. War (1921) Provisional* (London, 1921).

General Staff, *Infantry Training, ii. War* (London, 1926).
—— *Infantry Training, ii. War (1931)* (London, 1931).
—— *Infantry Training (Training and War) 1937* (London, 1937).
—— *Comrades in Arms. Three Talks to Junior Officers or Officer Cadets to Assist them in Handling their Men* (London, 1942).
—— *The Soldier's Welfare. Notes for Officers* (2nd edn., London, 1943).
—— *Infantry Training, vi. The Anti-tank Platoon (1943)* (London, 1943).
Joint Warfare Publications, *British Defence Doctrine* (London, 1997).
Jolsen, Lieutenant-Colonel H. F., *Orders of Battle. Second World War 1939–1945* (2nd edn., London, 1990).
Ministry of Information, *They Sought Out Rommel. A Diary of the Libyan Campaign* (London, 1942).
Report of the War Office Committee on Enquiry into 'Shell-Shock', Parliamentary Papers, 1922 (Cmd. 1734), xii.
War Office, *Royal Army Medical Corps Training, 1925* (London, 1925).
—— *Royal Army Medical Corps Training, 1935* (London, 1935).
—— *Regulations for the Territorial Army (Including the Territorial Army Reserve) and for County Associations 1936* (London, 1936).
—— *King's Regulations for the Army and Army Reserve 1928* (London, 1928).
—— *Manual of Military Law 1929. Reprinted 1939* (London, 1943).
—— *Notes on Administration of Discipline* (London, 1941).
—— *Training Regulations 1934* (London, 1934).

PUBLISHED PRIMARY SOURCES, MEMOIRS ETC.

The Alexander Memoirs 1940–45, ed. J. North (London, 1962).
Anon., 'Military Notes', *Journal of the Royal United Services Institute*, 65 (1920), 419–23.
—— 'Military Notes', *Journal of the Royal United Services Institute*, 68 (1923), 337–41, 529–33, 715–20.
—— 'Army Notes', *Journal of the Royal United Services Institute*, 78 (1933), 425–8.
—— 'Army Notes', *Journal of the Royal United Services Institute*, 80 (1935), 190–5, 414–36.
—— 'Army Notes', *Journal of the Royal United Services Institute*, 82 (1937), 430–1, 655, 886.
—— 'Army Notes', *Journal of the Royal United Services Institute*, 83 (1938), 437–48, 649–56, 877–84.
—— 'Army Notes', *Journal of the Royal United Services Institute*, 84 (1939), 202–10, 425–30, 643–52.
Anon., *Team Spirit. The Administration of the 53rd Welsh Division during 'Operation Overlord' June 1944 to May 1945* (Germany, 1945).
Barker, Major-General G. H., 'Army Recruiting', *Journal of the Royal United Services Institute*, 83 (1937), 69–83.
Bartlett, Sir Basil, *My First War: An Army Officer's Journal for May 1940* (London, 1940).

Beale, P., *Tank Tracks: 9ᵗʰ Battalion Royal Tank Regiment at War 1940–45* (Stroud, 1995).

Beauman, Brigadier A. B., *Then a Soldier* (London, 1960).

Belchem, Major-General D., *All in the Day's March* (London, 1978).

Berg, C., 'Clinical Notes on the Analysis of a War Neurosis', *The British Journal of Medical Psychology*, 19 (1941–3), 155–85.

Bishop, G. S. C., *The Battle: A Tank Officer Remembers* (Brighton [c.1969]).

Bishop, T., *One Young Soldier: The Memoirs of a Cavalryman* (Norwich, 1993).

Bogacz, T., 'War Neurosis and Cultural Change in England, 1914–22: The Work of the War Office Committee of Enquiry into "Shell-Shock"', *Journal of Contemporary History*, 24 (1989), 227–56.

Bowlby, A., *The Recollections of Rifleman Bowlby* (London, 1969).

Bowman, J. E., *Three Stripes and a Gun* (Braunton, Devon, 1987).

Brooke-Popham, Air Vice-Marshal H. R. M, 'Air Warfare', in Sir G. Aston (ed.), *The Study of War* (London, 1927), 149–72.

Brutton, P., *Ensign Italy: A Platoon Commander's Story* (London, 1992).

Bryant, A., *The Turn of the Tide 1939–42* (London, 1957).

Callwell, Colonel C. E., *Small Wars: Their Principles and Practice* (2nd edn., London, 1914).

Carrington, P., *Reflect on Things Past: The Memoirs of Lord Carrington* (London, 1989).

'Cato', *Guilty Men* (London, 1940).

Carver, Field Marshal Lord, *Out of Step. The Memoirs of Field Marshal Lord Carver* (London, 1989).

Cawston, R., *Before I Forget. Some Recollections of a Sharpshooter 1939–1945* (Bristol, 1993).

Cheetham, A. M., *Ubique* (London, 1987).

Cherry, Brigadier R. G., 'Territorial Army Staffs and Training', *Journal of the Royal United Services Institute*, 84 (1939), 548–52.

Chief of Staff. The Diaries of Lieutenant-General Sir Henry Pownall, i. 1933–39, ed. B. Bond (London, 1972).

Churchill, W. S., *The Second World War, i. The Gathering Storm* (London, 1948).

—— *The Second World War, ii. Their Finest Hour* (London, 1949).

—— *The Second World War, iii. The Grand Alliance* (London, 1950).

—— *The Second World War, iv. The Hinge of Fate* (London 1951).

Churchill and Roosevelt: The Complete Correspondence, i. Alliance Emerging, ed. W. F. Kimball (Princeton, NJ, 1984).

The Churchill War Papers, ii. Never Surrender, May–December 1940, ed. M. Gilbert (London, 1994).

Cochrane, P., *Charlie Company: In Service with C Company 2ⁿᵈ Queen's Own Cameron Highlanders 1940–44* (London, 1979).

Cole, D. H., *Imperial Military Geography: General Characteristics of the Empire in Relation to Defence* (London, 1939).

Colville, J., *The Fringes of Power. Downing Street Diaries 1939–1955* (London, 1985).

Craig, N., *The Broken Plume: A Platoon Commander's Story 1940–45* (London, 1982).

Crimp, R. L., *The Diary of a Desert Rat*, ed. Alex Bowlby (London, 1971).

Croft, Lieutenant-Colonel W. D., 'The Influence of Tanks upon Tactics', *Journal of the Royal United Services Institute*, 67 (1922), 41–52.

Cunningham, Lieutenant-Colonel A. G., 'The Training of the Army', *Journal of the Royal United Services Institute*, 9 (1934), 723–32.

Dundas, Lieutenant-Colonel J. C., 'Anti-Tank', *Journal of the Royal United Services Institute*, 67 (1992), 106–11.

Dunn, R., *Sword and Pen: Memoirs of a Lord Justice* (London, 1993).

Dyson, S., *Tank Twins: East End Brothers in Arms 1943–45* (London, 1994).

Eisenhower, D. D., *Crusade in Europe* (London, 1948).

Eke, C. R., *A Game of Soldiers* (Brighton, 1997).

Ellenberger, Major G. F., 'The Infantry Section—French, German and British', *Journal of the Royal United Services Institute*, 83 (1938), 539–51.

Fielden, P., *Swings and Roundabouts* (privately published, 1991).

Forman, D., *To Reason Why* (London, 1991).

Foster, Lieutenant R. D., 'Promotion by Merit in the Army', *Journal of the Royal United Services Institute*, 71 (1926), 685–92.

Fuller, Brevet Colonel J. F. C., 'The Application of Recent Developments in Mechanics and Other Scientific Knowledge to Preparation and Training for Future War on Land', *Journal of the Royal United Services Institute*, 65, (1920), 239–74.

Gale, Lieutenant-General Sir R. N., *With the Sixth Airborne Division in Normandy* (London, 1948).

The Gallup International Public Opinion Polls: Great Britain, 1937–1975, ed. G. H. Gallup, 2 vols. (New York, 1976).

Garforth, Colonel F. I. de la P., 'WOSBs (OCTU)', *Occupational Psychology*, 19 (1945), 97–106.

Gilbert, M. (ed.), *Winston S. Churchill, iv: Companion pt 2, Documents July 1919–March 1921* (London, 1977).

Goode, F. D., 'The War Office General Staff 1940–42—A Worm's Eye View', *Journal of the Royal United Services Institute*, 138 (1993), 31–5.

Graham, Brigadier C. A. L., *The Story of the Royal Regiment of Artillery* (Woolwich, 1939).

A Guards' General: The Memoirs of Major General Sir Alan Adair, ed. O. Lindsay (London, 1986).

Guderian, General H., *Panzer Leader* (London, 1974).

Gudgin, P., *With Churchills to War: 48th Battalion Royal Tank Regiment at War 1939–45* (Stroud, 1996).

Guingand, Major-General Sir F. de, *Operation Victory* (2nd edn., London, 1960).

—— *Generals at War* (London, 1964).

Gunner, C., *Front of the Line: Adventures with the Irish Brigade* (Antrim, 1991).

Gwynn, Major-General Sir C. W., *Imperial Policing* (London, 1934).

Hall, Captain P. A., 'The Training of Junior Leaders in a Country Territorial

Battalion', *Journal of the Royal United Services Institute*, 77 (1932), 586–8.

Hamerton, I. C., *Achtung Minen! The Making of a Flail Tank Troop Commander* (Lewes, Sussex, 1991).

Hamilton, S., *Armoured Odyssey: 8ᵗʰ Royal Tank Regiment in the Western Desert 1941–42. Palestine, Syria, Egypt, 1943–44: Italy 1944–45* (London, 1995).

Hamley, Sir E. B., *The Operations of War Explained and Illustrated* (rev. edn., London, 1907).

Harington, General Sir C., *Tim Harington Looks Back* (London, 1941).

Harrison, T., 'The British Soldier: Changing Attitudes', *British Journal of Psychology*, 35 (1944–5), 34–9.

Harvey, Colonel L. G. S., 'Military Umpiring', *Journal of the Royal United Services Institute*, 76 (1931), 557–62.

Healey, D., *The Time of My Life* (London, 1990).

Hennessey, P., *Young Man in a Tank* (Camberley, 1995).

Henniker, M., *An Image of War* (London, 1987).

Hillier, J., *The Long Road to Victory: War Diary of an Infantry Despatch Rider 1940–46* (Trowbridge, Wilts, 1995).

Hills, R. J. T., *Phantom Was There* (London, 1951).

Holding, R., *Since I Bore Arms* (Cirencester, Glous., 1987).

Horrocks, Lieutenant-General Sir B., *A Full Life* (London, 1960).

—— with E. Belfield and Major-General H. Essame, *Corps Commander* (London, 1977).

Houldsworth, D., *'One Day I'll Tell You'* (Marlborough, Wilts, 1994).

Hunt, Sir D., *A Don at War* (London, 1966).

The Ironside Diaries 1937–40, ed. Colonel R. Ironside and D. Kelly (London, 1962).

Jackson, Major-General Sir L. C., 'Possibilities of the Next War', *Journal of the Royal United Services Institute*, 65 (1920), 71–89.

Jary, S., *Eighteen Platoon* (Carshalton Beeches, Surrey, 1987).

Johnston, B., *Someone Who Was: Reflections on a Life of Happiness and Fun* (London, 1993).

Kennedy, Major-General Sir J., *The Business of War* (London, 1957).

Kennedy, Captain J. R., 'Army Training', *Journal of the Royal United Services Institute*, 77 (1932), 714–20.

—— *This, Our Army* (London, 1935).

Kiln, Major R., *D-Day to Arnhem with Hertfordshire's Gunners* (Welwyn, 1993).

Knappe, K., with Brusaw, T., *Soldat: Reflections of a German Soldier, 1936–1949* (Shrewsbury, 1993).

Lee Harvey, J. M., *D-Day Dodger* (London, 1979).

Liddell Hart, Sir B. H., 'Army Manoeuvres, 1925', *Journal of the Royal United Services Institute*, 70 (1925), 647–55.

—— *Europe in Arms* (London, 1937).

—— *The Memoirs of Captain Liddell Hart*, 2 vols. (London, 1965).

—— 'High Command in the Army', *The Times*, 16 Sept. 1937.

Lindsay, M., *So Few Got Through* (London, 1946).

Lindsell, Lieutenant-General W. G., *Military Organisation and Administration* (22 edn., Aldershot, 1939).

Linklater, Major E., *The Defence of Calais* (London, 1941).

Low, A. M., *Modern Armaments* (London, 1939).

Luck, H. von, *Panzer Commander: The Memoirs of Colonel Hans von Luck* (New York, 1989).

McCallum, N., *Journey with a Pistol* (London, 1959).

McLean, A. W., *Letters from a Soldier in Europe 1944 to 1946* (Gairloch, 1992.)

McMilling, Lieutenant-Colonel J., 'The Training of the Infantry Soldier', *Journal of the Royal United Services Institute*, 74 (1929), 515–19.

—— 'Individual Training', *Journal of the Royal United Services Institute*, 75 (1930), 794–80.

Macready, Colonel G. H., 'The Trend of Organization in the Army', *Journal of the Royal United Services Institute*, 80 (1935), 1–20.

Macready, Lieutenant-General Sir G., *In the Wake of the Great* (London, 1965).

Martel, Lieutenant-General Sir G., *An Outspoken Soldier: His Views and Memoirs* (London, 1949).

Mays, S., Fall Out the Officers (London, 1969).

Meyer, K., *Grenadiers* (Winnipeg, Man., 1994).

Montgomery and the Eighth Army: A Selection from the Diaries and Correspondence and Other Papers of Field Marshal the Viscount Montgomery of Alamein, August 1942 to December 1943, ed. S. Brooks (London, 1991).

Montgomery of Alamein, Field Marshal Viscount, *El Alamein to the River Sangro* (London, 1948).

—— *The Memoirs of Field-Marshal the Viscount Montgomery of Alamein* (London, 1958).

Moran, H. R., *In My Fashion: An Autobiography of the Last Ten Years* (London, 1945).

Morgan, General Sir F., *Peace and War: A Soldier's Life* (London, 1961).

Morris, B. S., 'Officer Selection in the British Army, 1942–45', *Occupational Psychology*, 23 (1949), 219–34.

Myers, C. S., 'The Selection of Army Personnel', *Occupational Psychology*, 18 (1943), 1–5.

Neame, Lieutenant-General Sir P., *Playing with Strife: The Autobiography of a Soldier* (London, 1947).

Nicholson, Lieutenant-Colonel W. N., 'The Training of an Infantry Battalion', *Journal of the Royal United Services Institute*, 74 (1929), 49–54.

Niven, D., *The Moon's a Balloon* (London, 1971).

Noakes, Major S. M., 'The New Leadership', *Journal of the Royal United Services Institute*, 81 (1936), 589–92.

Oldfield, Colonel L. C. L., 'Artillery and the Lessons We Have Learnt with Regard to the Late War', *Journal of the Royal United Services Institute*, 67 (1922), 579–99.

Prendergast, J., *Prender's Progress: A Soldier in India 1931–47* (London, 1979).

The Private Papers of Leslie Hore-Belisha, ed. R. J. Minney (London, 1960).

Rees, Brigadier J. R., *The Shaping of Psychiatry by War* (New York, 1945).

——'The Development of Psychiatry in the British Army', *Military Neuropsychiatry: Proceedings of the Association of Nervous and Mental Diseases, December 15–16 1944, New York* (Baltimore, Md., 1946), 48–53.

Reid, M., *Last on the List* (London, 1974).

Reynolds, Major B. T., 'Interviewing for the New Militia', *Journal of the Royal United Services Institute*, 84 (1939), 508–10.

Richardson, General Sir C., *Flashback: A Soldier's Story* (London, 1985).

Ritgen, H., *The Western Front 1944: Memoirs of a Panzer Lehr Officer* (Winnipeg, Man., 1995).

Roach, P., *The 8.15 to War: Memoirs of a Desert Rat* (London, 1982).

Roberts, Major-General G. P. B., *From the Desert to the Baltic* (London, 1987).

Robertson, Lieutenant-Colonel G. McM., 'The Army as a Career', *Journal of the Royal United Services Institute*, 76 (1931), 37–52.

The Rommel Papers, ed. Sir B. H. Liddell Hart (London, 1953).

Ross, P., *All Valiant Dust: An Irishman Abroad* (Dublin, 1992).

Sandilands, Colonel H. R., 'The Case for the Senior Officers' School', *Journal of the Royal United Services Institute*, 73 (1928), 235–8.

Seton-Watson, C., *Dunkirk–Alamein–Bologna: Letters and Diaries of an Artilleryman 1939–45* (London, 1993).

Sherbrooke, Major R. L., 'Regimental Depots', *Journal of the Royal United Services Institute*, 77 (1932), 571–7.

Sherbrooke, Lieutenant-Colonel R. L., 'The New Infantry Weapons', *Journal of the Royal United Services Institute*, 83 (1938), 136–44.

Siminson, J., *A Saturday Night Soldier* (London, 1994).

Sims, J., *Arnhem Spearhead. A Private Soldier's Story* (London, 1978).

Smith, Lieutenant-Colonel B. (rtd.), 'Promotion by Rejection in the Army', *Journal of the Royal United Services Institute*, 71 (1926), 52–7.

Smyth, Sir J., *The Only Enemy: An Autobiography* (London, 1959).

Stahlberg, A., *Bounden Duty: The Memoirs of a German Officer, 1932–45* (London, 1990).

The Strategic Air War against Germany 1939–1945: Report of the British Bombing Survey Unit, ed. S. Cox (London, 1998).

Strong, Major-General Sir K. *Intelligence at the Top: The Recollections of an Intelligence Officer* (London, 1968).

Taylor, Brigadier G., *Infantry Colonel* (Upton-upon-Severn, Worcs., 1990).

Thorner, A. P., 'The Treatment of Psychoneurosis in the British Army', *International Journal of Psychoanalysis*, 27 (1946), 52–9.

Tobler, Major D. H., *Intelligence in the Desert: The Recollections and Reflections of a Brigade Intelligence Officer* (Victoria, BC, 1978).

Trevelyan, G., *The Fortress: Anzio, 1944* (London, 1956).

Verney, J., *Going to the Wars: A Journey in Various Directions* (London, 1957).

Von Mellenthin, Major-General F. W., *Panzer Battles: A Study in the Employment of Armour in the Second World War* (Norman Okla., 1956).

Von Senger und Etterlin, F., *Neither Fear Nor Hope* (London, 1963).

Wade, A., *A Life on the Line* (Tunbridge Wells, 1988).

Walters, D., *Some Soldier: Adventures in the Desert War* (Yeovil, 1989).

Wardle, Major K., 'A Defence of Close Order Drill: A Reply to "Modern Infantry Discipline"', *Journal of the Royal United Services Institute*, 79 (1934), 715–22.

War Office, 'The Bren Light Machine Gun', *Journal of the Royal United Services Institute*, 81 (1936), 102–8.

Wavell, Brigadier A. P., 'The Training of the Army for War', *Journal of the Royal United Services Institute*, 78 (1933), 254–73.

Wavell, Field Marshal Lord, *Generals and Generalship* (London, 1941).

Westmorland, Captain H. C., 'The Training of the Army', *Journal of the Royal United Services Institute*, 75 (1930), 582–6.

Westphal, General S., *The German Army in the West* (London, 1951)

—— 'Notes on the Campaign in North Africa, 1941–43', *Journal of the Royal United Services Institute*, 105 (1960), 70–81.

Wingfield, Col. M. A., 'The Supply and Training of Officers for the Army', *Journal of the Royal United Services Institute*, 69 (1924), 432–41.

Wingfield, R. M., *The Only Way Out: An Infantryman's Autobiography of the North-West Europe Campaign August 1944–February 1945* (London, 1955).

Whitefield, R., *The Eyes and Ears of the Regiment: 67th Field Regiment RA, 1939–1946* (Upton on Severn, Worcs., 1995).

Whitehouse, S., and Bennett, G. B., *Fear is the Foe: A Footslogger from Normandy to the Rhine* (London, 1995).

PUBLISHED SECONDARY SOURCES

Ahrenfeldt, R. H., *Psychiatry in the British Army in the Second World War* (London, 1958).

Aldington, L. H., *The Blitzkrieg Era and the German General Staff 1865–1941* (New Brunswick, NJ, 1971).

Alexander, D. W., 'Repercussions of the Breda Variant', *French Historical Studies*, 8 (1974), 459–88.

Alexander, M. S., 'The Fall of France, 1940', *Journal of Strategic Studies*, 13 (1990), 10–44.

—— 'Maurice Gamelin and the Defeat of France, 1939–40', in B. Bond (ed.), *Fallen Stars: Eleven Studies of Twentieth Century Military Disasters* (London, 1991), 107–40.

—— *The Republic in Danger: General Maurice Gamelin and the Politics of French Defence, 1933–40* (Cambridge, 1992).

—— ' "Fighting to the Last Frenchman"? Reflections on the BEF's Deployment in France and the Strains of the Franco-British Alliance, 1939–40', *Historical Reflections/Reflexions Historiques*, 22 (1996), 235–62.

Anon., *Taurus Pursuant. A History of the 11th Armoured Division* (Germany, 1945).

Anon., *The Story of the Royal Army Service Corps 1939–1945* (London, 1955).

Applegate, Captain R. A. D., 'Why Armies Lose in Battle: An Organic Approach to Military Analysis', *Journal of the Royal United Services Institute*, 132 (1987), 45–54.

Bailey, J. B. A., *Field Artillery and Firepower* (Oxford, 1989).

Barclay, C. N., *The London Scottish in the Second World War* (London, 1952).

Barclay, Brigadier, C. N., *The History of the 53rd (Welsh) Division in the Second World War* (London, 1956).

Barker, R., *Conscience, Government and War* (London, 1982).

Barnett, C., *The Desert Generals* (2nd edn., London, 1983).

Bartov, O., 'Daily Life and Motivation in War: The Wehrmacht in the Soviet Union', *Journal of Strategic Studies*, 12 (1989), 200–14.

—— *Hitler's Army: Soldiers, Nazis and War in the Third Reich* (Oxford, 1991).

Beaver, D. R., '"Deuce and a Half": Selecting US Army Trucks, 1920–45', in J. A. Lynn (ed.), *Feeding Mars: Logistics in Western Warfare from the Middle Ages to the Present* (Boulder, Colo., 1993), 251–70.

Bennett, R., *Behind the Battle: Intelligence in the War with Germany 1939–45* (London, 1994).

Bidwell, Brigadier S., 'The Gentleman versus the Players', *Journal of the Royal United Services Institute*, 121 (1976), 82–3.

—— 'After the Wall Came Tumbling Down: A Historical Perspective', *Journal of the Royal United Services Institute*, 135 (1990), 57–61.

—— and Graham, D., *Fire-Power: British Army Weapons and Theories of War 1904–1945* (London, 1982).

Bielecki, C., 'Mail and Morale in the British Army during World War Two', MA diss. (University College London, 1997).

Birdwood, Lord, *The Worcestershire Regiment, 1922–1950* (Aldershot, 1952).

Blaxland, G., *The Plain Cook and the Great Showman: The First and Eighth Armies in North Africa* (London, 1977).

Bond, B., *Britain, France and Belgium, 1939–40* (2nd edn., London, 1990).

—— *Liddell Hart: A Study of his Military Thought* (London, 1977).

—— *British Military Policy between the Two World Wars* (Oxford, 1980).

—— and Murray, W., 'British Military Effectiveness, 1918–39', in A. R. Millett and W. Murray (eds.), *Military Effectiveness, ii. The Interwar Period* (London, 1988), 98–130.

Brereton, J. M., *The British Soldier: A Social History from 1661 to the Present Day* (London, 1986).

Brown, I., 'The Evolution of the British Army's Logistical and Administrative Infrastructure and its Influence on GHQ's Operational and Strategic Decision-Making on the Western Front, 1914–1918', Ph.D. thesis (London, 1996).

Brown, Major J. S., 'Colonel Trevor N. Dupuy and the Mythos of the Wehrmacht Superiority: A Reconsideration', *Military Affairs*, 50 (1986), 16–20.

—— 'The Wehrmacht Myth Revisited: A Challenge to Colonel Trevor N. Dupuy', *Military Affairs*, 51 (1987), 146–7.

Butler, J. R. M., *Grand Strategy* (London, 1957), ii.

Callaghan, R., 'Two Armies in Normandy: Weighing British and Canadian Military Performance', in T. A. Wilson (ed.), *D-Day 1944* (Lawrence, Kan., 1994), 261–81.

Carrington, Lieutenant-Colonel C. E., 'Army-Air Co-Operation, 1939–43', *Journal of the Royal United Services Institute*, 115 (1970), 37–41.

Carver, M., *Tobruk* (London, 1964).

—— *Dilemmas of the Desert War: A New Look at the Libyan Campaign 1940–42* (London, 1986).

Carver, Brigadier R. M. P., 'Tank and Anti-Tank', *Journal of the Royal United Services Institute*, 91 (1946), 38–51.

—— 'Operations—Higher Formations. A Post-War Review of Field Service Regulations Vol. III', *Journal of the Royal United Services Institute*, 91 (1946), 367–75.

Carver, Lieutenant-Colonel R. M. P., 'Tanks and Infantry—The Need for Speed', *Journal of the Royal United Services Institute*, 96 (1951), 452–6.

Chapman, Brigadier O. E., 'The Influence of the Late War on Tank Design', *Journal of the Royal United Services Institute*, 96 (1951), 47–65.

Childs, D. J., 'British Tanks 1915–1918, Manufacture and Employment', Ph.D. thesis, (Glasgow, 1996).

Clay, E. W., *The Path of the 50ᵗʰ* (Aldershot, 1950).

Collier, B., *The Defence of the United Kingdom* (London, 1957).

Collini, S., 'The Idea of "Character" in Victorian Political Thought', *Transactions of the Royal Historical Society*, 35 (1985), 29–50.

—— *Public Moralists: Political Thought and Intellectual Life in Britain 1850–1930* (Oxford, 1991).

Colls, R., 'Englishness and Political culture' in R. Colls and P. Dodd (eds.), *Englishness: Politics and Culture 1880–1920* (London, 1986), 29–61.

Colville, J. R., *Man of Valour, Field-Marshal Lord Gort* (London, 1972).

Cooper, M., *The German Army 1933–45: Its Political and Military Failure* (London, 1978).

Copp, T. J., 'Battle Exhaustion and the Canadian Soldier in Normandy', *British Army Review*, 85 (1987), 46–54.

—— and McAndrew, B., *Battle Exhaustion: Soldiers and Psychiatrists in the Canadian Army, 1939–1945* (Montreal and Kingston, Ont., 1990).

Corum, J. S., *The Roots of Blitzkrieg: Hans von Seeckt and German Military Reform* (Kan., 1992).

—— 'The Luftwaffe's Army Support Doctrine, 1918-1941', *Journal of Military History*, 59 (1995), 53-76.

—— 'From Bi-planes to Blitzkrieg: The Development of German Air Doctrine between the Wars', *War in History*, 3 (1996), 85-101.

Crang, J. A. 'Politics on Parade. Army Education and the 1945 General Election', *History*, 81 (1997), 215-27.

—— 'The British Soldier on the Home Front: Army Morale Reports, 1940-45', in P. Addison and A. Calder (eds.), *Time to Kill: The Soldier's Experience of War in the West 1939-45* (London, 1997), 60-74.

Crew, F. A. E. (ed.), *The Army Medical Services: Campaigns* (London, 1956), ii.

Dennis, P., *The Territorial Army 1907–1940* (London, 1987).

Doubler, M. D., *Closing With the Enemy: How GIs Fought the War in Europe, 1944-1945* (Lawrence, Kan, 1994).

Doughty, R. A., *The Seeds of Disaster: The Development of French Army*

Doctrine, 1919–1939 (Hamden, Conn., 1985).

—— 'The French Armed Forces, 1918-1940', in A. R. Millett and W. Murray (eds.), *Military Effectiveness, ii. The Interwar Period* (London, 1988), 39-69.

Dovey, H. O. 'The Eighth Assignment, 1941-42', *Intelligence and National Security*, 11 (1996), 672-95.

Dupuy, T. N., *A Genius for War: The German Army and General Staff, 1807–1945* (London, 1977).

—— *Numbers, Predictions and War: The Use of History to Evaluate and Predict the Outcome of Armed Conflict* (2nd edn., Fairfax, Va., 1985).

—— 'Mythos or Verity: The Quantified Judgement Model and German Combat Effectiveness', *Military Affairs*, 50 (1986), 204–10.

—— 'A Response to the "Wehrmacht Mythos" Revisited', *Military Affairs*, 51 (1987), 196–7.

Ellis, J., *Brute Force: Allied Strategy and Tactics in the Second World War* (London, 1990).

Ellis, Major L. F., *The War in France and Flanders 1939–40* (London, 1953).

—— *Victory in the West, i. The Battle for Normandy* (London, 1962).

—— and Warhurst, Lieutenant-Colonel A. E., *Victory in the West, ii. The Defeat of Germany* (2nd edn., London, 1994).

English, J. A., *On Infantry* (New York, 1984).

—— *The Canadian Army and the Normandy Campaign: A Study in the Failure of High Command* (New York, 1991).

Essame, Major-General H., *The 43rd Wessex Division at War 1944–45* (London, 1952).

Este, C. d', *Decision in Normandy* (New York, 1983).

—— 'The Army and the Challenge of War, 1939–45', in D. Chandler and I. Beckett (eds.), *The Oxford Illustrated History of the British Army* (Oxford, 1994), 298–9.

Farrar-Hockley, A., *Infantry Tactics 1939–1945* (London, 1976).

Ferris, J., 'The British "Enigma": Britain, Signals Security and Cipher Machines, 1906–1946', *Defence Analysis*, 3 (1987), 153–63.

—— 'The British Army, Signals and Security in the Desert Campaign, 1940–42', in M. Handel (ed.), *Intelligence and Military Operations* (London, 1990), 255–91.

—— (ed.), *The British Army and Signals Intelligence during the First World War* (London, 1992).

Fisher, Brigadier B. D. 'The Training of the Regimental Officer', *Journal of the Royal United Services Institute*, 74 (1929), 241–61.

Fletcher, D., *Vanguard of Victory: The 79th Armoured Division* (London, 1984).

—— *The Great Tank Scandal: British Armour in the Second World War, pt 1* (London, 1989).

—— *Mechanised Force: British Tanks between the Wars* (London, 1991).

—— *The Universal Tank: British Armour in the Second World War, pt 2* (London, 1993).

—— *British Military Transport 1829–1956* (London, 1998).

Förster, J., 'Motivation and Indoctrination in the Wehrmacht, 1933–45' in

P. Addison and A. Calder (eds.), *Time to Kill: The Soldiers' Experience of War in the West 1939–1945* (London, 1997), 263–73.

Fraser, D., *Alanbrooke* (London, 1982).

—— *And We Shall Shock Them: The British Army and the Second World War* (London, 1983).

French, D., *The British Way in Warfare, 1688–2000* (London, 1990).

—— 'Colonel Blimp and the British Army: British Divisional Commanders in the War against Germany, 1939–1945', *English Historical Review*, 111 (1996), 1182–1201.

—— '"Tommy is No Soldier": The Morale of the Second British Army in Normandy, June–August 1944', *Journal of Strategic Studies*, 19 (1996), 154–78.

—— 'Discipline and the Death Penalty in the British Army in the Second World War', *Journal of Contemporary History*, 33 (1998), 531–45.

Fritz, S. G., *Frontsoldaten: The German Soldier in World War Two* (Lexington, Ky, 1995).

—— '"We are Trying to Change the Face of the World"—Ideology and Motivation in the Wehrmacht on the Eastern Front: The View from Below', *Journal of Military History*, 60 (1996), 683–710.

Gibbs, N. H., *Grand Strategy, i. Rearmament Policy* (London, 1976).

Gladman, B., 'Air Power and Intelligence in the Western Desert Campaign, 1940–3', *Intelligence and National Security*, 13 (1998), 144–62.

Gooderson, I., *Air Power at the Battlefront: Allied Close Air Support in Europe 1943–45* (London: 1998).

Graham, D., 'Observations on the Dialectics of British Tactics, 1904–1945', in R. Haycock and K. Neilson (eds.), *Men: Machines and War* (Ontario, 1984), 47–74.

—— *Against Odds: Reflections on the Experiences of the British Army, 1914–45* (London, 1999).

Grant, Colonel C., 'The Use of History in the Development of Contemporary Doctrine', in J. Gooch (ed.), *The Origins of Contemporary Doctrine: Papers Presented at a Conference Sponsored by the Director General of Development and Doctrine at Larkhill, March 1996* (Camberley, 1996), 7–17.

Greenhous, B., 'Aircraft versus Armour: Cambrai to Yom Kippur', in T. Travers and C. Archer (eds.), *Men at War: Politics, Technology and Innovation in the Twentieth Century* (Chicago, 1982), 93–118.

Griffith, P., 'British Armoured Warfare in the Western Desert, 1940–43', in J. P. Harris and F. N. Toase (eds.), *Armoured Warfare* (London, 1990), 70–87.

—— *Battle Tactics of the Western Front: The British Army's Art of Attack 1916–18* (London, 1994).

—— (ed.), *British Fighting Methods in the Great War* (London, 1996).

Gudgin, P., *Armoured Firepower: The Development of Tank Armament 1939–45* (Stroud, 1997).

Hamilton, N., *The Making of a General 1887–1942* (London, 1981).

—— *Monty: Master of the Battlefield 1942–44* (London, 1983).

Hancock, W. K., and Gowing, M. M., *British War Economy* (London, 1949).

Handy, C., *Understanding Organisations* (London, 1993).

Harman, N., *Dunkirk. The Patriotic Myth* (New York, 1980).

Harris, J. P. 'British Armour and Rearmament in the 1930s', *Journal of Strategic Studies*, 11 no. 2 (1988), 220–44.

—— 'British Intelligence and the Rise of German Mechanised Forces, 1929–40', *Intelligence and National Security*, 6 (1991), 395–417.

—— *Men, Ideas and Tanks. British Military Thought and Armoured Forces, 1903–1939* (Manchester, 1995).

Harrison, M., 'Resource Mobilization for World War II: The US, UK, USSR and Germany, 1938–1945', *Economic History Review*, 41 (1988), 171–92.

Harrison-Place, T., 'British Perceptions of the German Army, 1938–40', *Intelligence and National Security*, 9 (1994), 495–519.

—— 'Tactical Doctrine and Training in the Infantry and Armoured Arms of the British Home Army, 1940–44', Ph.D. thesis (Leeds, 1997).

Hart, R. A. 'Feeding Mars: The Role of Logistics in the German Defeat in Normandy, 1944', *War in History*, 3 (1996), 418–35.

Hart, S. A., 'Field Marshal Montgomery, 21st Army Group, and North West Europe, 1944–45', Ph.D. thesis (London, 1995).

—— 'Montgomery, Morale Casualty Conservation and "Colossal Cracks": 21st Army Group's Operational Technique in North West Europe, 1944–45', *Journal of Strategic Studies*, 19 (1996), 132–53.

Harvey, A. D., 'The French Armée de l'Air May–June 1940: A Failure in Conception', *Journal of Contemporary History*, 25 (1990), 447–65.

Hastings, M., *Overlord. D-Day and the Battle for Normandy* (New York, 1984).

Hawkins T. H., and Trimble, L. J. F., *Adult Education: The Record of the British Army* (London, 1947).

Heyck, T. W., 'Myths and Meanings of Intellectuals in Twentieth Century British National Identity', *Journal of British Studies*, 37 (1998), 192–221.

Hinsley, F. H. et al., *British Intelligence in the Second World War: Its Influence on Strategy and Operations*, 3 vols. (London, 1979–88).

Hogg, I. V., *The Encyclopaedia of Infantry Weapons of World War II* (London, 1977).

—— *British and American Artillery of World War Two* (London, 1978).

Holden Reid, B., 'The Operational Level of War and Historical Experience', in Major-General J. J. Mackenzie and B. Holden Reid (eds.), *The British Army and the Operational Level of War* (London, 1989), 1–12.

—— 'Alexander', in J. Keegan (ed.), *Churchill's Generals* (London, 1991), 104–29.

Holmes, R., *Firing Line* (London, 1987).

Horne, A., with Montgomery, D., *The Lonely Leader: Monty, 1944–45* (London, 1994).

Howard, M., 'The Liddell Hart Memoirs', *Journal of the Royal United Services Institute*, 111 (1966), 58–61.

—— *British Intelligence in the Second World War, v. Strategic Deception* (London, 1990).

—— 'Men against Fire: The Doctrine of the Offensive in 1914', in M. Howard, *The Lessons of History* (Oxford, 1993), 97–112.

Institution of the Royal Army Service Corps, *The Story of the Royal Army Service Corps 1939–1945* (London, 1955).

Jackson, W. F., *Alexander of Tunis as Military Commander* (London, 1971).

—— *The Mediterranean and Middle East, vi. Victory in the Mediterranean, part 3: November 1944 to May 1945* (London, 1988).

Janowitz, M., and Little, R. W., *Sociology and the Military Establishment* (London and Beverly Hills, Calif., 1974).

Jeffery, K., 'The Post-War Army', in I. Beckett and K. Simpson (eds.), *A Nation in Arms: A Social Study of the British Army in the First World War* (Manchester, 1985), 211–34.

'J. P. R.', *A Short History of the 13th Hussars* (Aldershot, 1923).

Keegan, J., 'Regimental Ideology', in G. Best and A. Wheatcroft (eds.), *War, Economy and the Military Mind* (London, 1976).

Kennett, Brigadier B. B., and Tateman, Colonel J. A., *Craftsmen of the Army: The Story of the Royal Electrical and Mechanical Engineers* (London, 1970).

Kershaw, K. J., Lieutenant-Colonel, 'Lessons to be Derived from the Wehrmacht's Experience in the East, 1943–45', *Journal of the Royal United Services Institute*, 132 (1987), 61–8.

Kier, E., *Imagining War: French and British Military Doctrine Between the Wars* (Princeton, NJ, 1997).

Kiszeley, J., 'The British Army and Approaches to Warfare since 1945', *Journal of Strategic Studies*, 19 (1996), 179–206.

Knox, M, 'The Italian Armed Forces, 1940–43', in A. R. Millett and W. Murray (eds.), *Military Effectiveness, iii. The Second World War* (London, 1988), 136–79.

Larson, R. H., *The British Army and the Theory of Armoured Warfare, 1918–40* (Newark, NJ, 1984).

Lewin, R., *The Life and Death of the Afrika Korps* (London, 1977).

Liddell Hart, B. H., *The Other Side of the Hill* (London, 1951).

Lind, W. S., 'The Theory and Practice of Manoeuvre Warfare', in R. D. Hooker (ed.), *Maneuvre Warfare: An Anthology* (Novato, Calif., 1993), 3–18.

Lindsay, D., *Forgotten General: A Life of Sir Andrew Thorne* (London, 1987).

Lynn, J. A., *Bayonets of the Republic: Motivation and Tactics in the Army of Revolutionary France, 1791–1794* (2nd edn., Boulder Colo., 1996).

McHugh, J., 'The Labour Party and the Parliamentary Campaign to Abolish the Military Death Penalty, 1919–1930', *Historical Journal*, 42 (1999), 233–50.

Mackay-Dick, Brigadier I. C., 'The Desert War 1940–43: Are any of the Lessons Relevant to NATO's Central Front Today?' in Major-General J. J. Mackenzie and B. Holden Reid (eds.), *Central Region versus Out-of-Area: Future Commitments* (London, 1990), 219–46.

Mackenzie, S. P., *Politics and Military Morale: Current Affairs and Citizenship Education in the British Army 1914–1950* (Oxford, 1992).

—— 'Vox Populi: British Army Newspapers in the Second World War', *Journal of Contemporary History*, 24 (1989), 665–81.

—— 'The Treatment of POWs in World War Two', *Journal of Modern History*, 66 (1994), 487–520.

McKibbin, R., *Classes and Cultures: England 1918–1951* (Oxford, 1998).

McLaine, I., *Ministry of Morale: Home Front Morale and the Ministry of Information in World War II* (London, 1979).

Man, J., *The Penguin Atlas of D-Day and the Normandy Campaign* (London, 1994).

Maurice, Sir F., *British Strategy: A Study of the Application of the Principles of War* (London, 1931).

Meilinger, Colonel P. S., 'John C. Slessor and the Genesis of Air Interdiction', *Journal of the Royal United Services Institute*, 140 (1995), 43–8.

Messerschmidt, M., 'German Military Law in the Second World War', in W. Deist (ed.), *The German Military in the Age of Total War* (Leamington Spa, 1985), 315–30.

Miller, Major-General C. H., *History of the 13th/18th Royal Hussars (Queen Mary's Own) 1922–1947* (London, 1949).

Molony, Brigadier C. J. C., *The Mediterranean and Middle East, vi. Victory in the Mediterranean, pt 1. 1 April to 4 June 1944* (London, 1984).

—— *The Mediterranean and Middle East, vi. Victory in the Mediterranean. pt 2. June to October 1944* (London, 1987).

Moreman, T. R., ' "Small Wars" and "Imperial Policing": The British Army and the Theory and Practice of Colonial Warfare in the British Empire, 1919–39', *Journal of Strategic Studies*, 19 (1996), 105–31.

Morgan, D., and Evans, M., *The Battle for Britain: Citizenship and Ideology in the Second World War* (London, 1993).

Muir, R., *Tactics and the Experience of Battle in the Age of Napoleon* (London, 1998).

Muller, R. R., 'Close Air Support: The German, British and American Experiences, 1918–41', in W. Murray and A. R. Millett (eds.), *Military Innovation in the Interwar Period* (Cambridge, 1996), 144–90.

Murray, W., *Luftwaffe: Strategy for Defeat 1939–45* (London, 1988).

—— 'British Military Effectiveness in the Second World War', in A. R. Millett and W. Murray (eds.), *Military Effectiveness, iii: The Second World War* (London, 1988), 90–135.

Natzio, G., 'British Army Servicemen and Women 1939–45: Their Selection, Care and Management', *Journal of the Royal United Services Institute*, 138 (1993), 36–43.

Neilson, K., ' "That Dangerous and Difficult Enterprise": British Military Thinking and the Russo-Japanese War', *War and Society*, 9 (1991), 17–37.

Nicol, G., *Uncle George: Field-Marshal Lord Milne of Salonika and Rubislaw* (London, 1976).

Osley, A., *Persuading the People: Government Publicity in the Second World War* (London, 1995).

Overy, R., *Why the Allies Won* (London, 1995).

Palmer, I., Lieutenant-Colonel, 'Battle Stress and its Treatment', *Journal of the Royal United Services Institute*, 143 (1998), 65–6.

Peden, G., *British Rearmament and the Treasury, 1932–39* (Edinburgh, 1979).

Perry, F. W., *The Commonwealth Armies: Manpower and Organisation in Two World Wars* (Manchester, 1988).

Pick, D., *War Machine: The Rationalisation of Slaughter in the Modern Age*

(London and New Haven, 1993).

Pittman, Major S., *Second Royal Gloucester Hussars: Libya–Egypt 1941–42* (London, 1950).

Playfair, Major-General I. S. O., *The Mediterranean and Middle East, i: The Early Successes against Italy (to May 1941)* (London, 1954).

—— *The Mediterranean and Middle East, ii:The Germans Come to Help their Ally (1941)* (London, 1956).

—— *The Mediterranean and Middle East, iii: British Fortunes Reach their Lowest Ebb (September 1941 to September 1942)* (London, 1960).

—— *The Mediterranean and Middle East, iv: The Destruction of the Axis Forces in Africa* (London, 1960).

Postan, M. M., *British War Production* (London, 1952).

—— Hay, D., and Scott, J. D., *Design and Development of Weapons: Studies in Government and Industrial Organisation* (London, 1964).

Prior, R., and Wilson, T., *Command on the Western Front: The Military Career of Sir Henry Rawlinson 1914–18* (Oxford, 1992).

Reisman, W. M., and Antoniou, C. T., *The Laws of War: A Comprehensive Collection of Primary Documents on International Laws Governing Armed Conflict* (New York, 1994).

Richards, D., and Saunders, H. St. G., *Royal Air Force 1939–45, ii: The Fight Avails* (London, 1953).

Rosen, S. P., *Winning the Next War: Innovation and the Modern Military* (Ithica, NY, 1994).

Rosse, Captain the Earl of, and Hill, Colonel E. R., *The Story of the Guards Armoured Division* (London, 1956).

Ryder, R., *Oliver Leese* (London, 1987).

Sadkovich, J. J., 'Understanding Defeat: Reappraising Italy's Role in World War II', *Journal of Contemporary History*, 24 (1989), 27–61.

—— 'Of Myths and Men: Rommel and the Italians in North Africa, 1940–42', *International History Review*, 13 (1991), 284–313.

Salmond, J. B., *The History of the 51st Highland Division 1939–45* (Edinburgh, 1953).

Samuels, M., 'Directive Command and the German General Staff', *War in History*, (1995), 22–42.

—— *Command or Control? Command, Training and Tactics in the British and German Armies 1888–1918* (London, 1995).

Scarfe, N., *Assault Division. A History of the 3rd Division from the Invasion of Normandy to the Surrender of Germany* (London, 1947).

Schulte, T. J., 'The German Soldier in Occupied Russia', in P. Addison and A. Calder (eds.), *Time to Kill. The Soldiers' Experience of War in the West 1939–1945* (London, 1997), 275–83.

Scott, Major G. L., 'British and German Operational Styles in World War Two', *Military Review*, 65 (1985), 37–41.

Shay, R. P., *British Rearmament in the Thirties: Politics and Profits* (Princeton, NJ, 1977).

Sheffield, G. D., 'Officer-Men Relations, Morale and Discipline in the British Army, 1902–22', Ph.D. thesis (London, 1994).

—— 'The Shadow of the Somme: The Influence of the First World War on British Soldiers' Perceptions and Behaviour in the Second World War', in P. Addison and A. Calder (eds.), *Time to Kill. The Soldier's Experience of War in the West 1939–45* (London, 1997), 29–39.

Shils, E., and Janowitz, M., 'Cohesion and Disintegration in the Wehrmacht', *Public Opinion Quarterly*, 12 (1948), 280–315.

Simkins, P., 'Co-Stars or Supporting Cast? British Divisions in "The Hundred Days", 1918', in P. Griffith (ed.), *British Fighting Methods in the Great War* (London, 1996).

Simpson, K., 'The Officers', in I. Beckett and K. Simpson (eds.), *A Nation in Arms. A Social Study of the British Army in the First World War* (Manchester, 1985), 63–98.

Sixsmith, Major-General E. K. G., 'The British Army in May 1940—A Comparison with the BEF, 1914', *Journal of the Royal United Services Institute*, 127 (1982), 8–10.

Skillen, H., *Spies of the Airwaves: A History of Y Sections During the Second World War* (Pinner, Middx., 1989).

Smurthwaite, D., *'Against All Odds'. The British Army of 1939–40* (London, 1990).

Sokoloff, S., 'Soldiers or Civilians? The Impact of Army Service in World War Two on Birmingham Men', *Oral History*, 25 (1997), 59–66.

Solomon, D. N., 'Civilian to Soldier: Three Sociological Studies of Infantry Recruit Training', *Canadian Journal of Psychology*, 8 (1954), 87–94.

Stein, A., 'International Law and Soviet Prisoners of War', in B. Wegner (ed.), *From Peace to War: Germany, Soviet Russia and the World, 1939* (Providence, RI), 293–308.

Stephenson, J., 'Political Thought, Elites, and the State in Modern Britain', *Historical Journal*, 42 (1999), 251–68.

Sullivan, B. R., 'The Italian Soldier in Combat, June 1940 to September 1943: Myths, Realities and Explanations', in P. Addison and A. Calder (eds.), *Time to Kill. The Soldiers' Experience of War in the West 1939–1945* (London, 1997), 177–205.

Surridge, K., ' "All you Soldiers are what we Call pro-Boer": The Military Critique of the South African War, 1899–1902', *History*, 82 (1997), 582–600.

Tank Museum, *Data Book of Wheeled Vehicles: Army Transport 1939–45* (London, 1983).

Travers, T., 'A Particular Style of Command: Haig and GHQ, 1916–1918', *Journal of Strategic Studies*, 10 (1987), 363–76.

—— *The Killing Ground. The British Army and the Emergence of Modern Warfare 1900–1918* (London, 1987).

—— *How the War Was Won: Command and Technology in the British Army on the Western Front, 1917–18* (London, 1992).

Tuker, Lieutenant-General Sir F., *Approach to Battle, A Commentary: Eighth Army November 1941 to May 1943* (London, 1963).

Van Creveld, M., *Supplying War: Logistics from Wallenstein to Patton* (Cambridge, 1977).

Van Creveld, M., *Fighting Power: German and US Army Performance 1939–1945* (London, 1983).

—— *Command in War* (Cambridge, Mass., 1985).

Ventham, P., and Fletcher, D., *Moving the Guns: The Mechanisation of the Royal Artillery 1854 to 1939* (London, 1990).

Verney, Major-General G. L., *The Desert Rats: The History of the 7th Armoured Division 1938 to 1945* (London, 1954).

—— *The Guards Armoured Division: A Short History* (London, 1955).

Warner, P., *The Battle of France 1940* (London, 1990).

Weight, R., 'State, Intelligensia and the Promotion of National Culture in Britain', *Historical Research*, 69 (1996), 83–101.

Weigley, R., *Eisenhower's Lieutenants: The Campaign of France and Germany 1944–45* (Bloomington, Ind., 1981).

Weinberg, G. L., *A World At Arms: A Global History of World War II* (Cambridge, 1994).

White, B. T., *Tanks and Other Armoured Vehicles of World War Two* (London, 1972).

Williams, D., *The Black Cats at War: The Story of the 56th (London) Division T.A., 1939–45* (London, 1995).

Wilmot, C., *The Struggle for Europe* (2nd edn., London, 1954).

Index